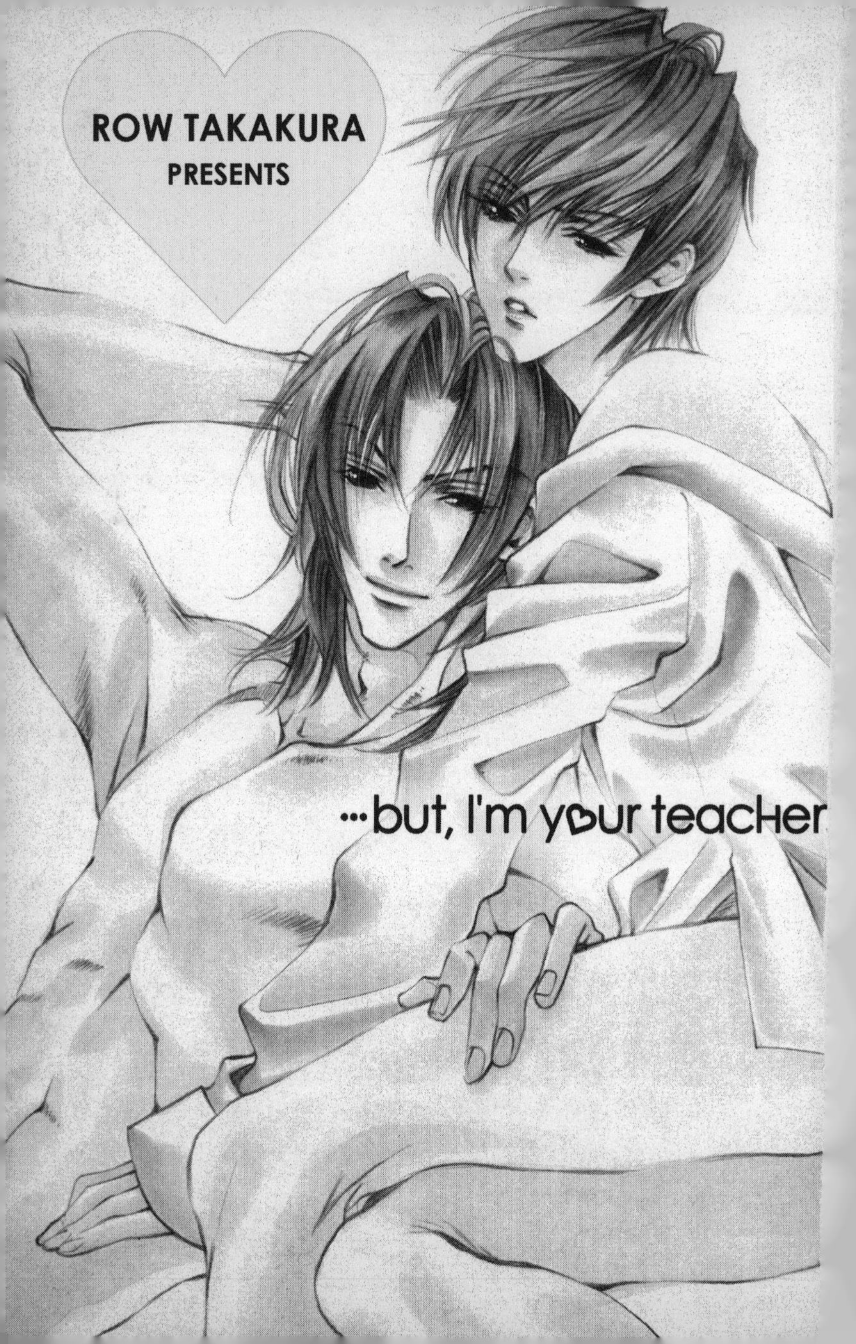
ROW TAKAKURA
PRESENTS
...but, I'm your teacher

3

···but, I'm your teacher.

35

···but, I'm your teacher.

59

bloom!

83

honey happy baby

107

voice box

139

scandal kiss

155

the view through the lens

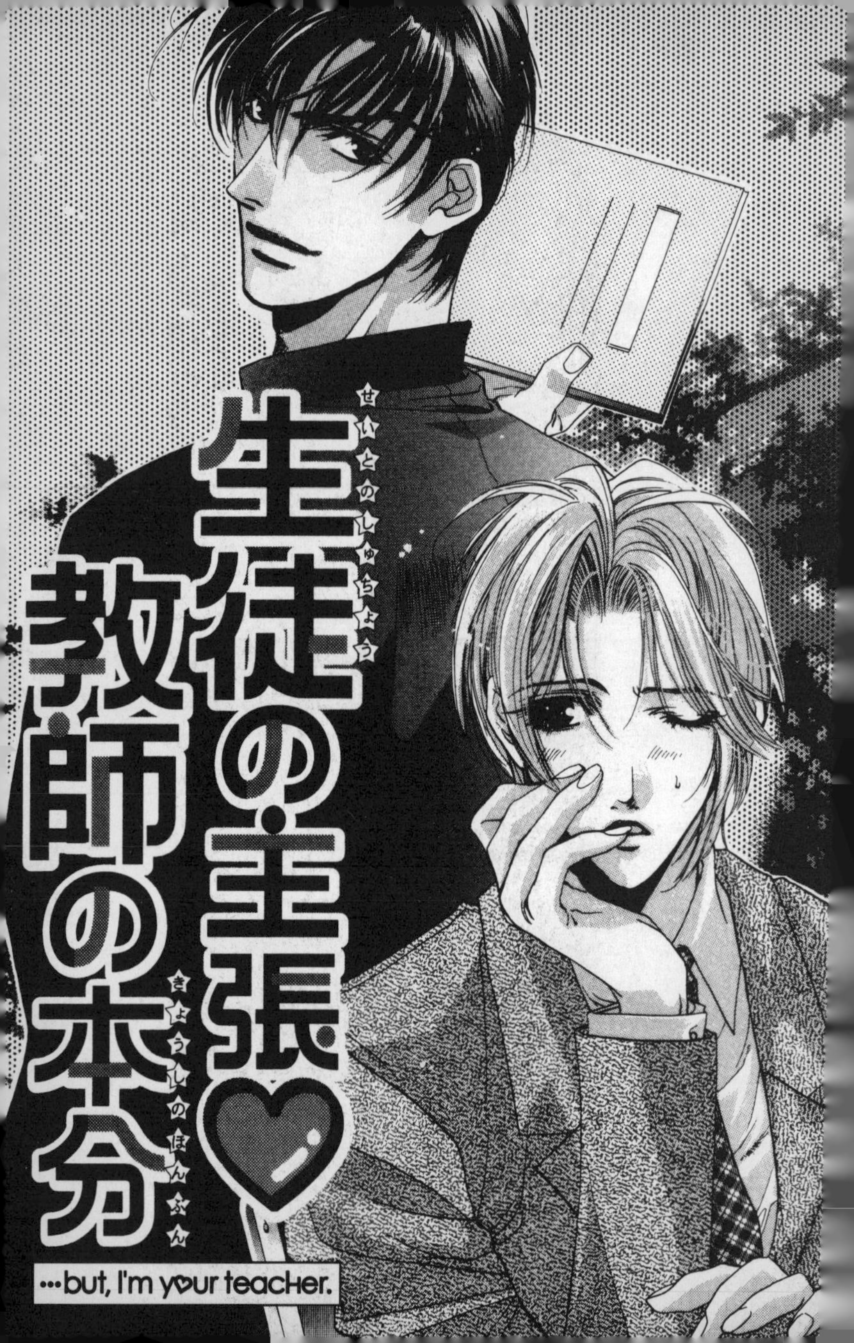
生徒の主張
教師の本分
...but, I'm your teacher.

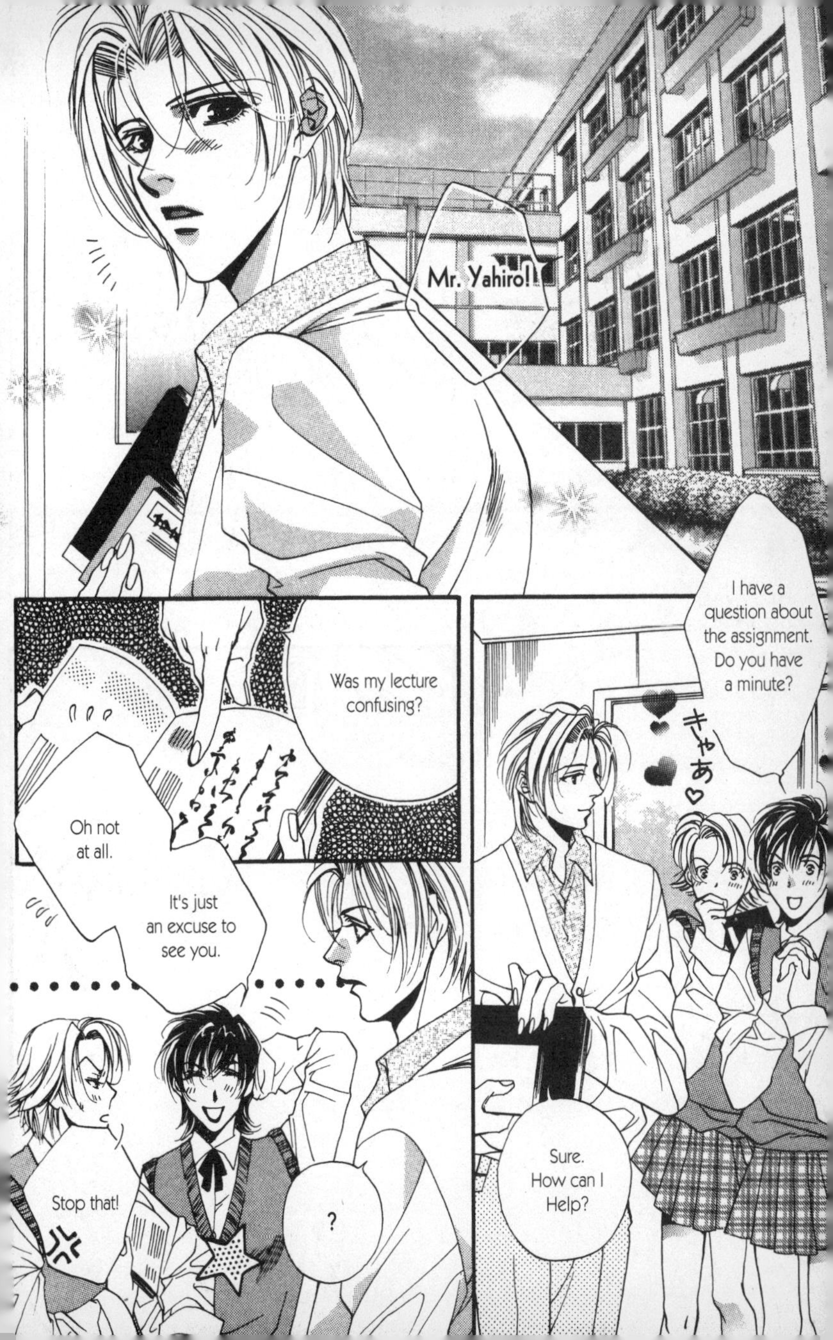
Mr. Yahiro!!
I have a question about the assignment. Do you have a minute?
きゃあ♡
Sure. How can I Help?
Was my lecture confusing?
Oh not at all.
It's just an excuse to see you.
?
Stop that!

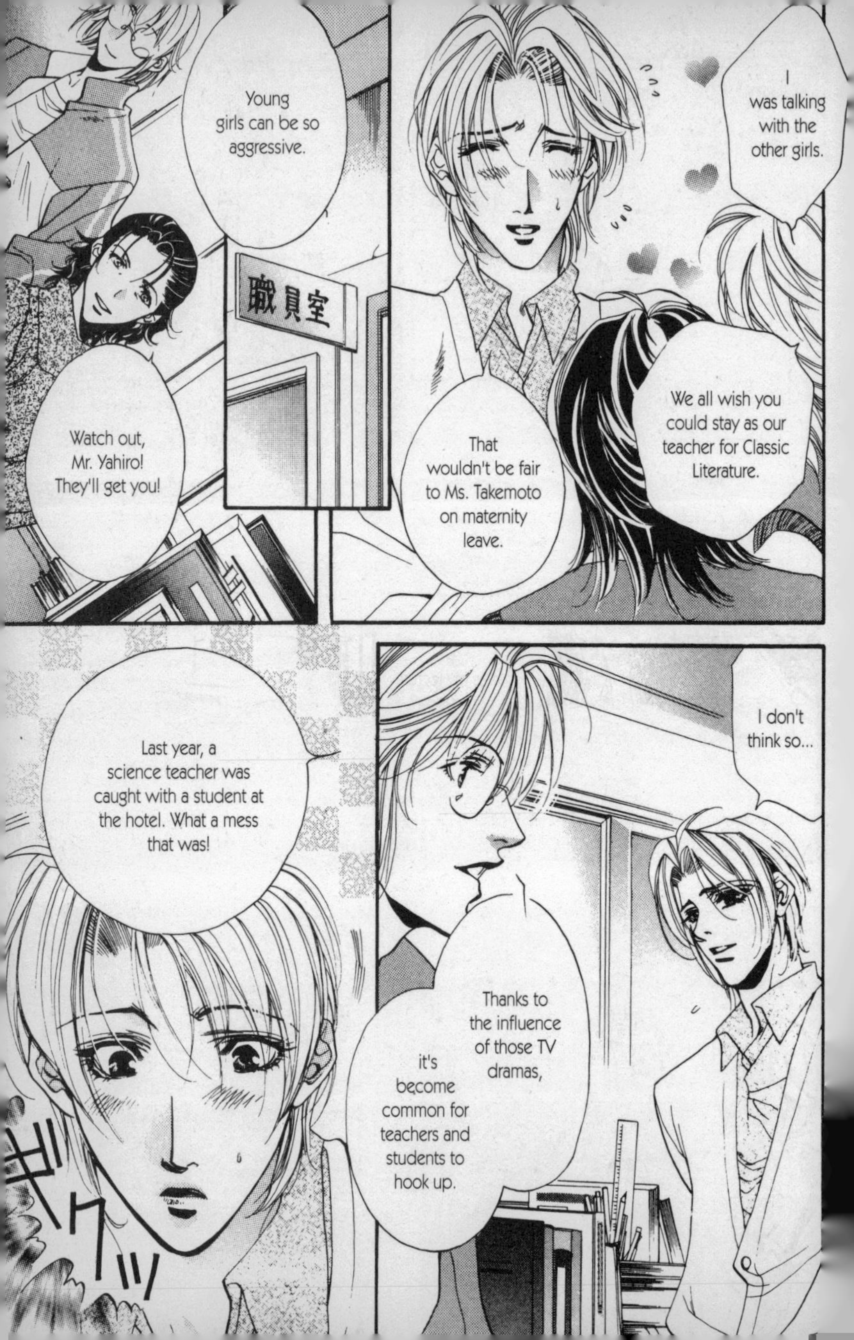
I was talking with the other girls.
We all wish you could stay as our teacher for Classic Literature.
That wouldn't be fair to Ms. Takemoto on maternity leave.
職員室
Young girls can be so aggressive.
Watch out, Mr. Yahiro! They'll get you!
I don't think so...
Thanks to the influence of those TV dramas,
it's become common for teachers and students to hook up.
Last year, a science teacher was caught with a student at the hotel. What a mess that was!
ギクッ

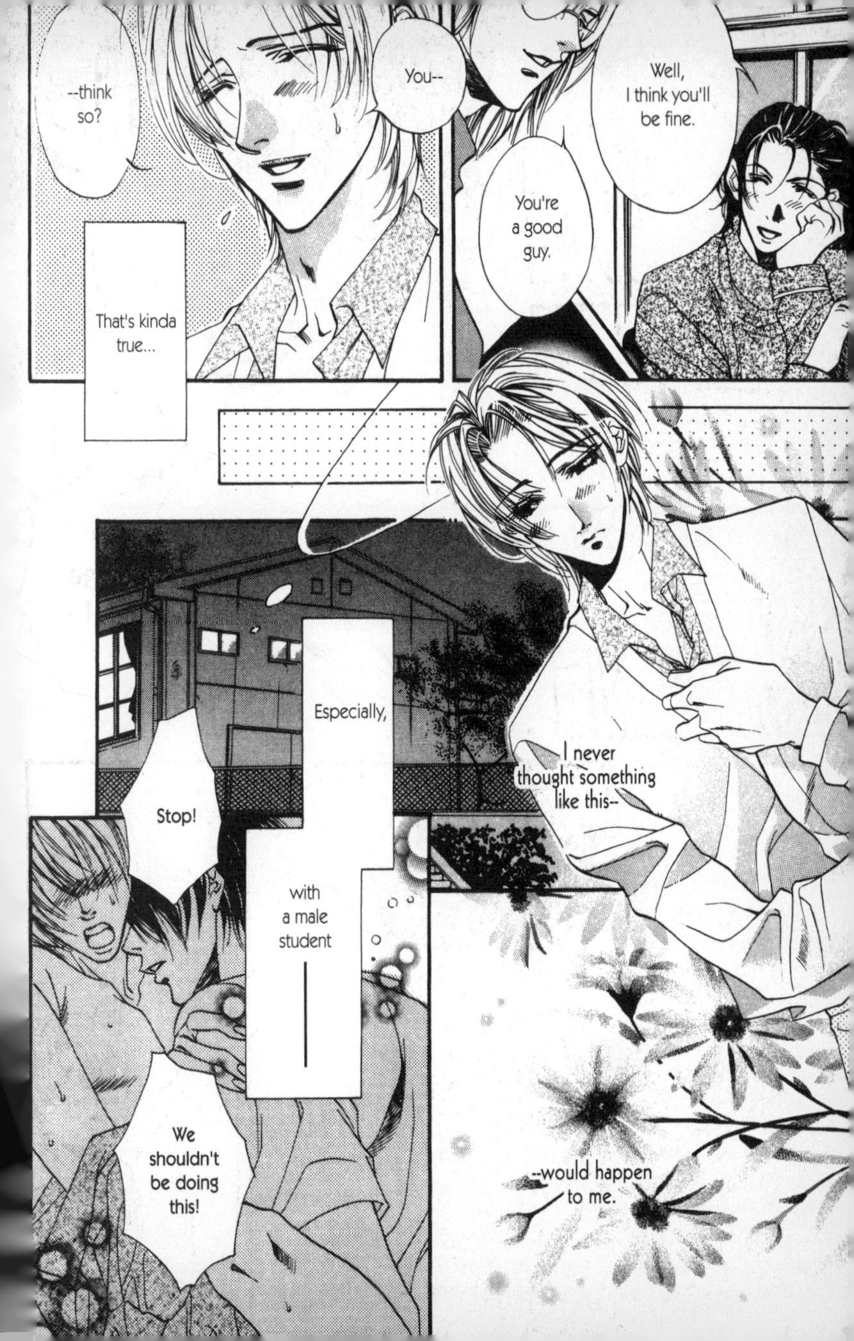

Well, I think you'll be fine.
You're a good guy.
You--
--think so?
That's kinda true...
I never thought something like this--
--would happen to me.
Especially,
with a male student
Stop!
We shouldn't be doing this!

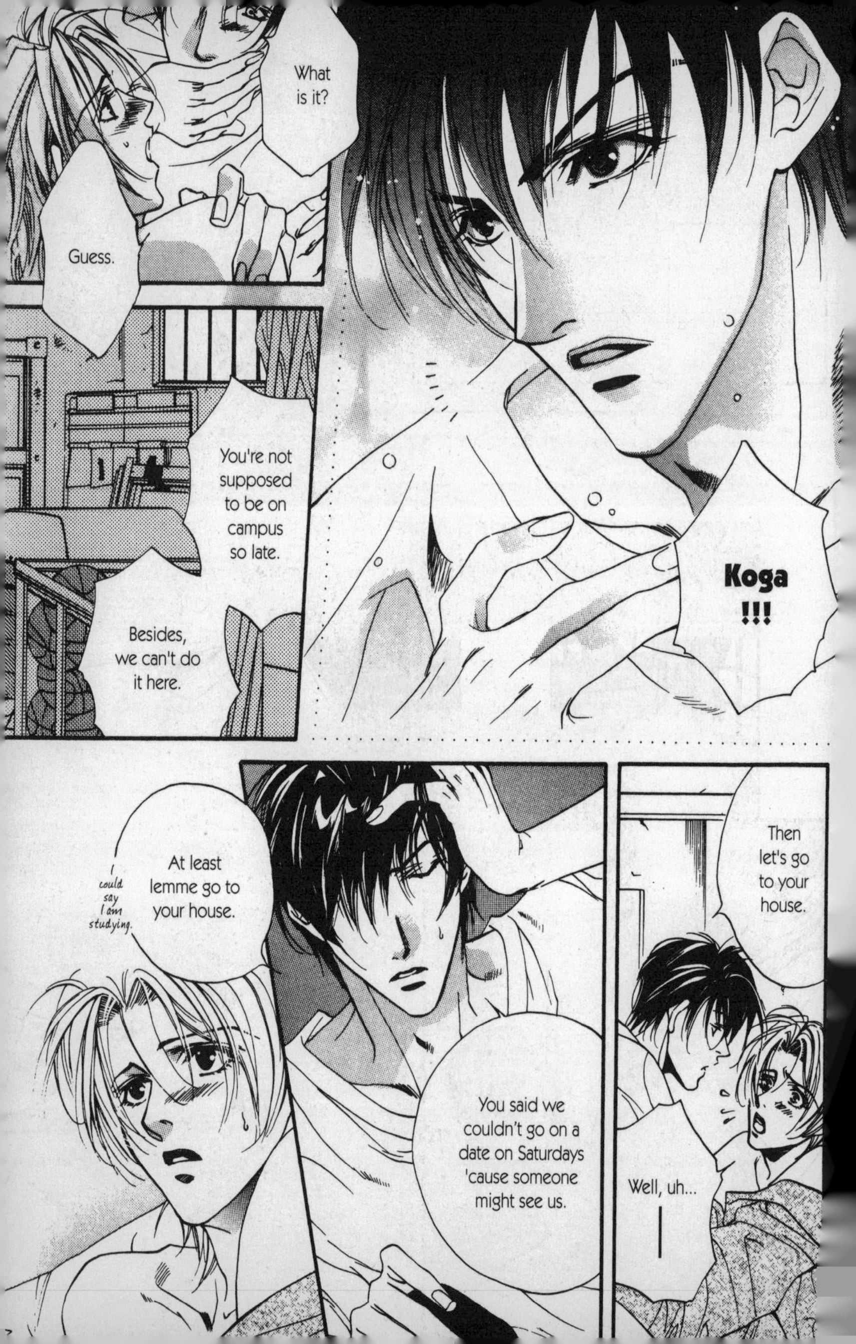
Koga !!!
What is it?
Guess.
You're not supposed to be on campus so late.
Besides, we can't do it here.
Then let's go to your house.
Well, uh...
You said we couldn't go on a date on Saturdays 'cause someone might see us.
At least lemme go to your house.
I could say I am studying.

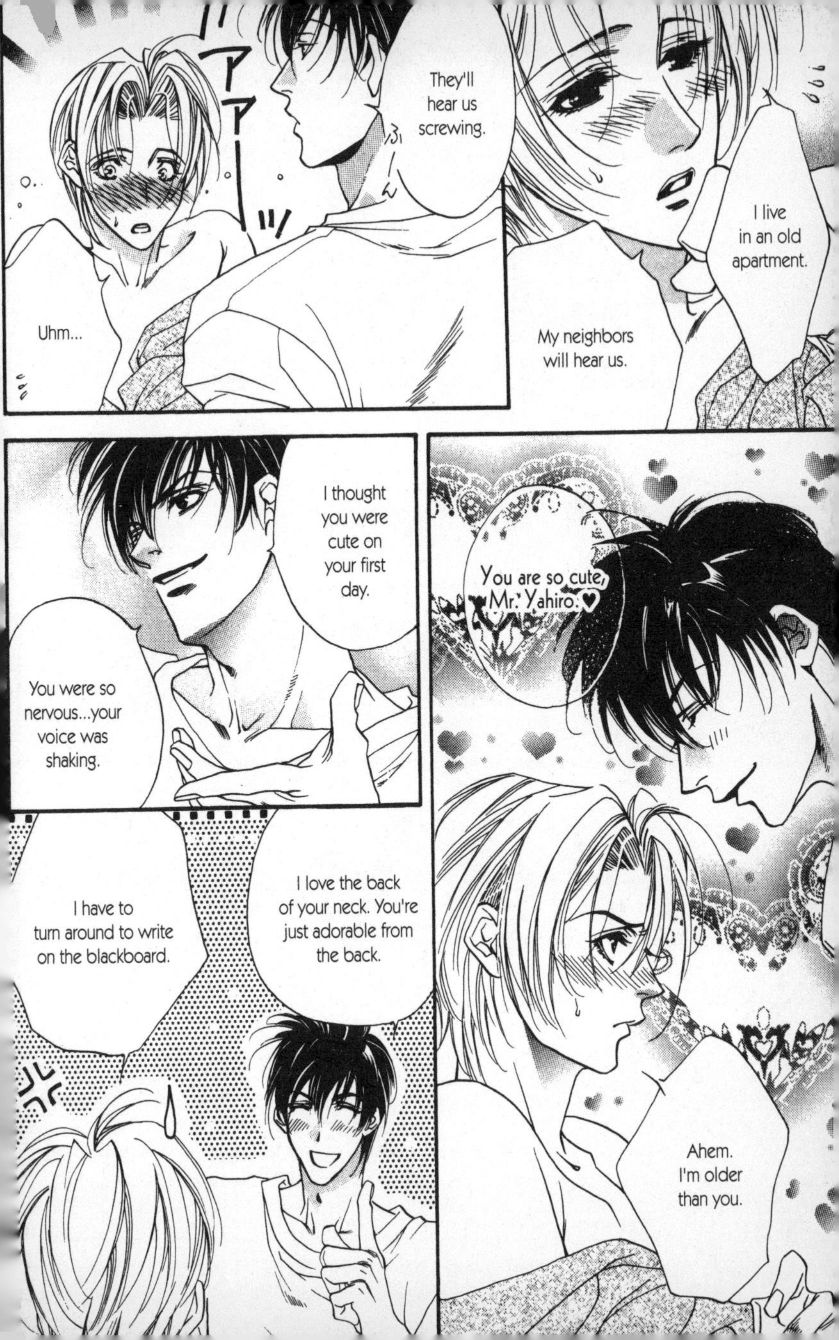

I live in an old apartment.
My neighbors will hear us.
They'll hear us screwing.
Uhm...
I thought you were cute on your first day.
You were so nervous...your voice was shaking.
I have to turn around to write on the blackboard.
I love the back of your neck. You're just adorable from the back.
You are so cute, Mr. Yahiro.♥
Ahem. I'm older than you.

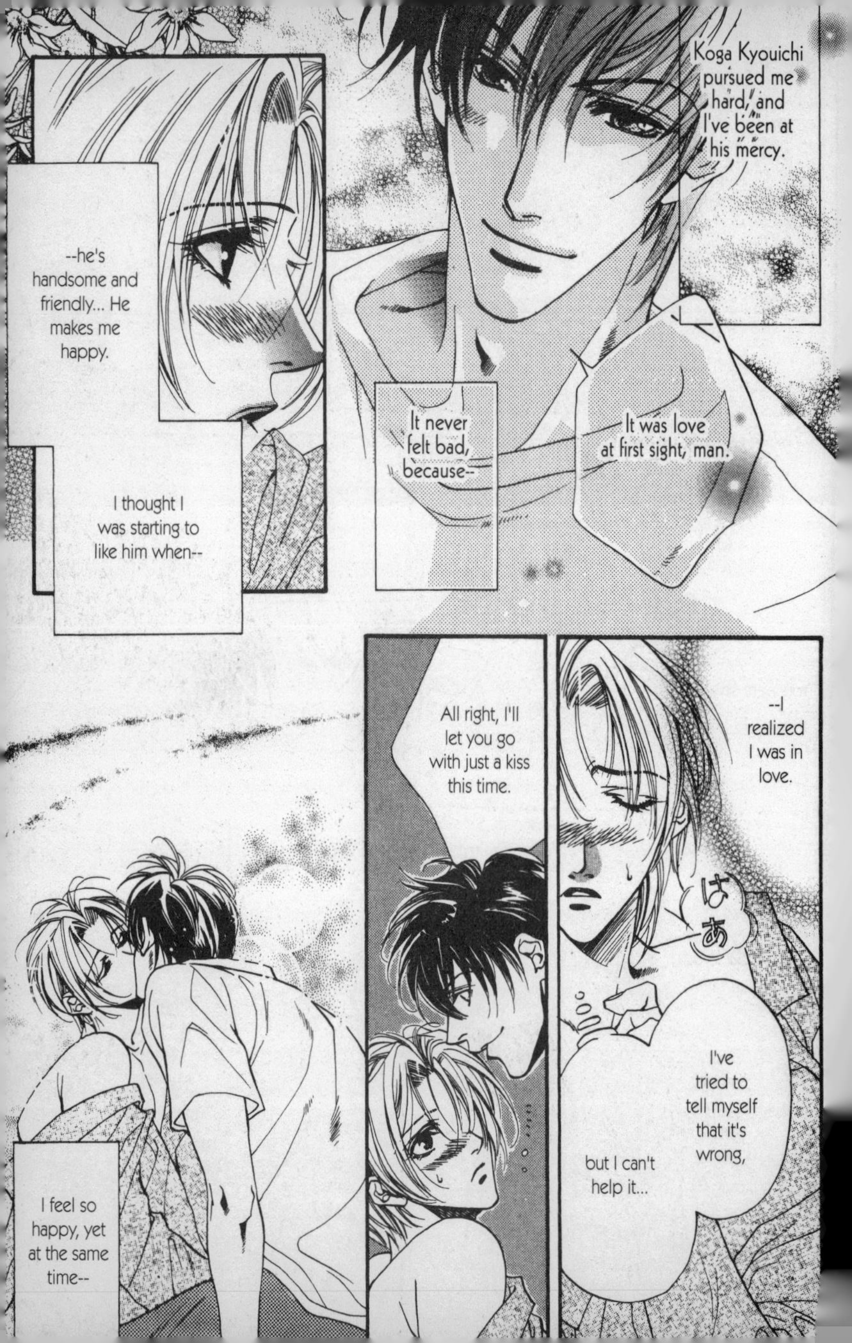
Koga Kyouichi pursued me hard, and I've been at his mercy.
It was love at first sight, man.
It never felt bad, because--
--he's handsome and friendly... He makes me happy.
I thought I was starting to like him when--
--I realized I was in love.
はあ
I've tried to tell myself that it's wrong,
but I can't help it...
All right, I'll let you go with just a kiss this time.
I feel so happy, yet at the same time--

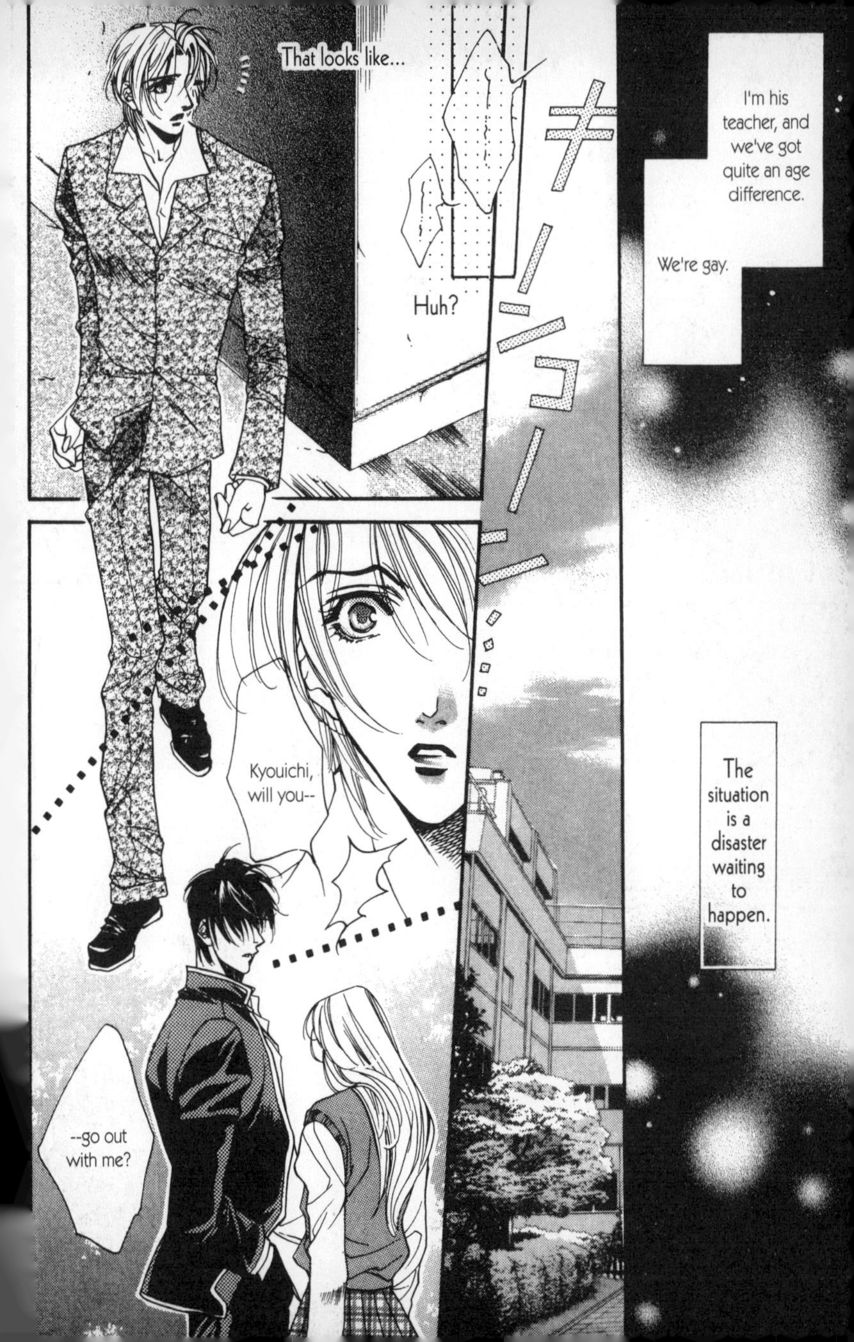
I'm his teacher, and we've got quite an age difference.
We're gay.
The situation is a disaster waiting to happen.
キーンコーン
Huh?
That looks like...
Kyouichi, will you--
--go out with me?

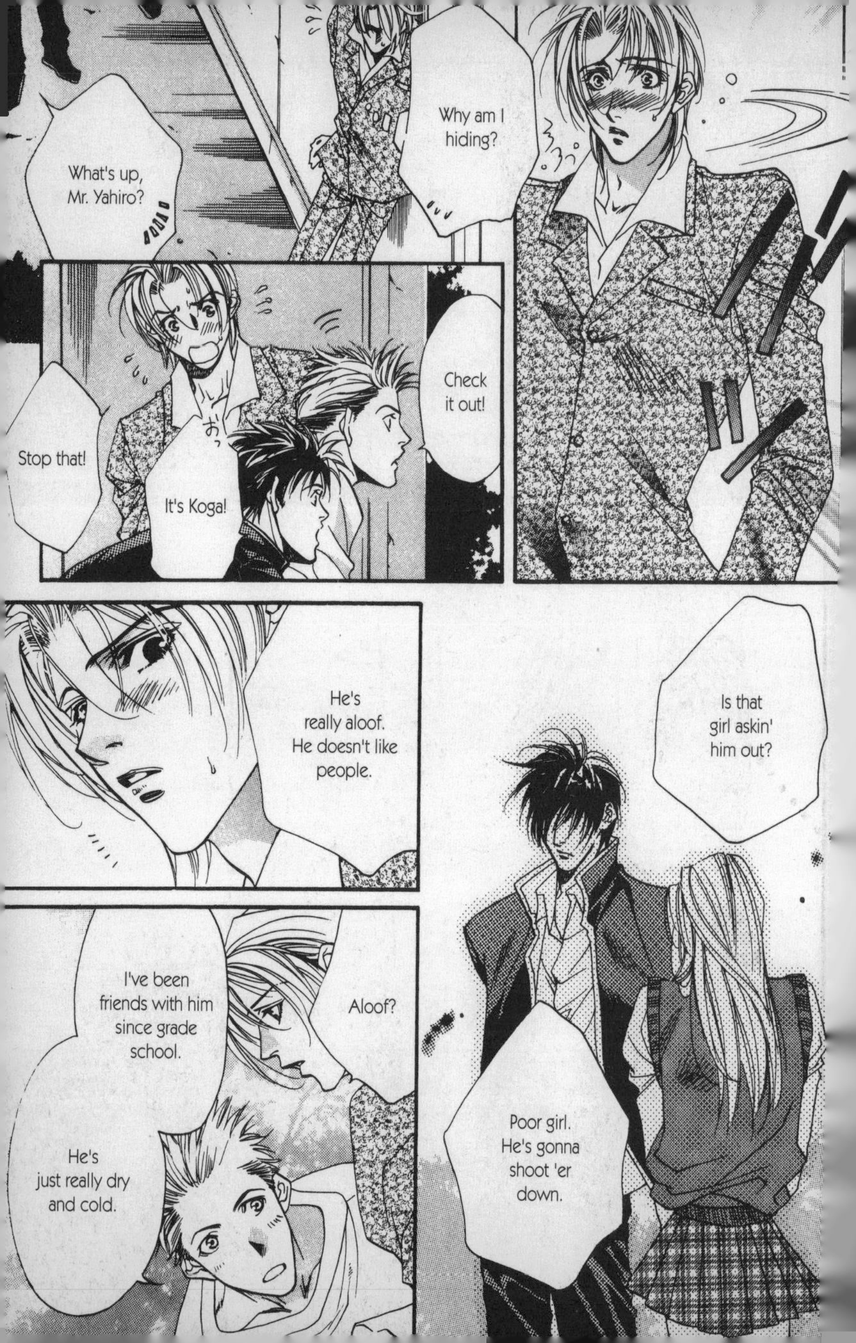
Why am I hiding?
What's up, Mr. Yahiro?
Check it out!
It's Koga!
Stop that!
Is that girl askin' him out?
Poor girl. He's gonna shoot 'er down.
He's really aloof. He doesn't like people.
Aloof?
I've been friends with him since grade school.
He's just really dry and cold.

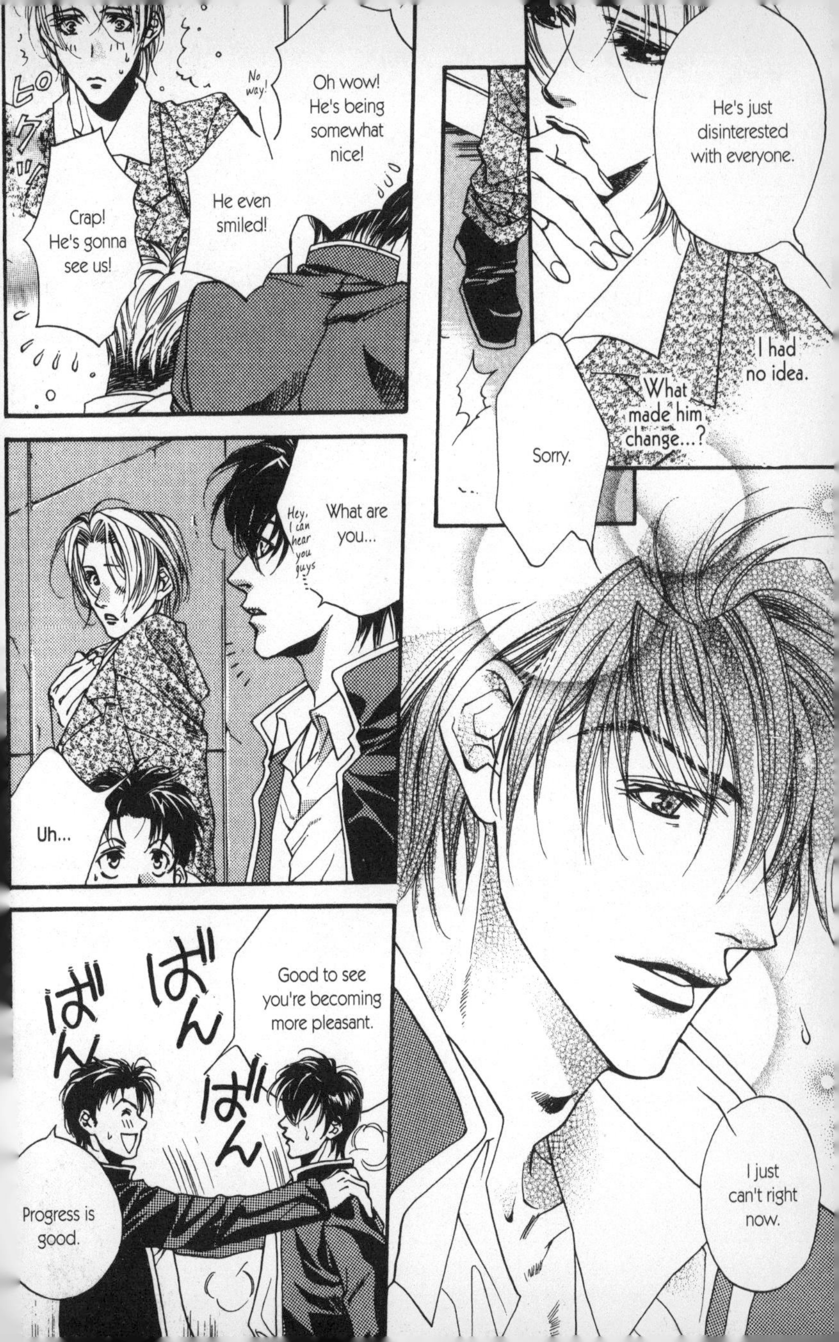
He's just disinterested with everyone.
I had no idea.
What made him change...?
Sorry.
I just can't right now.
Oh wow! He's being somewhat nice!
No way!
He even smiled!
Crap! He's gonna see us!
What are you...
Hey, I can hear you guys
Uh...
Good to see you're becoming more pleasant.
ばん ばん ばん
Progress is good.

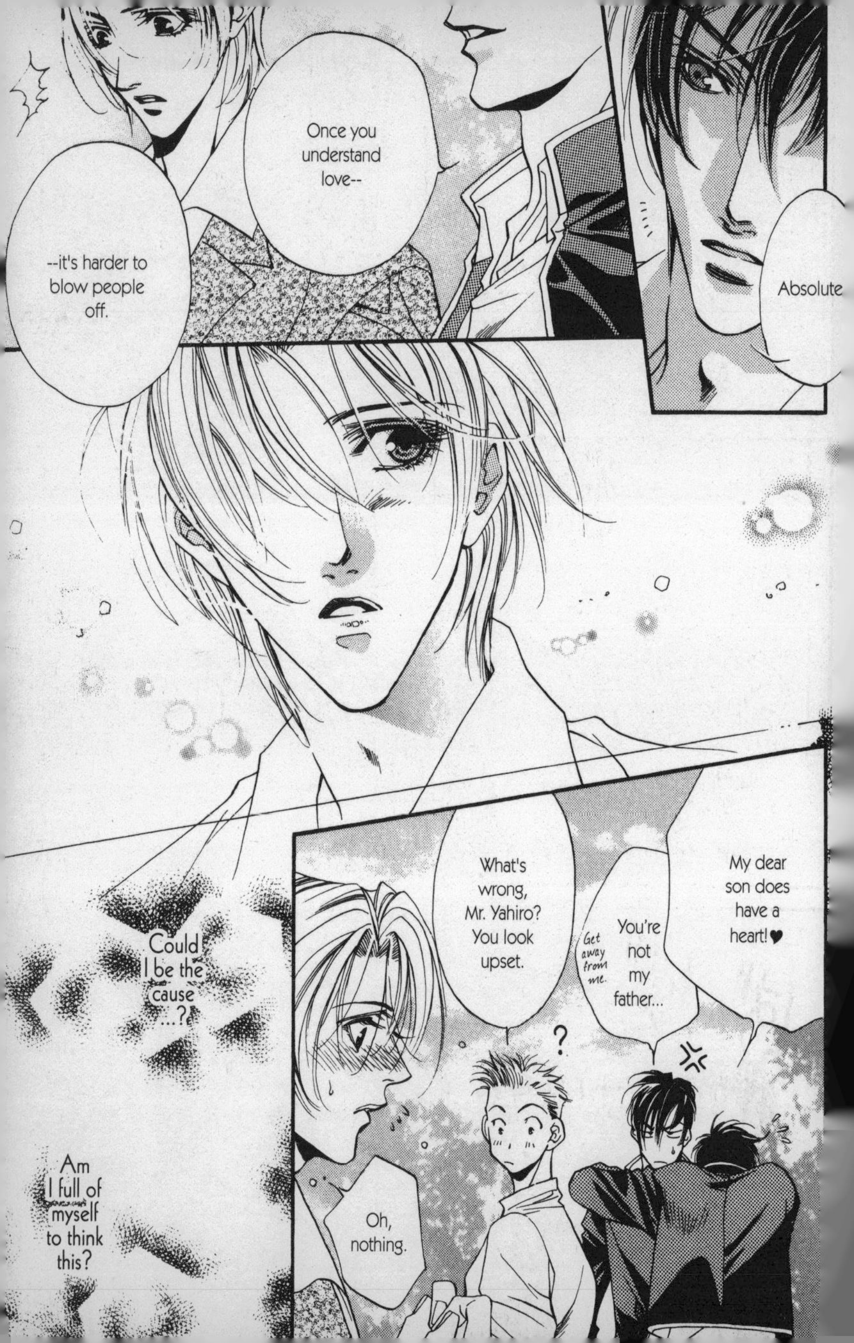
Absolute
Once you understand love--
--it's harder to blow people off.
My dear son does have a heart!♥
You're not my father...
Get away from me.
What's wrong, Mr. Yahiro? You look upset.
Oh, nothing.
Could I be the cause ...?
Am I full of myself to think this?

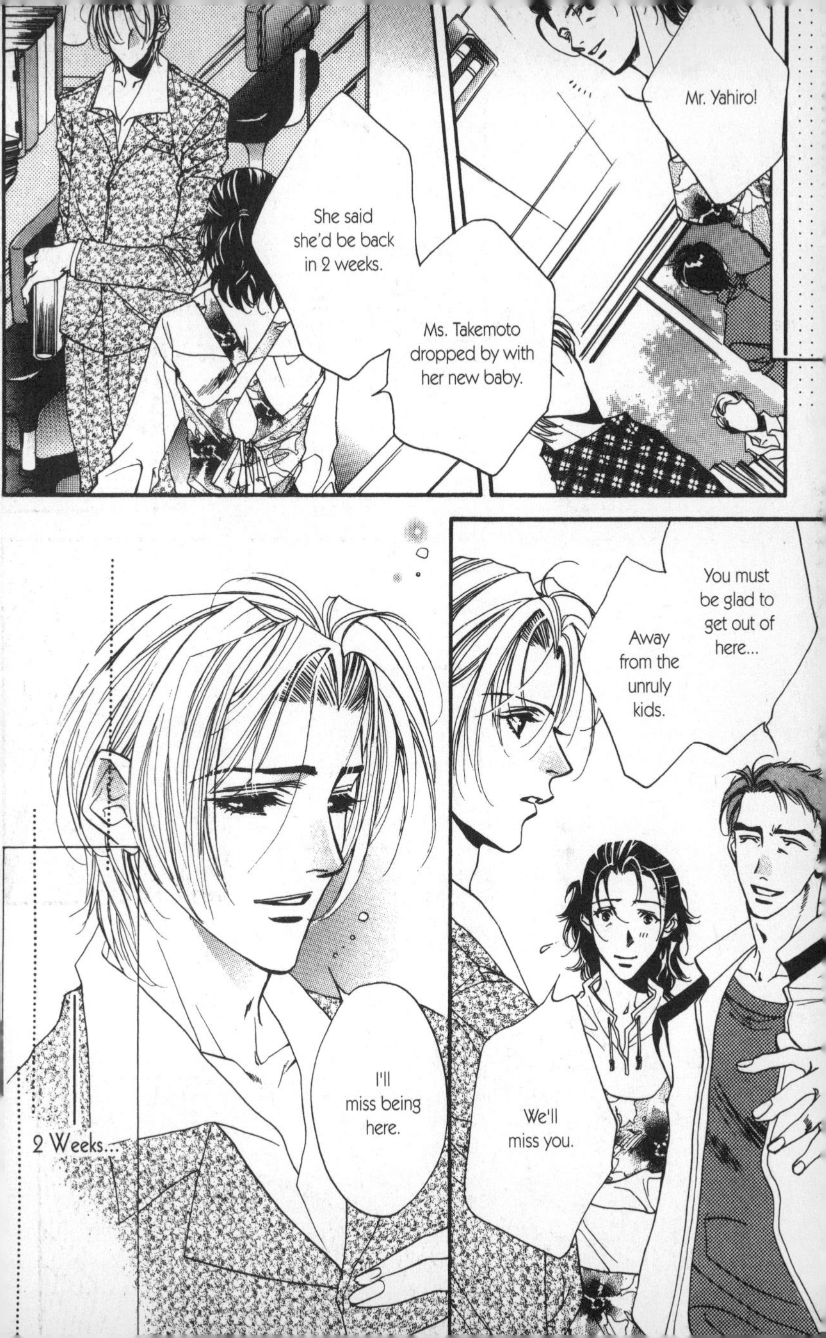
Mr. Yahiro!
Ms. Takemoto dropped by with her new baby.
She said she'd be back in 2 weeks.
You must be glad to get out of here...
Away from the unruly kids.
We'll miss you.
I'll miss being here.
2 Weeks...

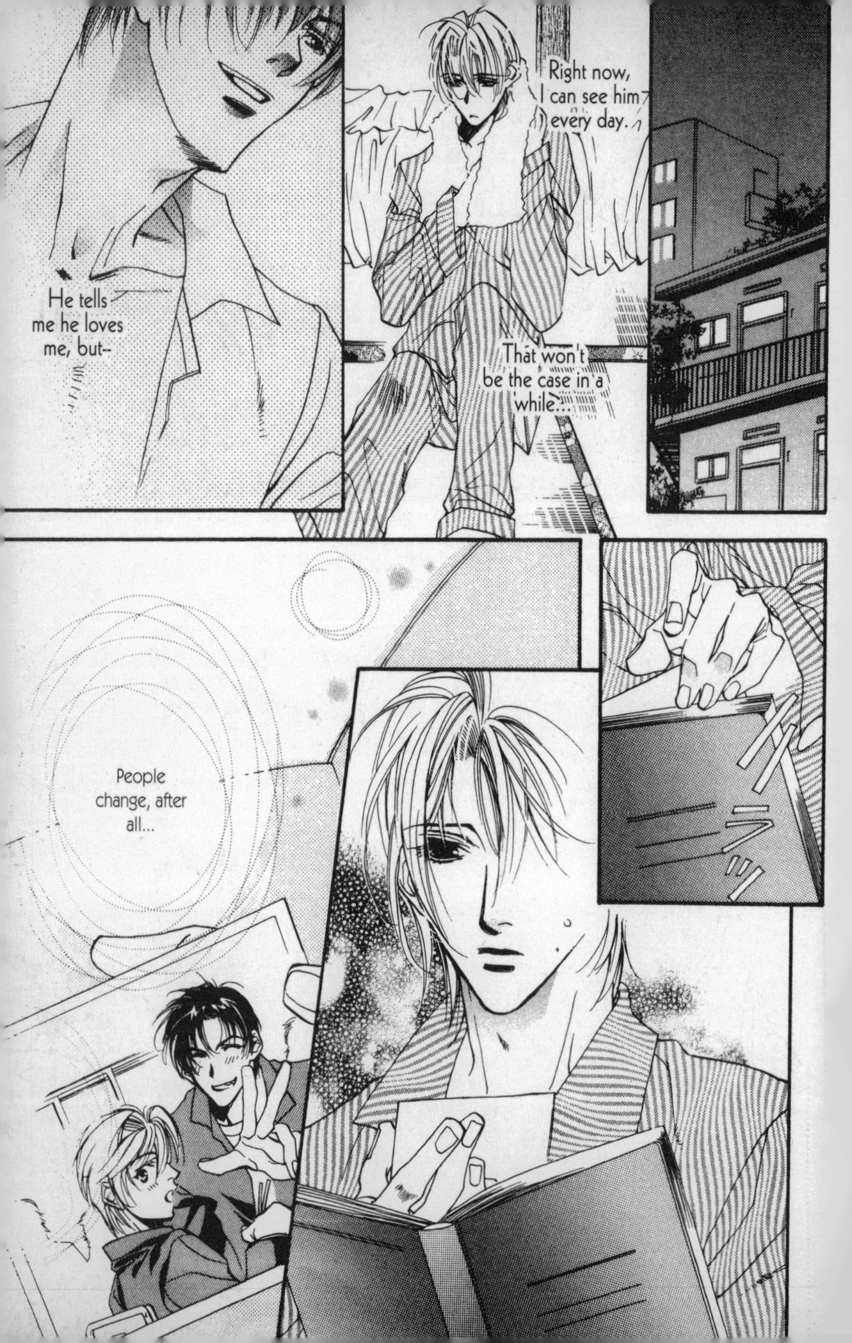
Right now, I can see him every day.
That won't be the case in a while...
He tells me he loves me, but--
People change, after all...

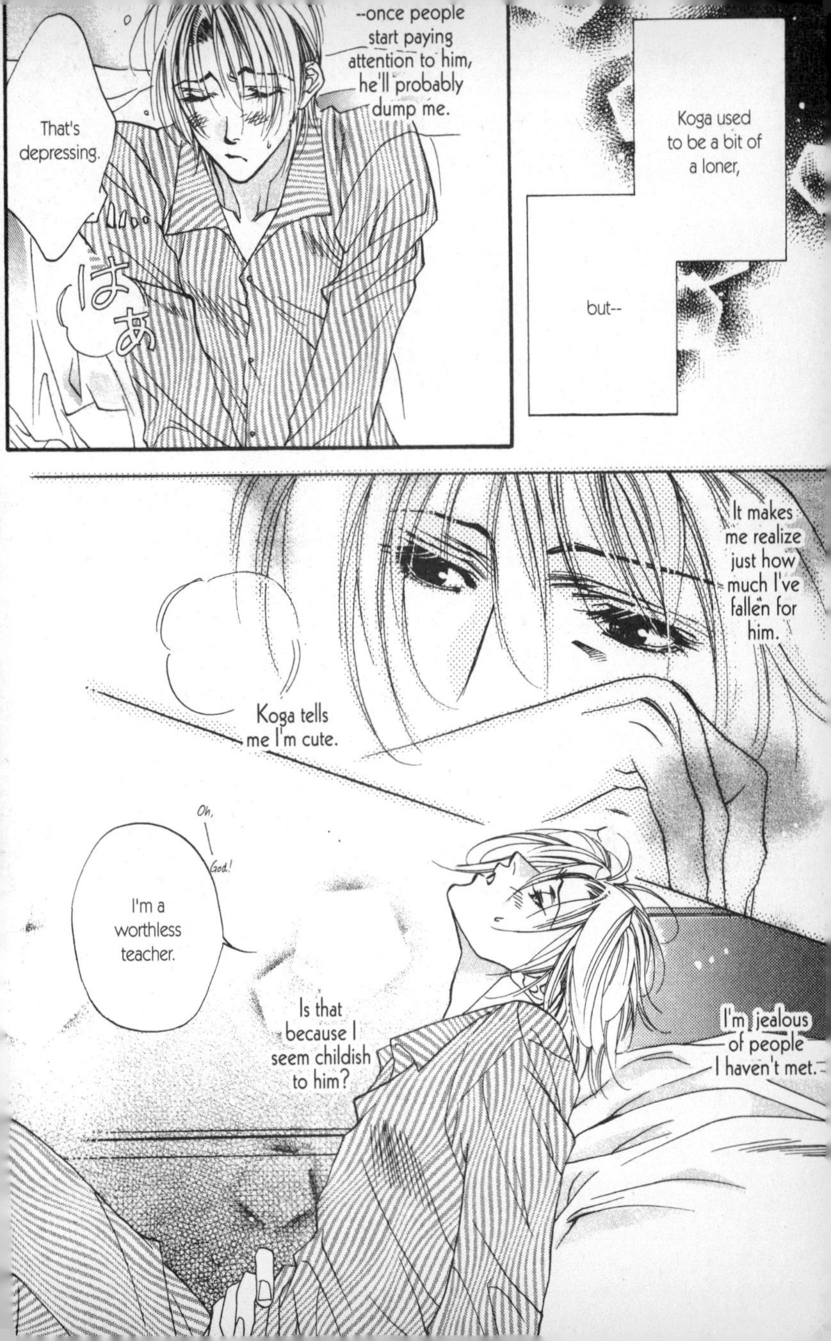
Koga used to be a bit of a loner,
but--
--once people start paying attention to him, he'll probably dump me.
That's depressing.
はあ
It makes me realize just how much I've fallen for him.
Koga tells me I'm cute.
I'm jealous of people I haven't met.
Is that because I seem childish to him?
I'm a worthless teacher.
Oh, God!

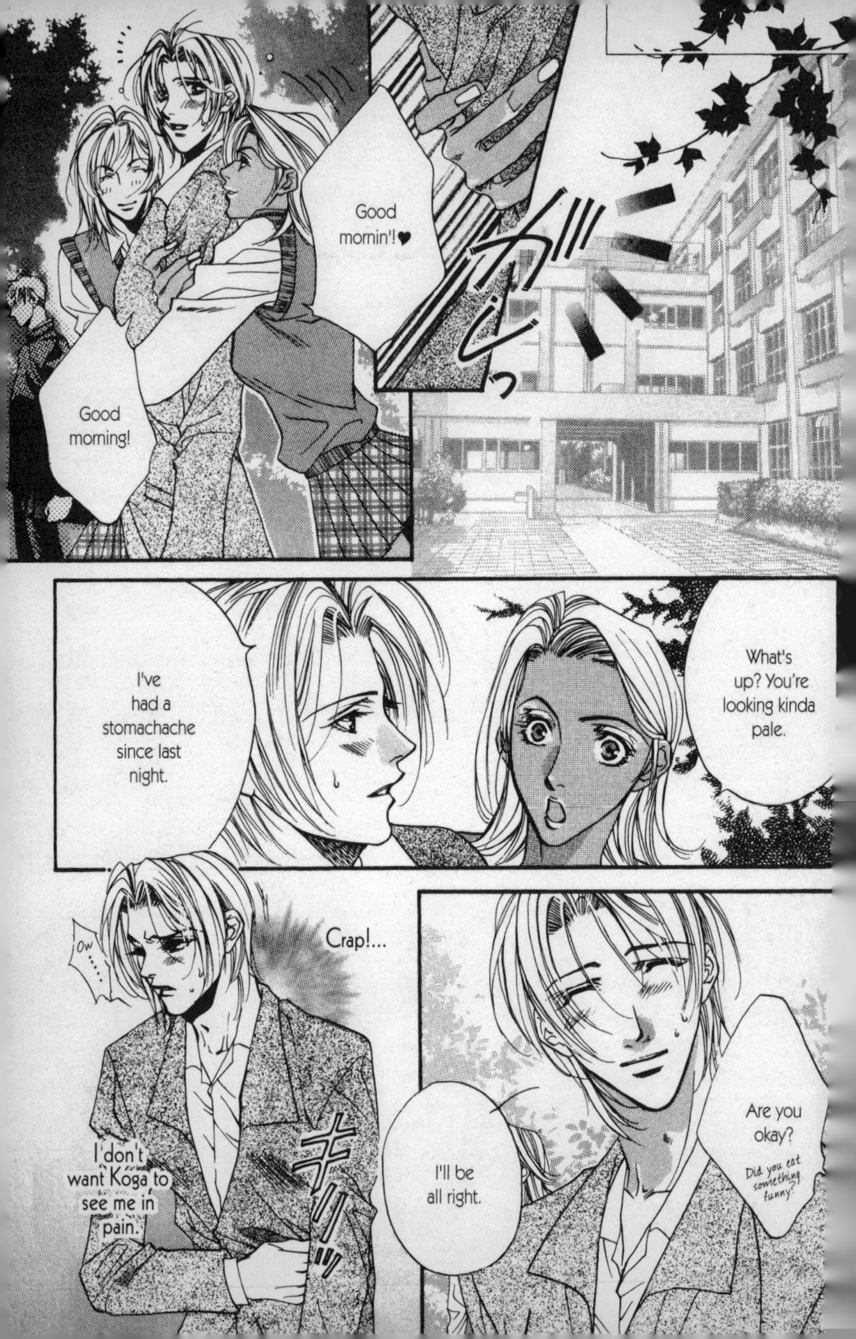
Good mornin'!♥
Good morning!
What's up? You're looking kinda pale.
I've had a stomachache since last night.
Are you okay?
Did you eat something funny?
I'll be all right.
Ow...
Crap!...
I don't want Koga to see me in pain.

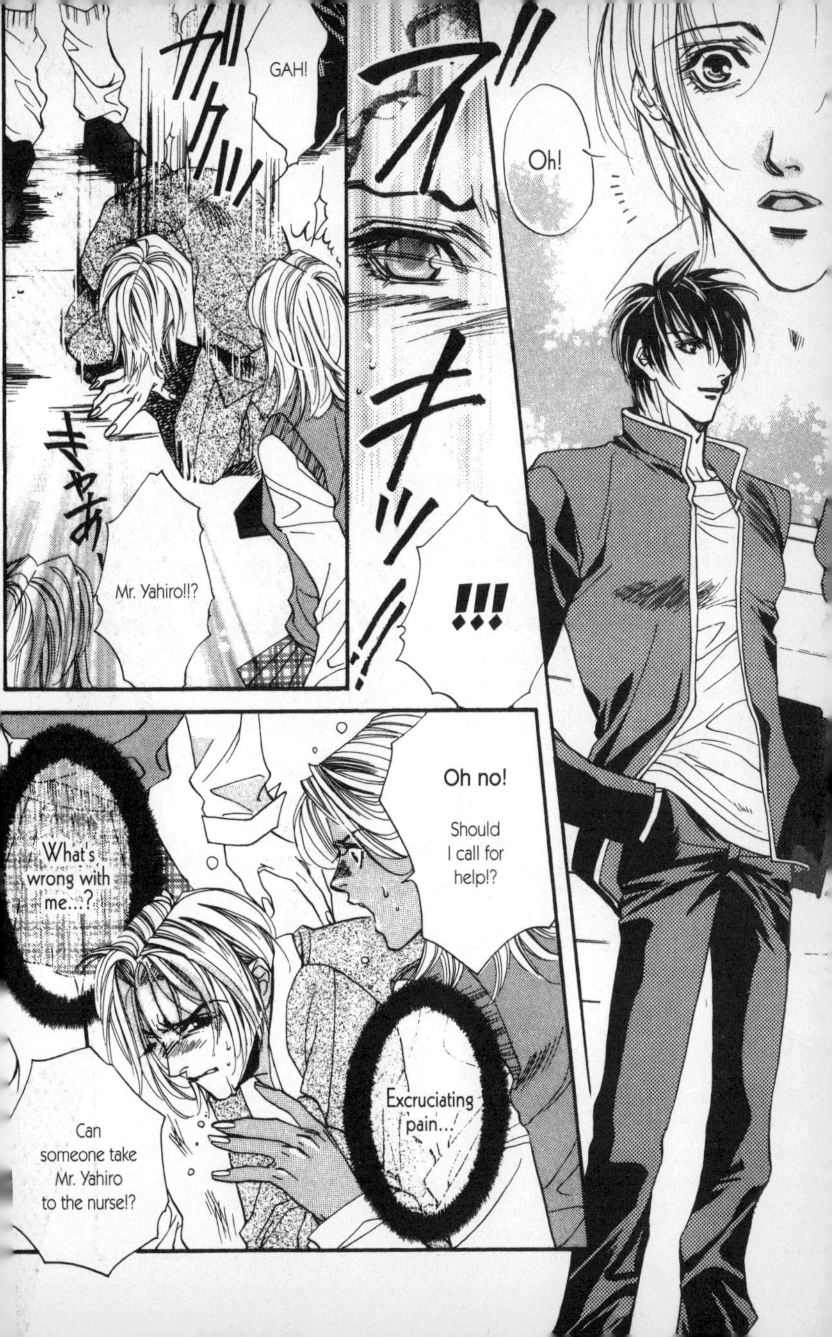
Oh!
!!!
GAH!
ガクッ
きゃあ
Mr. Yahiro!!?
Oh no!
Should I call for help!?
What's wrong with me...?
Excruciating pain...
Can someone take Mr. Yahiro to the nurse!?

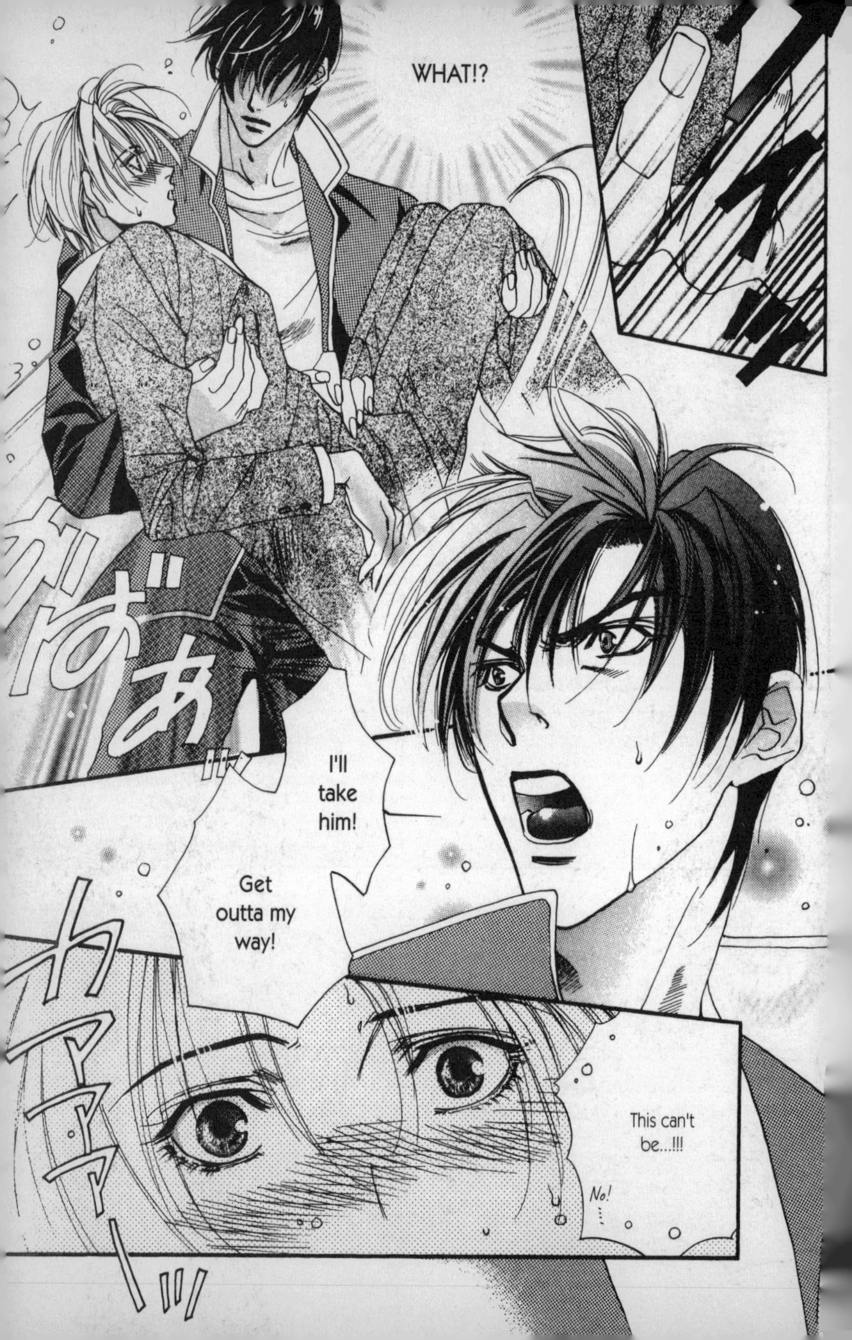
WHAT!?
I'll take him!
Get outta my way!
This can't be...!!!
No!

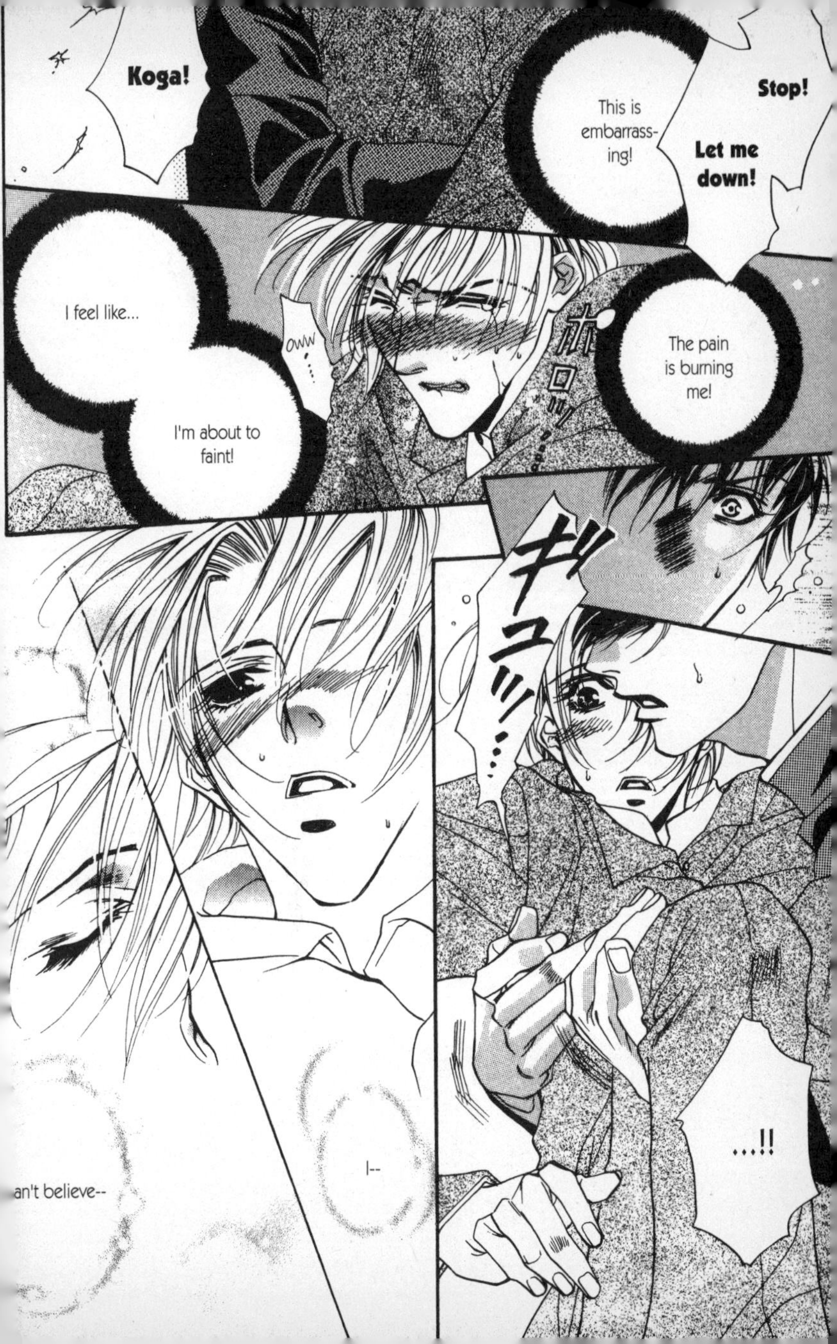
Stop!
Let me down!
This is embarrass-ing!
Koga!
The pain is burning me!
OWW...
I feel like...
I'm about to faint!
...!!
I--
an't believe--

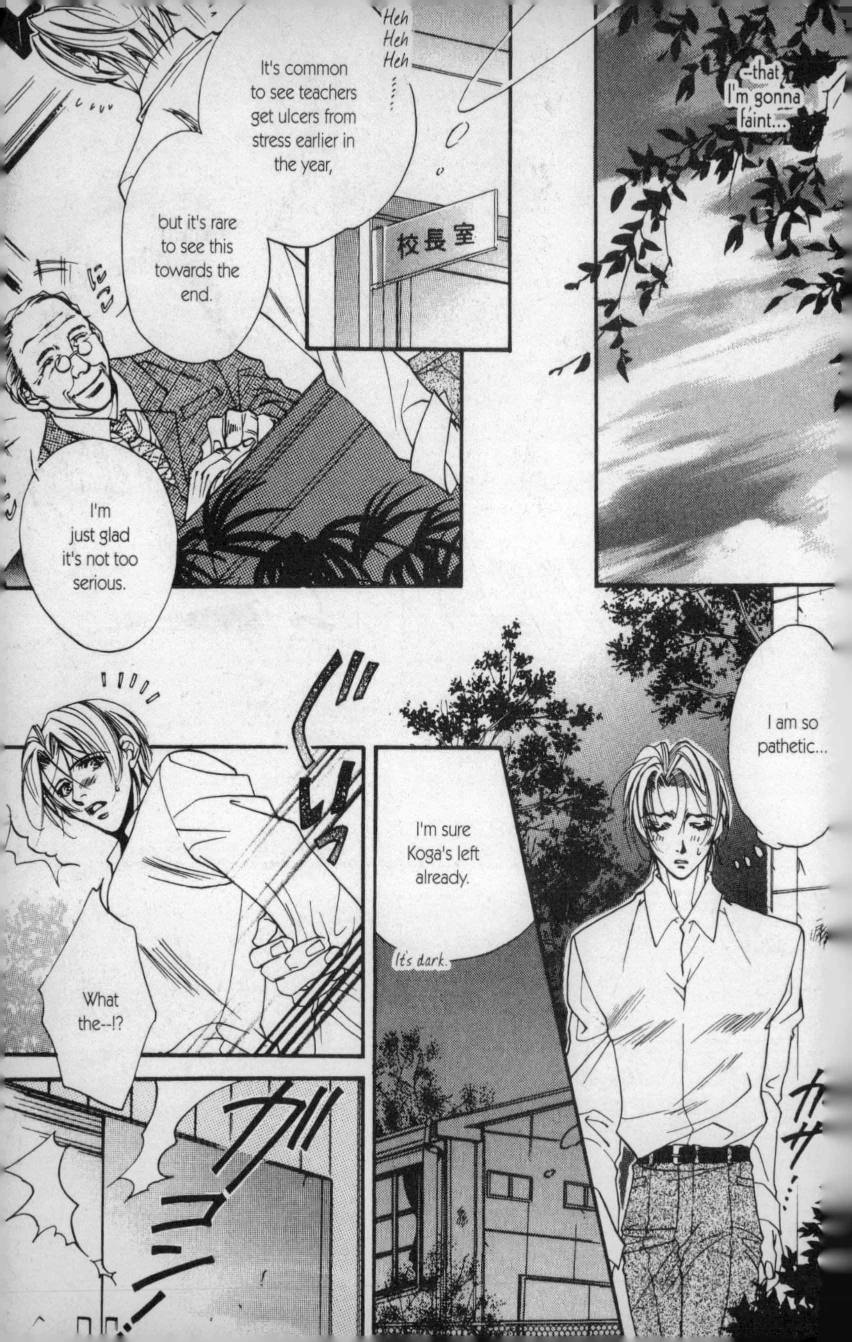

--that I'm gonna faint...
Heh Heh Heh
It's common to see teachers get ulcers from stress earlier in the year,
but it's rare to see this towards the end.
校長室
I'm just glad it's not too serious.
I am so pathetic...
I'm sure Koga's left already.
It's dark.
What the--!?

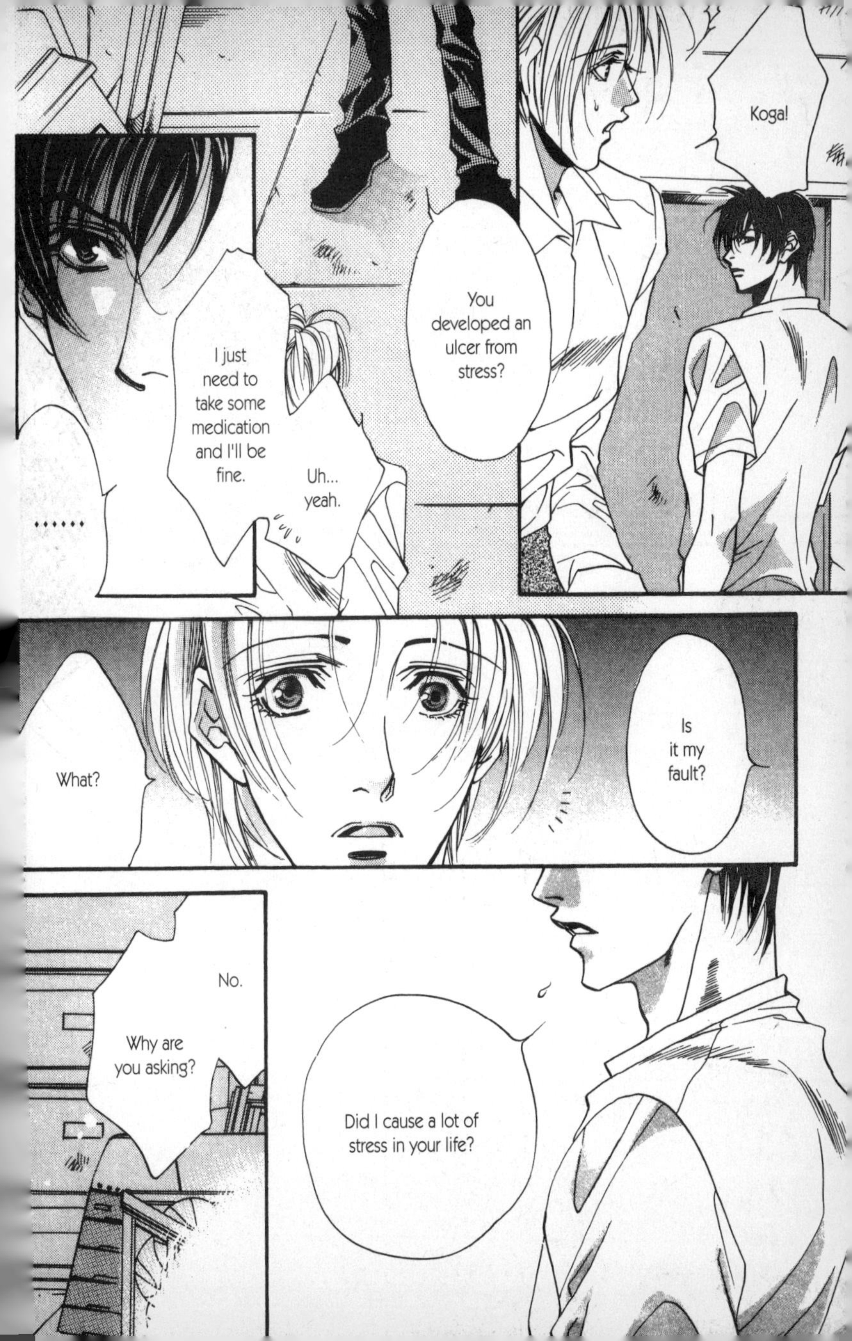
Koga!
You developed an ulcer from stress?
Uh... yeah.
I just need to take some medication and I'll be fine.
......
Is it my fault?
What?
Did I cause a lot of stress in your life?
No.
Why are you asking?

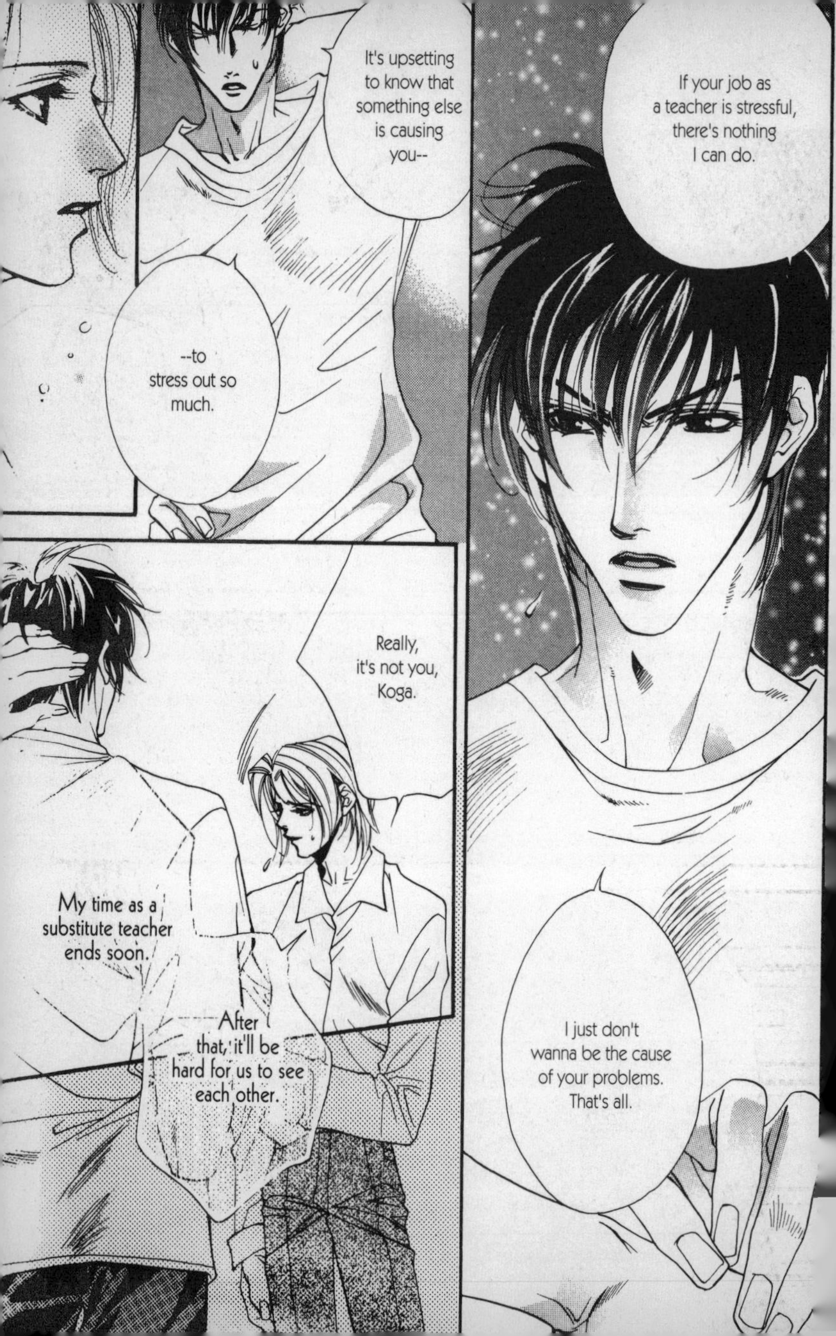

It's upsetting to know that something else is causing you--
--to stress out so much.
If your job as a teacher is stressful, there's nothing I can do.
I just don't wanna be the cause of your problems. That's all.
Really, it's not you, Koga.
My time as a substitute teacher ends soon.
After that, it'll be hard for us to see each other.

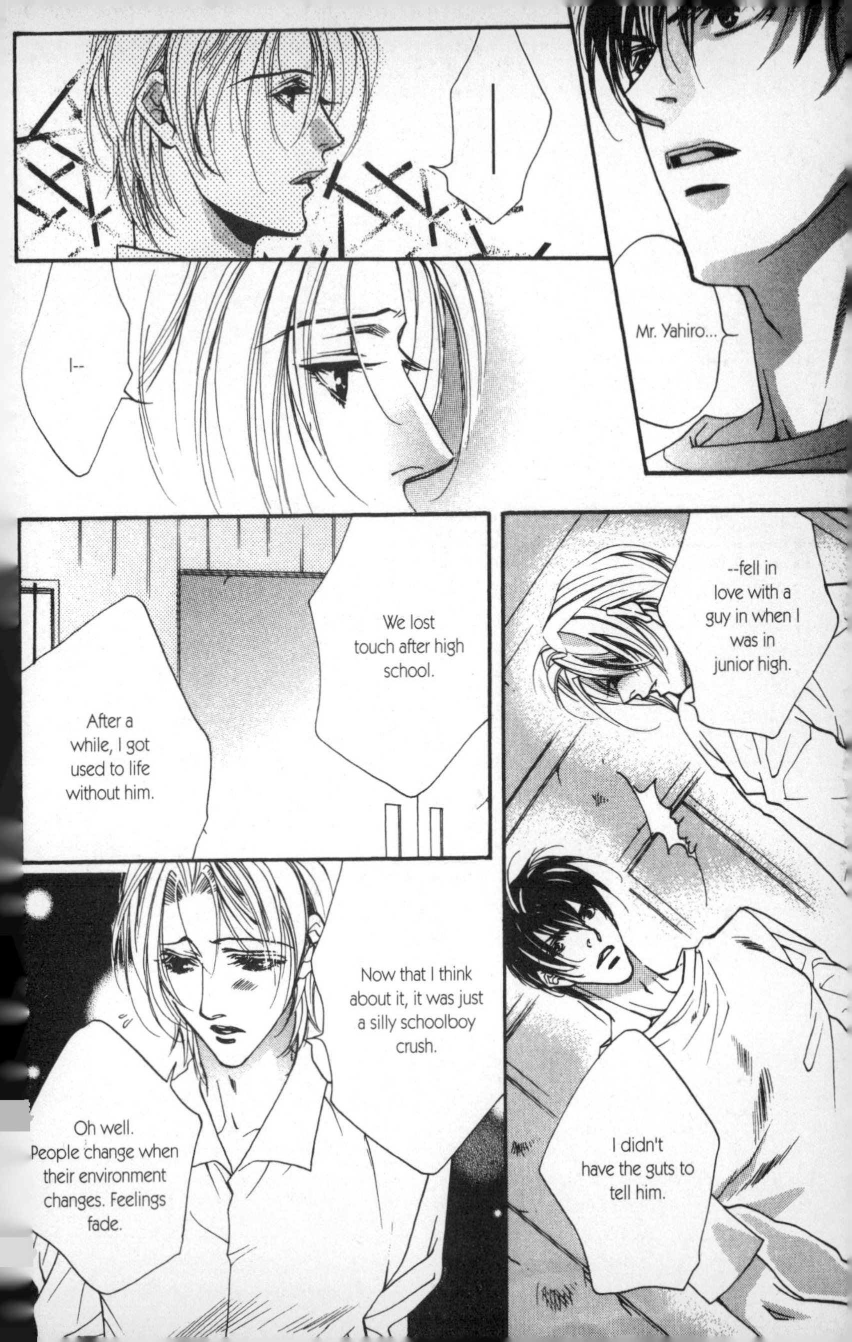

Mr. Yahiro...
I--
--fell in love with a guy in when I was in junior high.
I didn't have the guts to tell him.
We lost touch after high school.
After a while, I got used to life without him.
Now that I think about it, it was just a silly schoolboy crush.
Oh well. People change when their environment changes. Feelings fade.

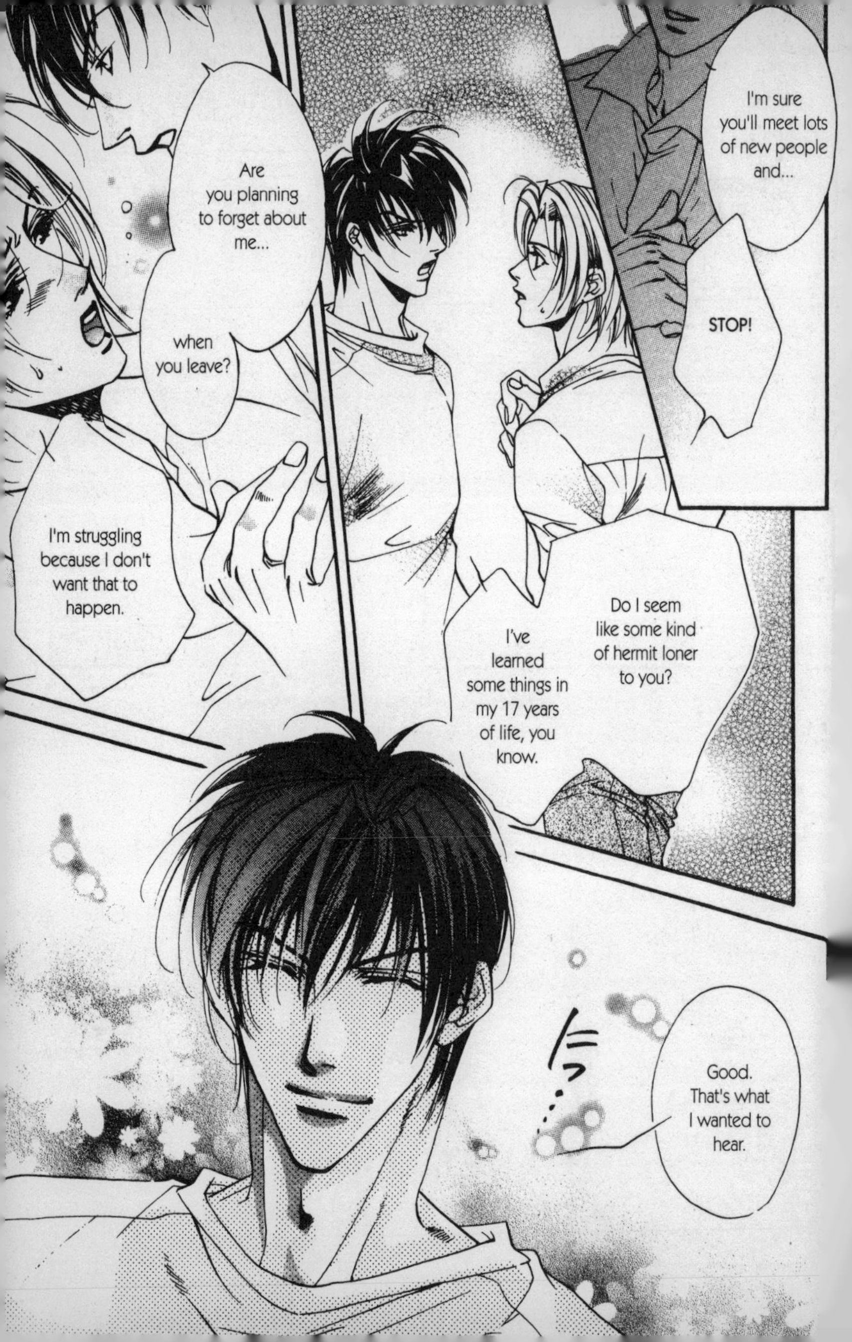
I'm sure you'll meet lots of new people and...
STOP!
Are you planning to forget about me...
when you leave?
I'm struggling because I don't want that to happen.
Do I seem like some kind of hermit loner to you?
I've learned some things in my 17 years of life, you know.
Good. That's what I wanted to hear.

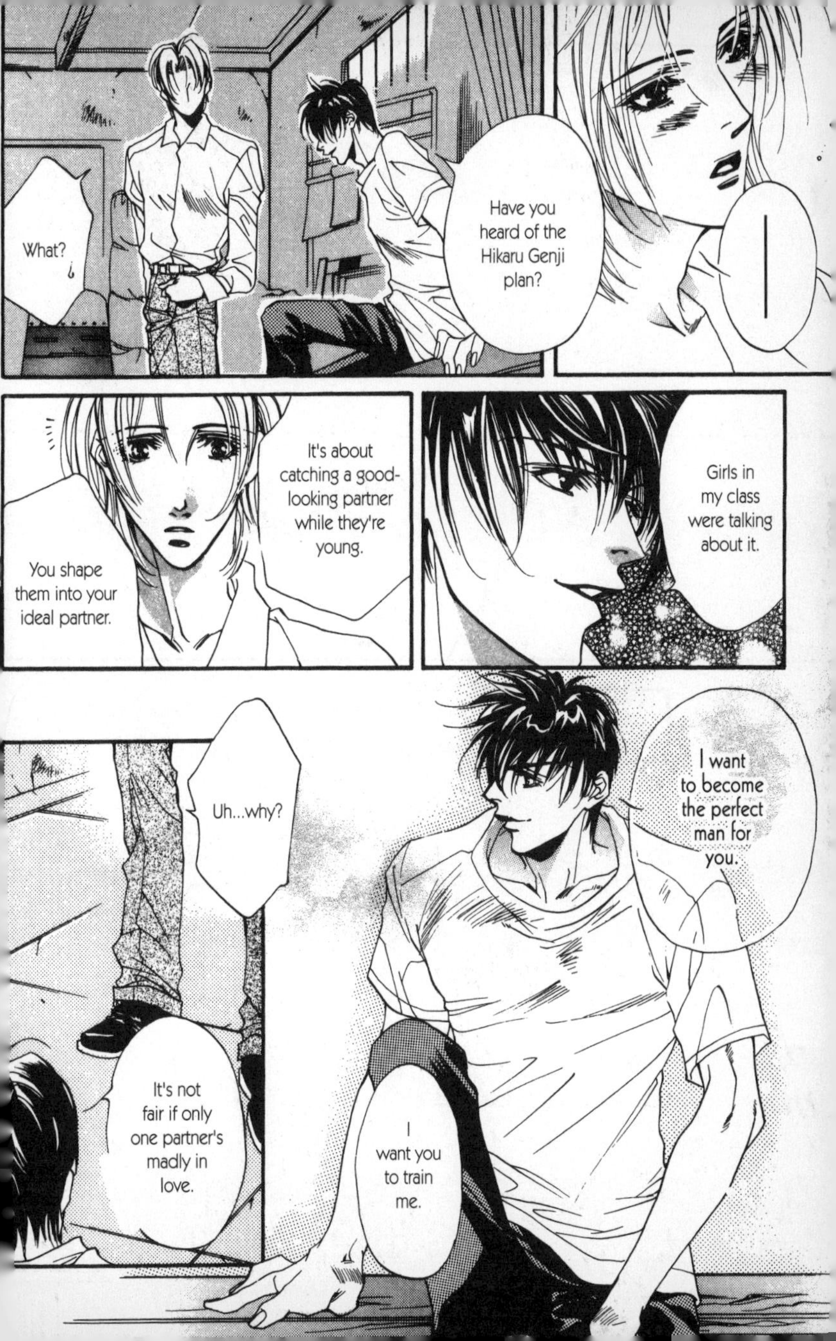
Have you heard of the Hikaru Genji plan?
What?
Girls in my class were talking about it.
It's about catching a good-looking partner while they're young.
You shape them into your ideal partner.
I want to become the perfect man for you.
Uh...why?
It's not fair if only one partner's madly in love.
I want you to train me.

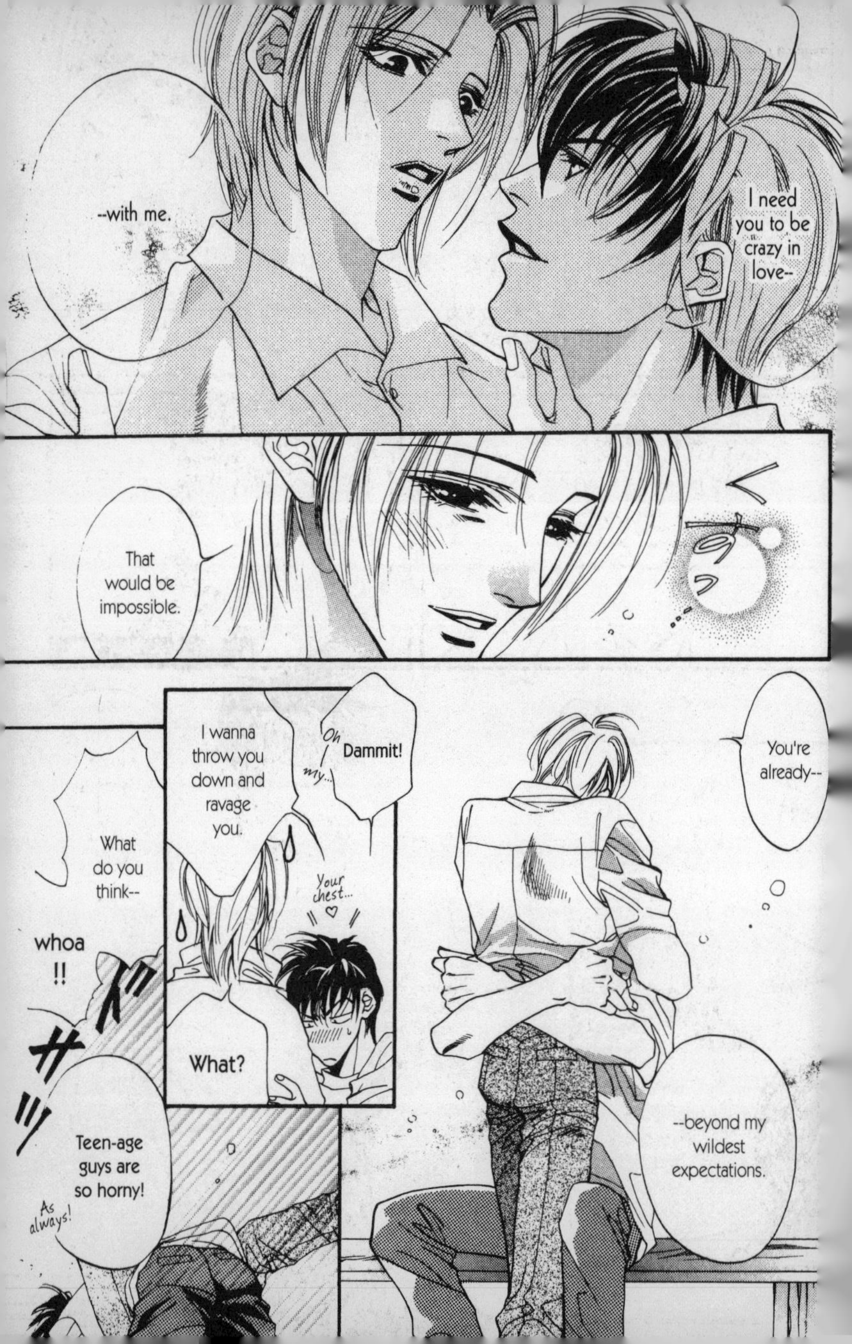
I need you to be crazy in love--
--with me.
That would be impossible.
You're already--
--beyond my wildest expectations.
Dammit!
Oh my...
I wanna throw you down and ravage you.
Your chest...
What?
What do you think--
whoa !!
Teen-age guys are so horny!
As always!

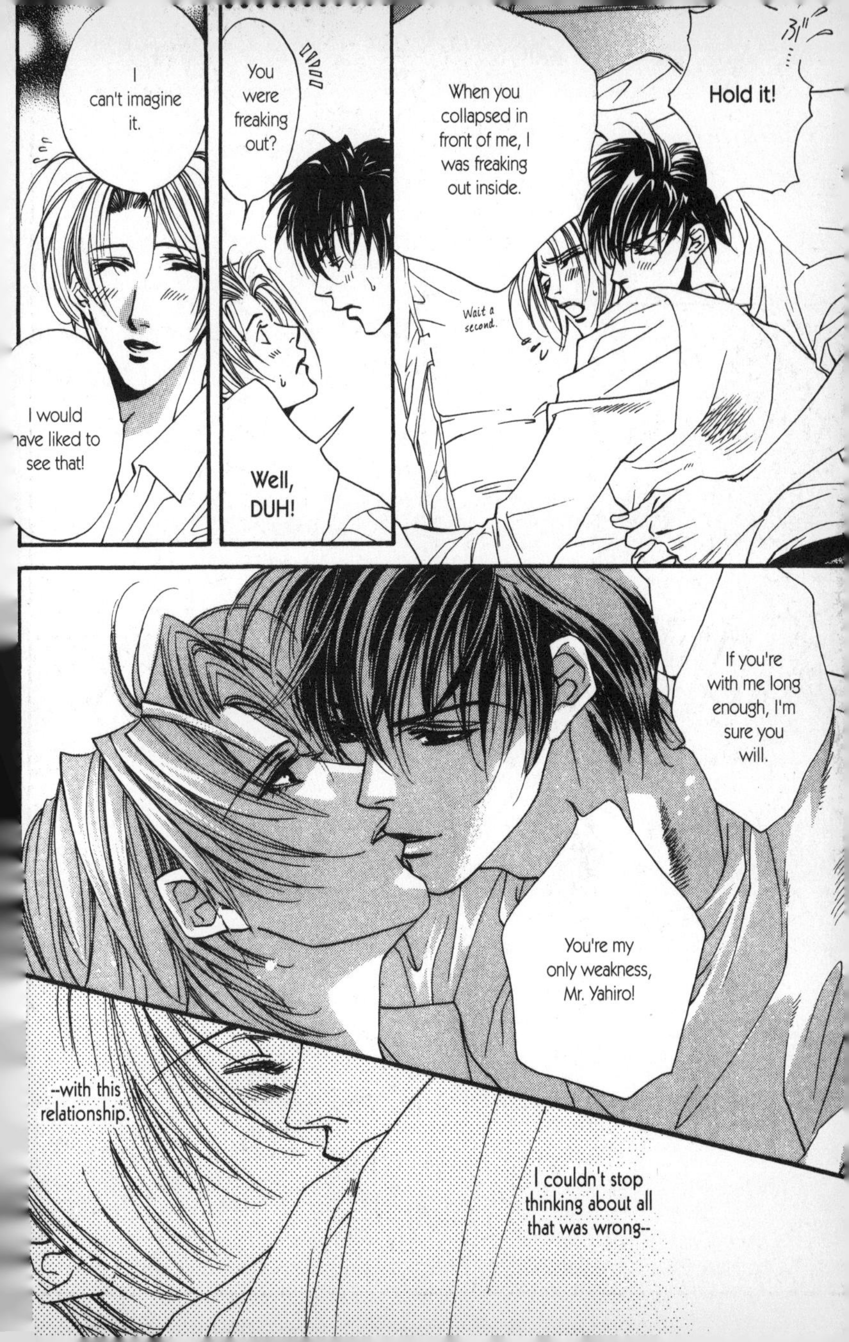

Hold it!
When you collapsed in front of me, I was freaking out inside.
Wait a second.
You were freaking out?
Well, DUH!
I can't imagine it.
I would have liked to see that!
If you're with me long enough, I'm sure you will.
You're my only weakness, Mr. Yahiro!
I couldn't stop thinking about all that was wrong--
--with this relationship.

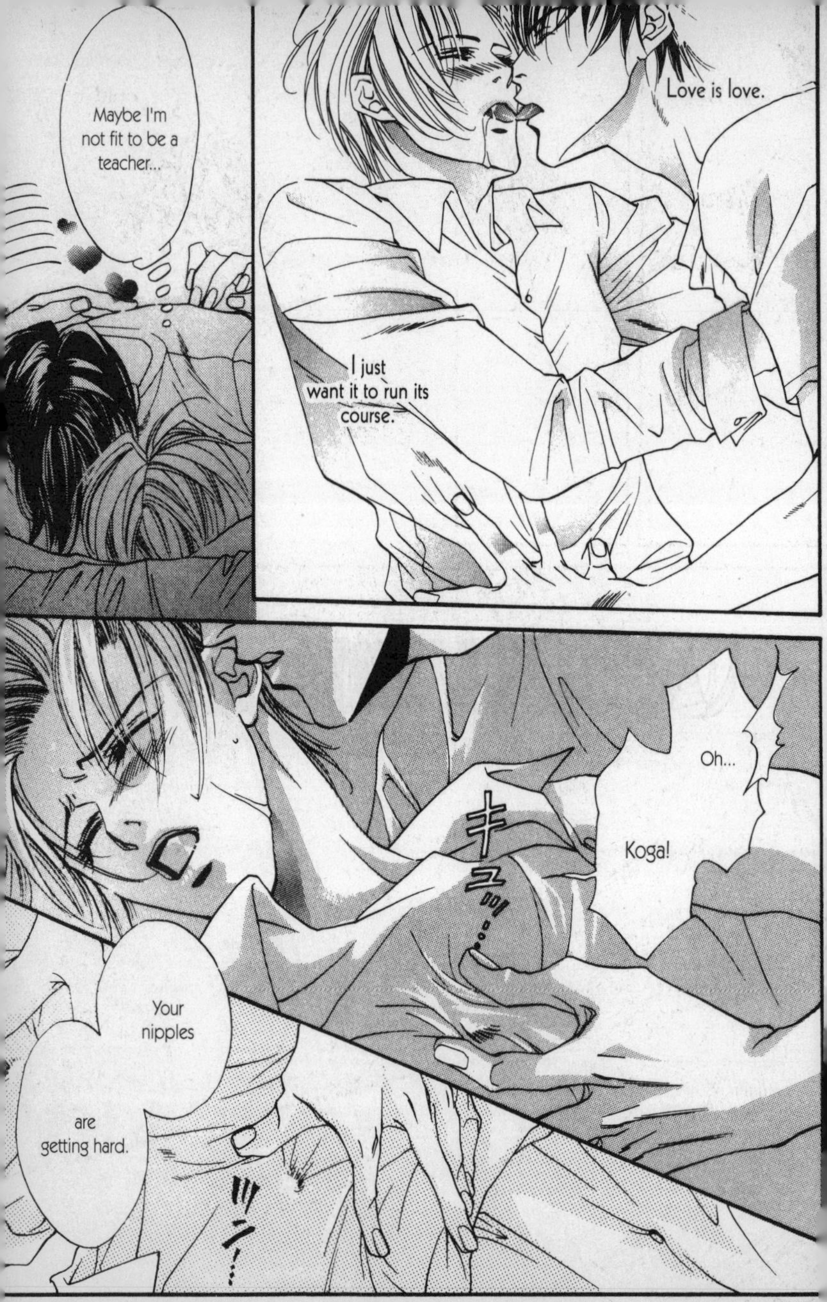
Love is love.
I just want it to run its course.
Maybe I'm not fit to be a teacher...
Oh...
Koga!
Your nipples are getting hard.

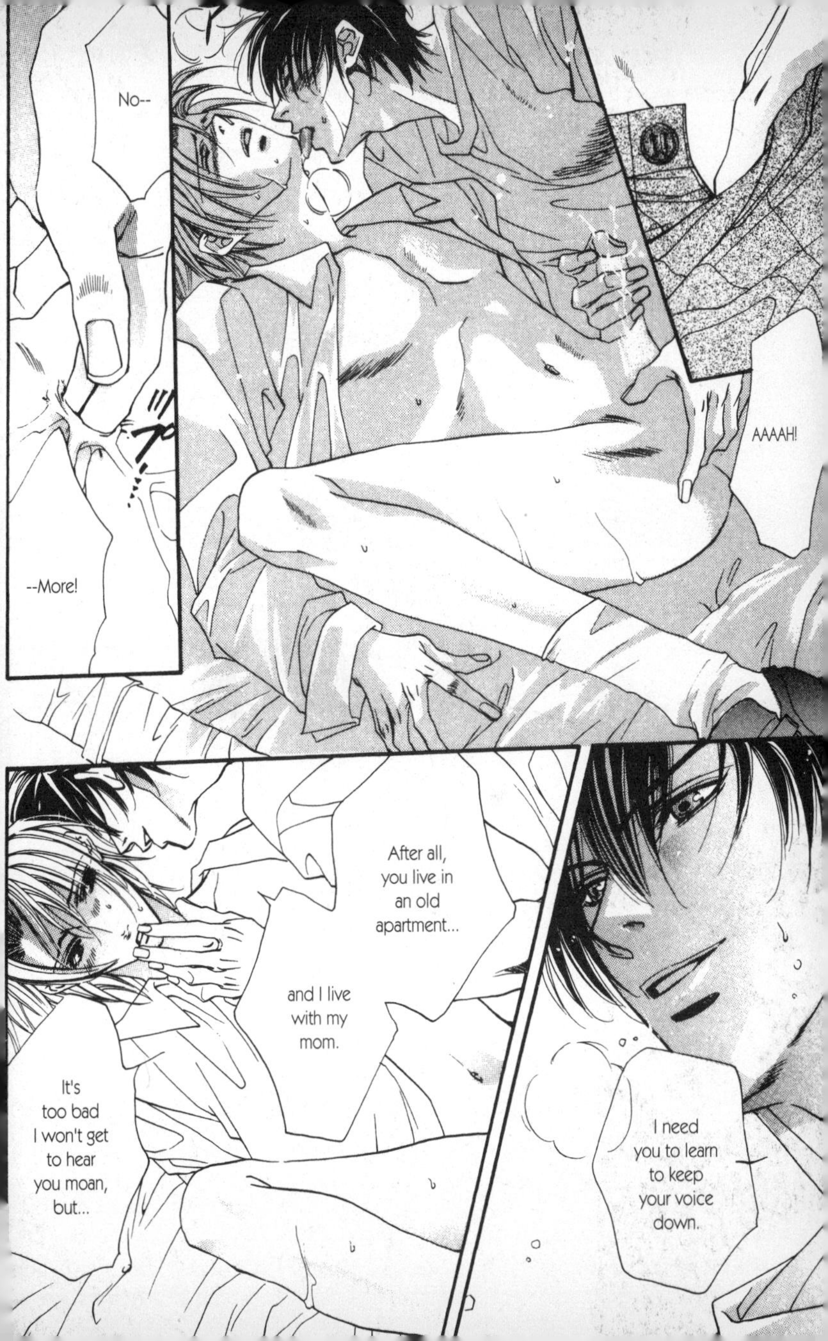
AAAAH!
No--
--More!
After all, you live in an old apartment...
and I live with my mom.
It's too bad I won't get to hear you moan, but...
I need you to learn to keep your voice down.

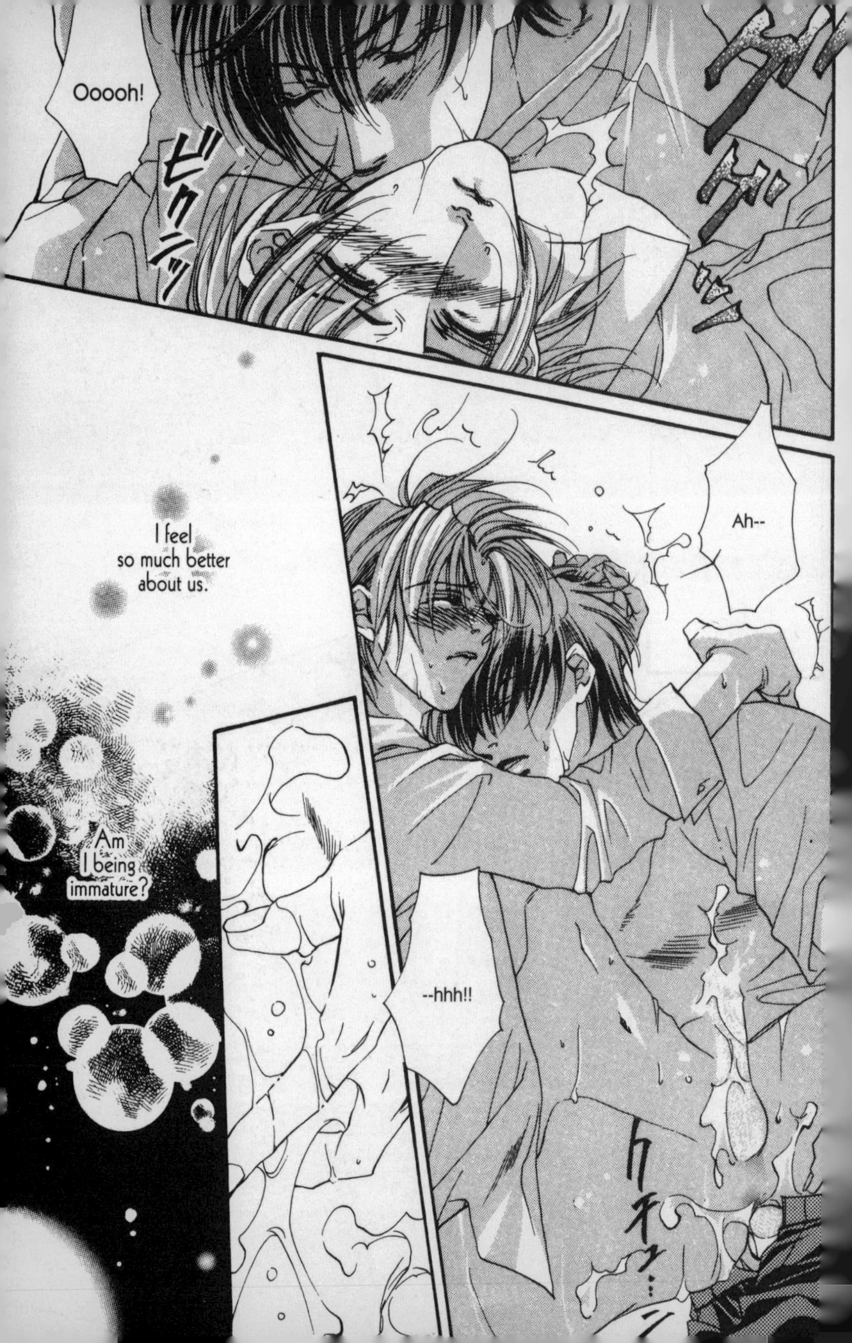
Ooooh!
ビクンッ
Ah--
--hhh!!
I feel so much better about us.
Am I being immature?

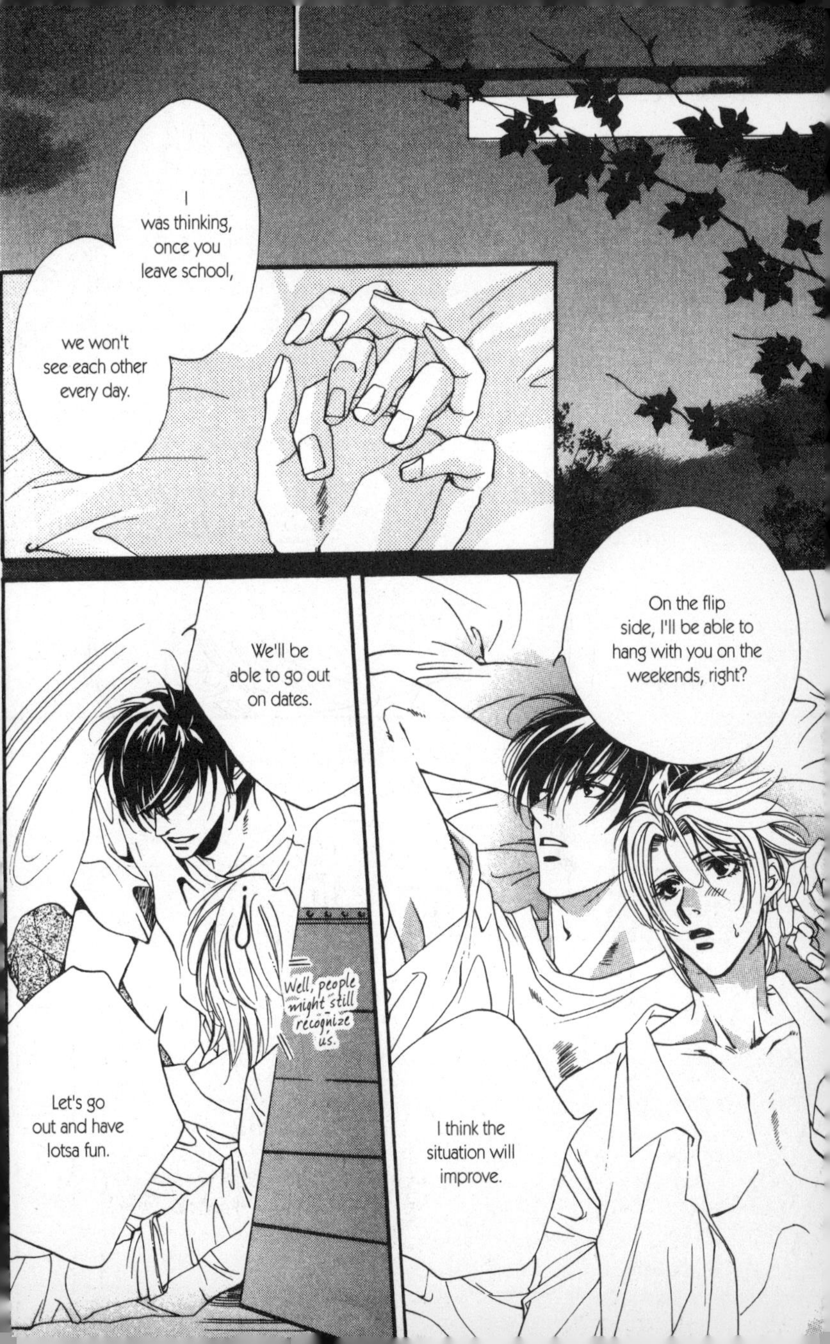
I was thinking, once you leave school,
we won't see each other every day.
On the flip side, I'll be able to hang with you on the weekends, right?
I think the situation will improve.
We'll be able to go out on dates.
Well, people might still recognize us.
Let's go out and have lotsa fun.

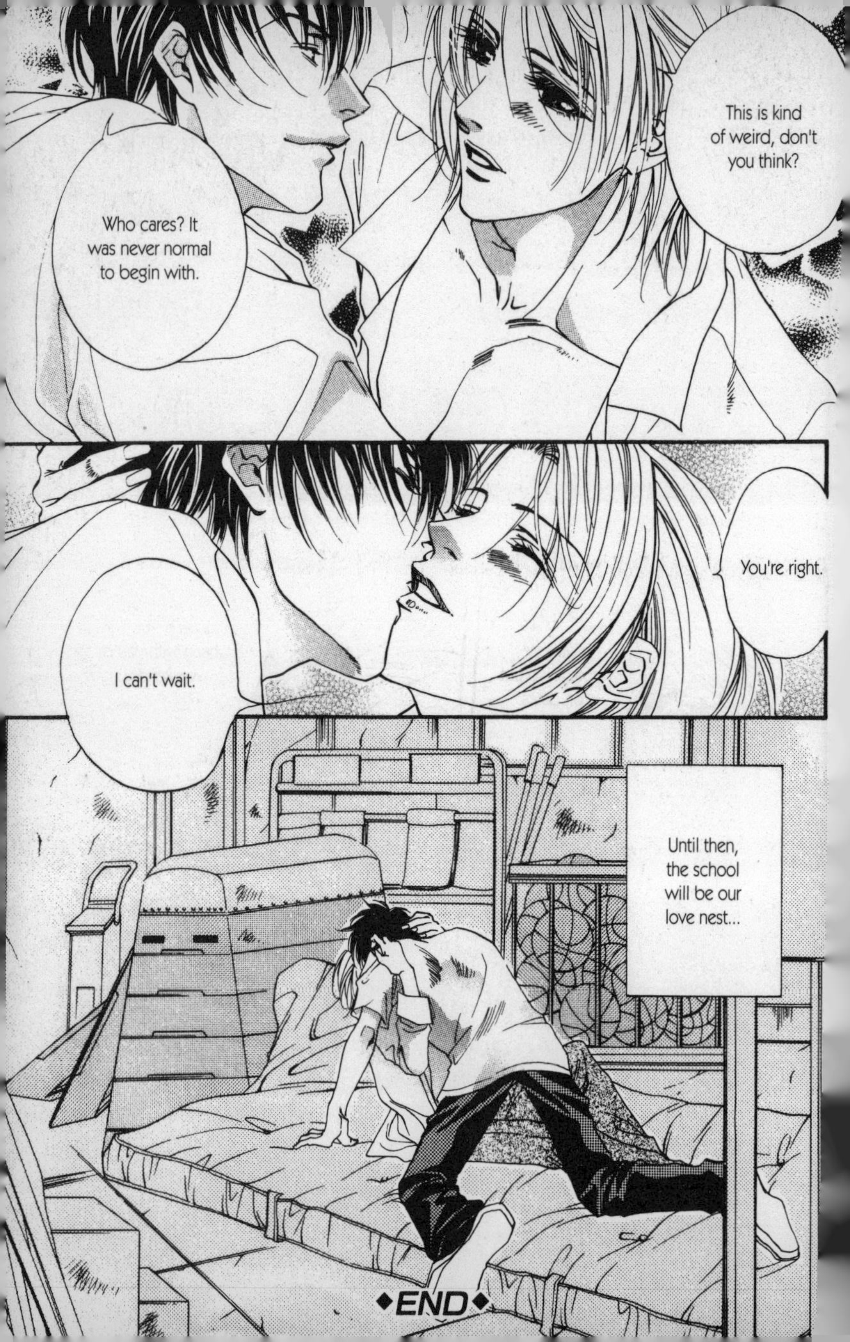
This is kind of weird, don't you think?
Who cares? It was never normal to begin with.
You're right.
I can't wait.
Until then, the school will be our love nest...
◆END◆

....:::but, I'm your teacher.

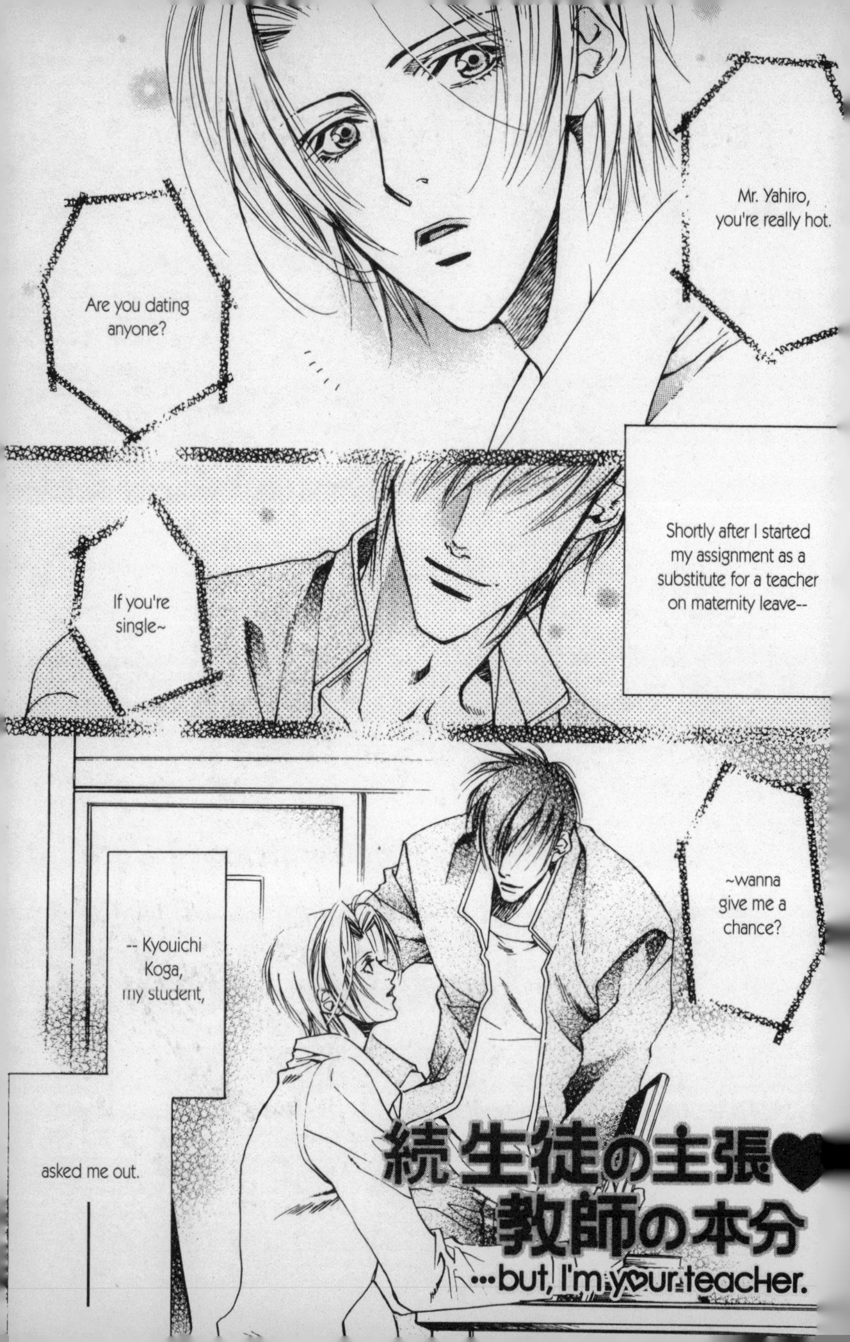
Mr. Yahiro, you're really hot.
Are you dating anyone?
Shortly after I started my assignment as a substitute for a teacher on maternity leave--
If you're single~
~wanna give me a chance?
-- Kyouichi Koga, my student,
asked me out.
続 生徒の主張♥教師の本分
…but, I'm your teacher.

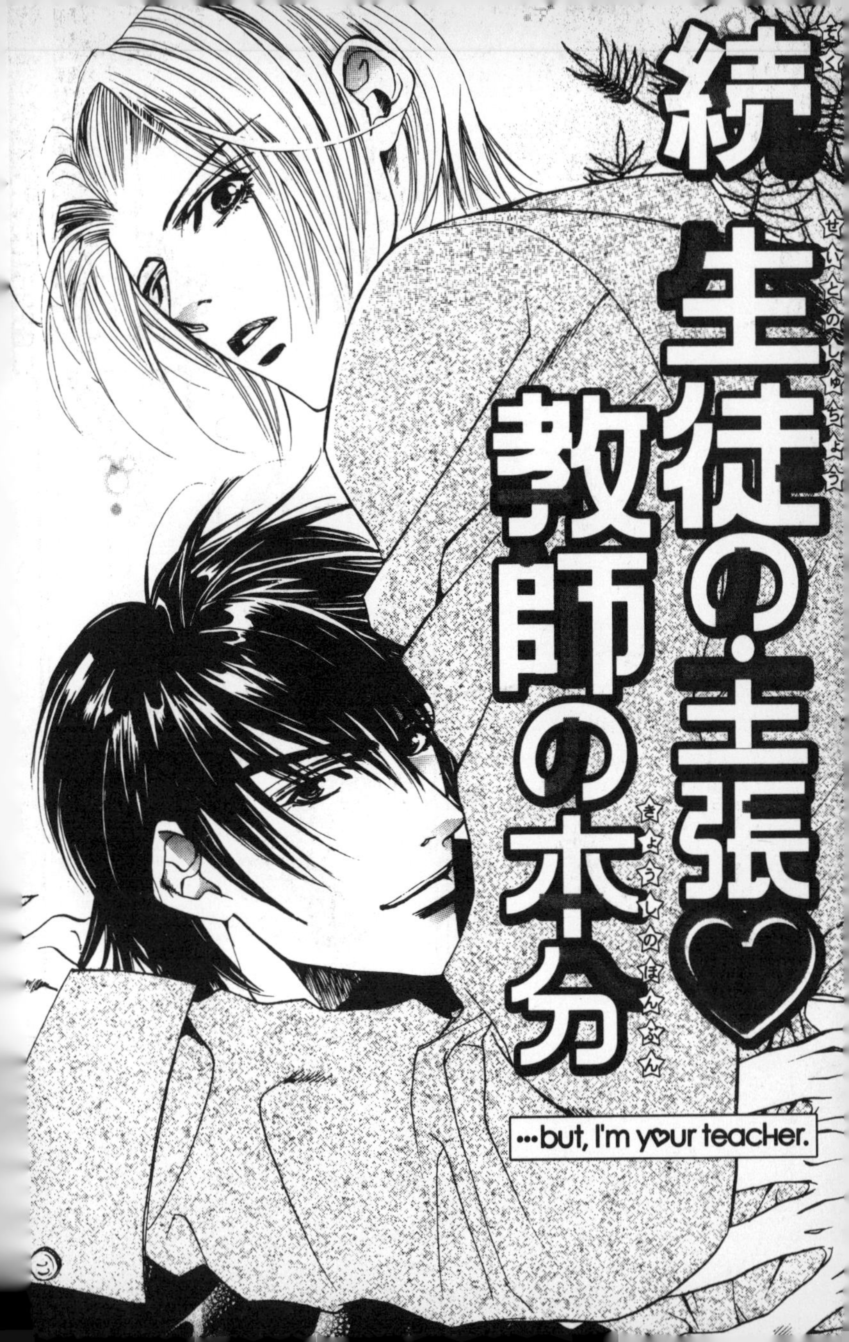
続生徒の主張♥
教師の本分
...but, I'm your teacher.

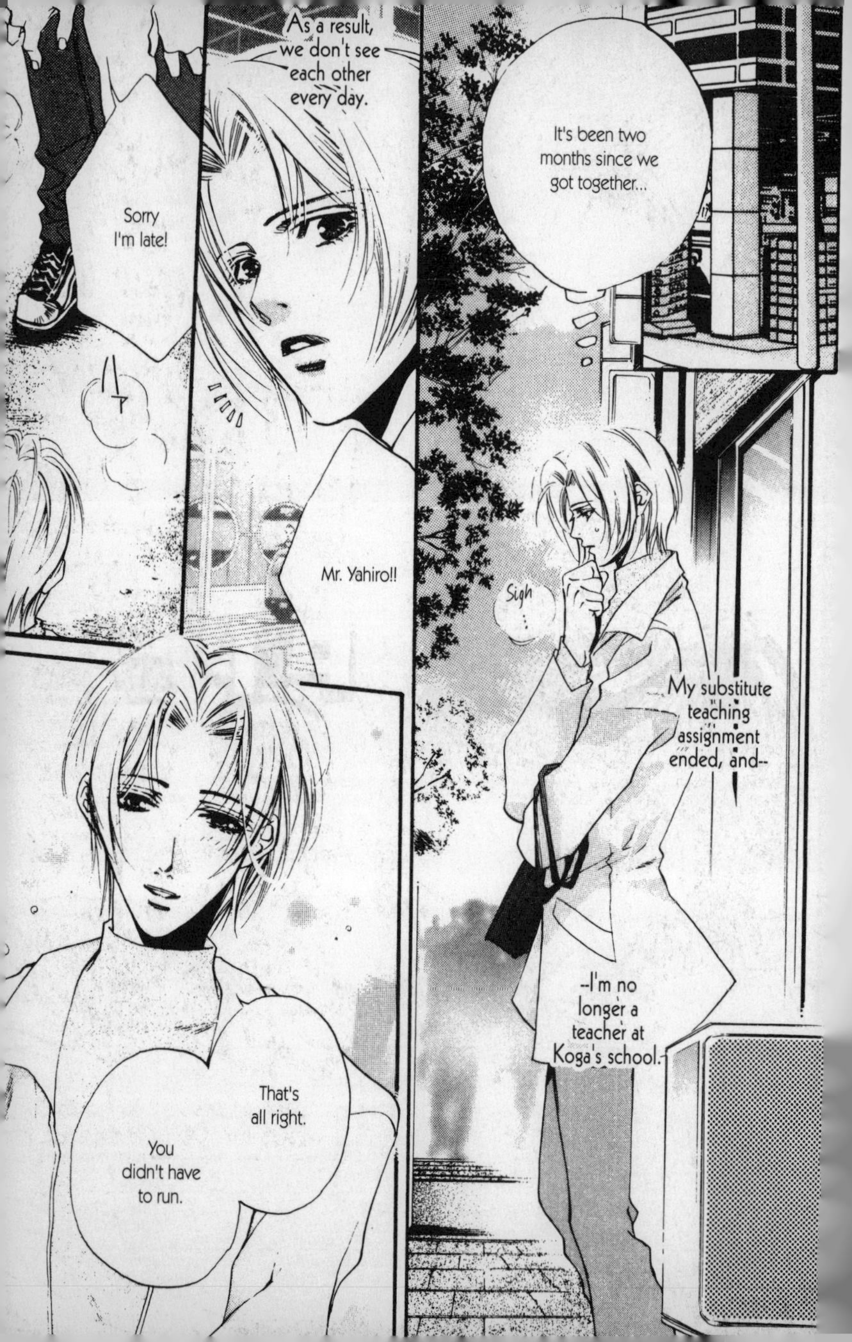
It's been two months since we got together...
Sigh...
My substitute teaching assignment ended, and--
--I'm no longer a teacher at Koga's school.
As a result, we don't see each other every day.
Mr. Yahiro!!
Sorry I'm late!
That's all right.
You didn't have to run.

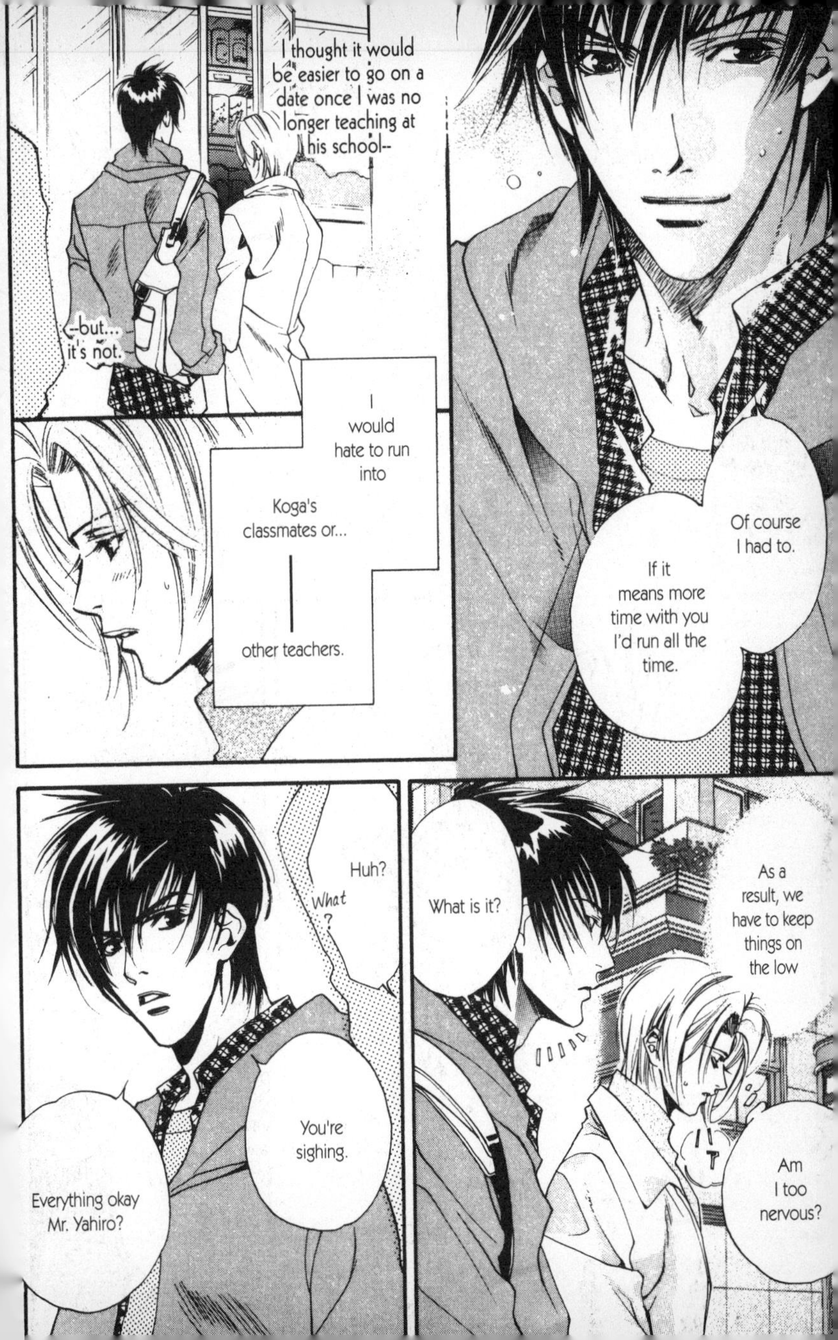

Of course I had to.
If it means more time with you I'd run all the time.
I thought it would be easier to go on a date once I was no longer teaching at his school--
--but... it's not.
I would hate to run into
Koga's classmates or...
other teachers.
As a result, we have to keep things on the low
Am I too nervous?
What is it?
Huh?
What?
You're sighing.
Everything okay Mr. Yahiro?

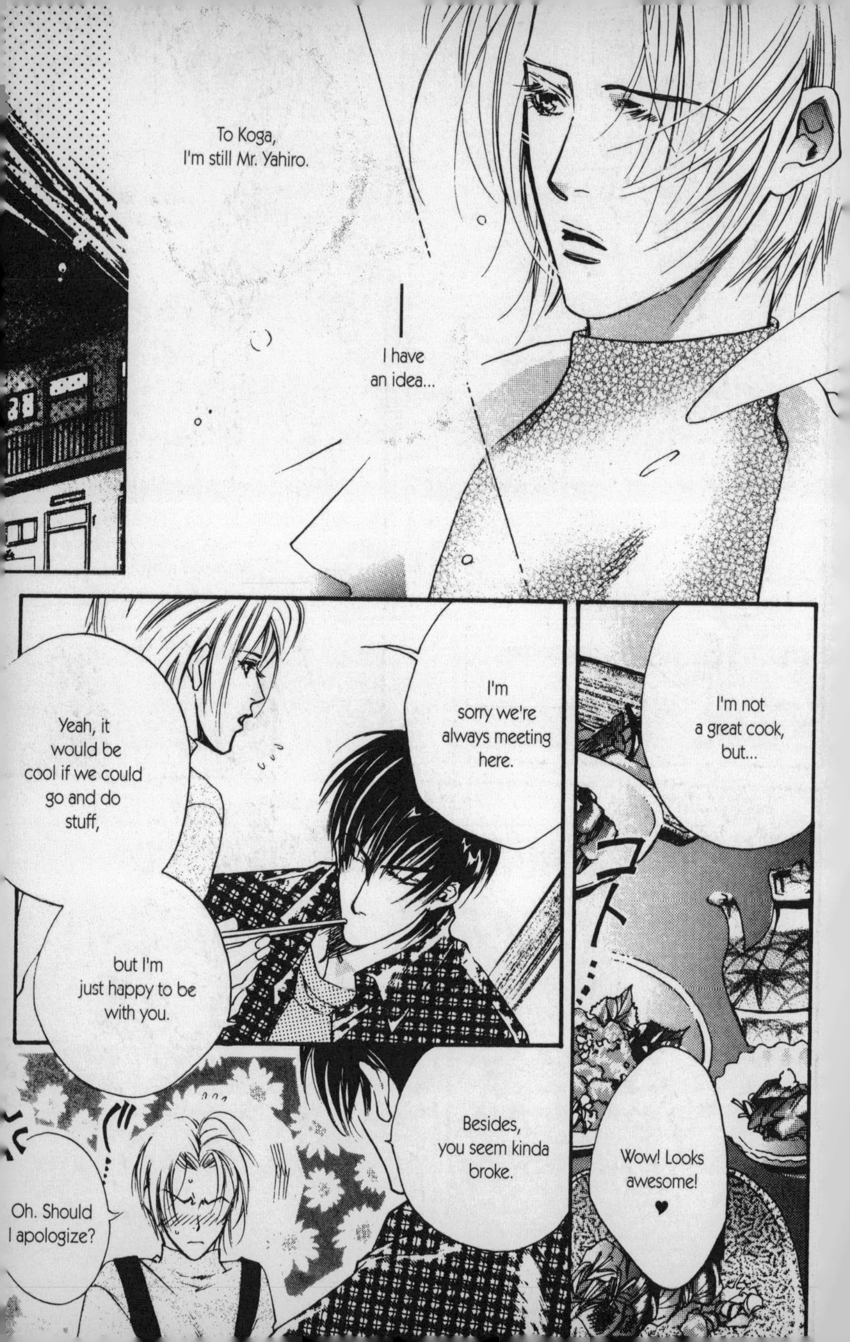

To Koga, I'm still Mr. Yahiro.
I have an idea...
I'm not a great cook, but...
I'm sorry we're always meeting here.
Yeah, it would be cool if we could go and do stuff,
but I'm just happy to be with you.
Wow! Looks awesome! ♥
Besides, you seem kinda broke.
Oh. Should I apologize?

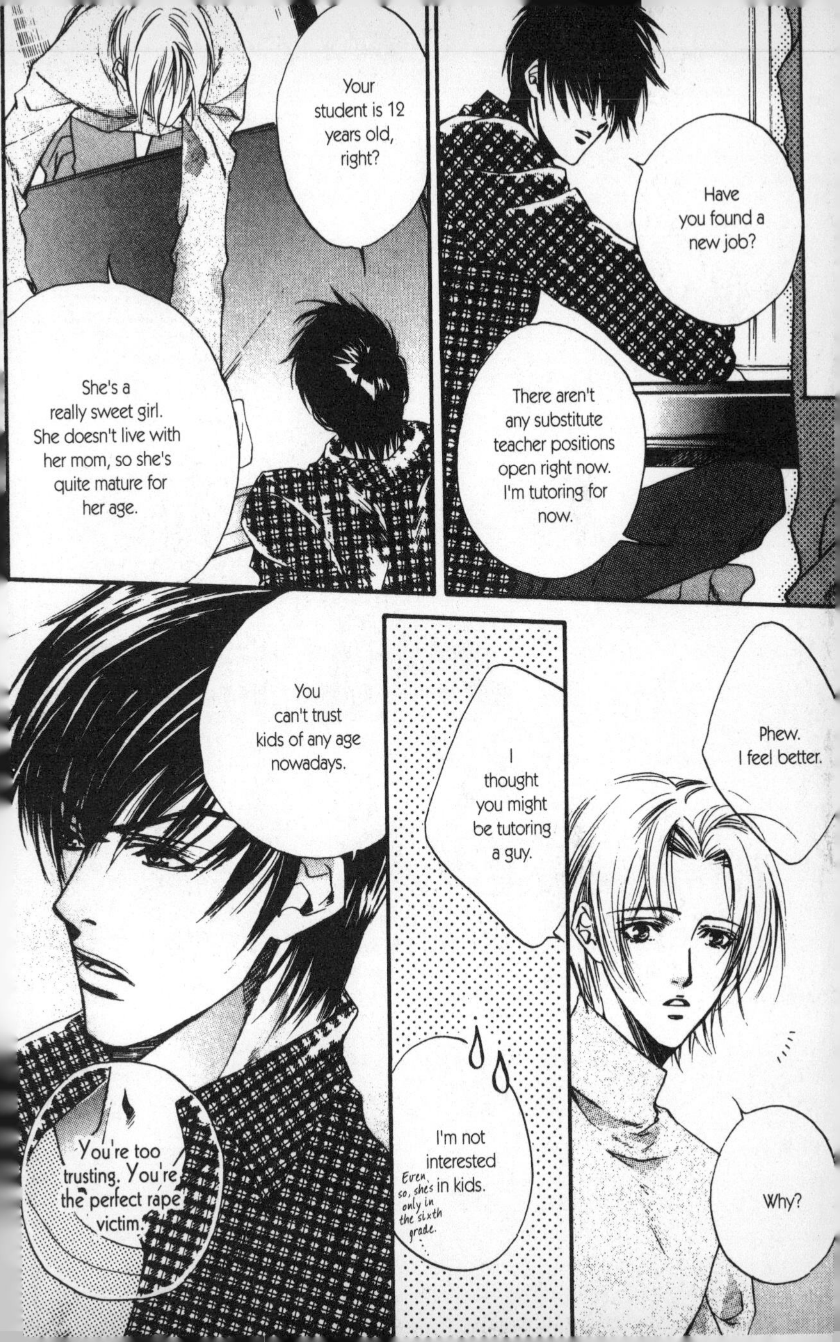
Have you found a new job?
There aren't any substitute teacher positions open right now. I'm tutoring for now.
Your student is 12 years old, right?
She's a really sweet girl. She doesn't live with her mom, so she's quite mature for her age.
Phew. I feel better.
Why?
I thought you might be tutoring a guy.
I'm not interested in kids.
Even so, she's only in the sixth grade.
You can't trust kids of any age nowadays.
You're too trusting. You're the perfect rape victim.

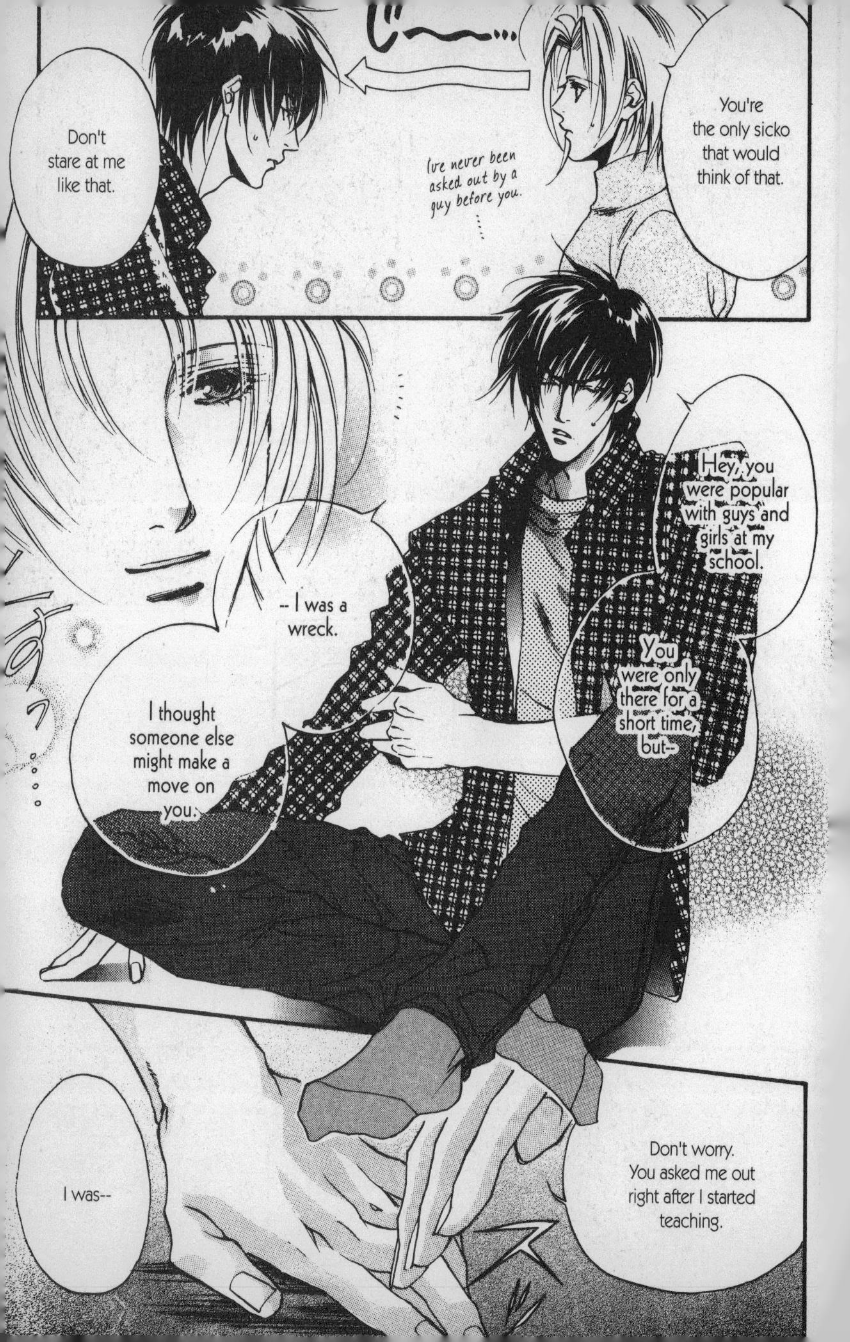

You're the only sicko that would think of that.
I've never been asked out by a guy before you. ...
じ〜〜…
Don't stare at me like that.
Hey, you were popular with guys and girls at my school.
You were only there for a short time, but--
-- I was a wreck.
I thought someone else might make a move on you.
Don't worry. You asked me out right after I started teaching.
I was--

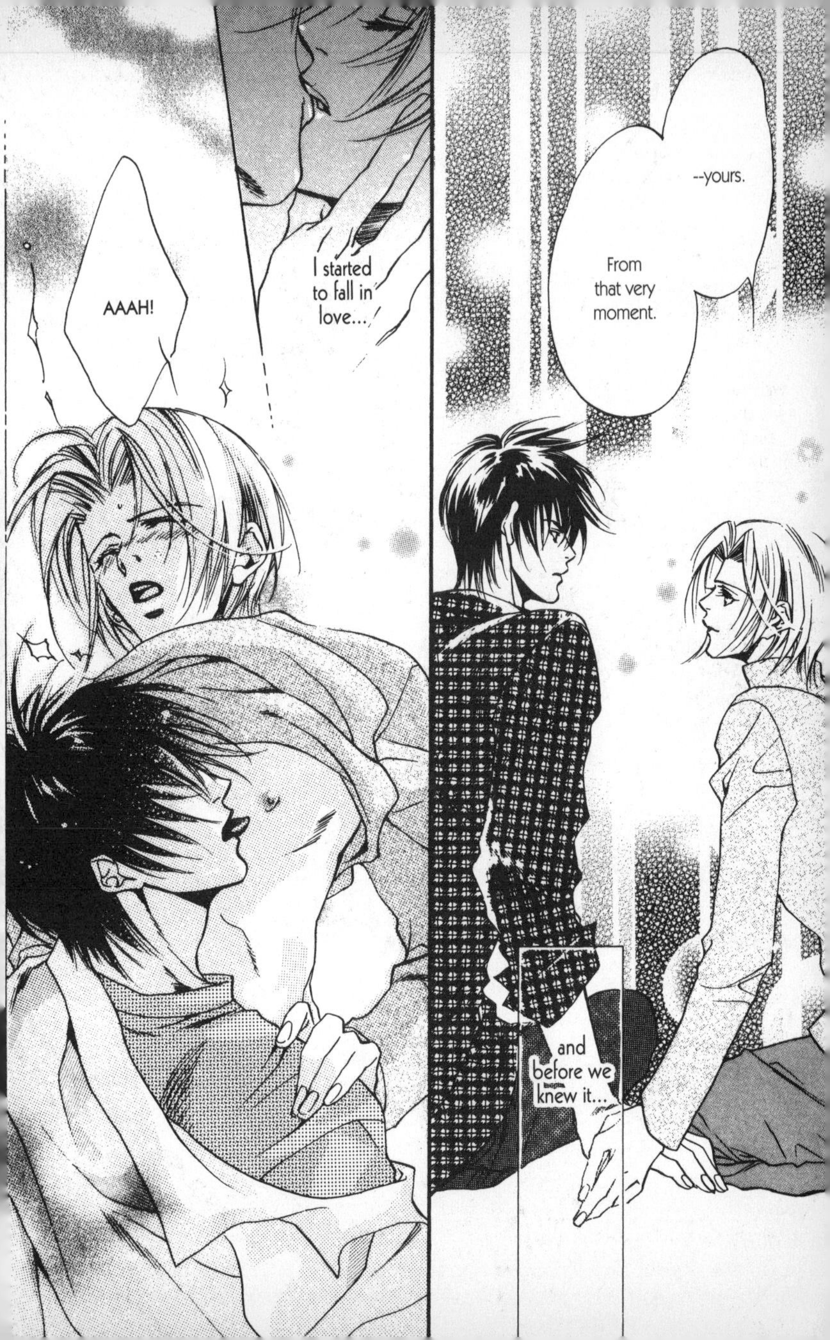
--yours.
From that very moment.
and before we knew it...
I started to fall in love...
AAAH!

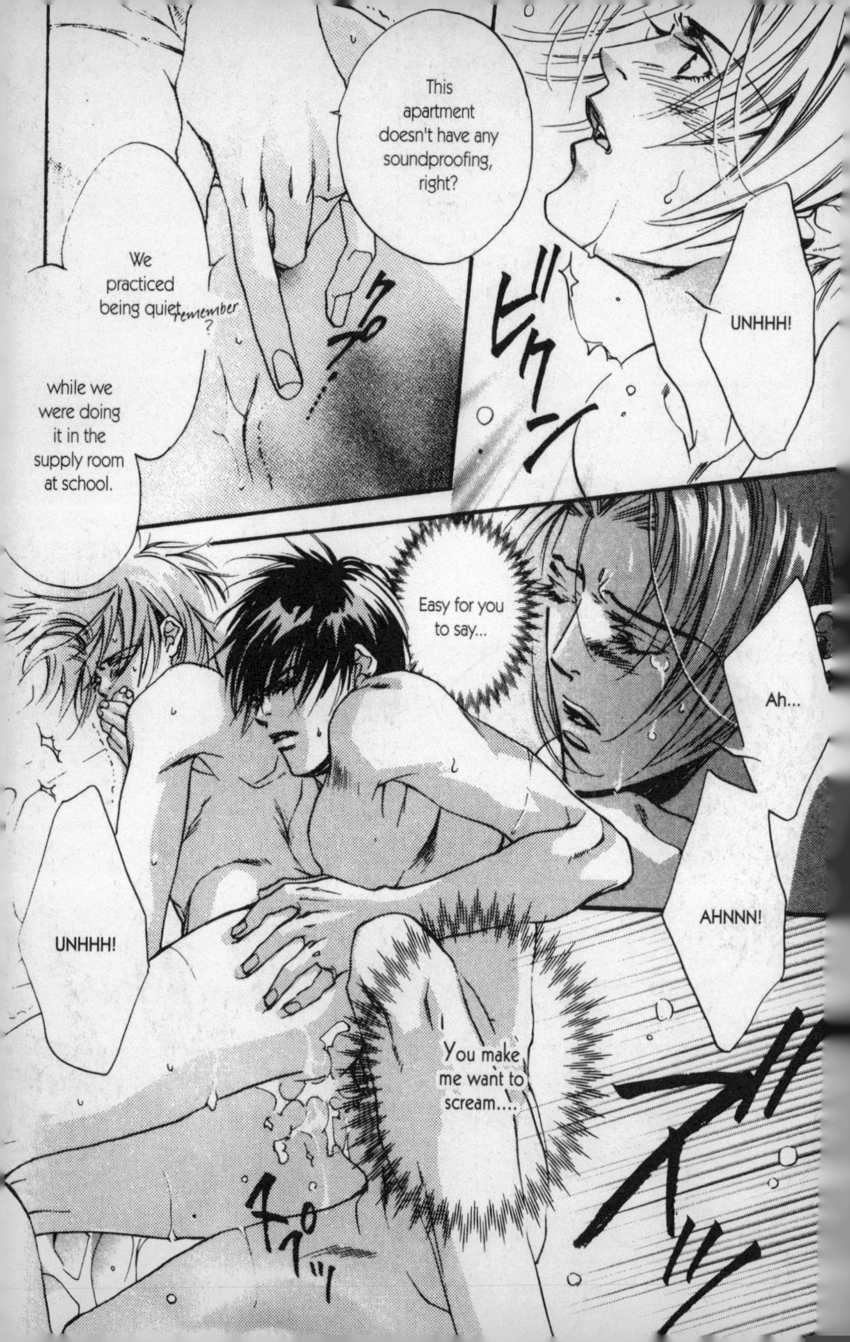
This apartment doesn't have any soundproofing, right?
UNHHH!
ビクン
We practiced being quiet remember?
while we were doing it in the supply room at school.
Easy for you to say...
Ah...
AHNNN!
UNHHH!
You make me want to scream....

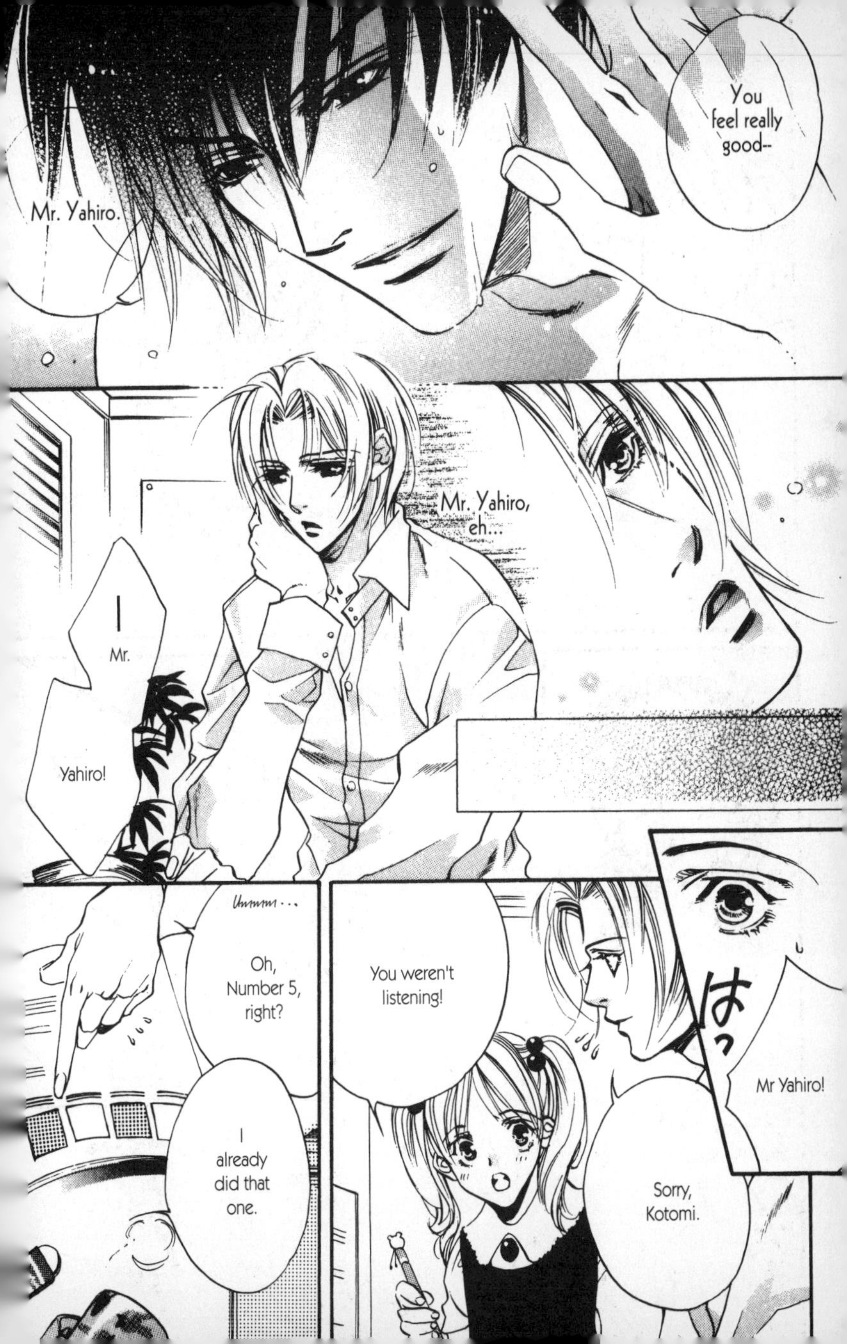

You feel really good--
Mr. Yahiro.
Mr. Yahiro, eh...
Mr. Yahiro!
はっ
Mr Yahiro!
You weren't listening!
Sorry, Kotomi.
Ummm...
Oh, Number 5, right?
I already did that one.

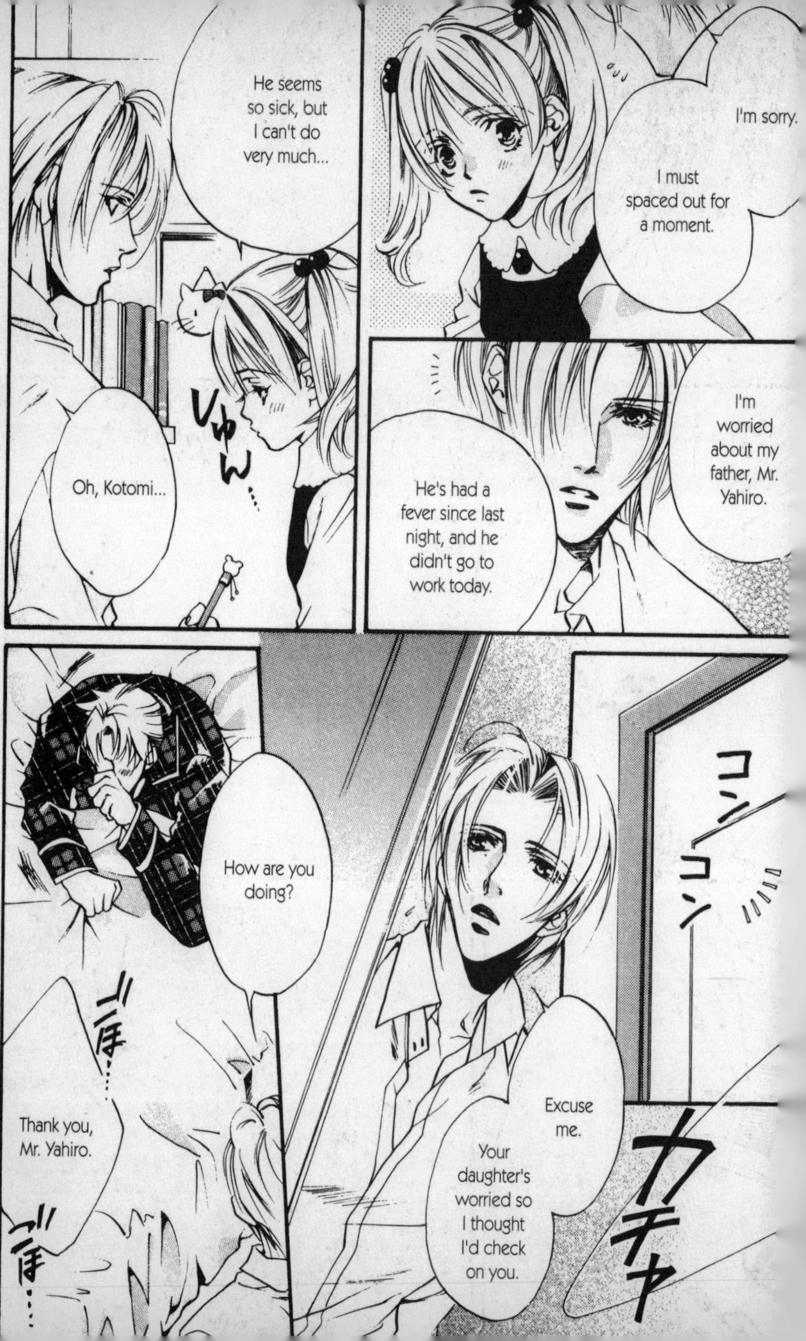

I'm sorry.
I must spaced out for a moment.
I'm worried about my father, Mr. Yahiro.
He's had a fever since last night, and he didn't go to work today.
He seems so sick, but I can't do very much...
しゅん…
Oh, Kotomi...
コンコン
カチャ
Excuse me.
Your daughter's worried so I thought I'd check on you.
How are you doing?
ごほ…
Thank you, Mr. Yahiro.
ごほ…

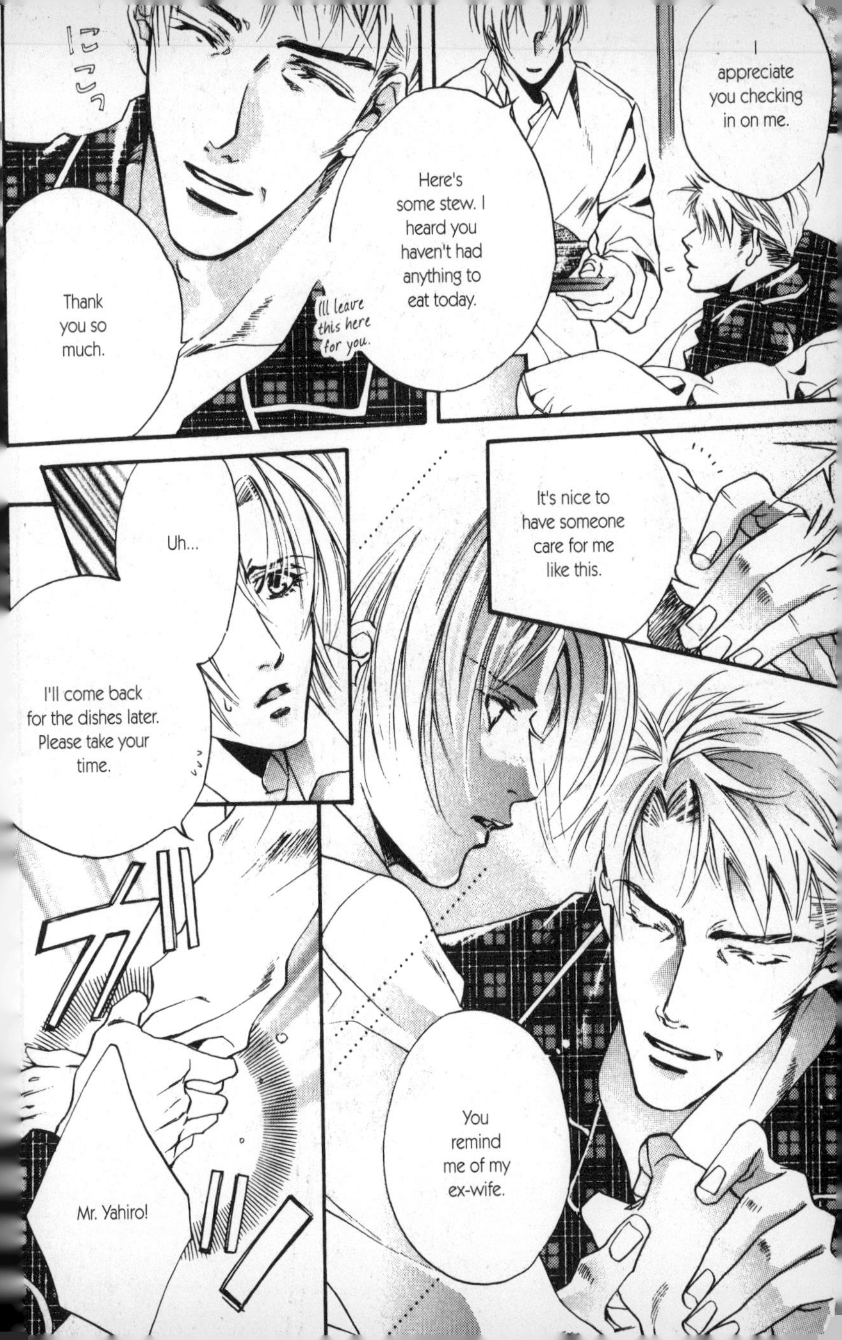
I appreciate you checking in on me.
Here's some stew. I heard you haven't had anything to eat today.
Ill leave this here for you.
Thank you so much.
It's nice to have someone care for me like this.
You remind me of my ex-wife.
Uh...
I'll come back for the dishes later. Please take your time.
Mr. Yahiro!

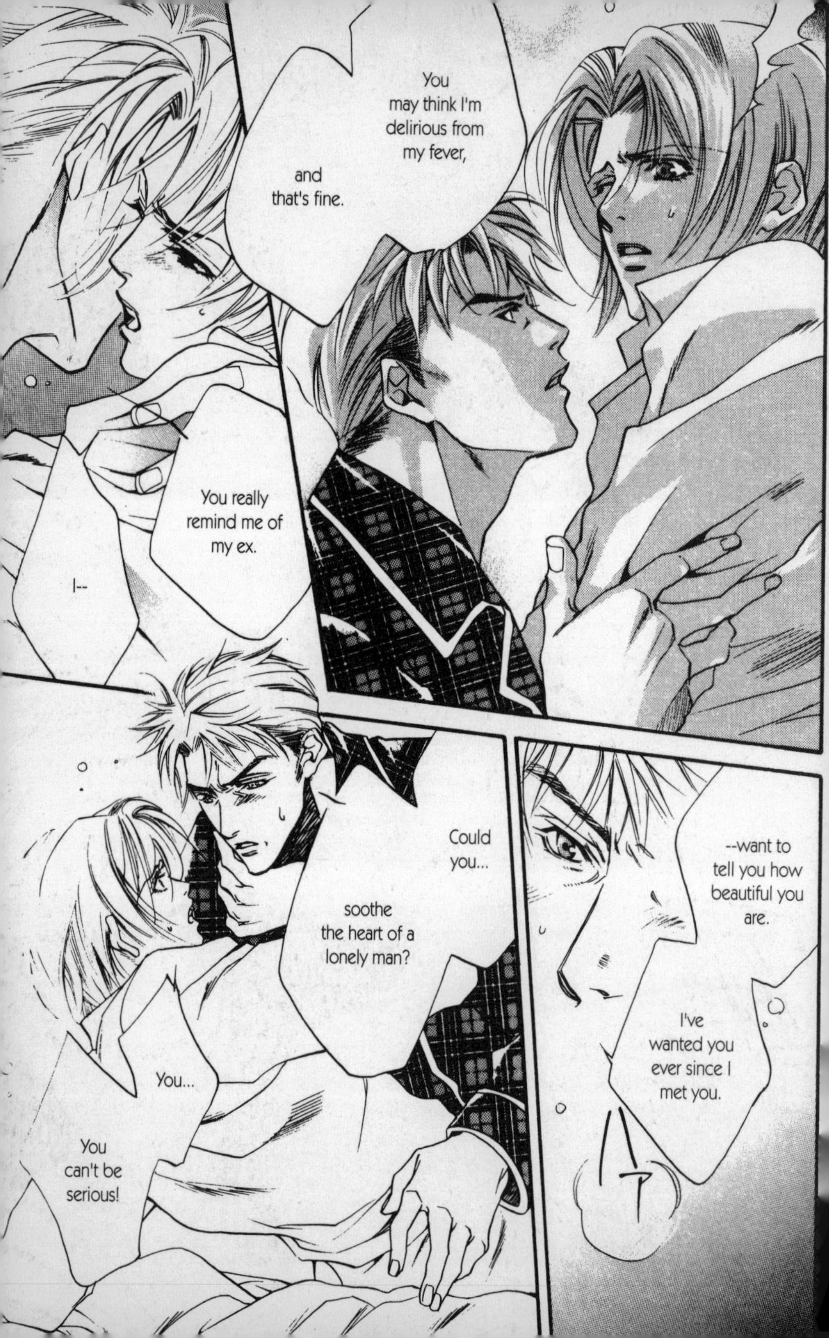
You may think I'm delirious from my fever,
and that's fine.
You really remind me of my ex.
I--
--want to tell you how beautiful you are.
I've wanted you ever since I met you.
Could you...
soothe the heart of a lonely man?
You...
You can't be serious!

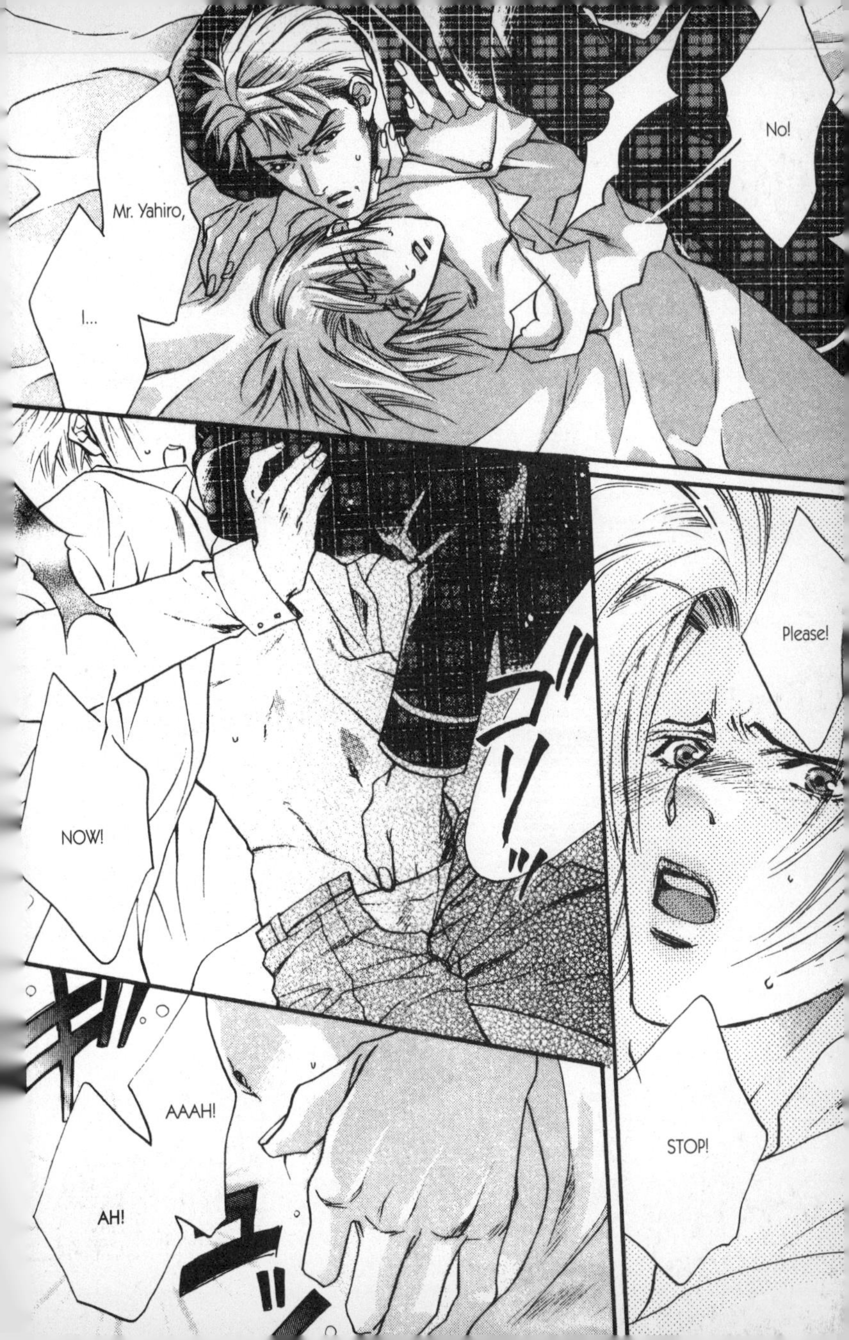
No!
Mr. Yahiro,
I...
Please!
NOW!
STOP!
AAAH!
AH!

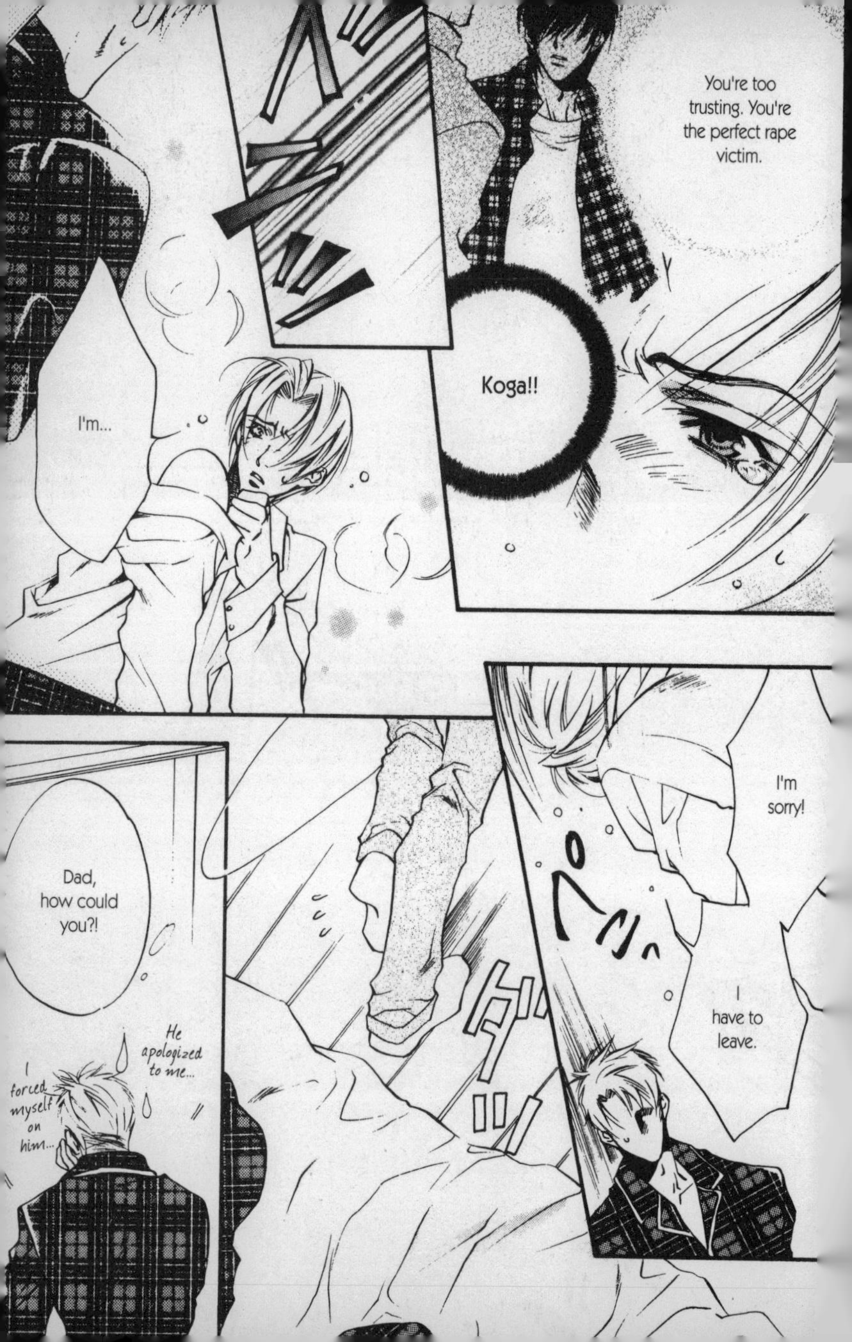

You're too trusting. You're the perfect rape victim.
Koga!!
I'm...
I'm sorry!
I have to leave.
Dad, how could you?!
He apologized to me...
I forced myself on him...

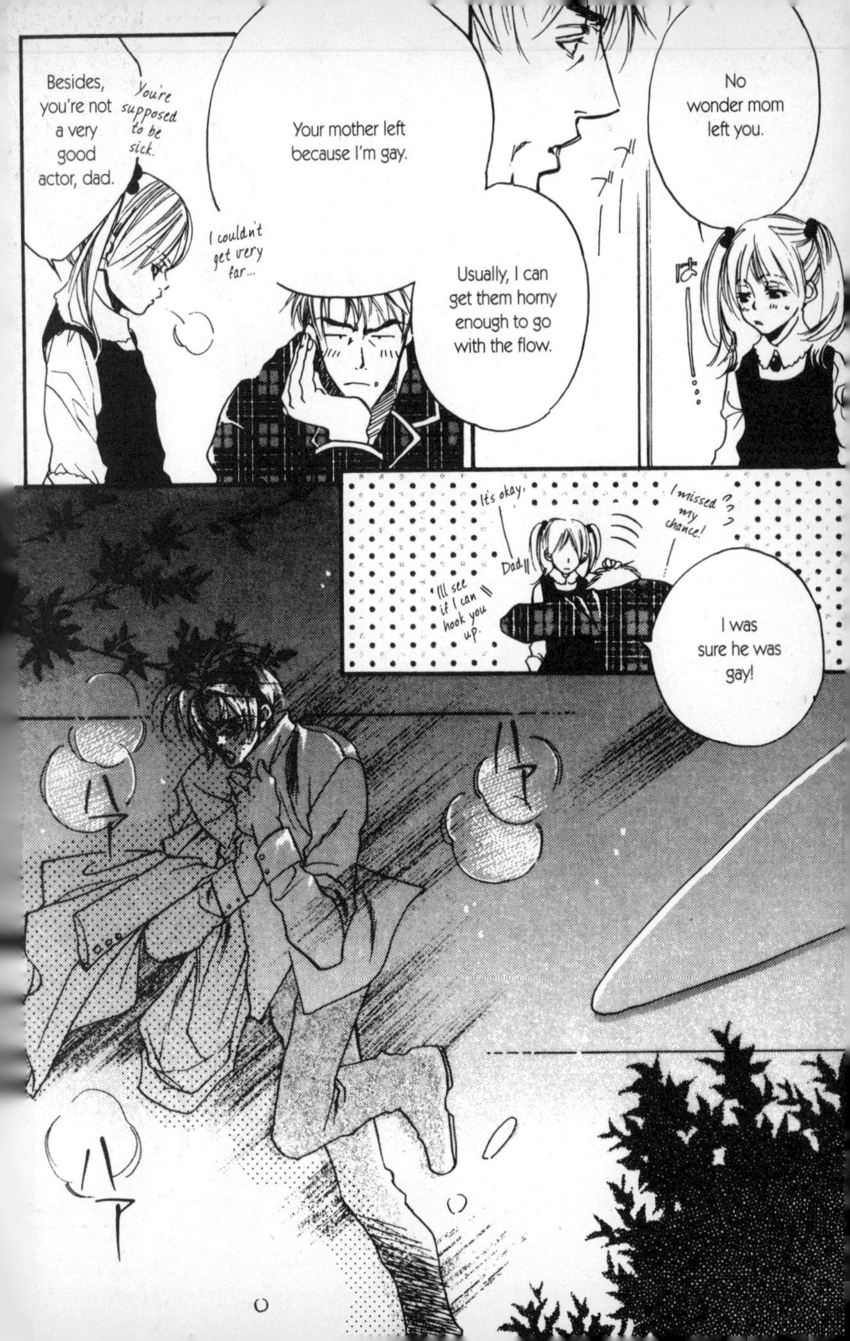
No wonder mom left you.
Your mother left because I'm gay.
Besides, you're not a very good actor, dad.
You're supposed to be sick.
Usually, I can get them horny enough to go with the flow.
I couldn't get very far...
I missed my chance!
It's okay, Dad
I'll see if I can hook you up.
I was sure he was gay!

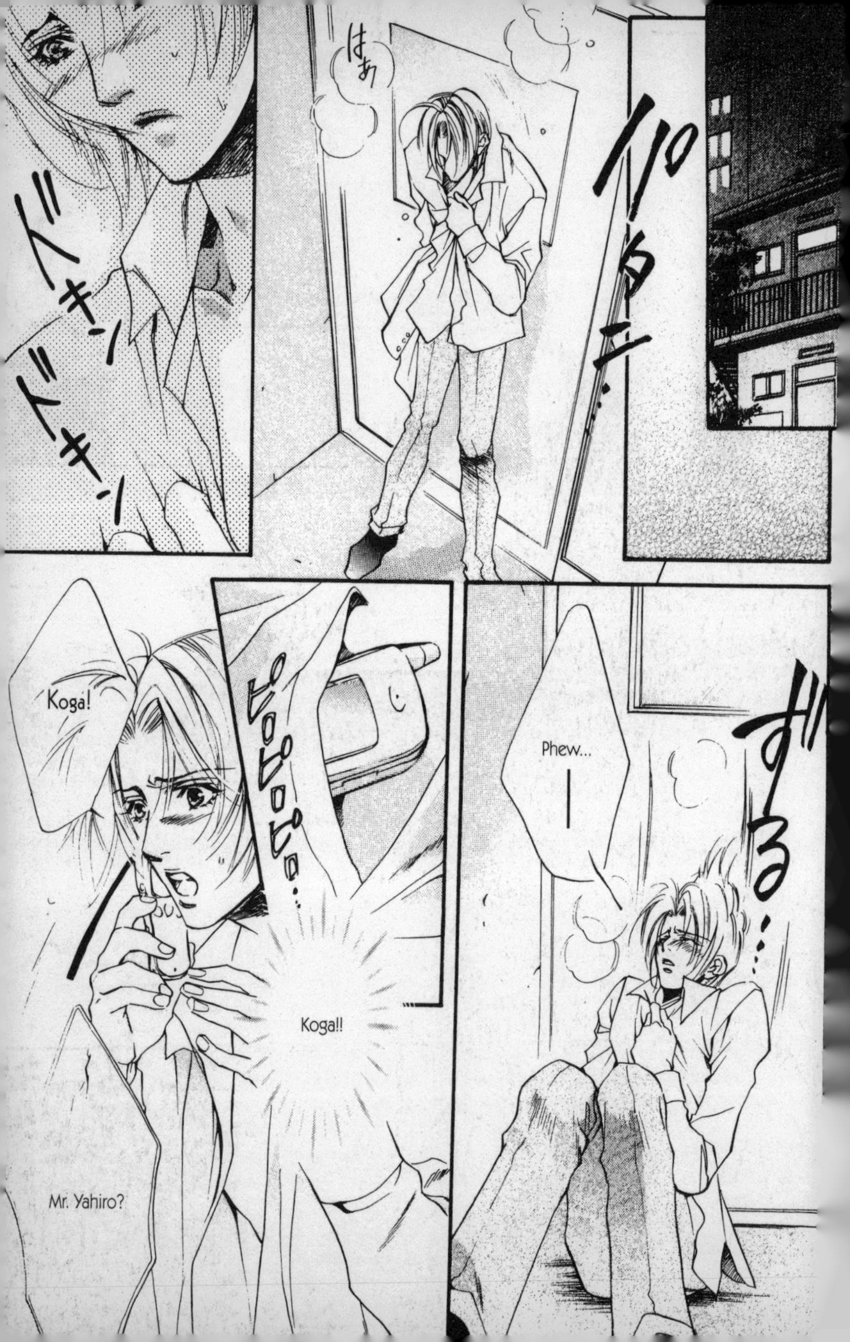
パタ…
はあ
ドキンドキン
ずる…
Phew…
ピッピッピッ…
Koga!
Koga!!
Mr. Yahiro?

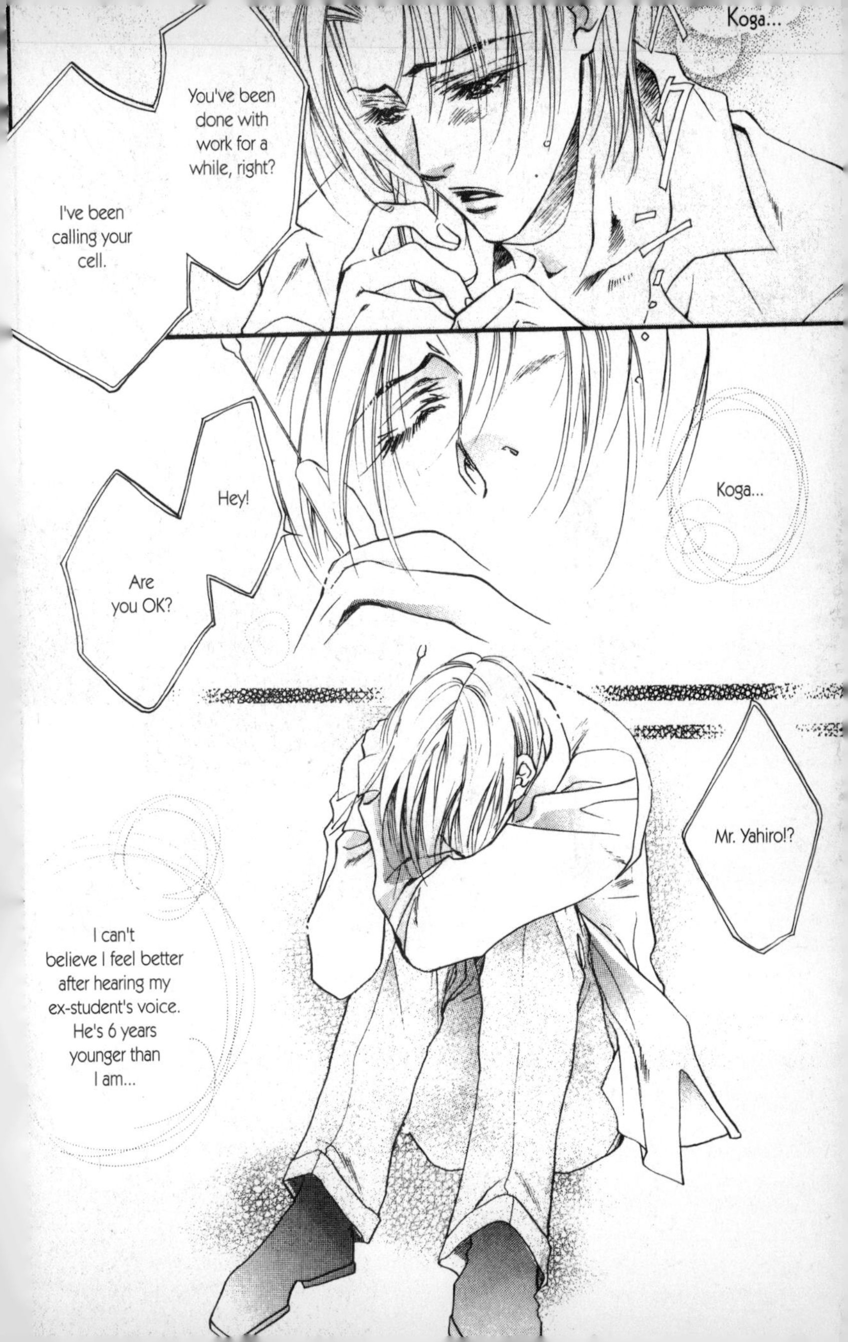
Koga...
You've been done with work for a while, right?
I've been calling your cell.
Koga...
Hey!
Are you OK?
Mr. Yahiro!?
I can't believe I feel better after hearing my ex-student's voice. He's 6 years younger than I am...

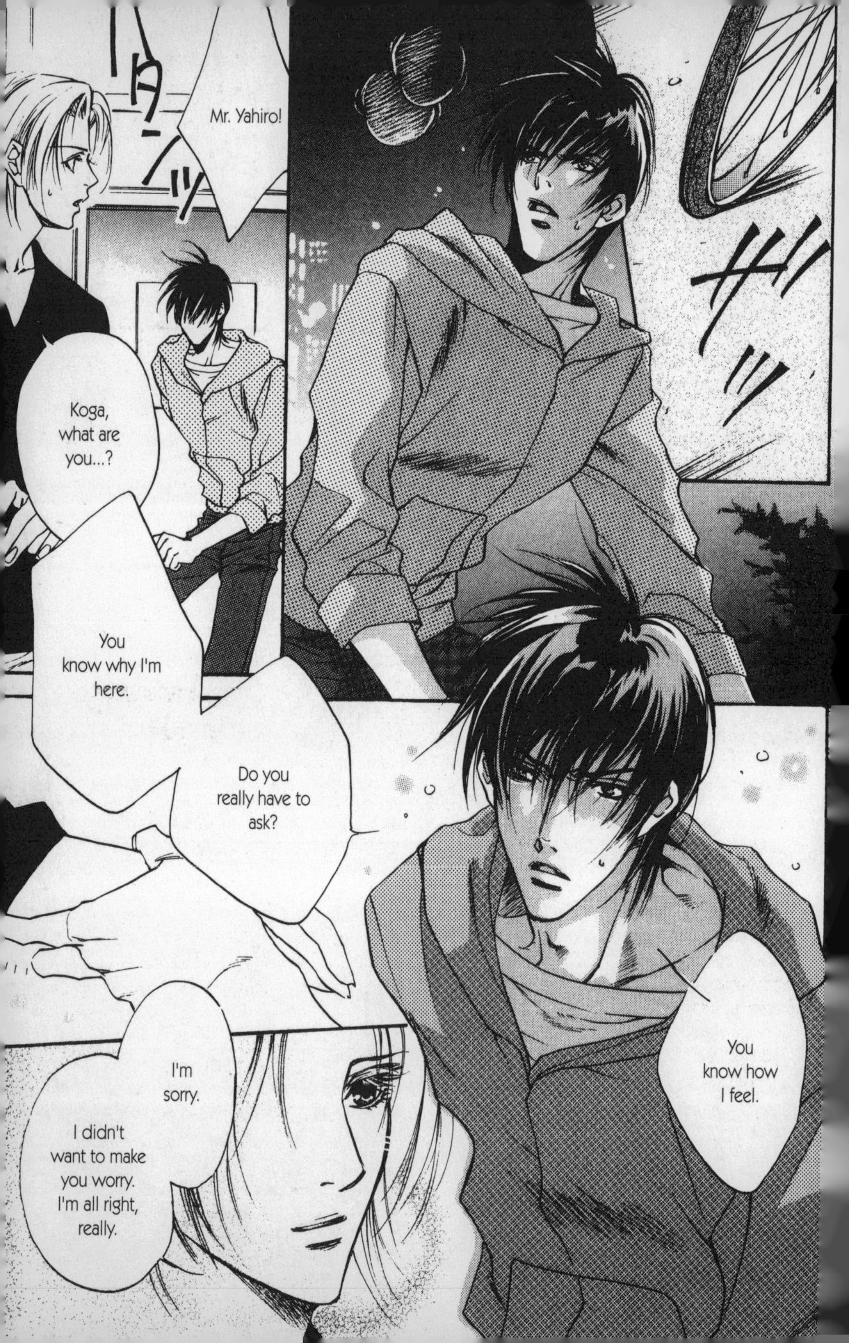
Mr. Yahiro!
Koga, what are you...?
You know why I'm here.
Do you really have to ask?
You know how I feel.
I'm sorry.
I didn't want to make you worry. I'm all right, really.

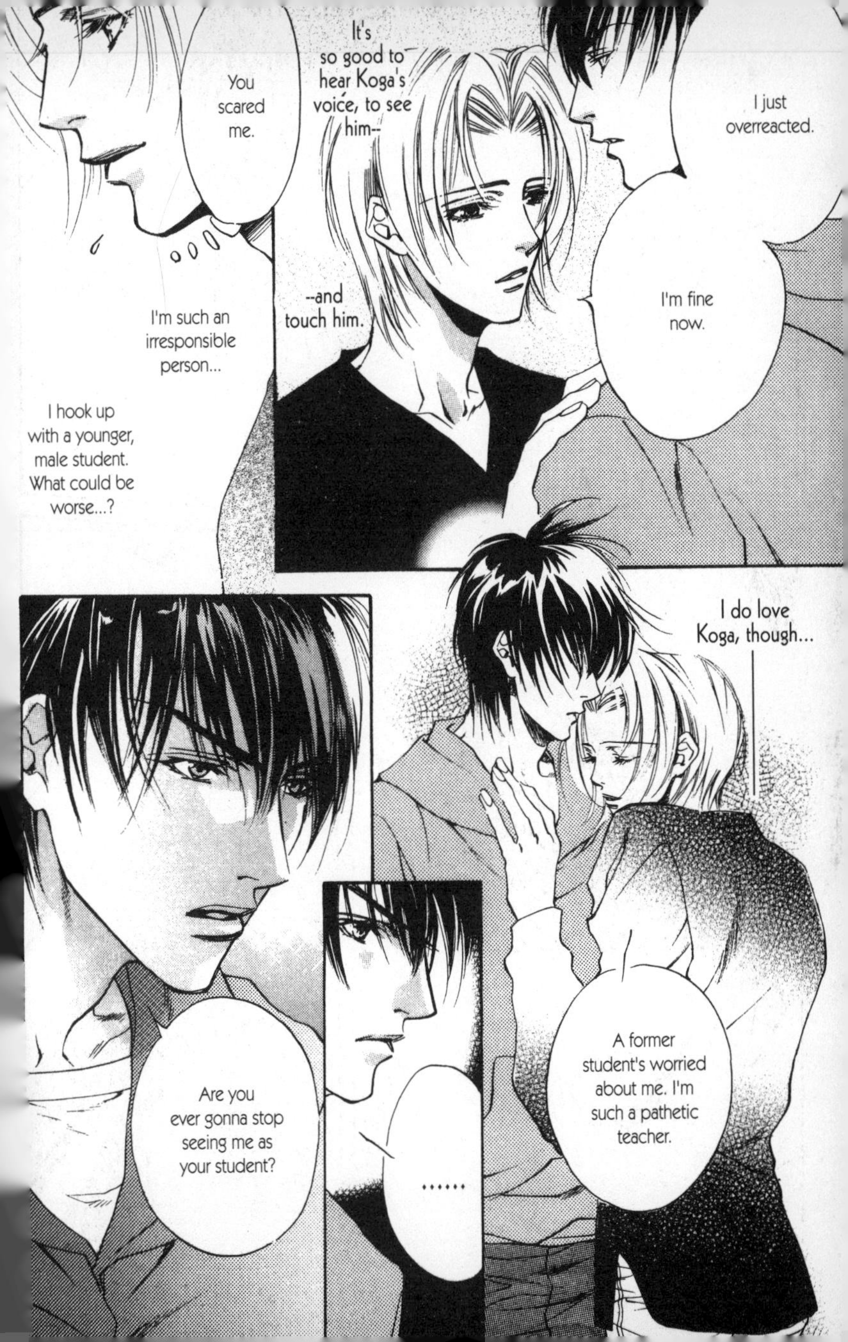
I just overreacted.
I'm fine now.
It's so good to hear Koga's voice, to see him--
--and touch him.
You scared me.
I'm such an irresponsible person...
I hook up with a younger, male student. What could be worse...?
I do love Koga, though...
A former student's worried about me. I'm such a pathetic teacher.
......
Are you ever gonna stop seeing me as your student?

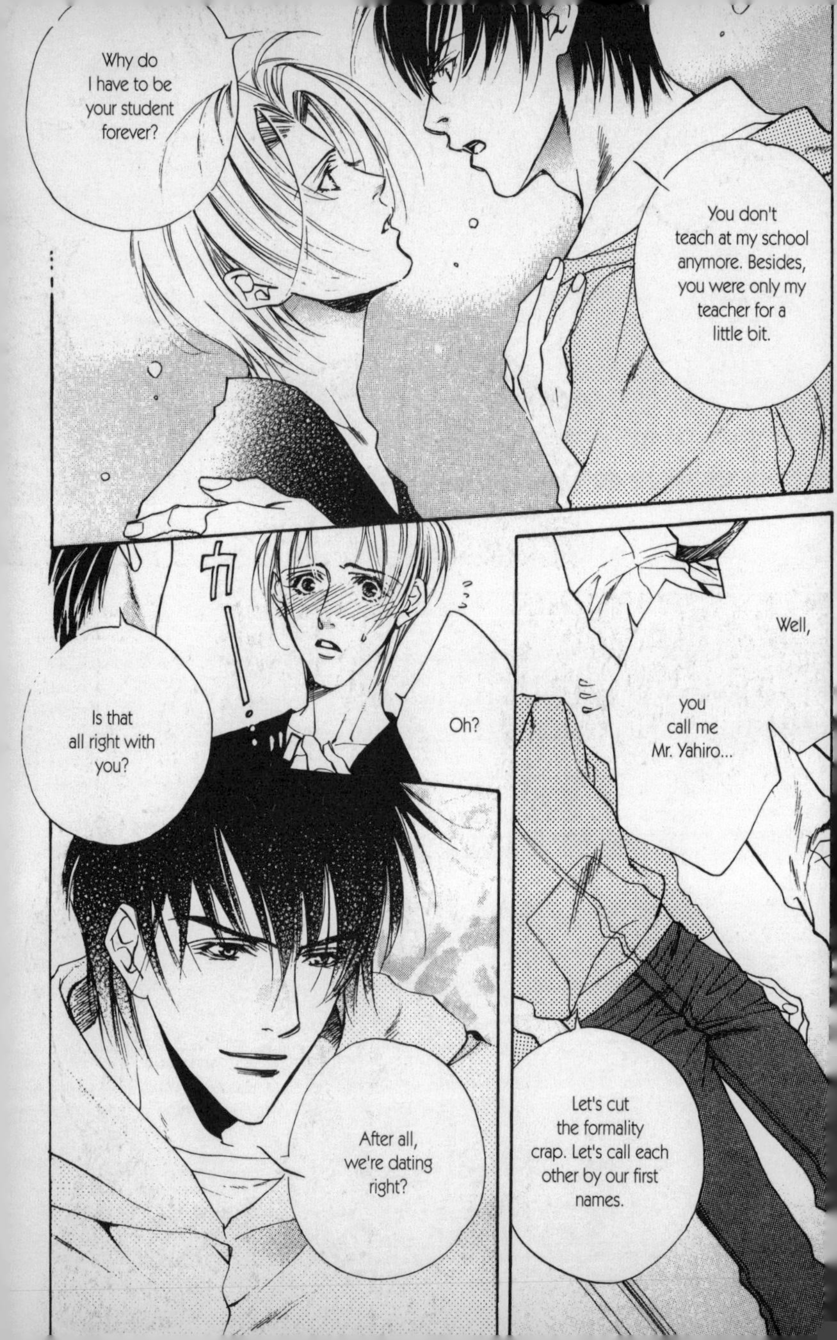
You don't teach at my school anymore. Besides, you were only my teacher for a little bit.
Why do I have to be your student forever?
Well, you call me Mr. Yahiro...
Let's cut the formality crap. Let's call each other by our first names.
カー
Oh?
Is that all right with you?
After all, we're dating right?

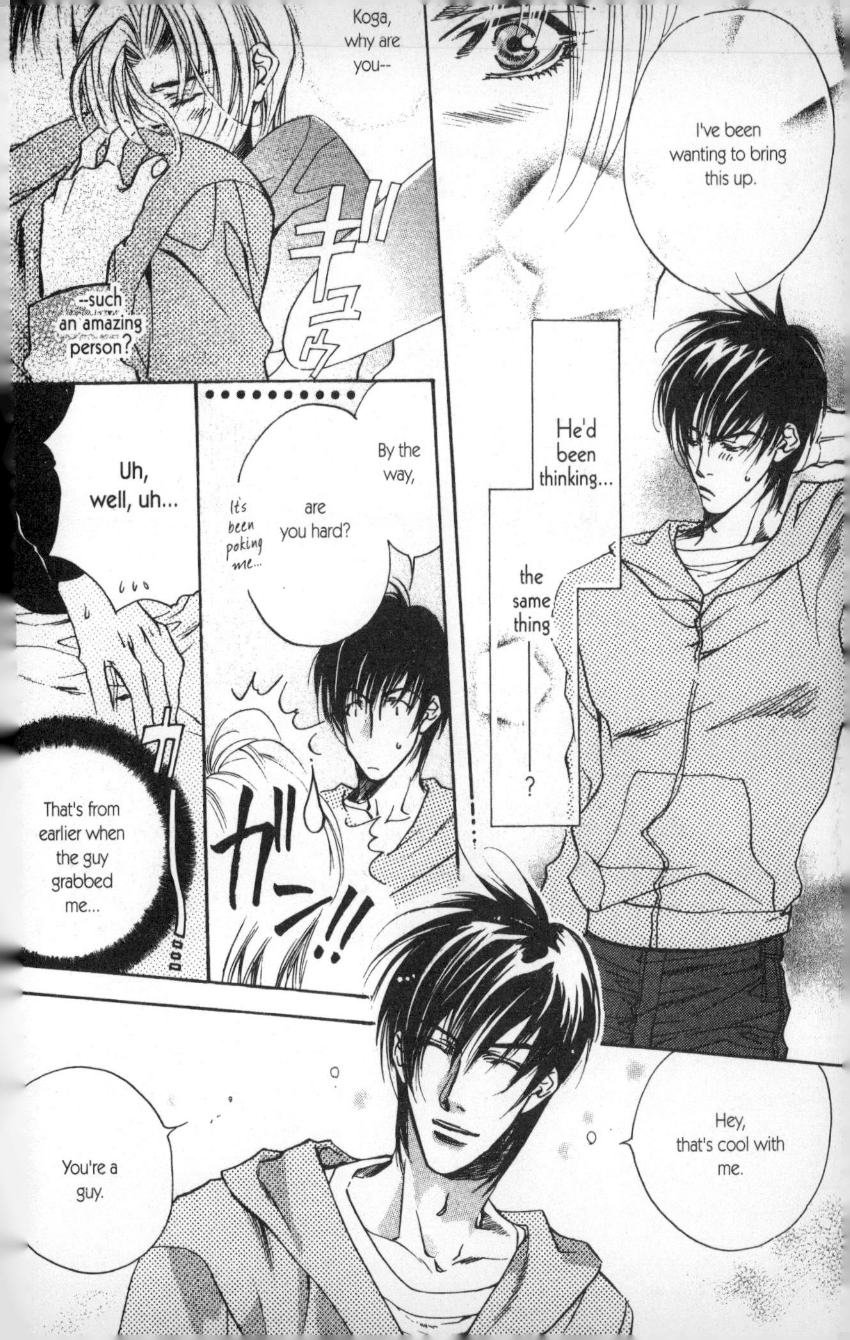
I've been wanting to bring this up.
Koga, why are you--
--such an amazing person?
ギュウ
He'd been thinking...
the same thing —?
By the way, are you hard?
It's been poking me...
ガーン!!
Uh, well, uh...
That's from earlier when the guy grabbed me...
Hey, that's cool with me.
You're a guy.

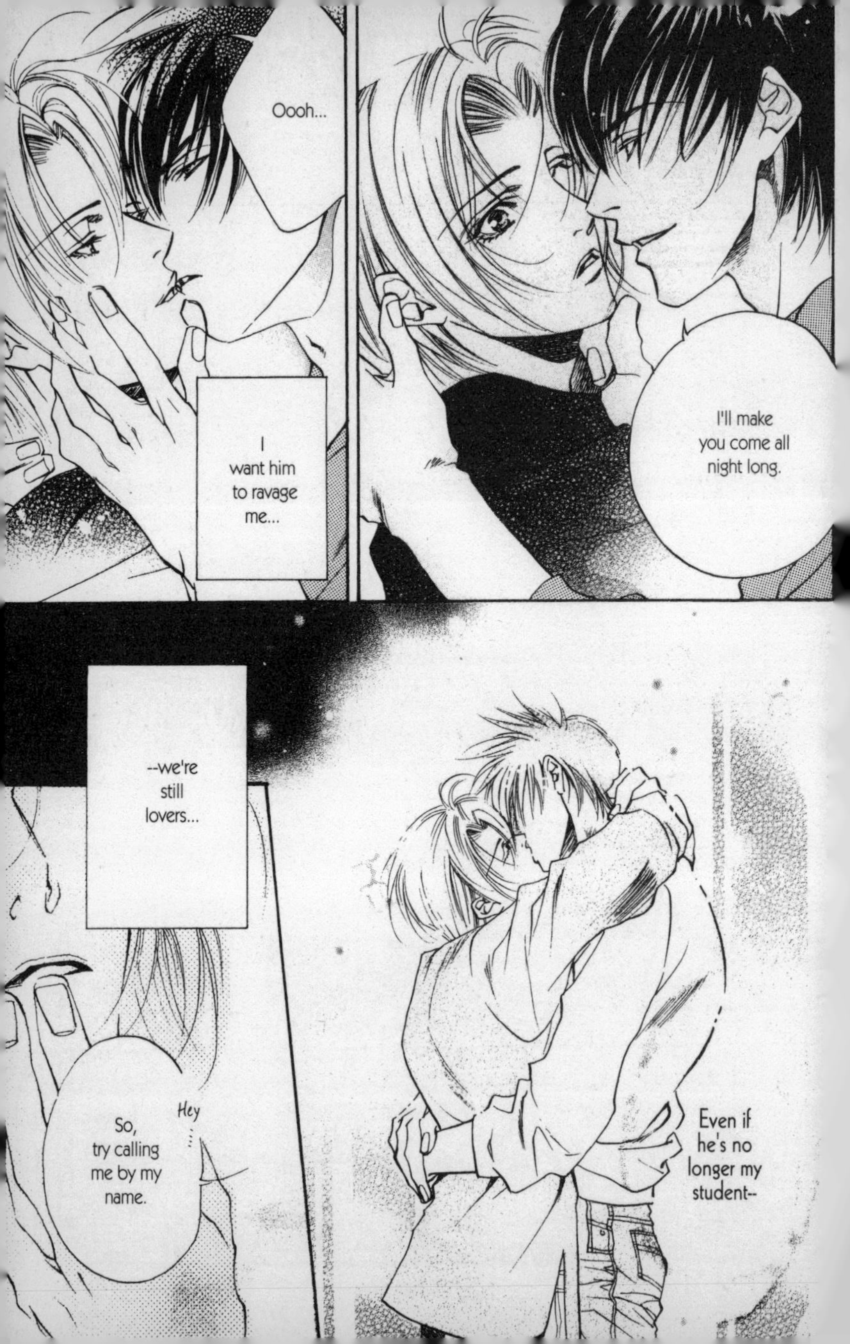
I'll make you come all night long.
Oooh...
I want him to ravage me...
Even if he's no longer my student--
--we're still lovers...
Hey...
So, try calling me by my name.

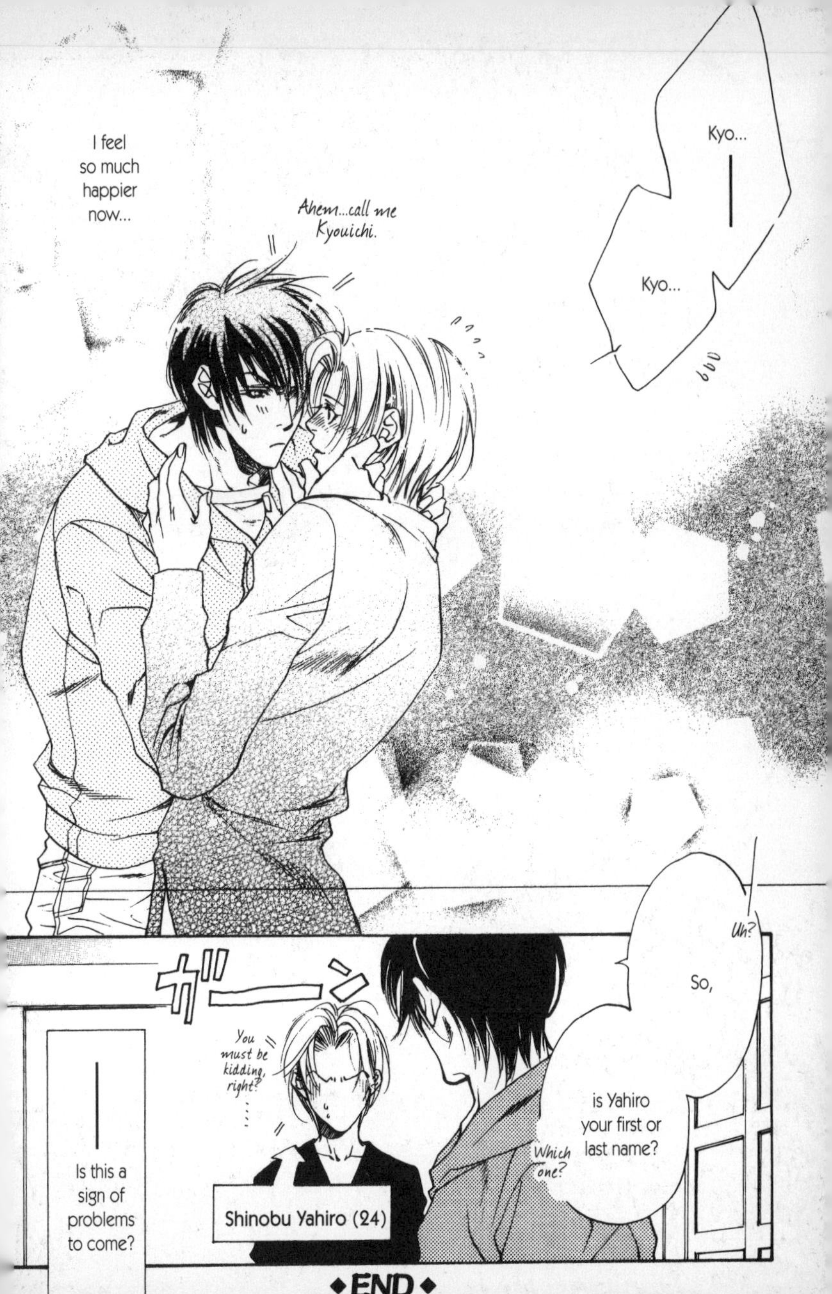
Kyo...
Kyo...
Ahem...call me Kyouichi.
I feel so much happier now...
Uh?
So,
is Yahiro your first or last name?
Which one?
ガーン
You must be kidding, right?
...
Shinobu Yahiro (24)
Is this a sign of problems to come?
◆END◆

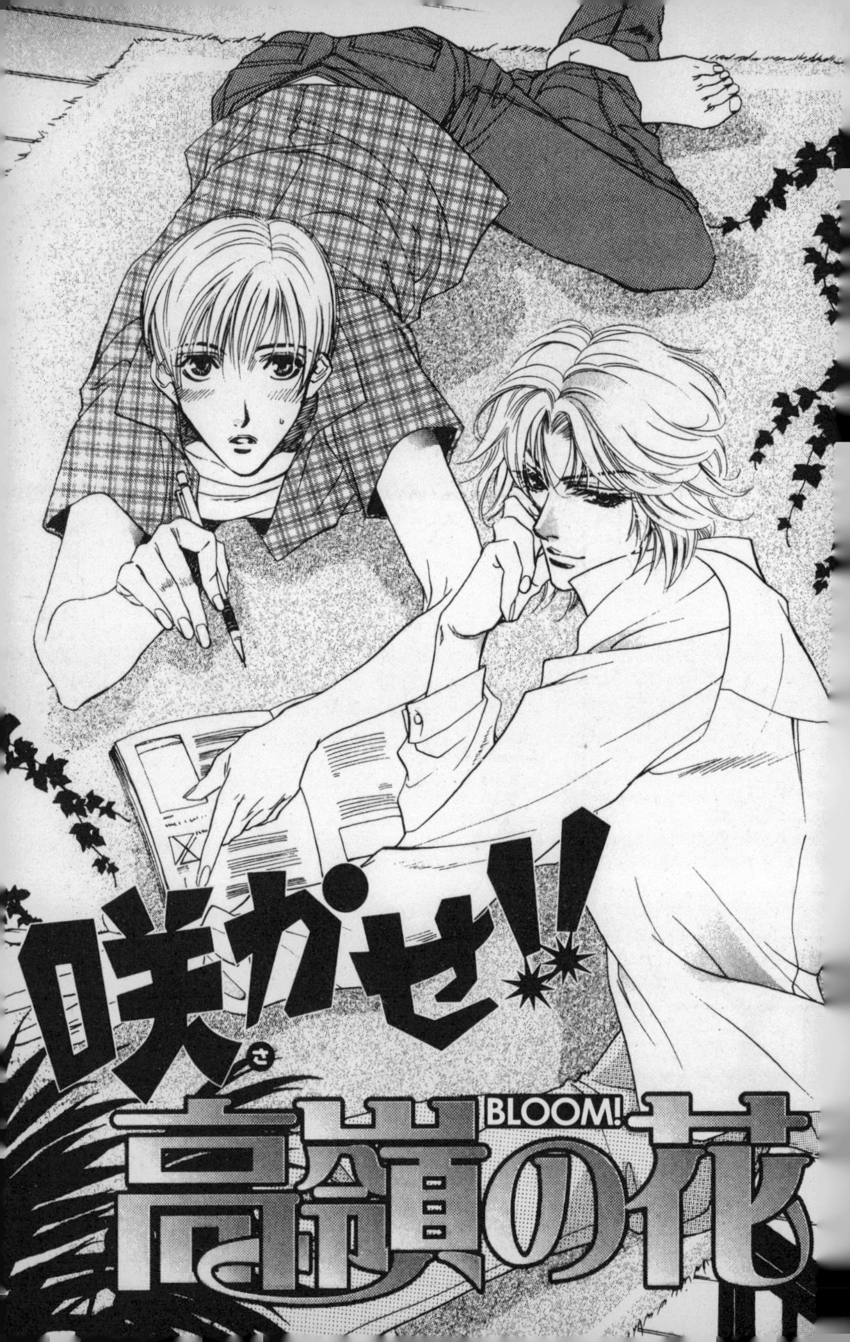
咲かせ!!
さ
BLOOM!
高嶺の花

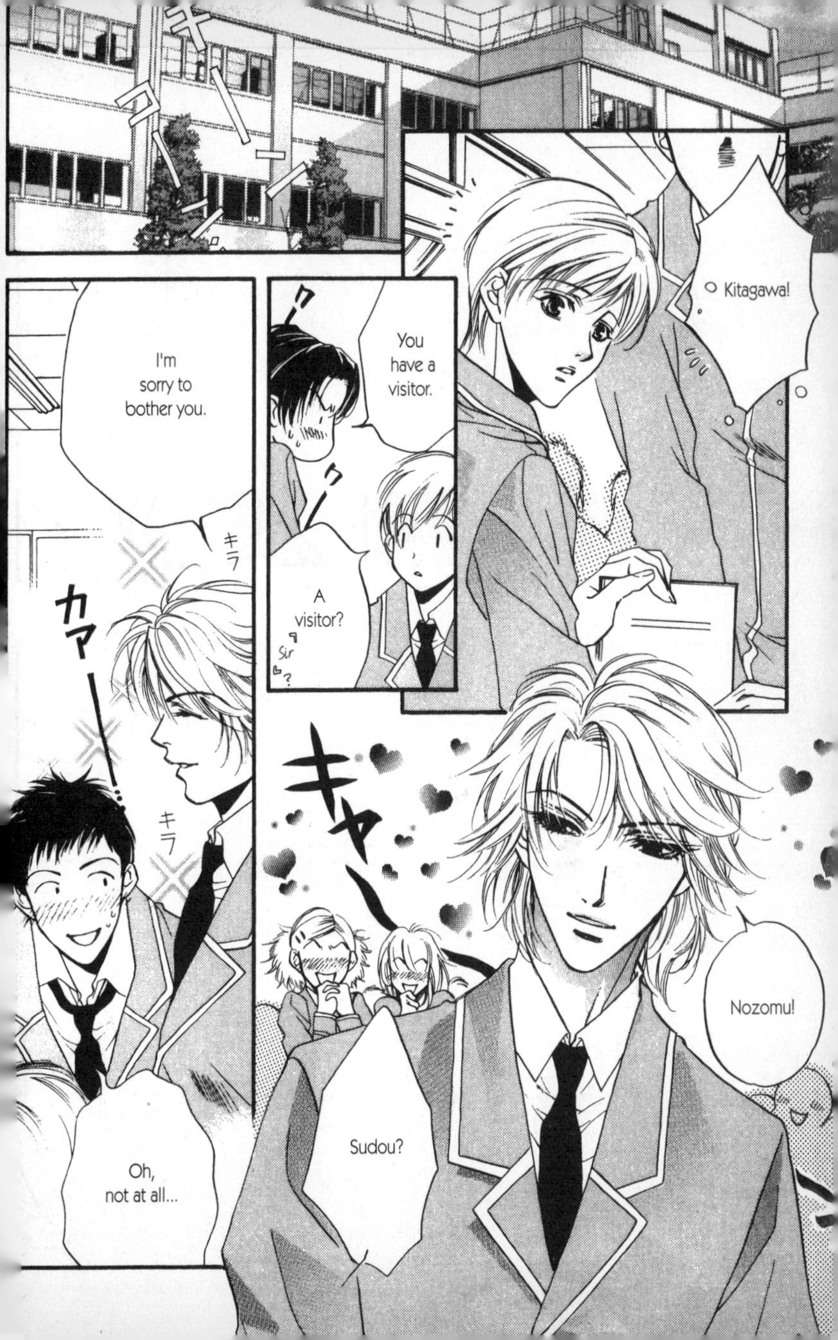

キーンコーンカーンコーン
Kitagawa!
You have a visitor.
A visitor?
Sir?
I'm sorry to bother you.
キラ
カァー
キラ
キャー
Nozomu!
Sudou?
Oh, not at all...

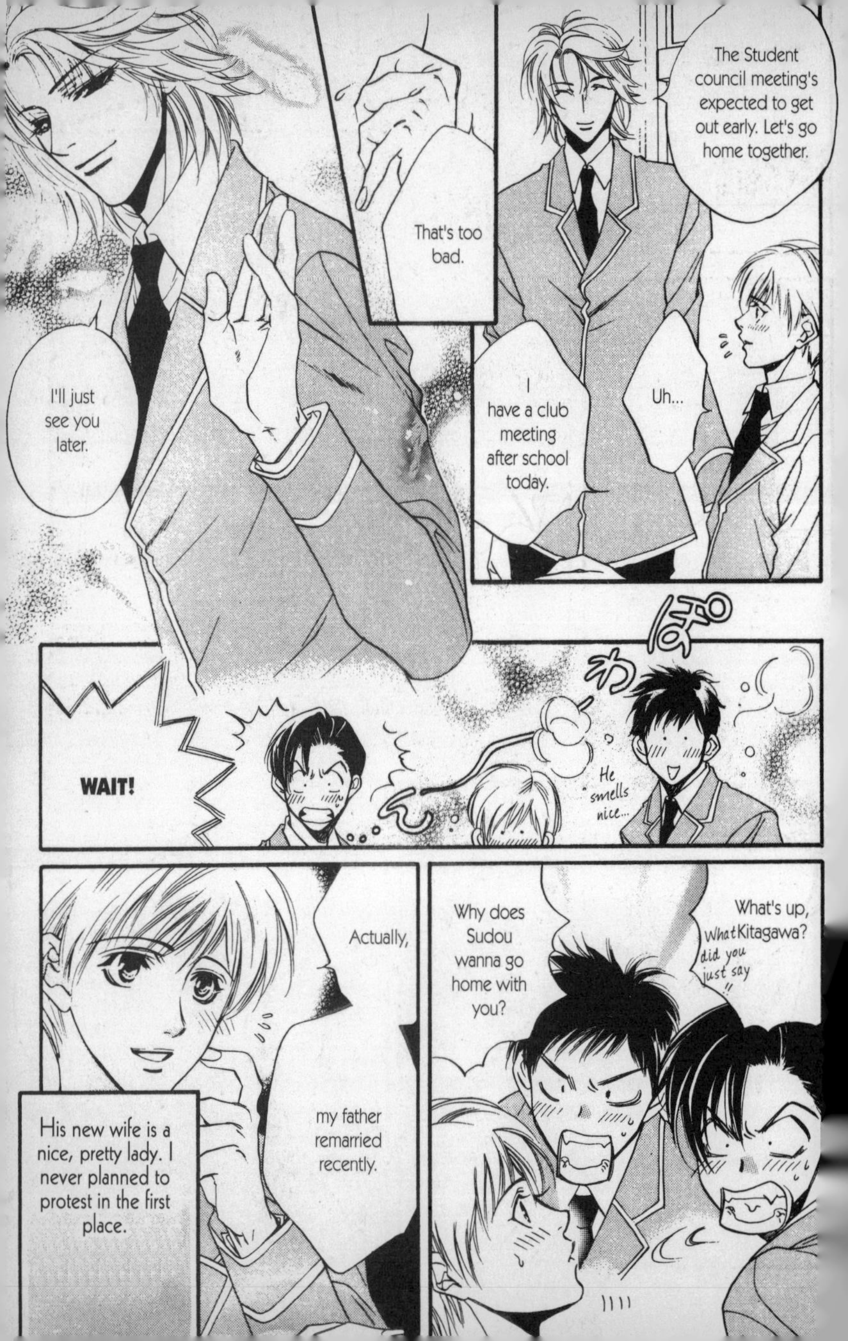

The Student council meeting's expected to get out early. Let's go home together.
Uh...
I have a club meeting after school today.
That's too bad.
I'll just see you later.
ぽわ
He smells nice...
WAIT!
What's up, Kitagawa?
What did you just say!!
Why does Sudou wanna go home with you?
Actually,
my father remarried recently.
His new wife is a nice, pretty lady. I never planned to protest in the first place.

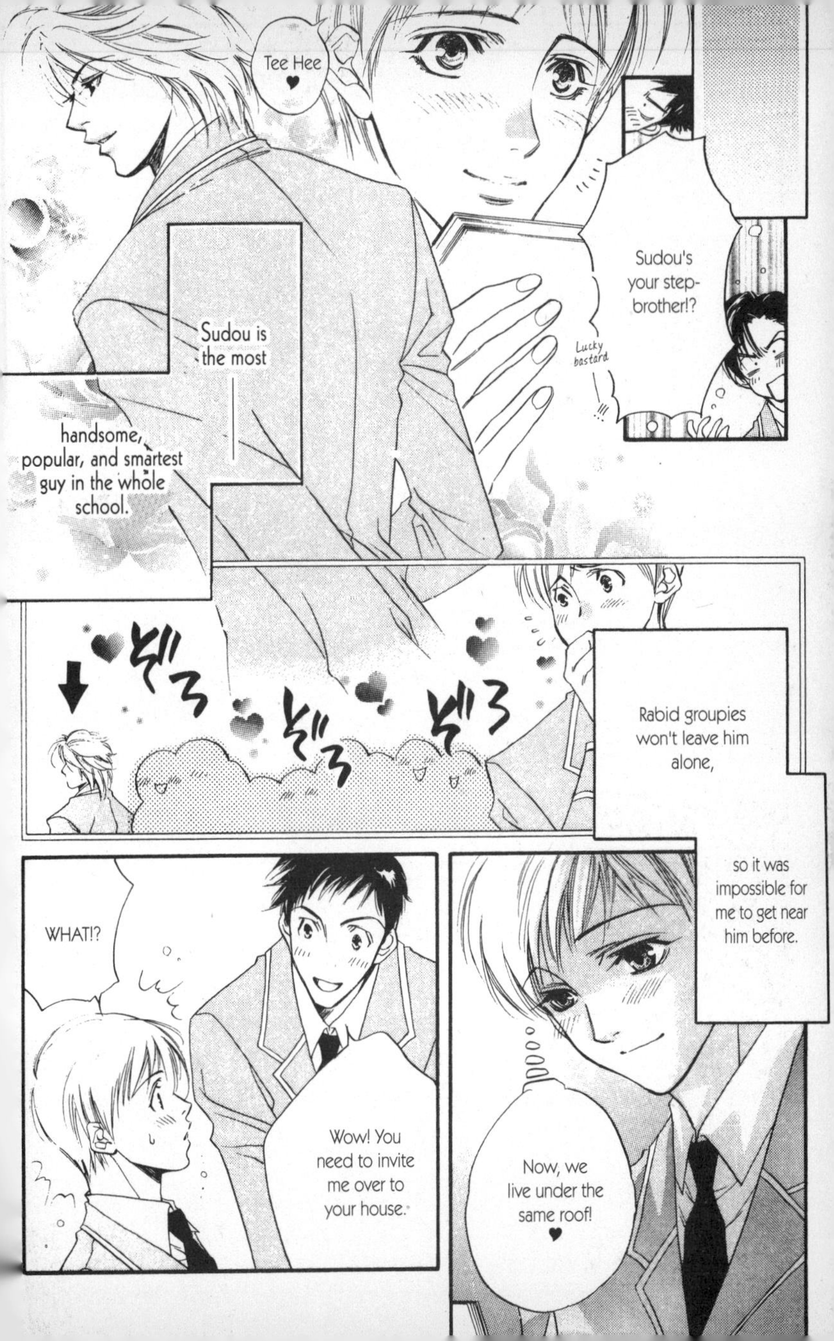
Tee Hee ♥
Sudou is the most —
handsome, popular, and smartest guy in the whole school.
Sudou's your step-brother!?
Lucky bastard
Rabid groupies won't leave him alone,
so it was impossible for me to get near him before.
WHAT!?
Wow! You need to invite me over to your house.
Now, we live under the same roof! ♥

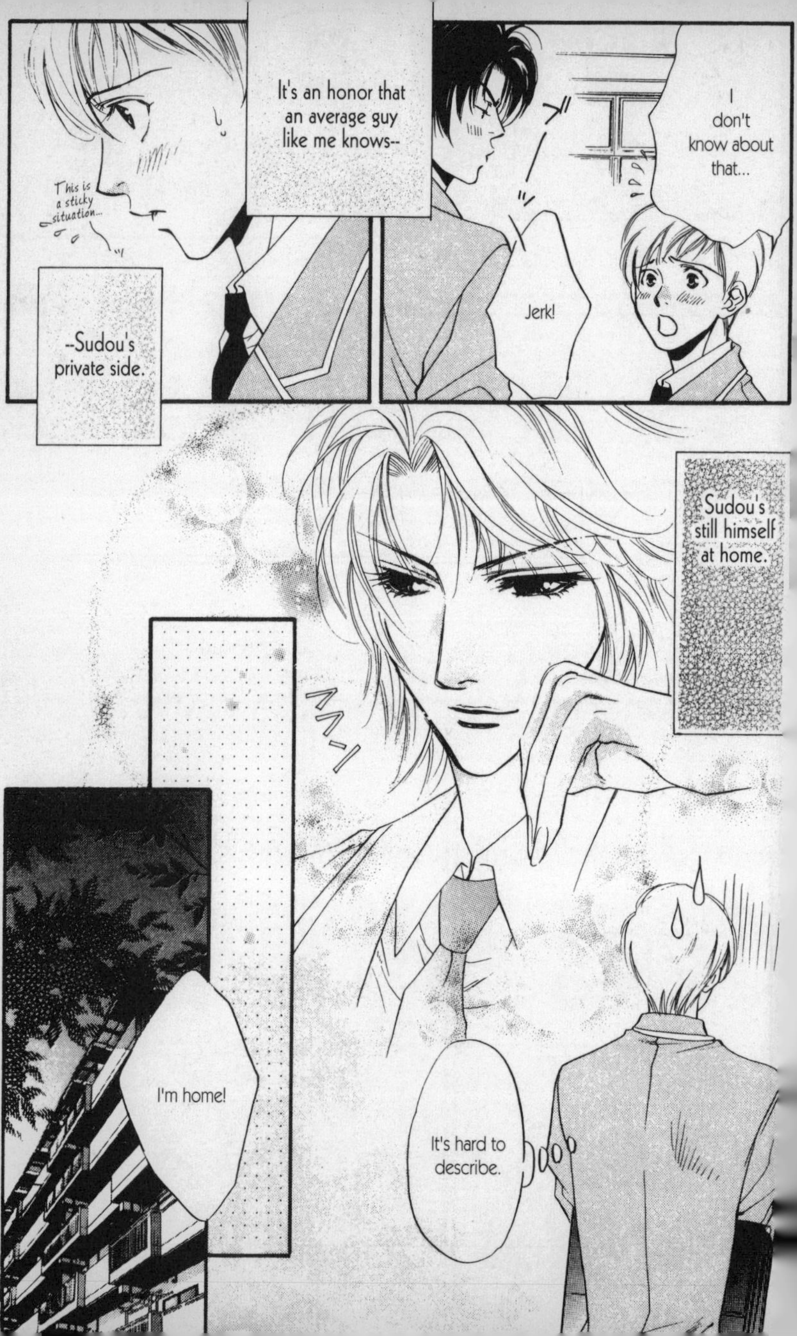

I don't know about that...
Jerk!
It's an honor that an average guy like me knows--
This is a sticky situation...
--Sudou's private side.
Sudou's still himself at home.
It's hard to describe.
I'm home!

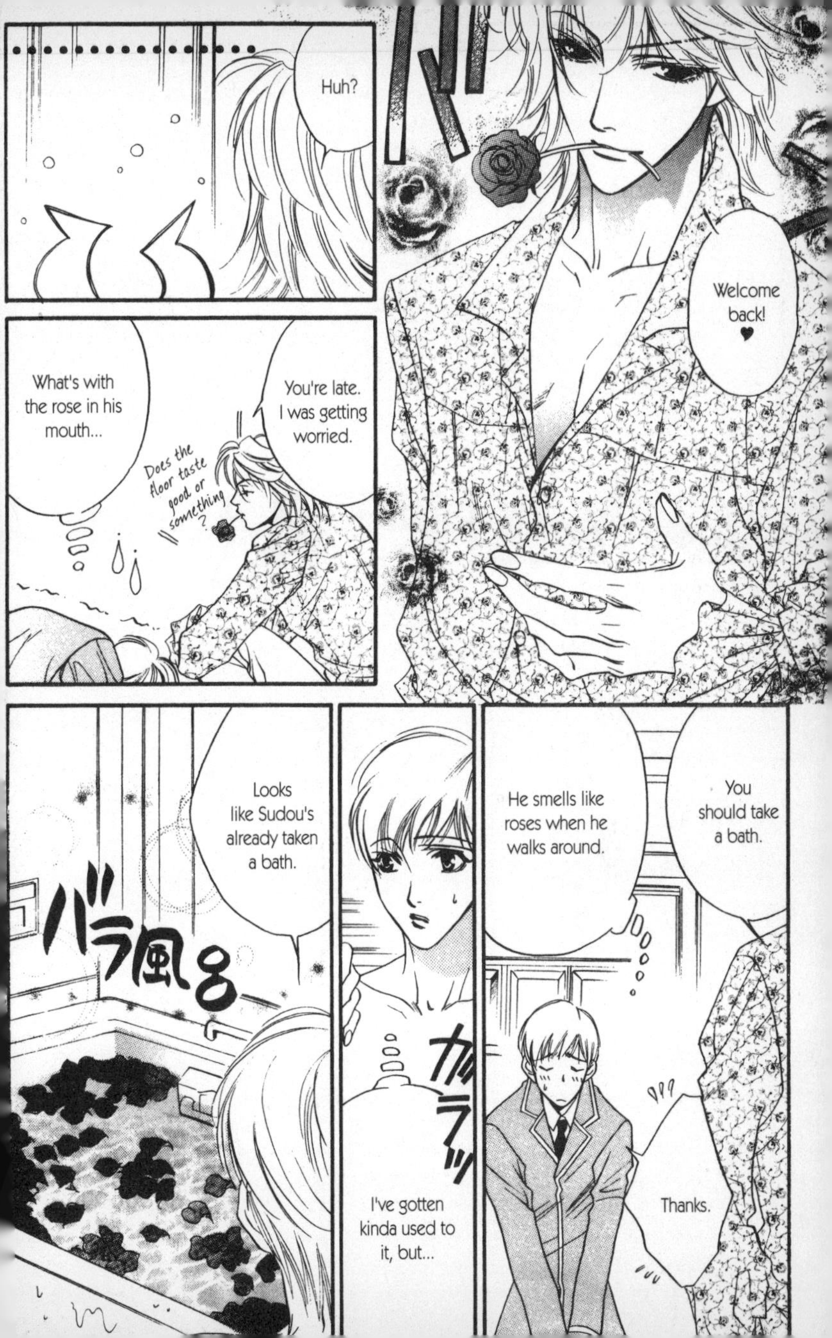
Welcome back! ♥
Huh?
You're late. I was getting worried.
What's with the rose in his mouth...
Does the floor taste good or something?
You should take a bath.
Thanks.
He smells like roses when he walks around.
I've gotten kinda used to it, but...
カラッ
Looks like Sudou's already taken a bath.
バラ風呂

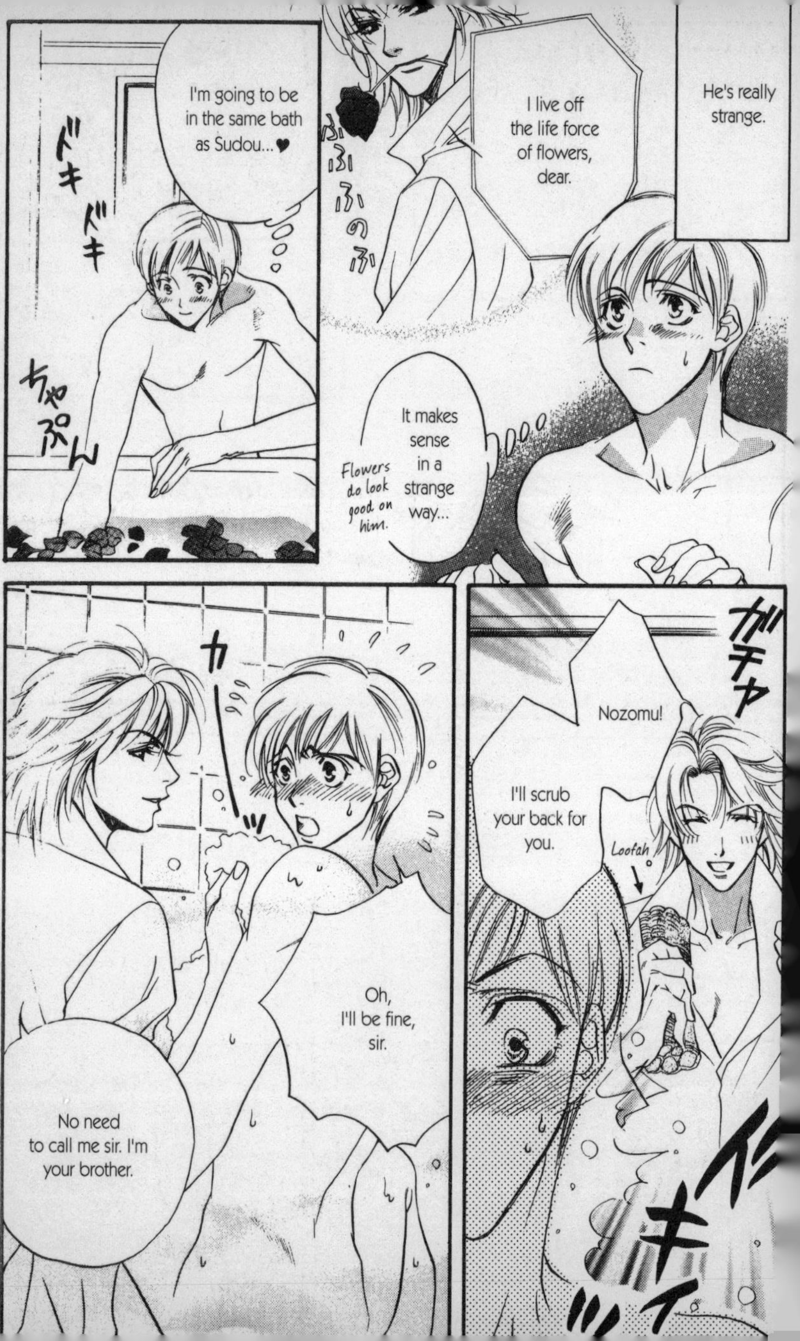

He's really strange.
I live off the life force of flowers, dear.
ふふふのふ
It makes sense in a strange way...
Flowers do look good on him.
I'm going to be in the same bath as Sudou...♥
ドキドキ
ちゃぷん
ガチャ
Nozomu!
I'll scrub your back for you.
Loofah
カーッ
Oh, I'll be fine, sir.
No need to call me sir. I'm your brother.

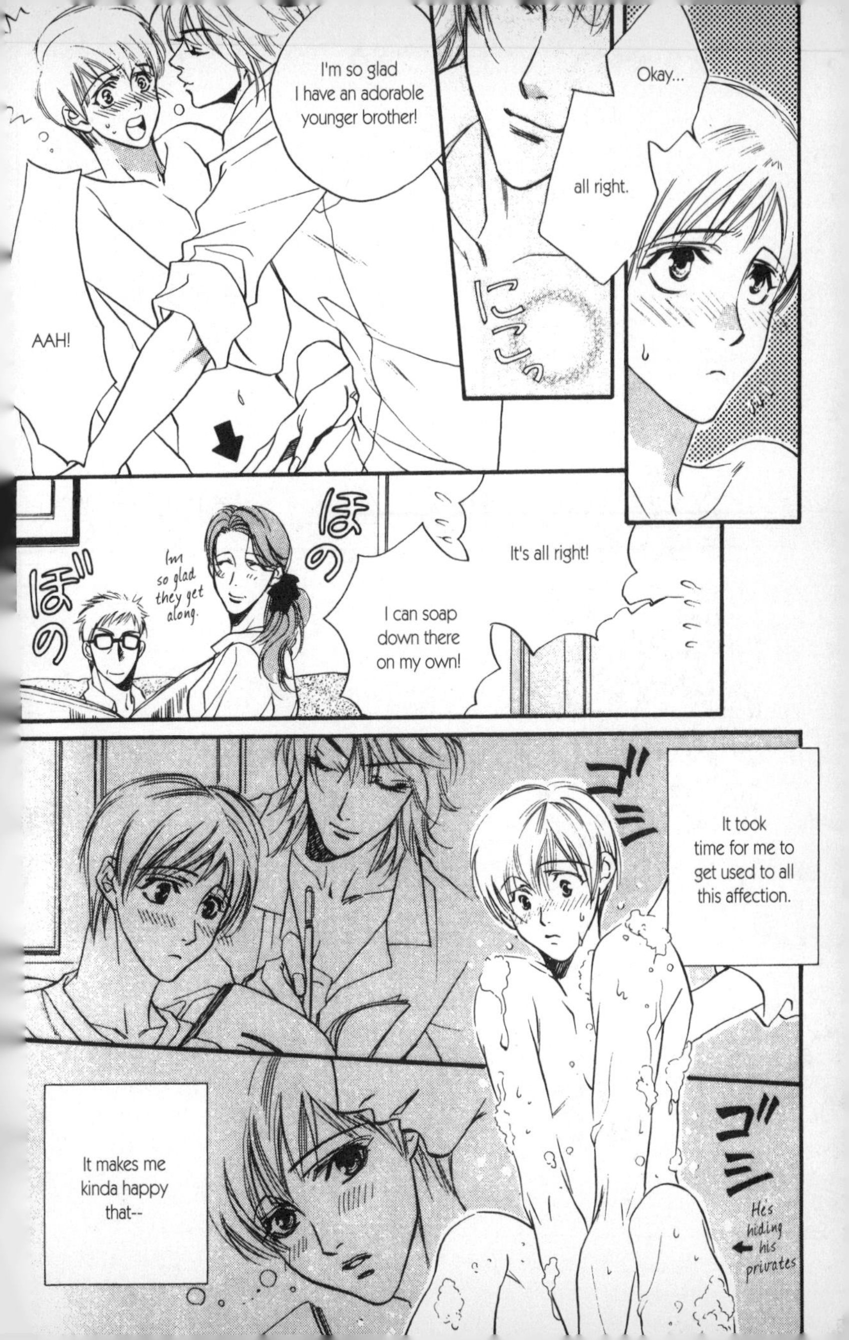

Okay...
all right.
にこっ
I'm so glad I have an adorable younger brother!
AAH!
It's all right!
I can soap down there on my own!
ほのぼの
I'm so glad they get along.
It took time for me to get used to all this affection.
ゴシ
ゴシ
He's hiding his privates
It makes me kinda happy that--

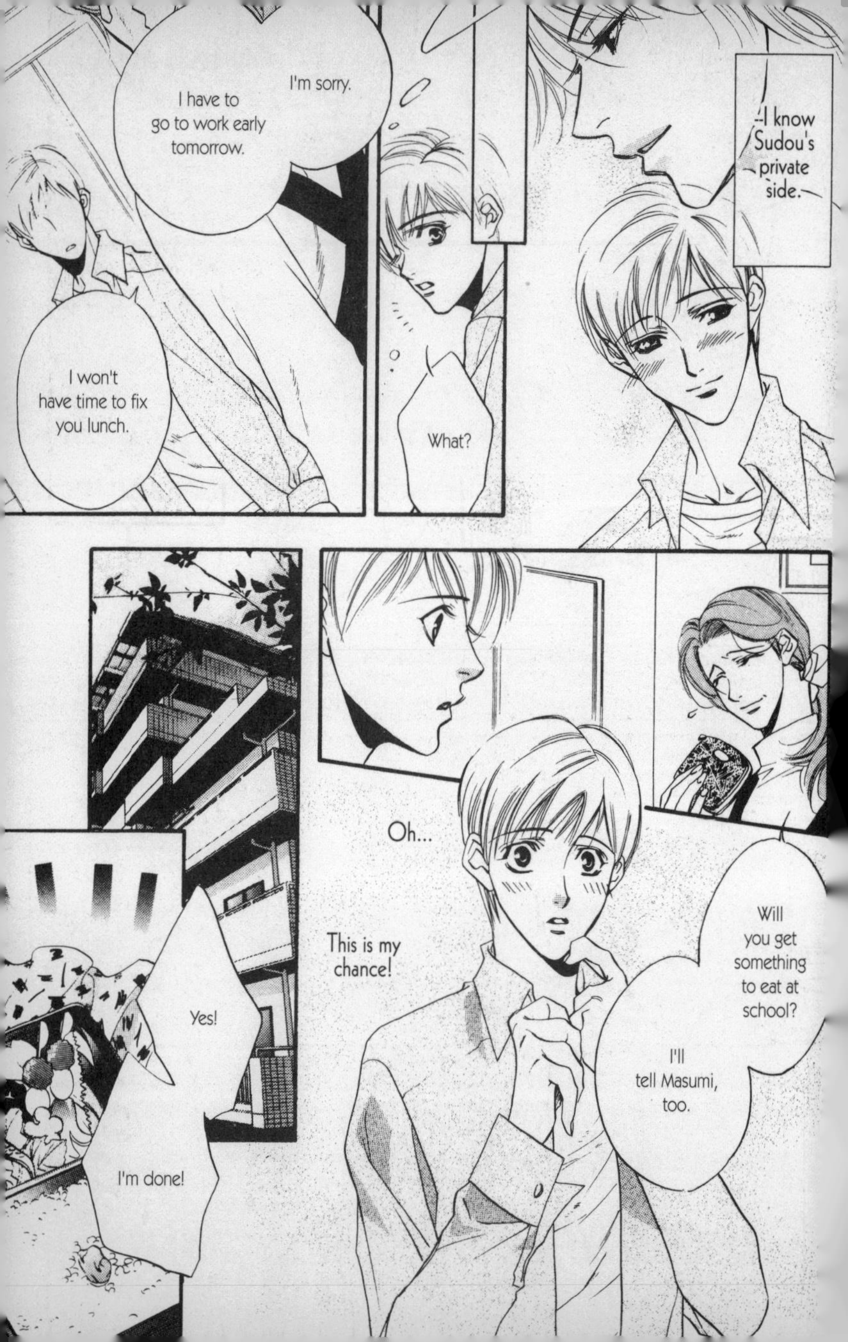

I'm sorry.
I have to go to work early tomorrow.
I won't have time to fix you lunch.
What?
--I know Sudou's private side.--
Will you get something to eat at school?
I'll tell Masumi, too.
Oh...
This is my chance!
Yes!
I'm done!

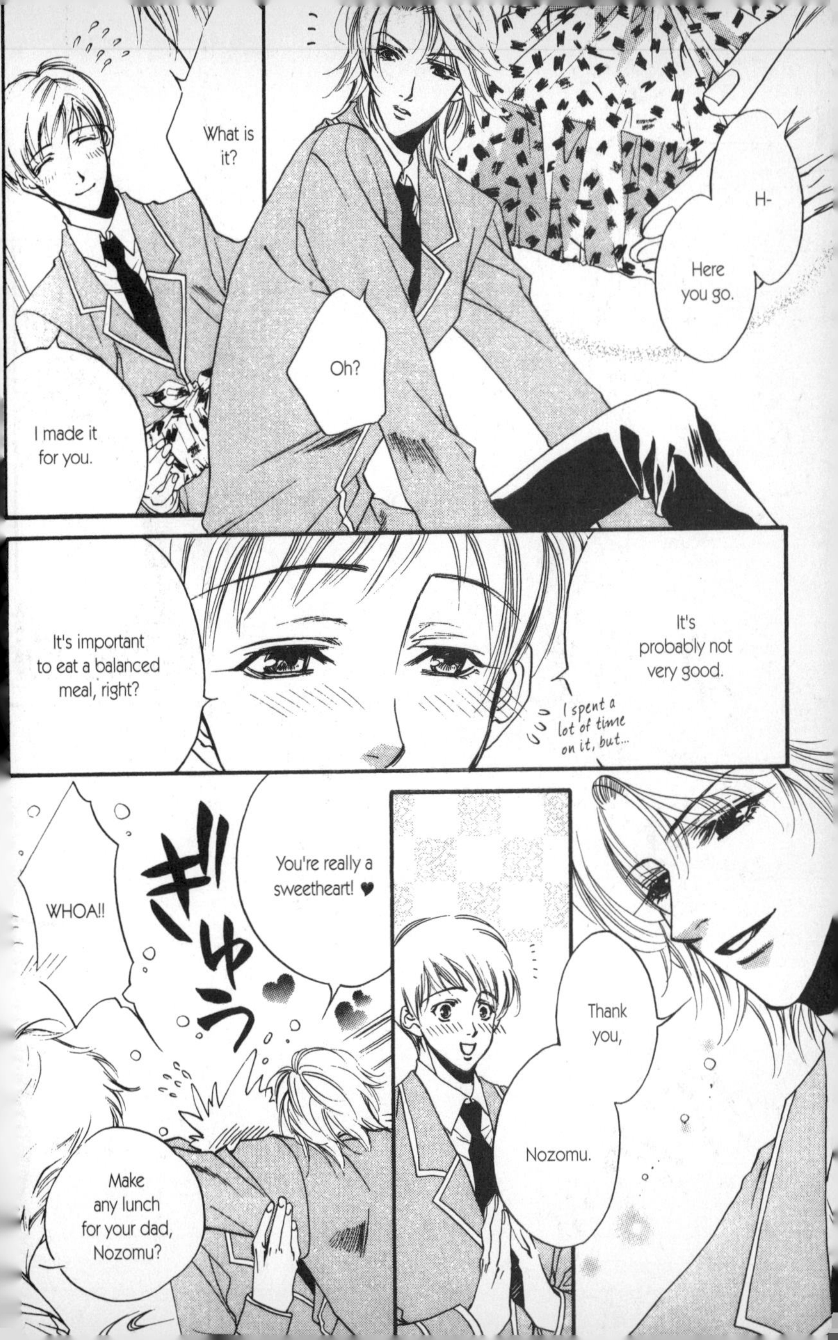
H-
Here you go.
Oh?
What is it?
I made it for you.
It's probably not very good.
I spent a lot of time on it, but...
It's important to eat a balanced meal, right?
Thank you,
Nozomu.
You're really a sweetheart! ♥
ぎゅう
WHOA!!
Make any lunch for your dad, Nozomu?

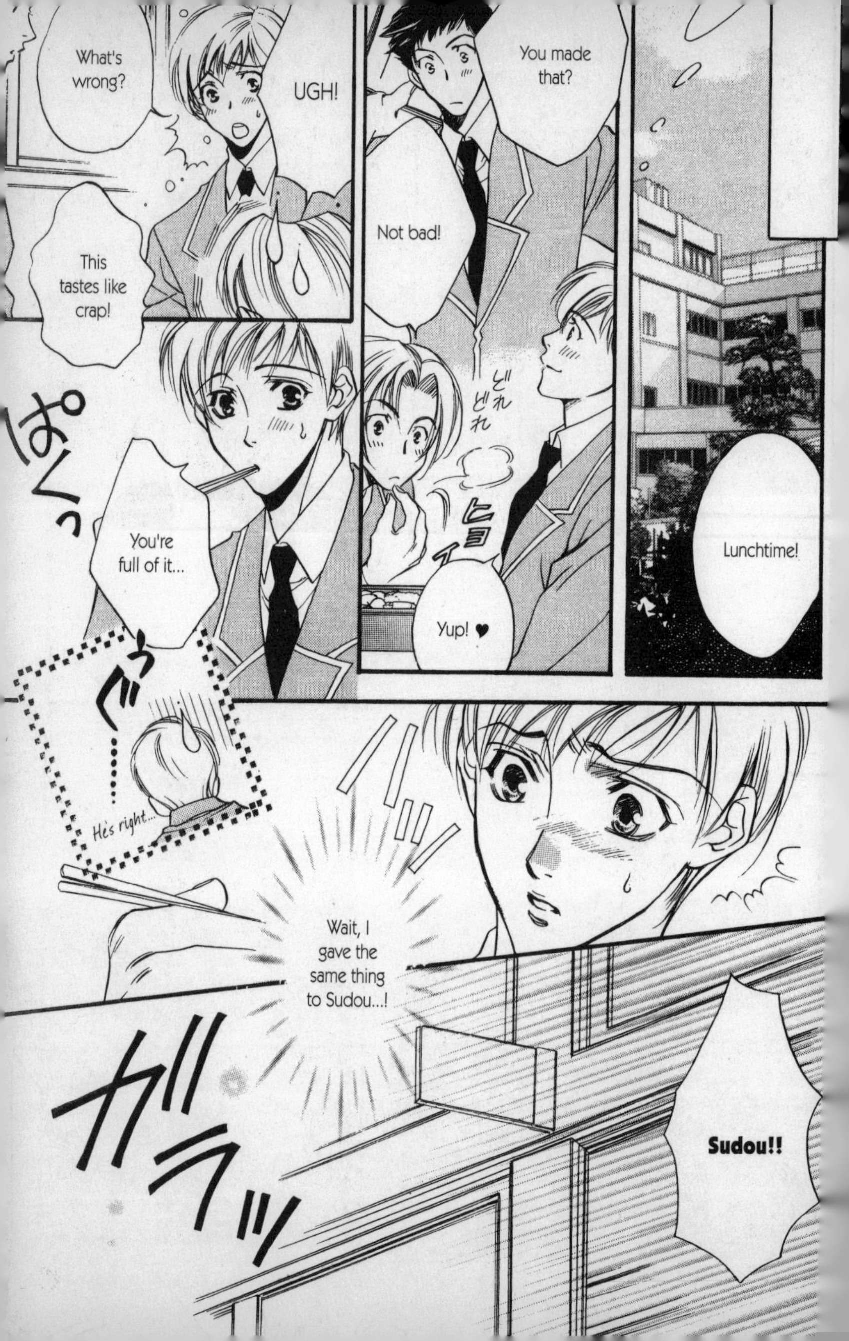
Lunchtime!
You made that?
どれどれ
Not bad!
ヒョイ
Yup! ♥
ぱくっ
UGH!
What's wrong?
This tastes like crap!
You're full of it...
うぐ...
He's right...
Wait, I gave the same thing to Sudou...!
ガラッ
Sudou!!

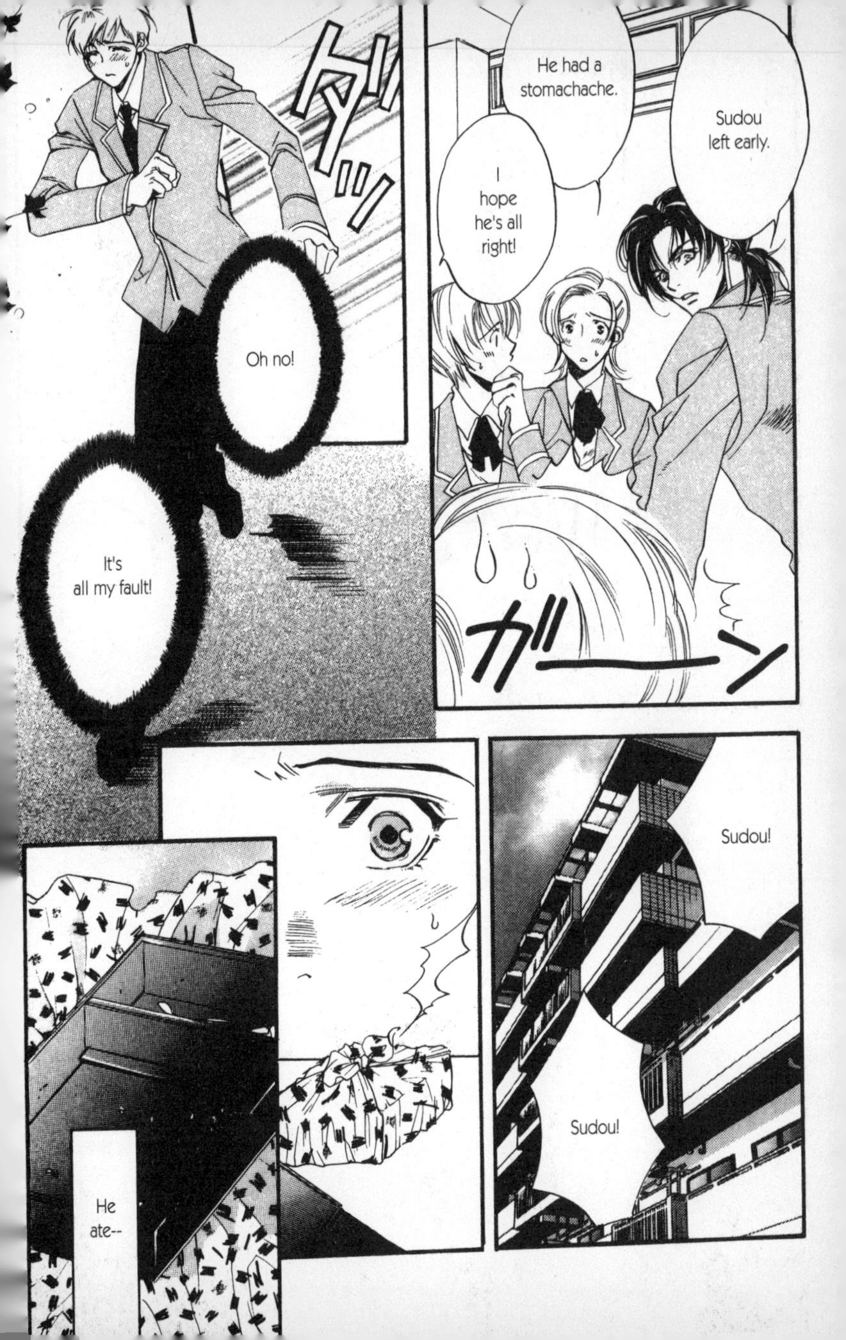
Sudou left early.
He had a stomachache.
I hope he's all right!
ガーン
ダッ
Oh no!
It's all my fault!
Sudou!
Sudou!
He ate--

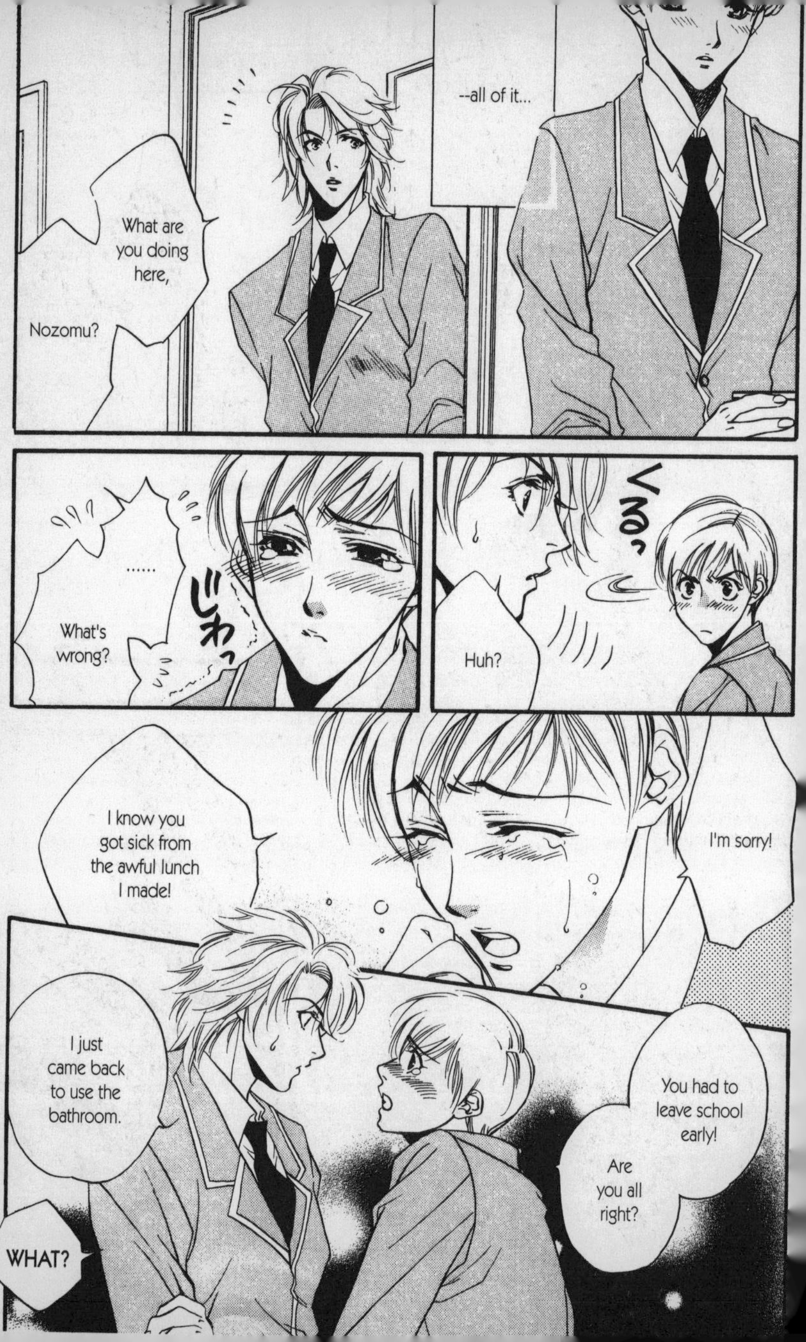
--all of it...
What are you doing here,
Nozomu?
......
What's wrong?
じわっ
くるっ
Huh?
I'm sorry!
I know you got sick from the awful lunch I made!
You had to leave school early!
Are you all right?
I just came back to use the bathroom.
WHAT?

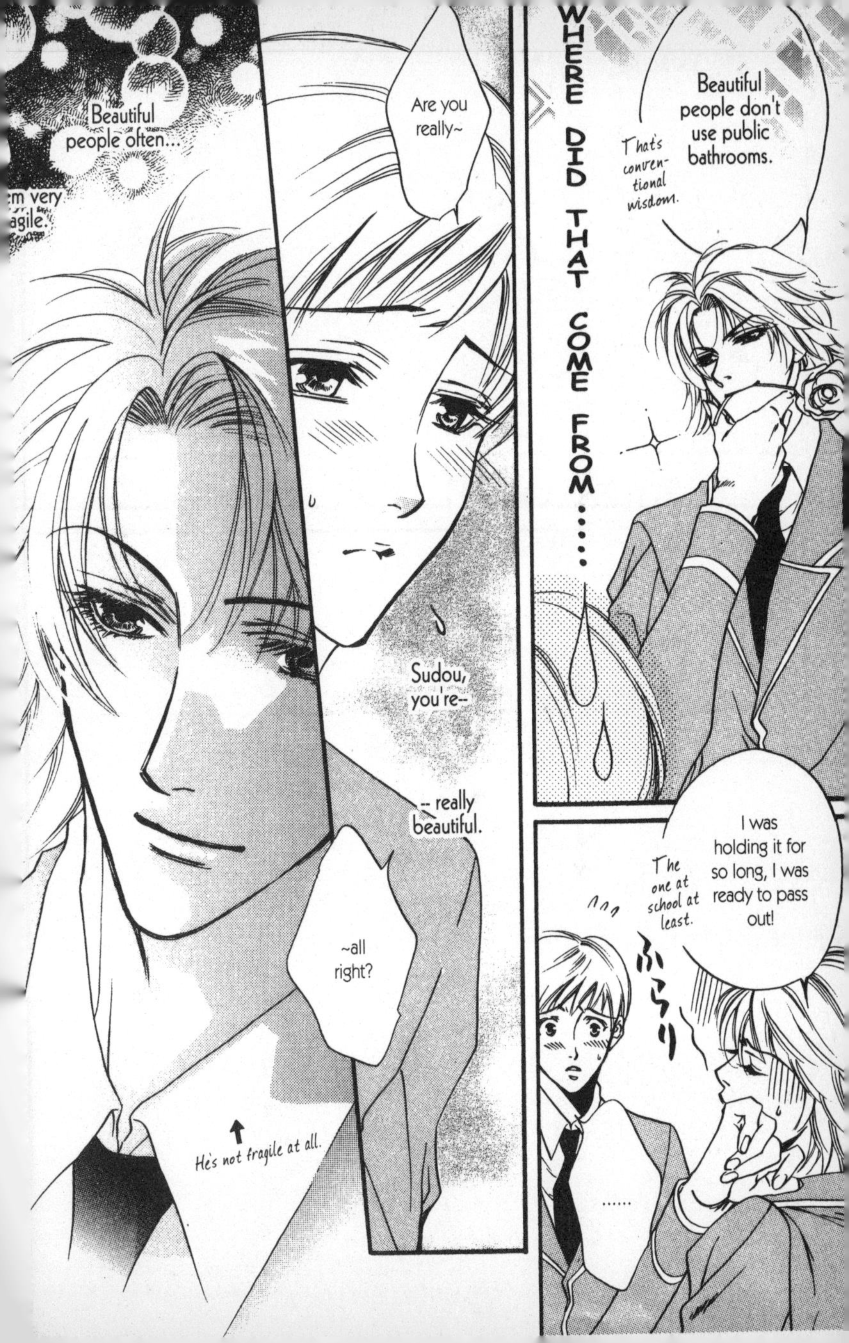
Beautiful people don't use public bathrooms.
That's conventional wisdom.
WHERE DID THAT COME FROM.....
I was holding it for so long, I was ready to pass out!
The one at school at least.
ふらり
......
Are you really~
~all right?
Sudou, you're--
-- really beautiful.
Beautiful people often...
em very agile.
He's not fragile at all.

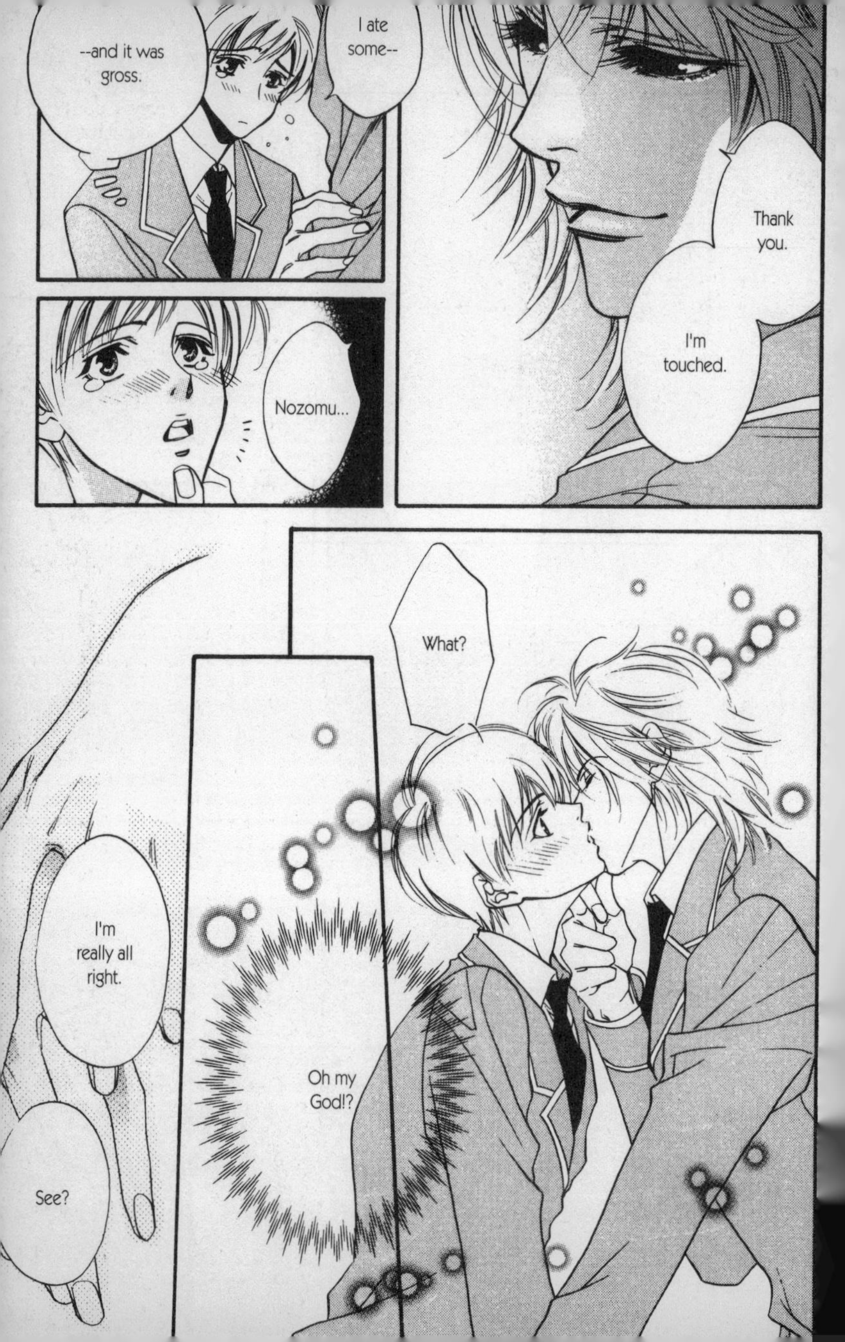
I ate some--
--and it was gross.
Thank you.
I'm touched.
Nozomu...
What?
Oh my God!?
I'm really all right.
See?

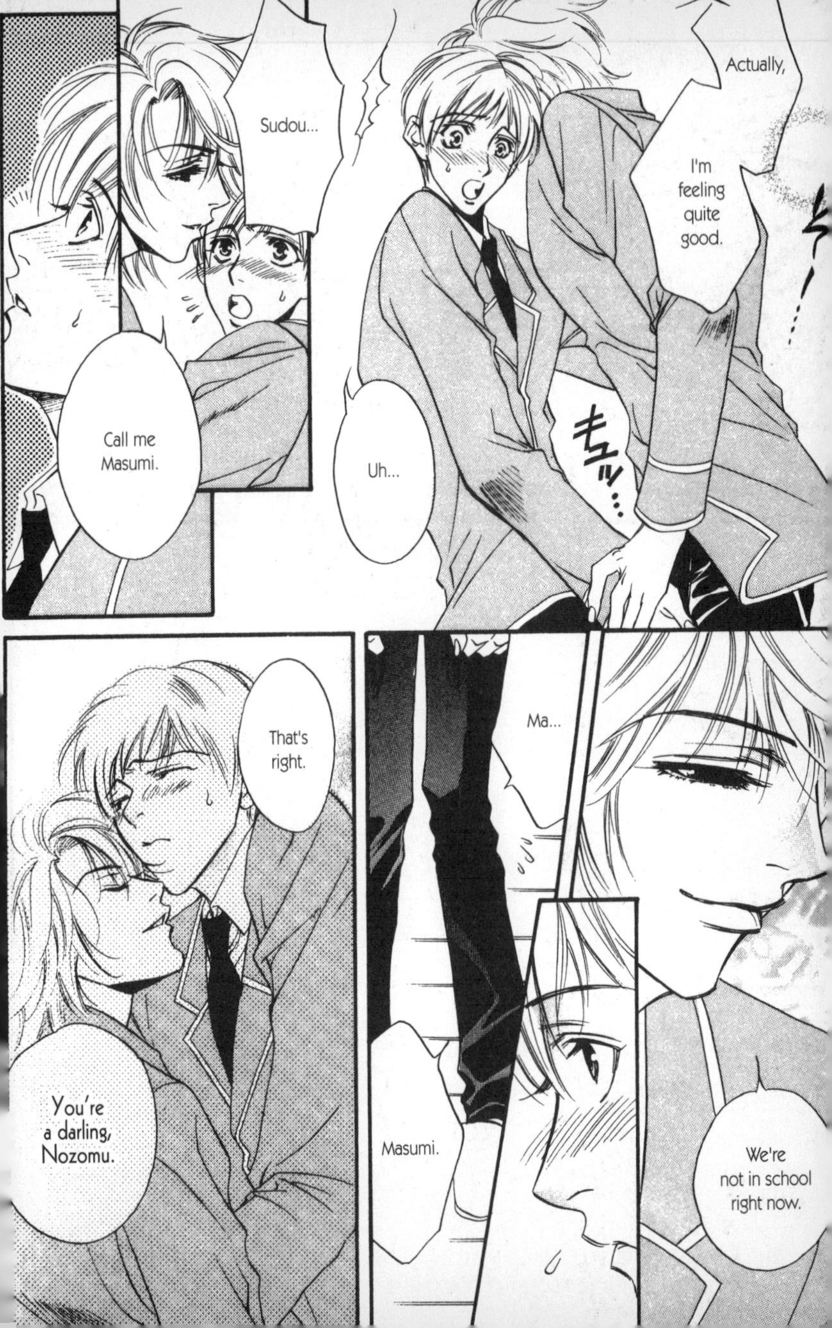
Actually,
I'm feeling quite good.
Uh...
Sudou...
Call me Masumi.
We're not in school right now.
Ma...
Masumi.
That's right.
You're a darling, Nozomu.

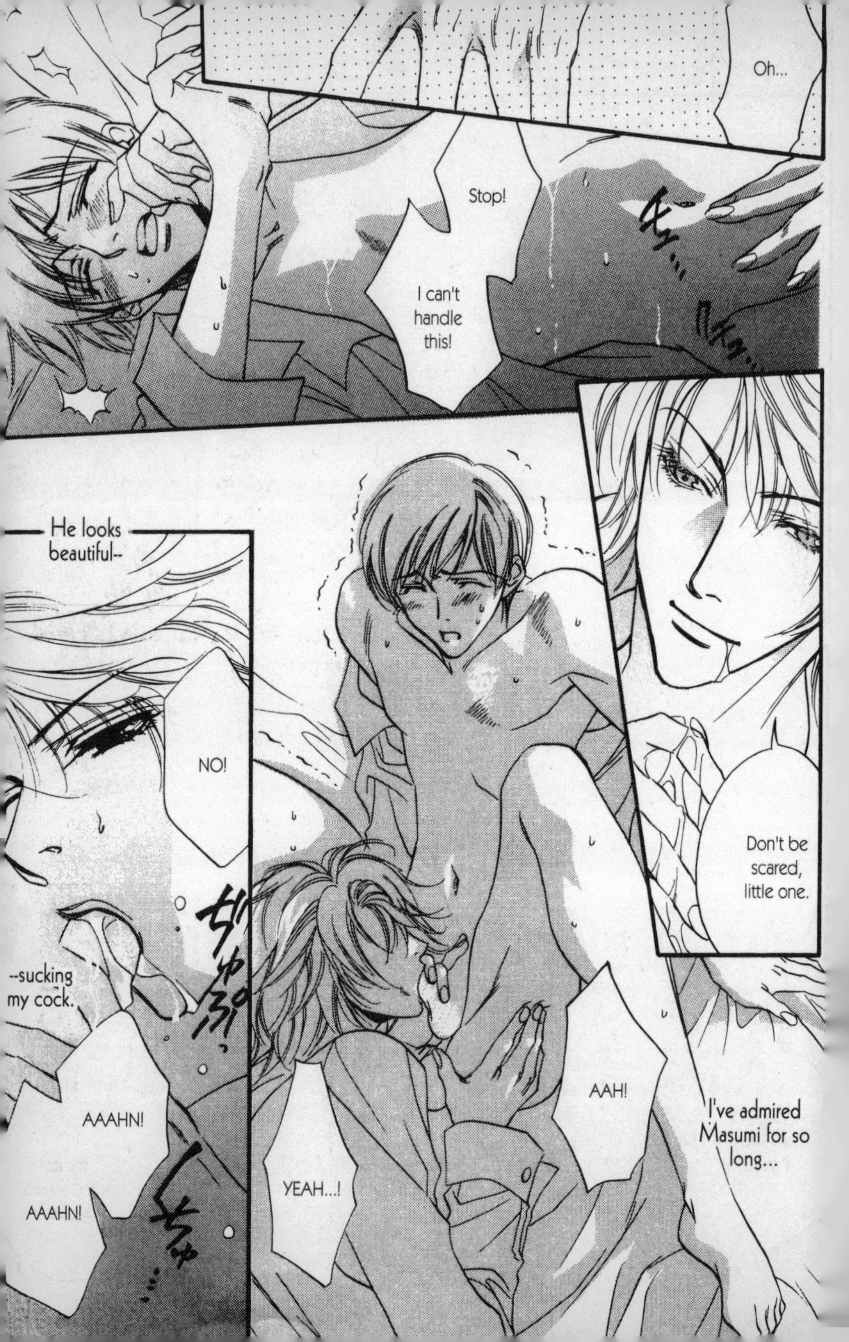
Oh...
Stop!
I can't handle this!
Don't be scared, little one.
I've admired Masumi for so long...
AAH!
YEAH...!
He looks beautiful--
NO!
--sucking my cock.
AAAHN!
AAAHN!

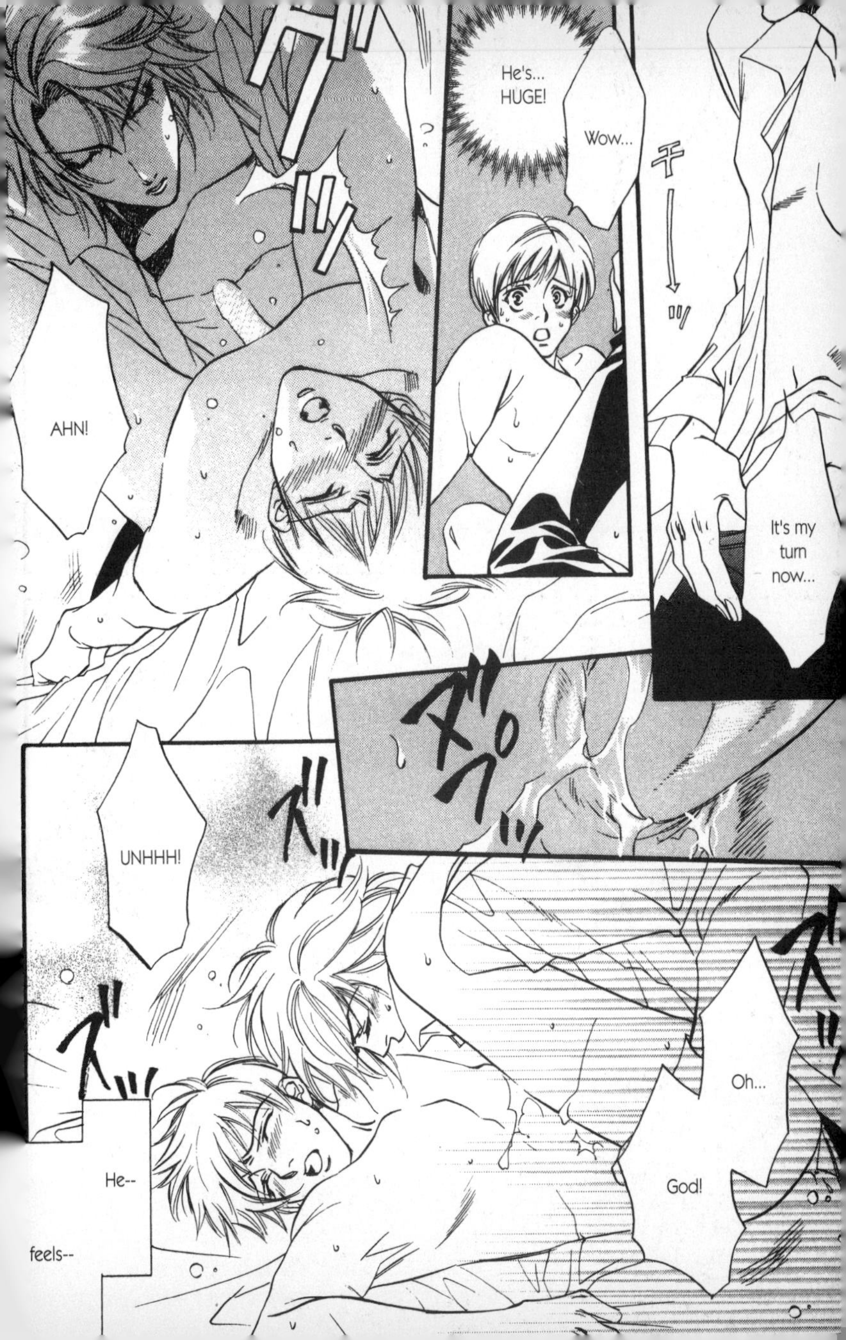
It's my turn now...
Wow...
He's... HUGE!
AHN!
UNHHH!
Oh...
God!
He--
feels--

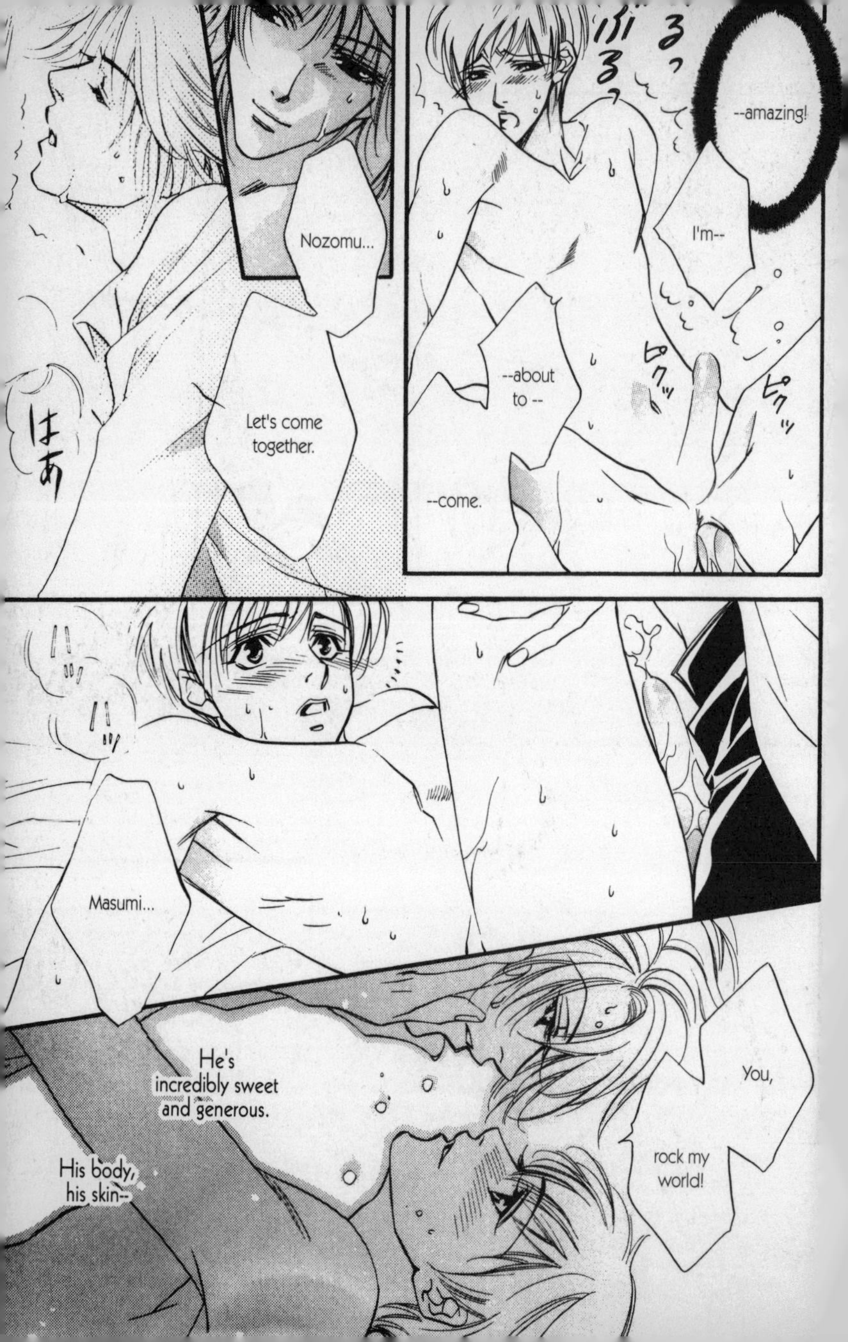

ぶるっ
--amazing!
I'm--
--about to --
--come.
ピクッ
ピクッ
Nozomu...
Let's come together.
はあ
Masumi...
You,
rock my world!
He's incredibly sweet and generous.
His body, his skin--

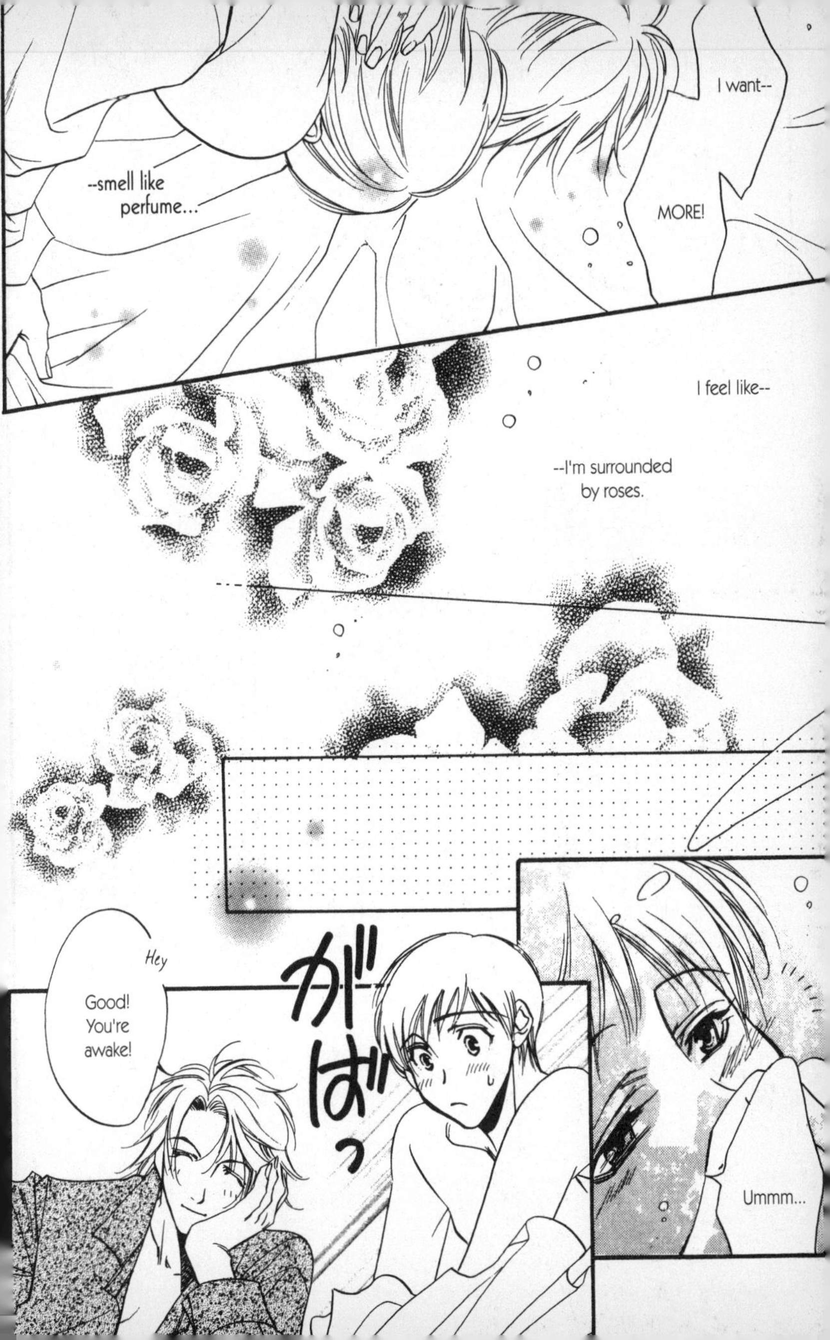
I want--
MORE!
--smell like perfume...
I feel like--
--I'm surrounded by roses.
Ummm...
がばっ
Hey
Good! You're awake!

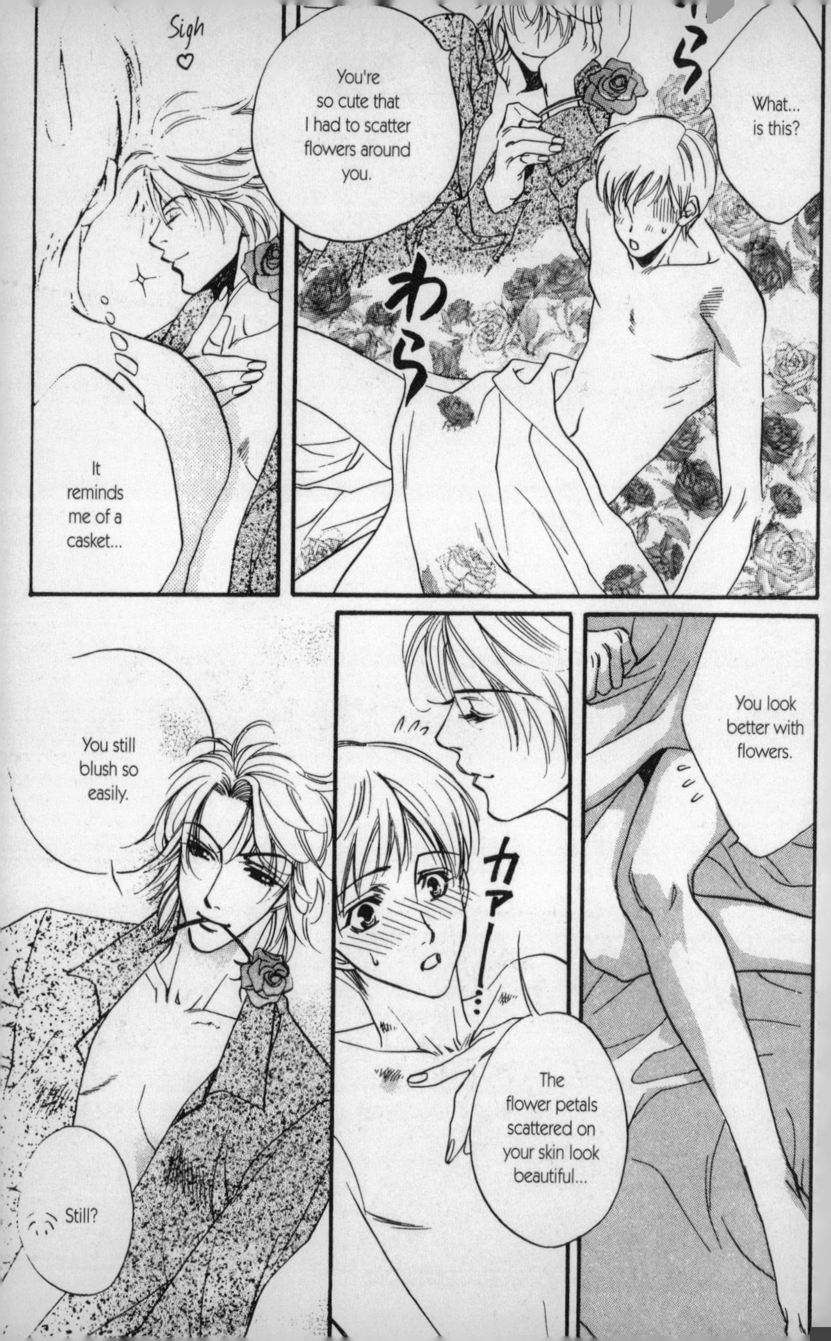
What... is this?
You're so cute that I had to scatter flowers around you.
わら
Sigh ♡
It reminds me of a casket...
You look better with flowers.
カァー
The flower petals scattered on your skin look beautiful...
You still blush so easily.
Still?

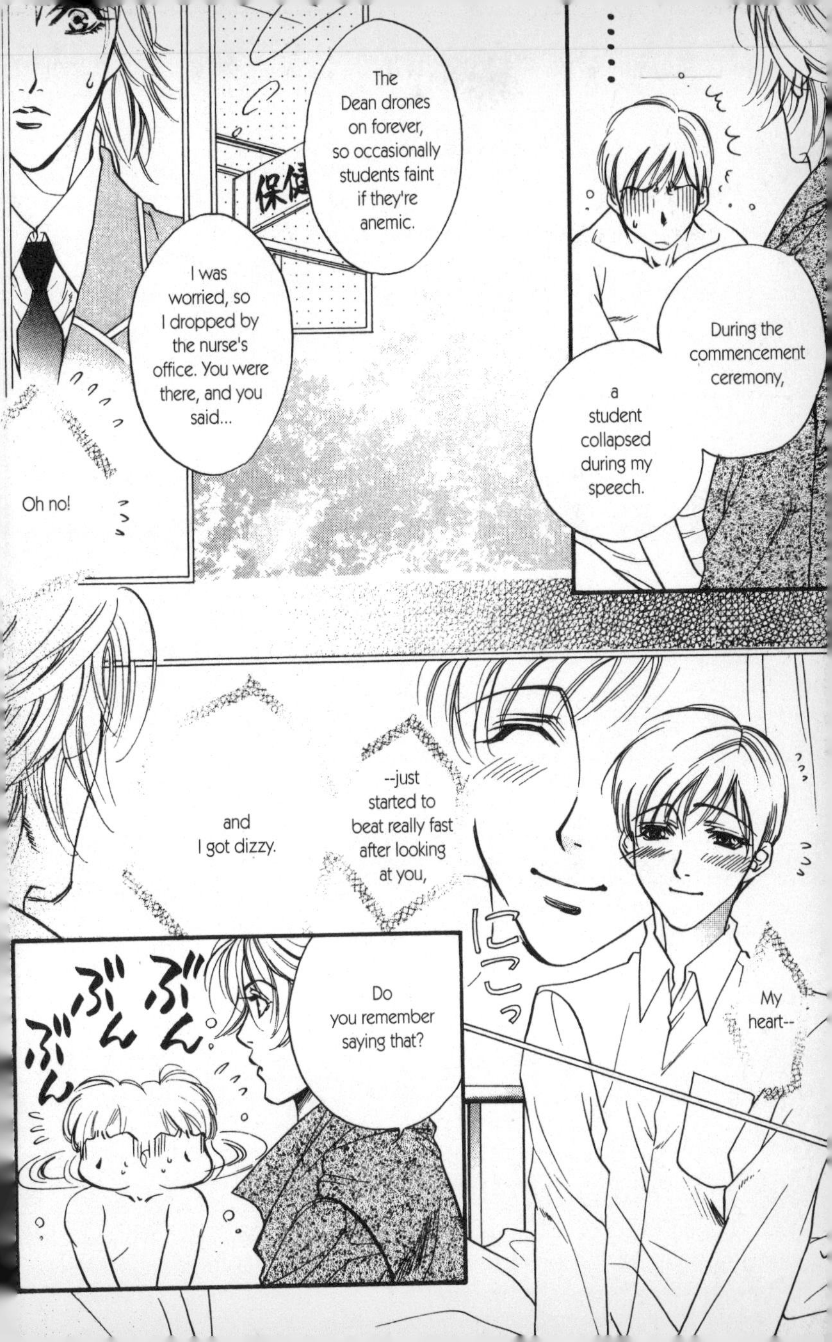
During the commencement ceremony,
a student collapsed during my speech.
The Dean drones on forever, so occasionally students faint if they're anemic.
I was worried, so I dropped by the nurse's office. You were there, and you said...
Oh no!
My heart--
--just started to beat really fast after looking at you,
and I got dizzy.
にこっ
Do you remember saying that?
ぶんぶんぶん

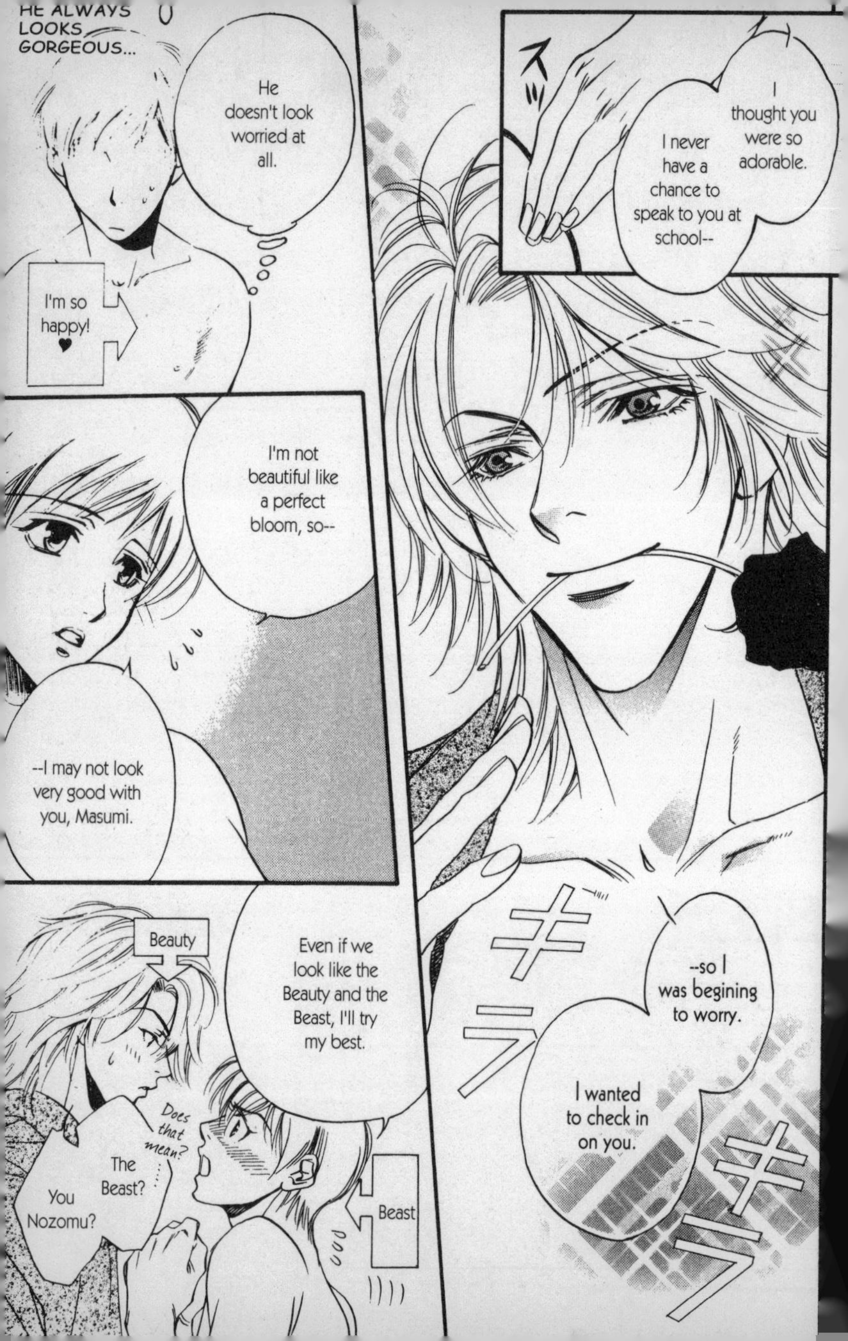

スッ
I thought you were so adorable.
I never have a chance to speak to you at school--
--so I was begining to worry.
I wanted to check in on you.
キラ
キラ
HE ALWAYS LOOKS GORGEOUS...
He doesn't look worried at all.
I'm so happy! ♥
I'm not beautiful like a perfect bloom, so--
--I may not look very good with you, Masumi.
Even if we look like the Beauty and the Beast, I'll try my best.
Beauty
Beast
Does that mean?
The Beast?
You Nozomu?

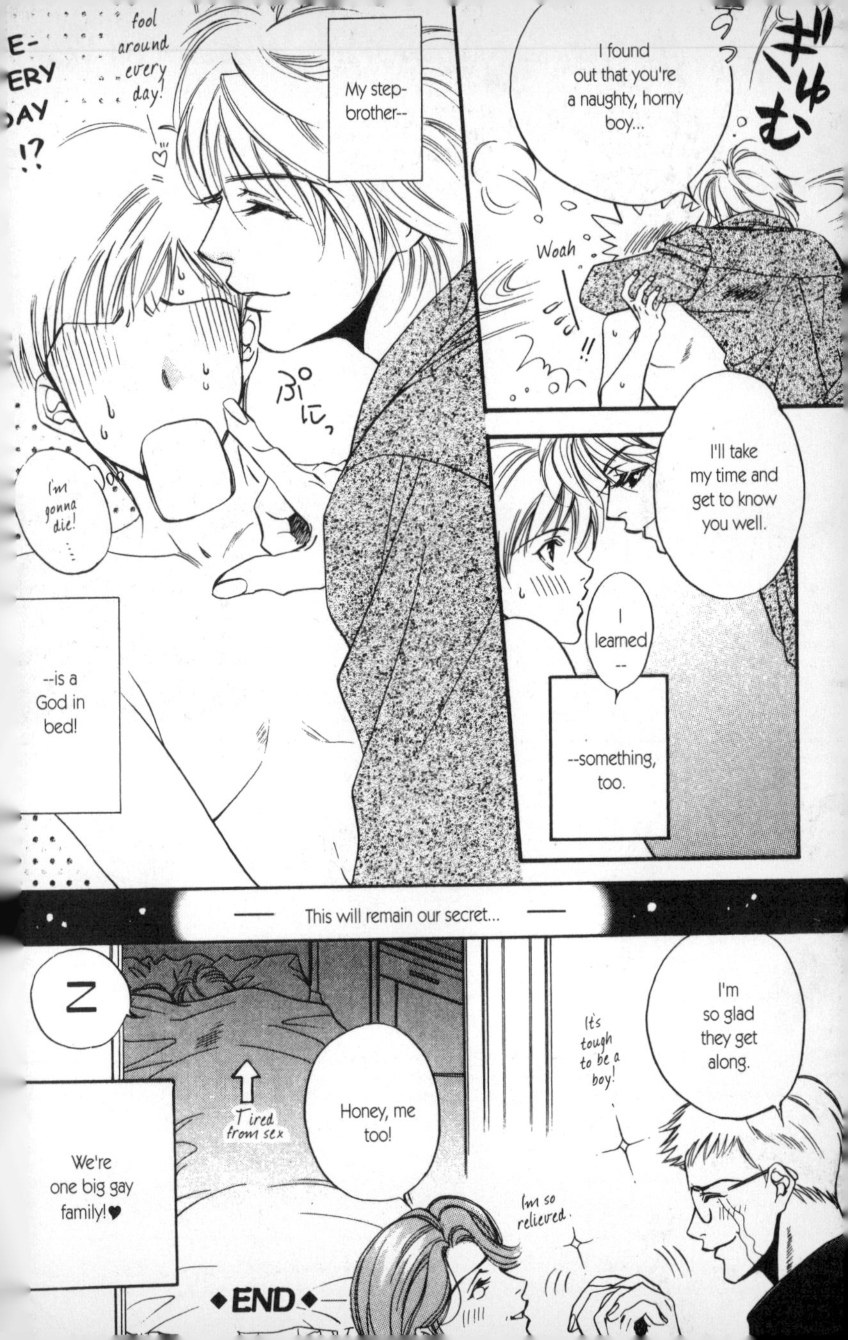

ぎゅむ
すっ
I found out that you're a naughty, horny boy...
Woah
!!
I'll take my time and get to know you well.
I learned--
--something, too.
My step-brother--
E-VERY DAY!?
fool around every day!
ぷにっ
I'm gonna die!
--is a God in bed!
— This will remain our secret... —
I'm so glad they get along.
It's tough to be a boy!
I'm so relieved.
Honey, me too!
Tired from sex
Z
We're one big gay family!♥
◆END◆

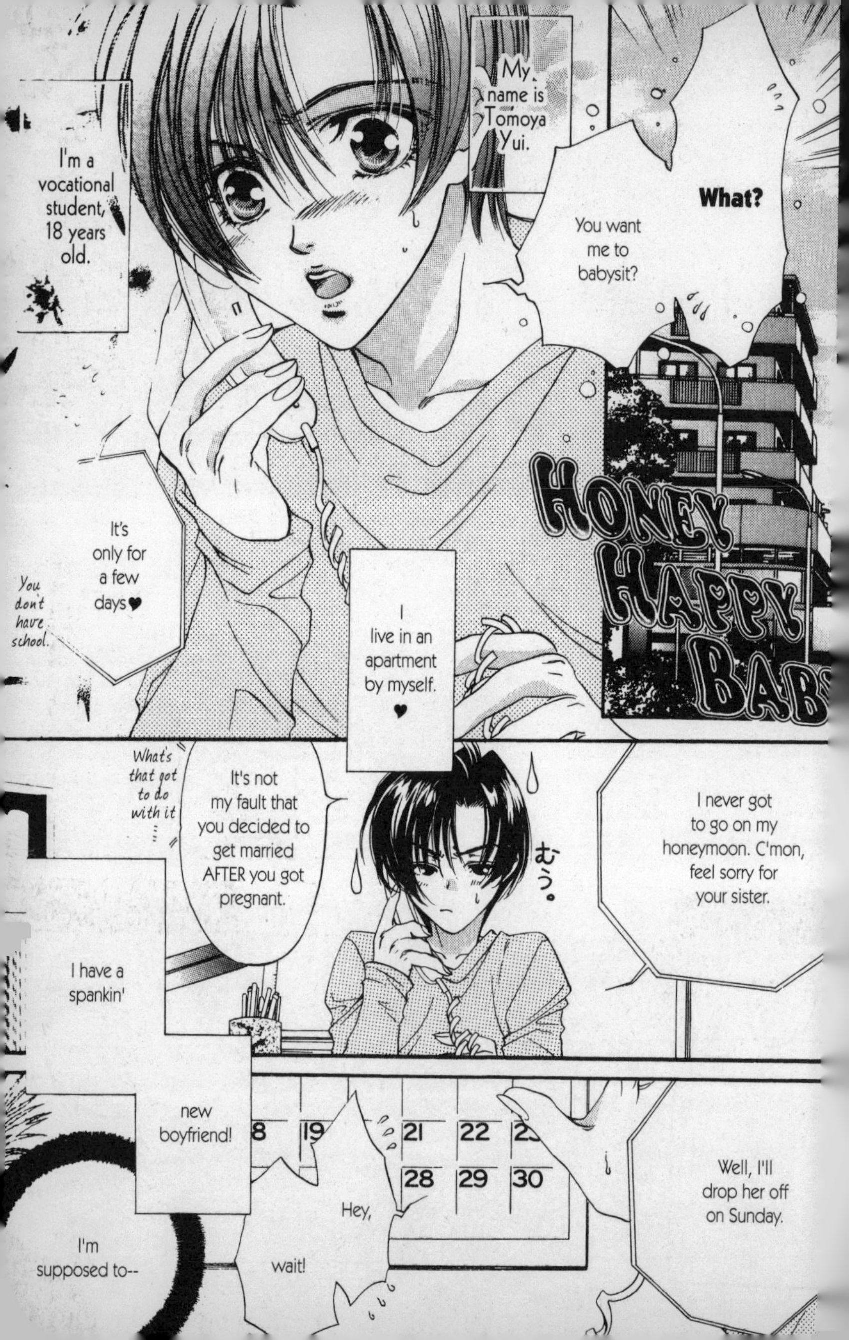

HONEY HAPPY BAB
What?
You want me to babysit?
My name is Tomoya Yui.
I'm a vocational student, 18 years old.
It's only for a few days♥
You don't have school.
I live in an apartment by myself. ♥
I never got to go on my honeymoon. C'mon, feel sorry for your sister.
むう。
It's not my fault that you decided to get married AFTER you got pregnant.
What's that got to do with it...
I have a spankin'
new boyfriend!
Well, I'll drop her off on Sunday.
Hey,
wait!
I'm supposed to--

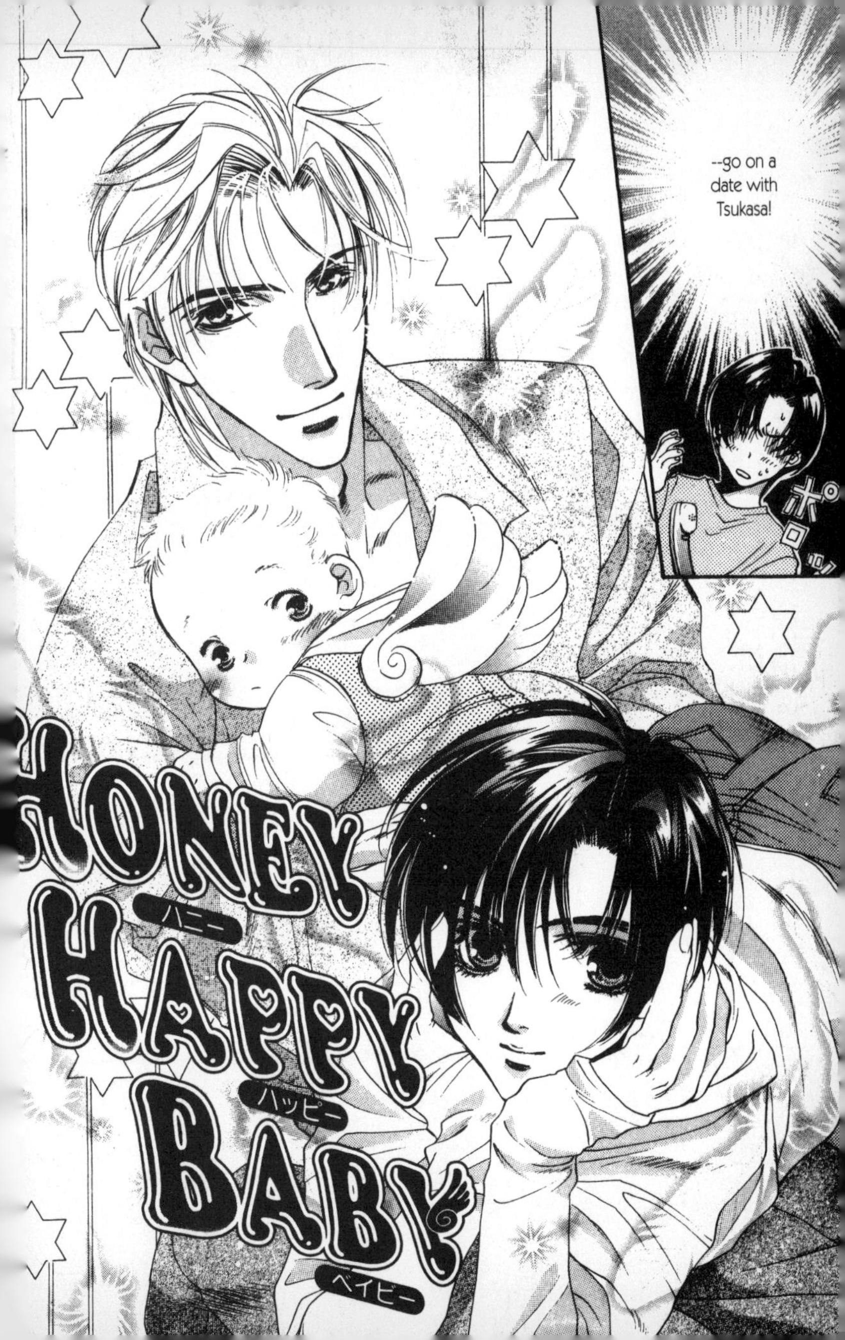
--go on a date with Tsukasa!
ポロッ
HONEY
ハニー
HAPPY
ハッピー
BABY
ベイビー

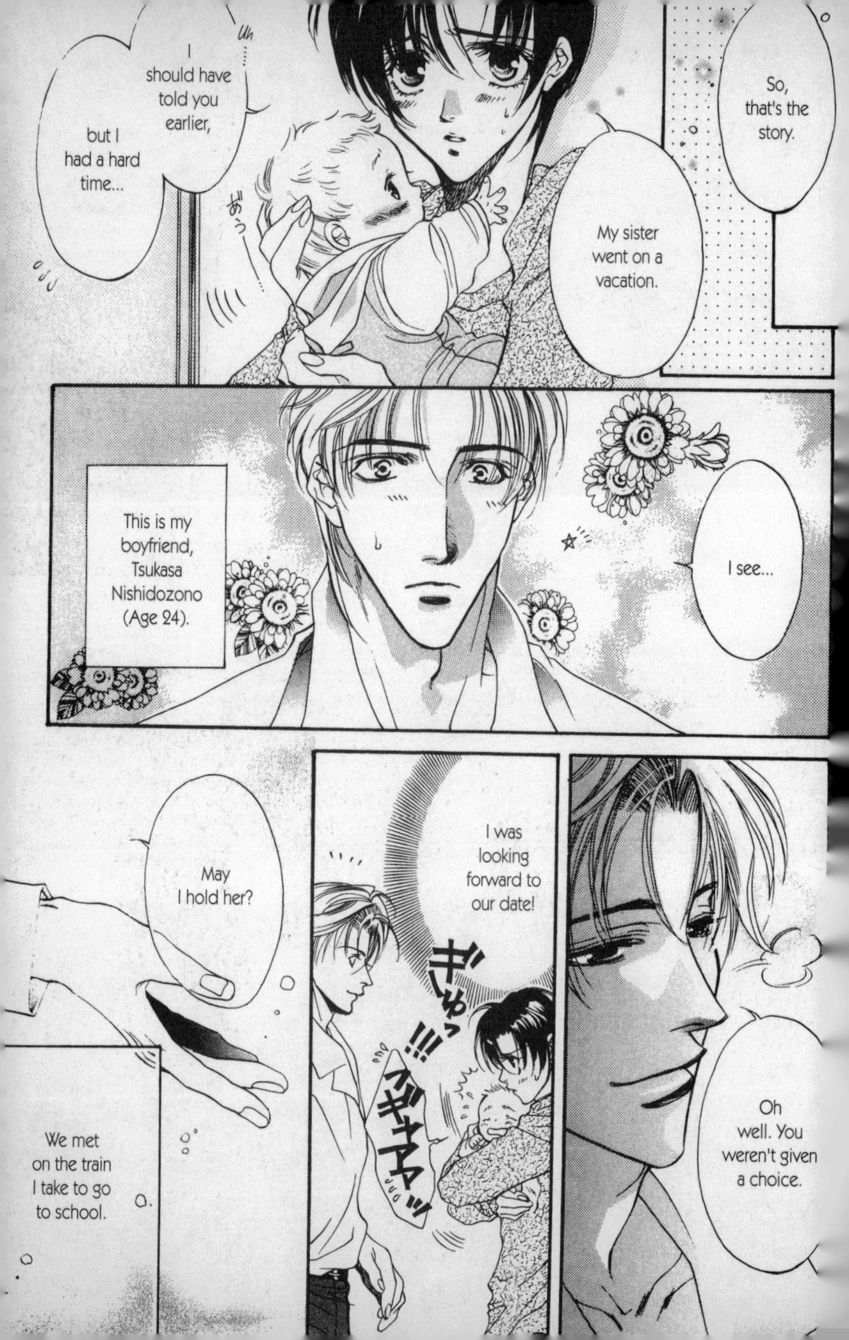
So, that's the story.
My sister went on a vacation.
I should have told you earlier,
but I had a hard time...
I see...
This is my boyfriend, Tsukasa Nishidozono (Age 24).
Oh well. You weren't given a choice.
I was looking forward to our date!
May I hold her?
We met on the train I take to go to school.

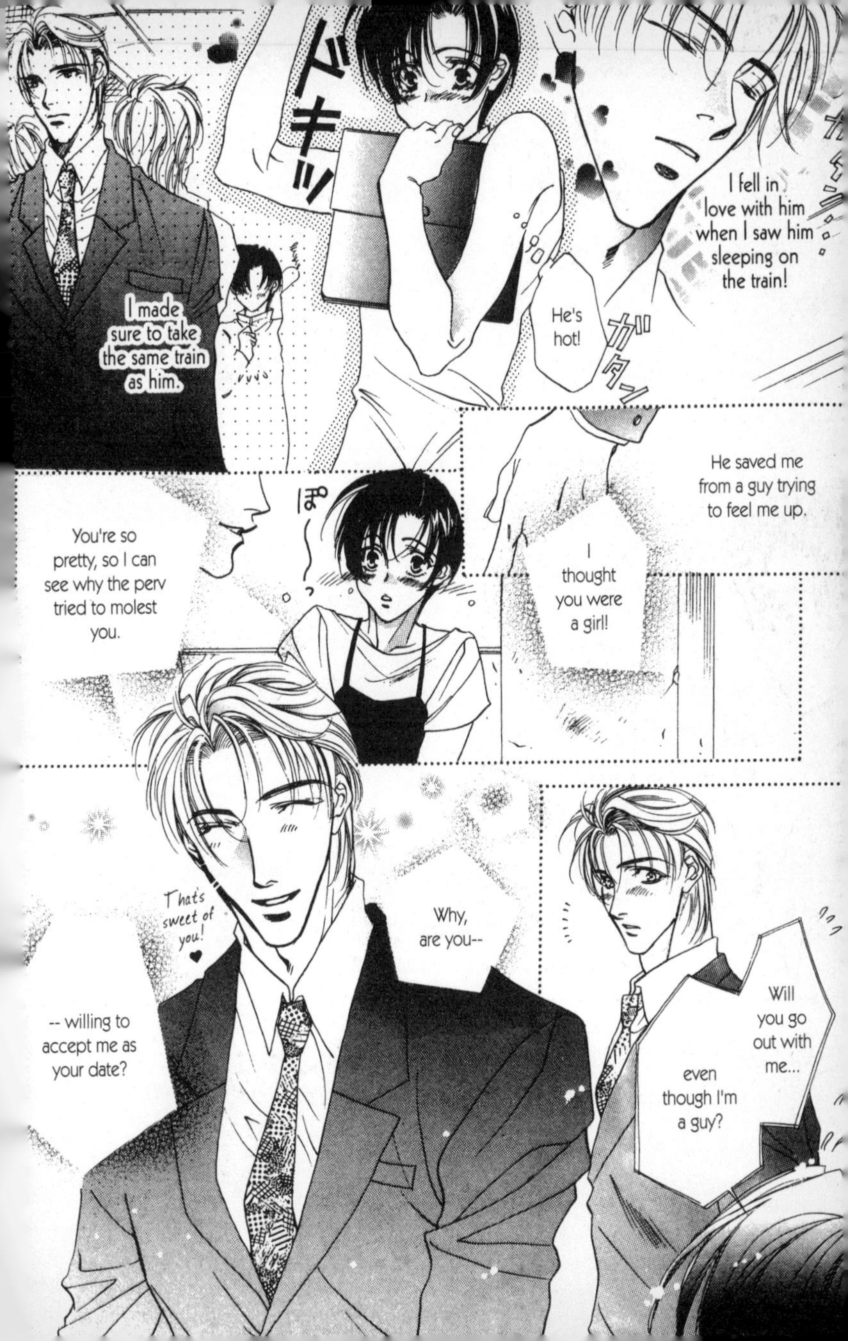
I fell in love with him when I saw him sleeping on the train!
ドキッ
He's hot!
ガタン
I made sure to take the same train as him.
He saved me from a guy trying to feel me up.
I thought you were a girl!
You're so pretty, so I can see why the perv tried to molest you.
Will you go out with me...
even though I'm a guy?
Why, are you--
-- willing to accept me as your date?
That's sweet of you!

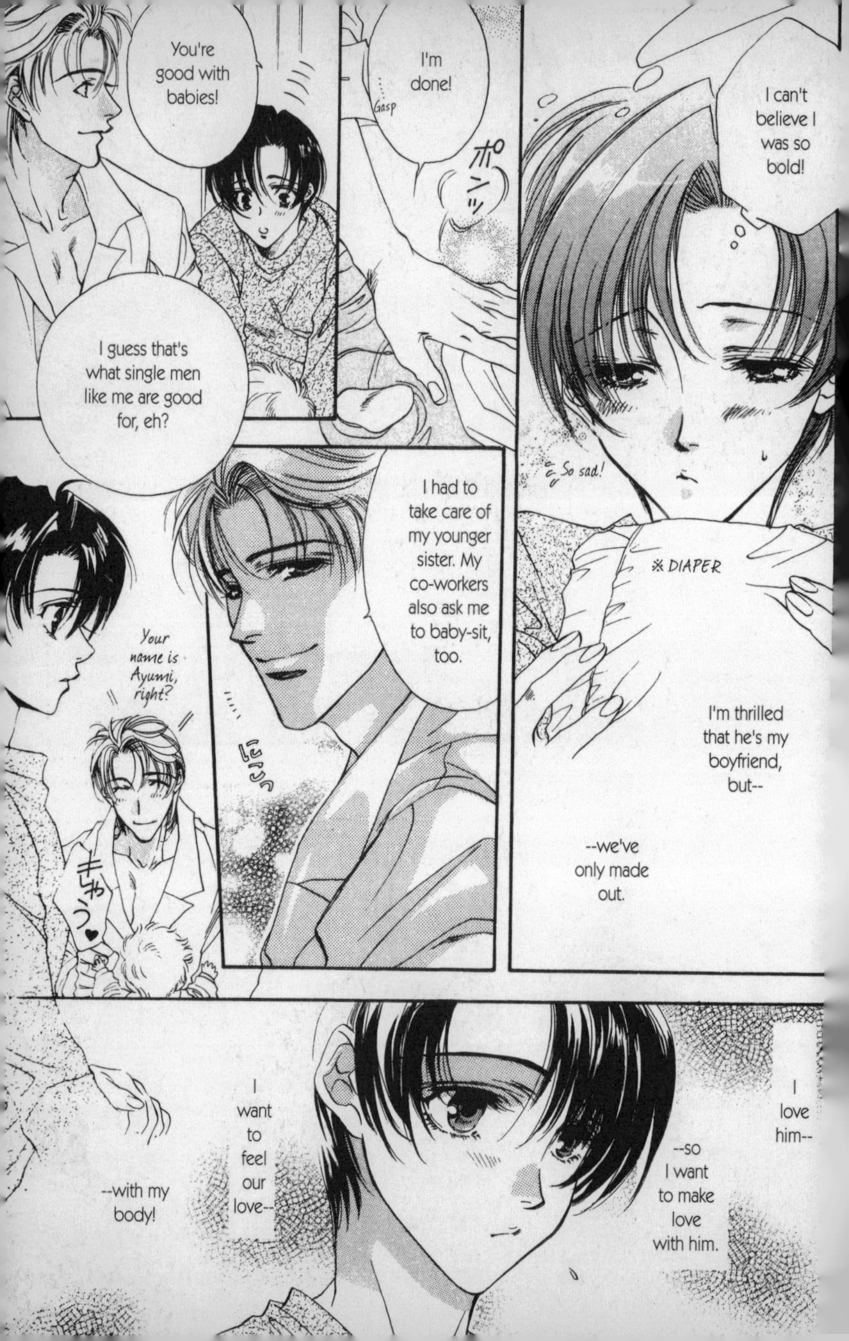

I'm done!
Gasp
ポンッ
You're good with babies!
I guess that's what single men like me are good for, eh?
I had to take care of my younger sister. My co-workers also ask me to baby-sit, too.
Your name is Ayumi, right?
I can't believe I was so bold!
So sad!
※DIAPER
I'm thrilled that he's my boyfriend, but--
--we've only made out.
I love him--
--so I want to make love with him.
I want to feel our love--
--with my body!

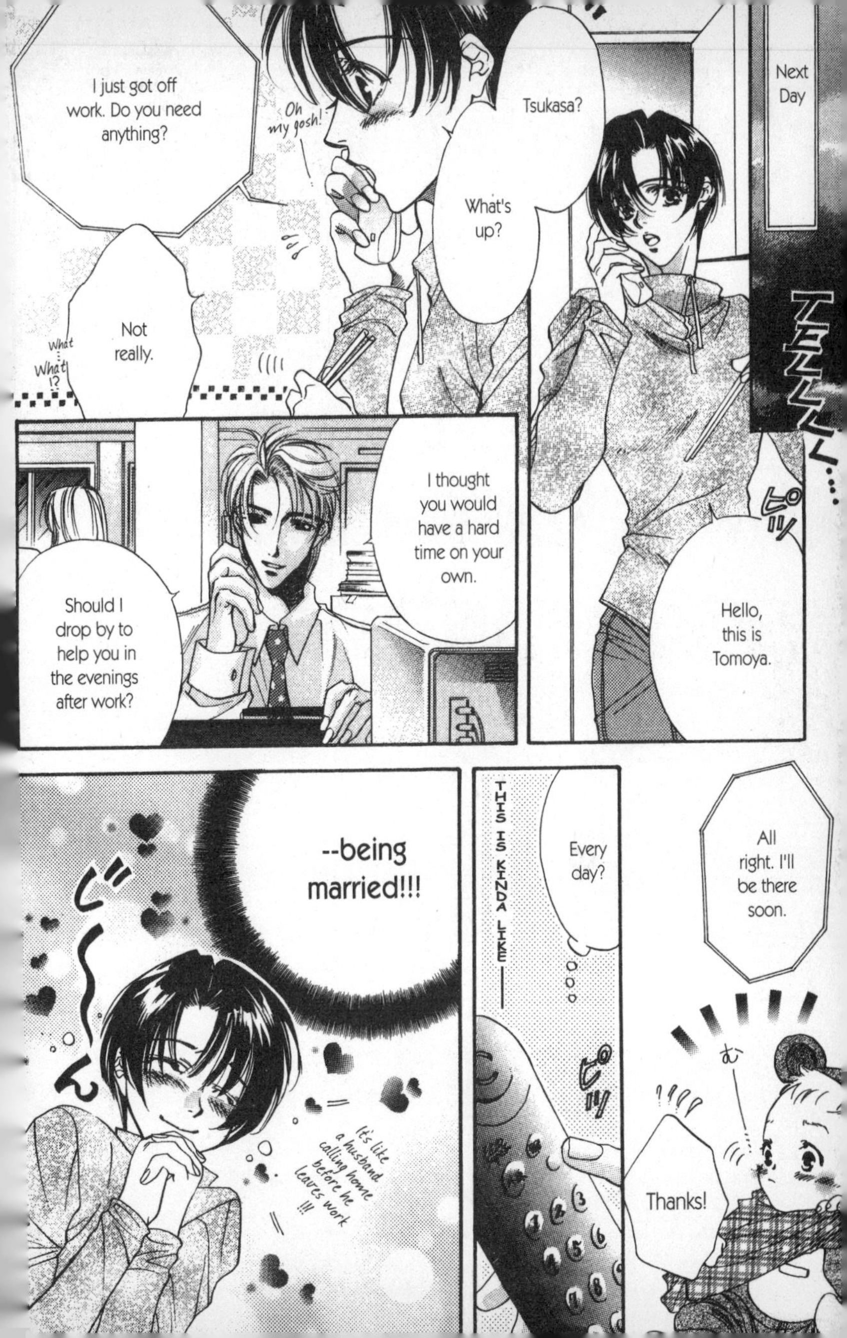
Next Day
TELLL...
ピッ
Hello, this is Tomoya.
Tsukasa?
What's up?
Oh my gosh!
I just got off work. Do you need anything?
Not really.
What What !?
I thought you would have a hard time on your own.
Should I drop by to help you in the evenings after work?
All right. I'll be there soon.
む
Thanks!
Every day?
ピッ
THIS IS KINDA LIKE ——
--being married!!!
It's like a husband calling home before he leaves work !!!
じ~~ん

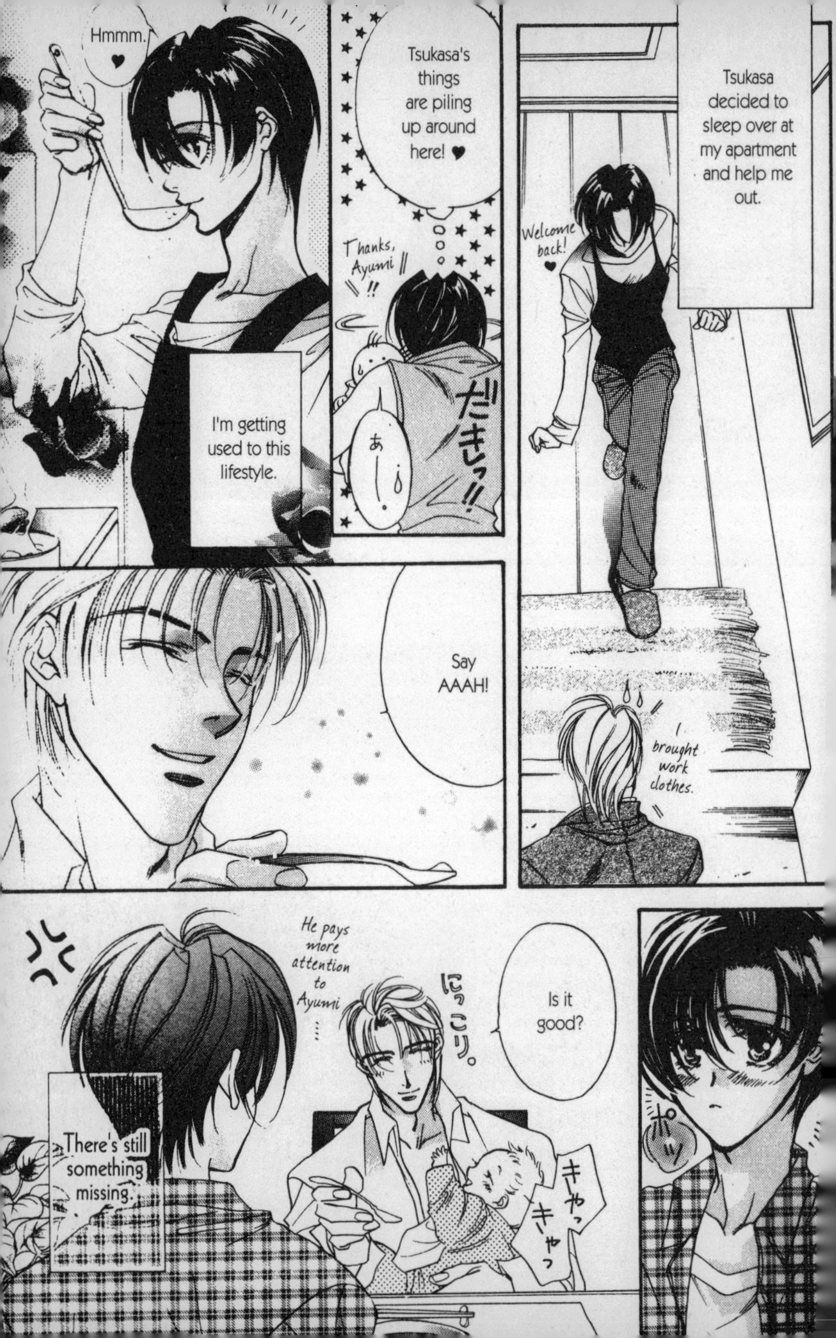

Tsukasa decided to sleep over at my apartment and help me out.
Welcome back! ♥
I brought work clothes.
Tsukasa's things are piling up around here! ♥
Thanks, Ayumi!!
だきっ!!
あー。
Hmmm. ♥
I'm getting used to this lifestyle.
Say AAAH!
Is it good?
キャッキャッ
にっこり。
He pays more attention to Ayumi...
There's still something missing.

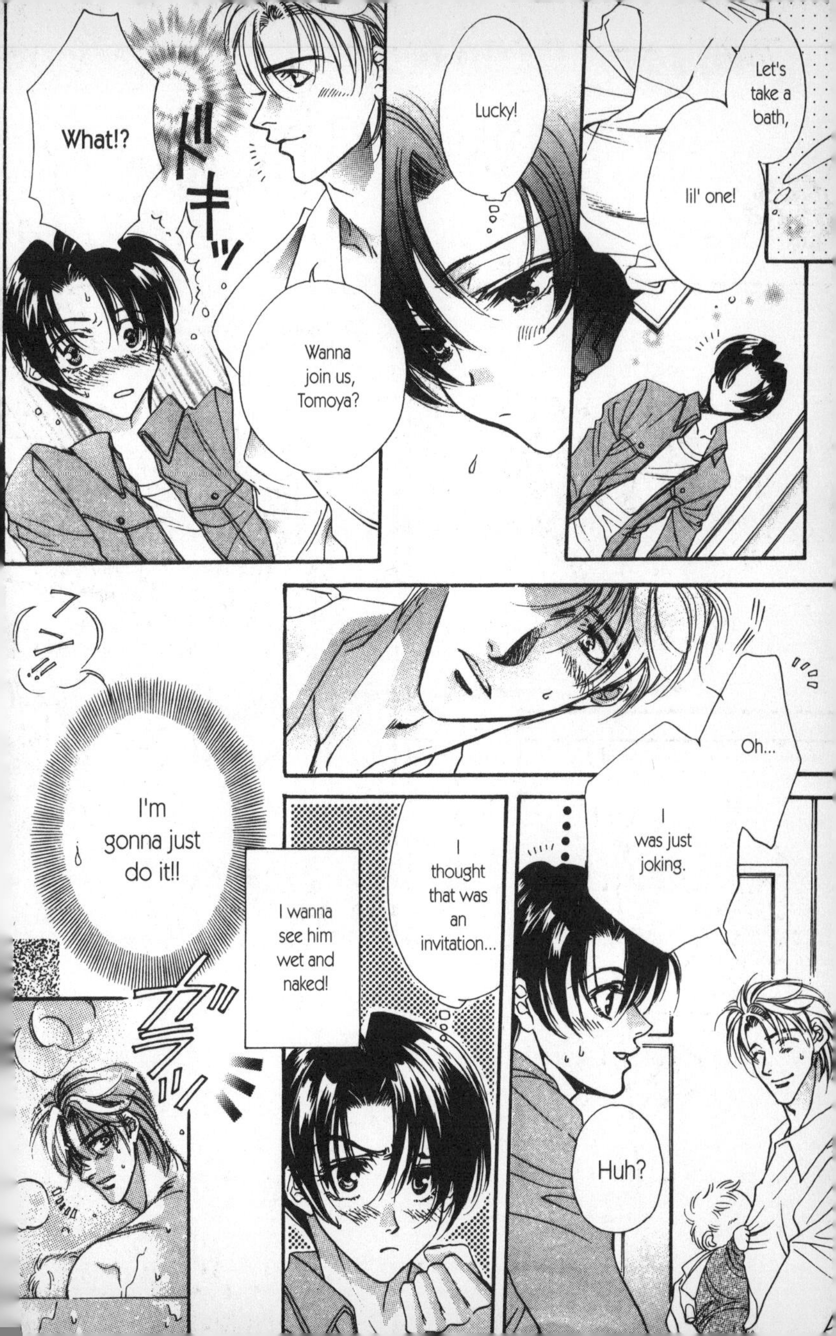
Let's take a bath,
lil' one!
Lucky!
Wanna join us, Tomoya?
ドキッ
What!?
Oh...
I was just joking.
Huh?
I thought that was an invitation...
I wanna see him wet and naked!
I'm gonna just do it!!

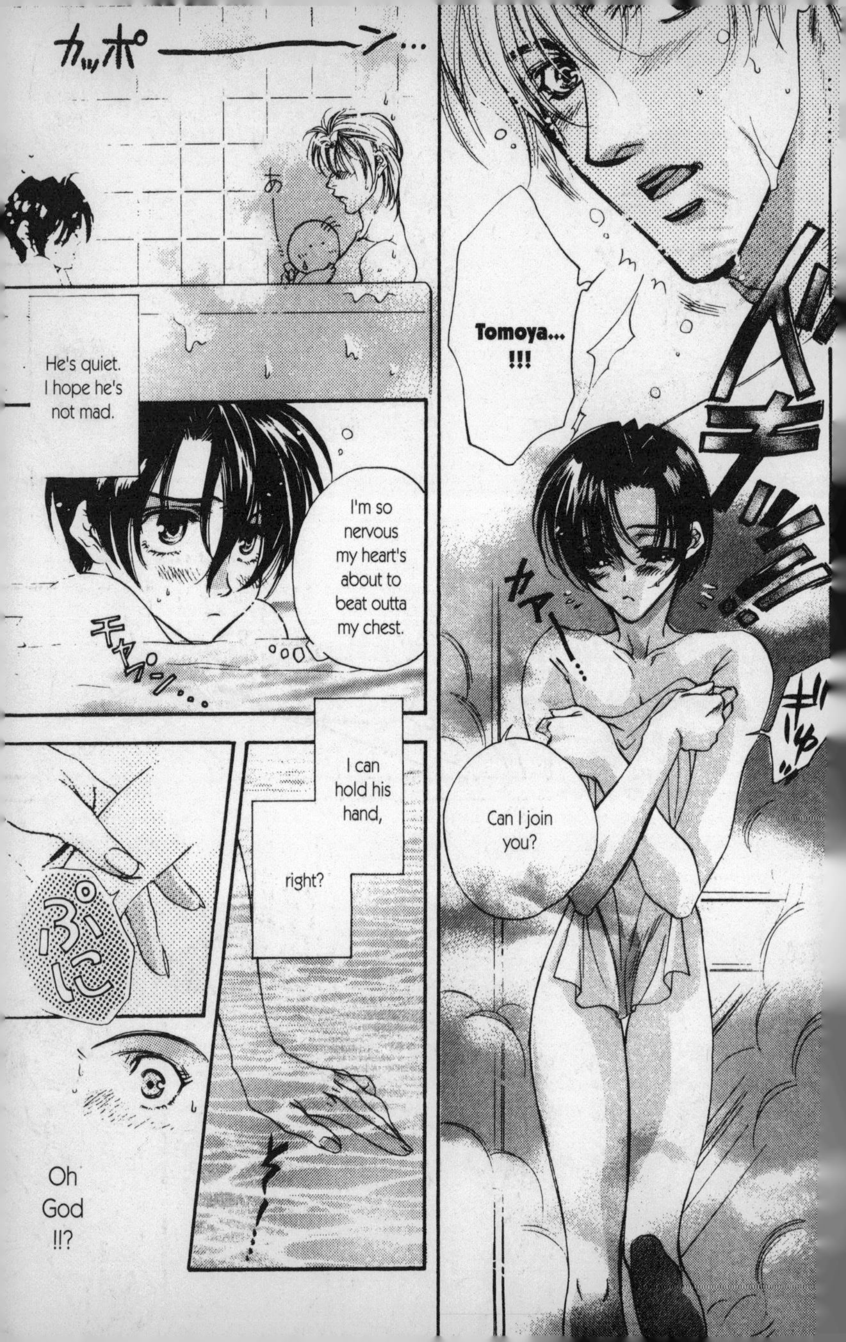

Tomoya... !!!
Can I join you?
カッポーーーン…
He's quiet. I hope he's not mad.
I'm so nervous my heart's about to beat outta my chest.
チャプーン…
I can hold his hand, right?
ぷに
Oh God !!?

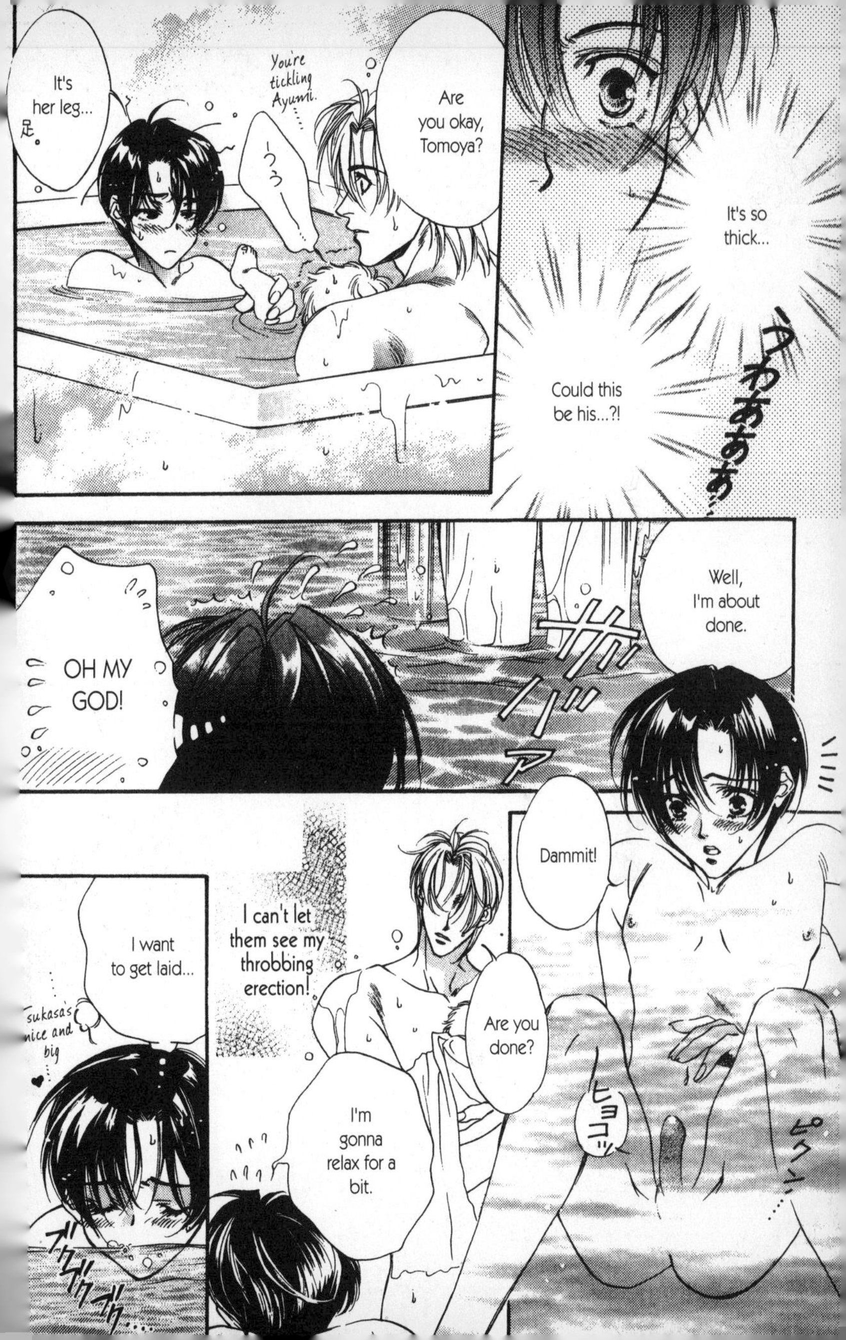

It's so thick...
Could this be his...?!
うわあああ
Are you okay, Tomoya?
You're tickling Ayumi.
うう
It's her leg...
足。
Well, I'm about done.
ザバァ
OH MY GOD!
Dammit!
Are you done?
I'm gonna relax for a bit.
ヒョコッ
ピクン…
I can't let them see my throbbing erection!
I want to get laid...
Tsukasa's nice and big

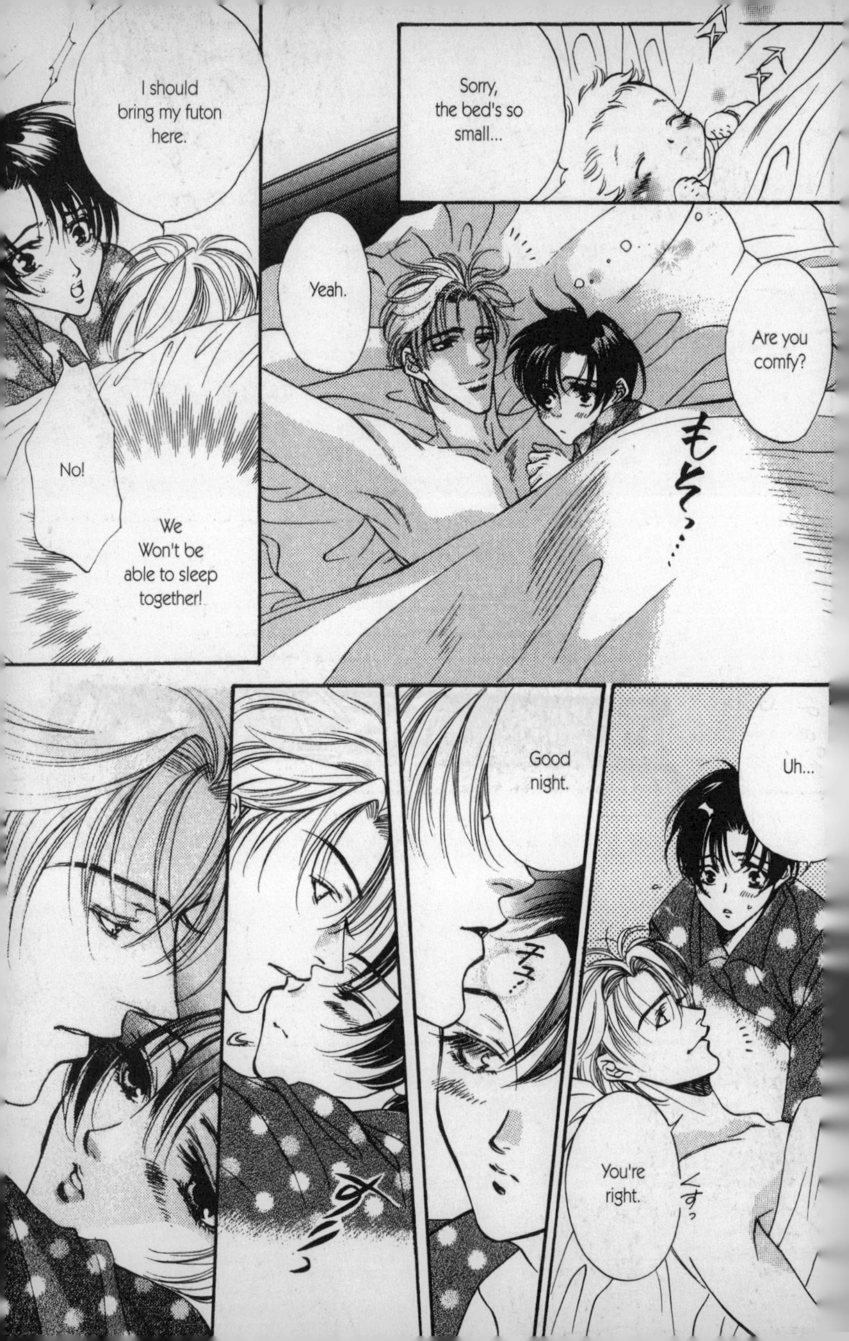
Sorry, the bed's so small...
Are you comfy?
Yeah.
もぞっ…
I should bring my futon here.
No!
We Won't be able to sleep together!
Uh...
You're right.
くすっ
Good night.

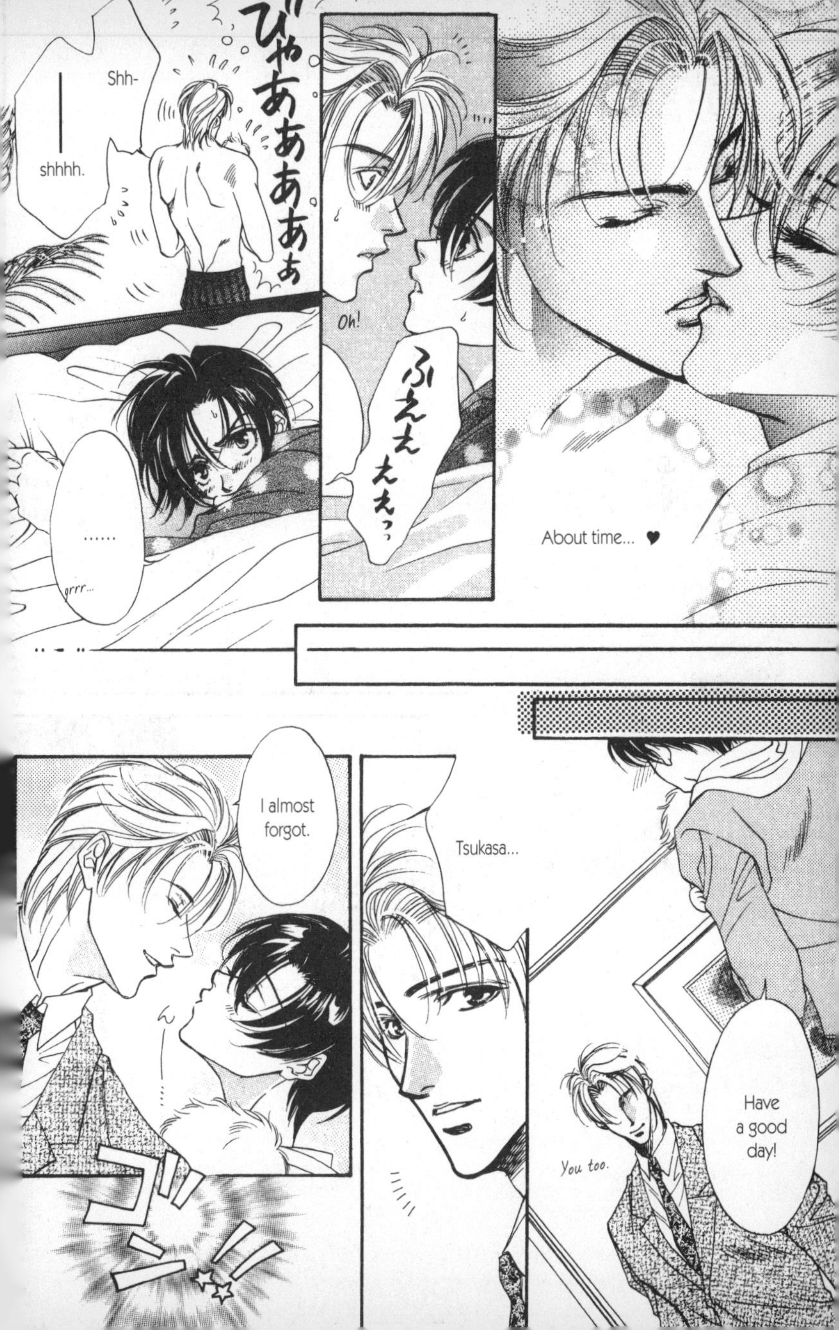
About time... ♥
Oh!
ふえええええっ
びゃあああああ
Shh-
shhhh.
......
grrr...
Have a good day!
You too.
Tsukasa...
I almost forgot.
ゴン!!

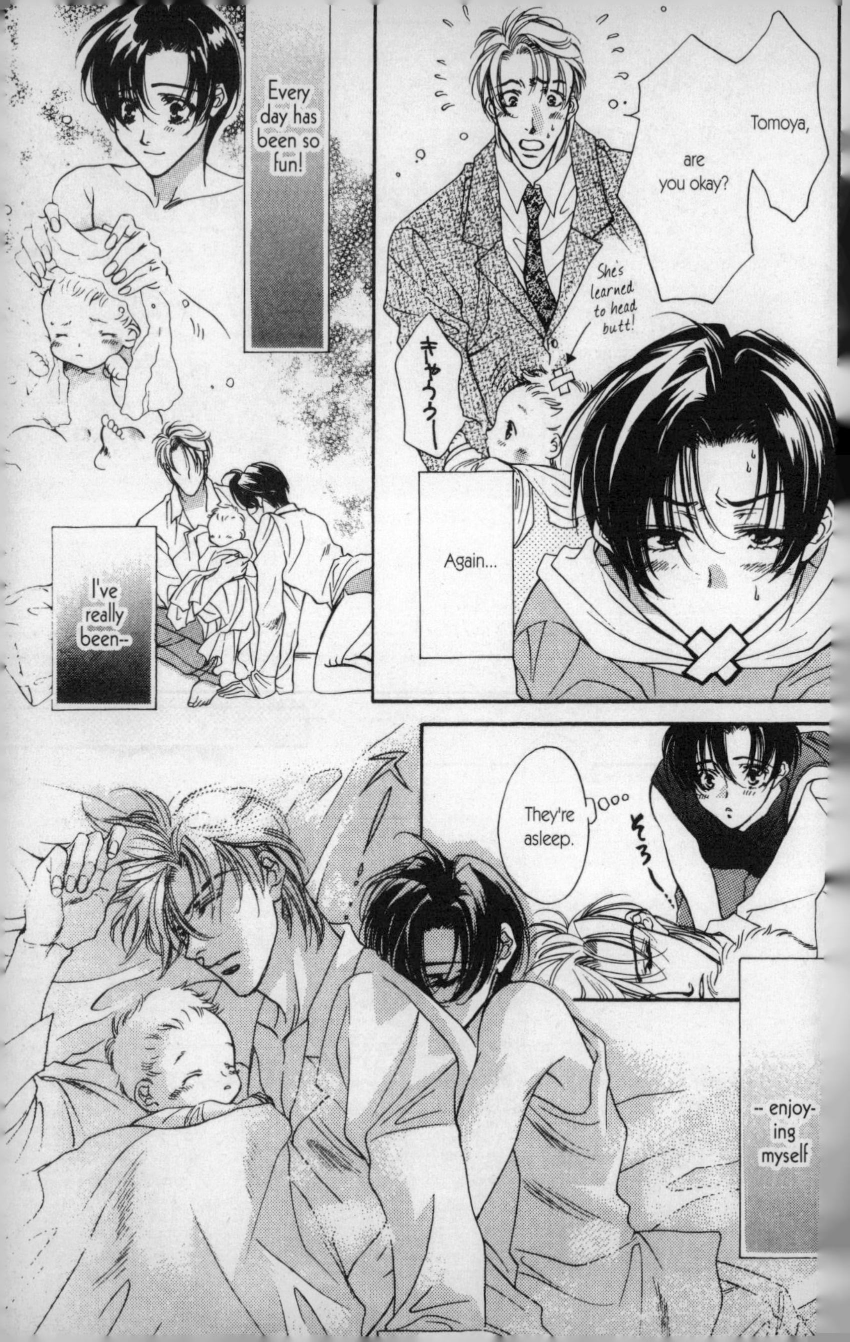
Tomoya,
are you okay?
She's learned to head butt!
きゃうう〜
Again...
Every day has been so fun!
I've really been--
They're asleep.
そろ〜
-- enjoying myself

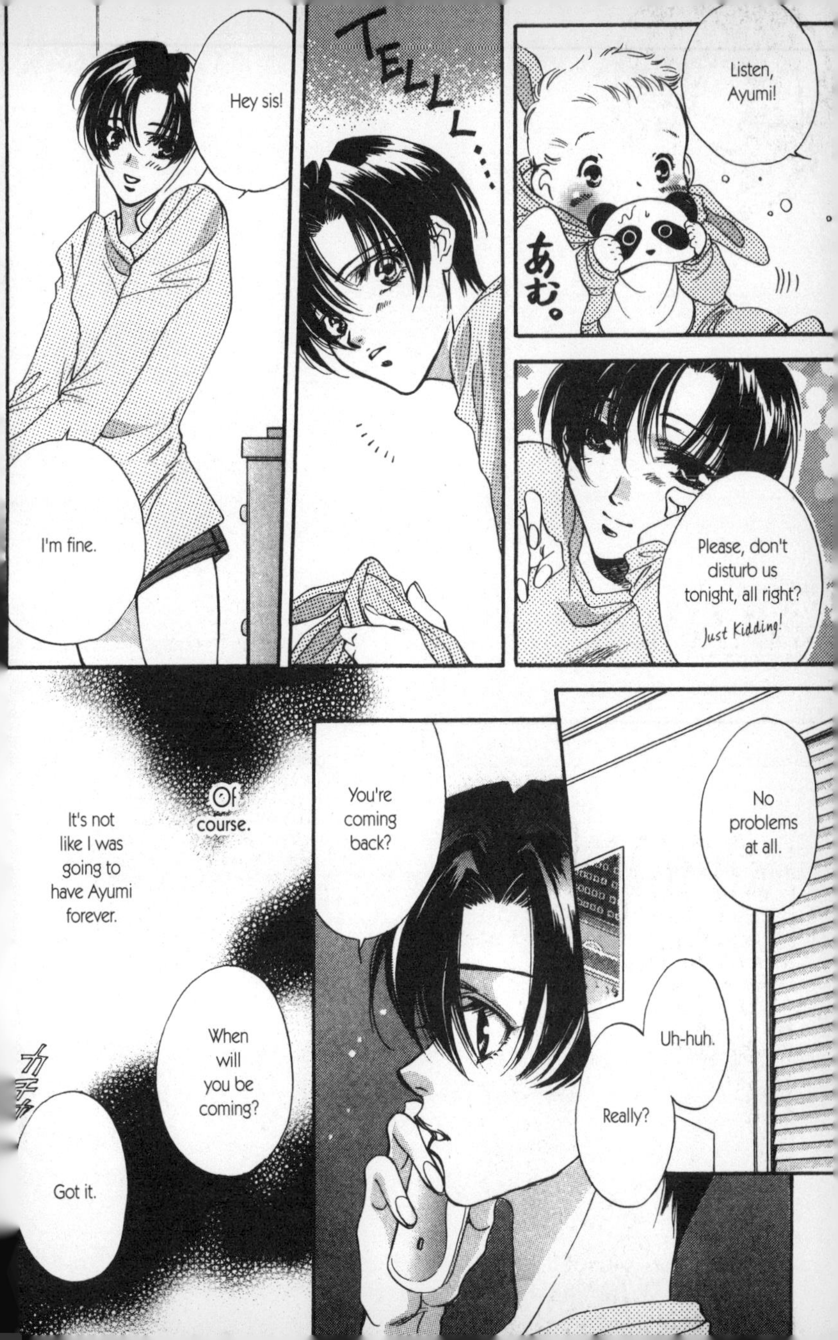

Listen, Ayumi!
あむ。
Please, don't disturb us tonight, all right?
Just Kidding!
TELLL...
Hey sis!
I'm fine.
No problems at all.
Uh-huh.
Really?
You're coming back?
Of course.
It's not like I was going to have Ayumi forever.
When will you be coming?
Got it.

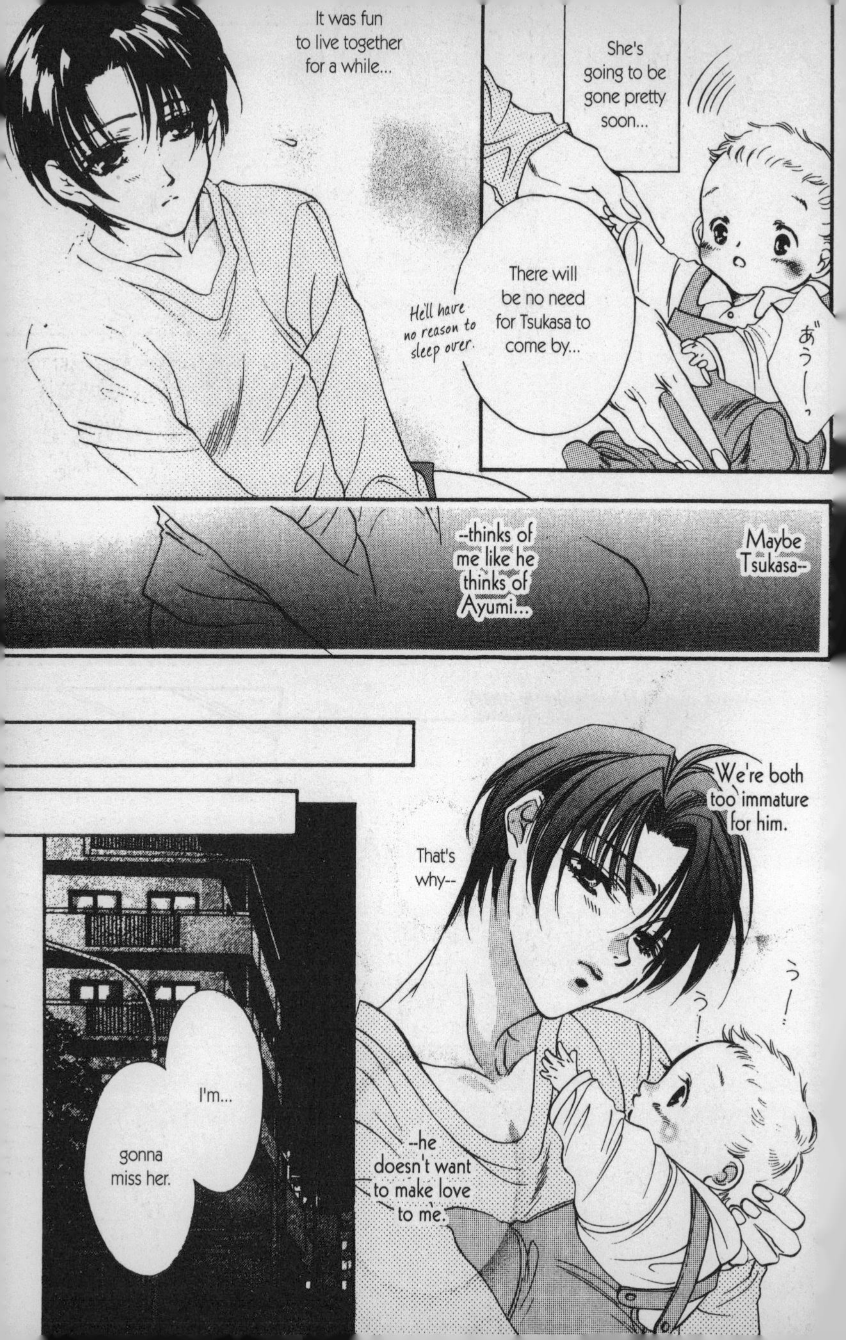

It was fun to live together for a while...
She's going to be gone pretty soon...
There will be no need for Tsukasa to come by...
He'll have no reason to sleep over.
あうー っ
Maybe Tsukasa--
--thinks of me like he thinks of Ayumi...
We're both too immature for him.
That's why--
--he doesn't want to make love to me.
う ー！
う！
I'm...
gonna miss her.

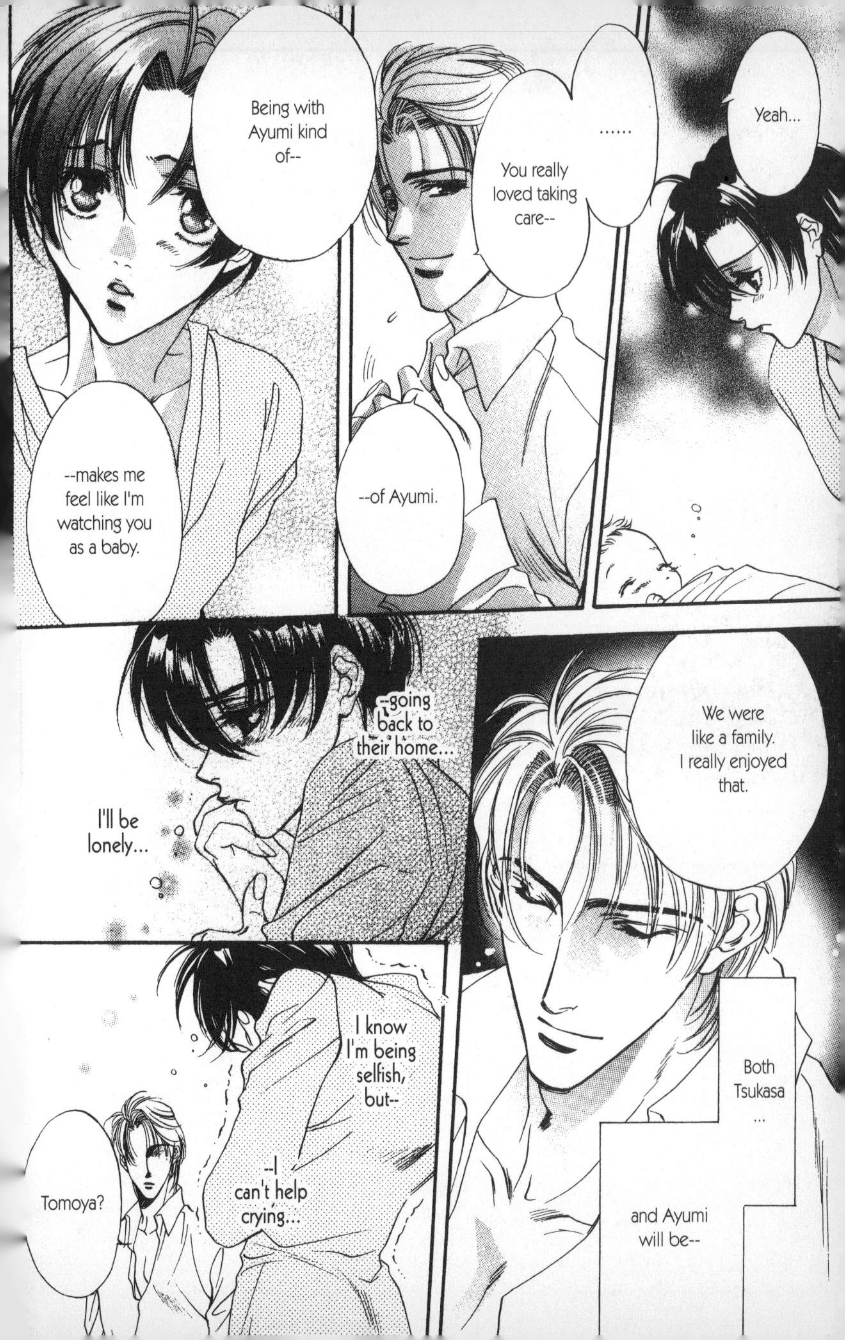
Being with Ayumi kind of--
--makes me feel like I'm watching you as a baby.
......
You really loved taking care--
--of Ayumi.
Yeah...
We were like a family. I really enjoyed that.
Both Tsukasa ...
and Ayumi will be--
--going back to their home...
I'll be lonely...
I know I'm being selfish, but--
--I can't help crying...
Tomoya?

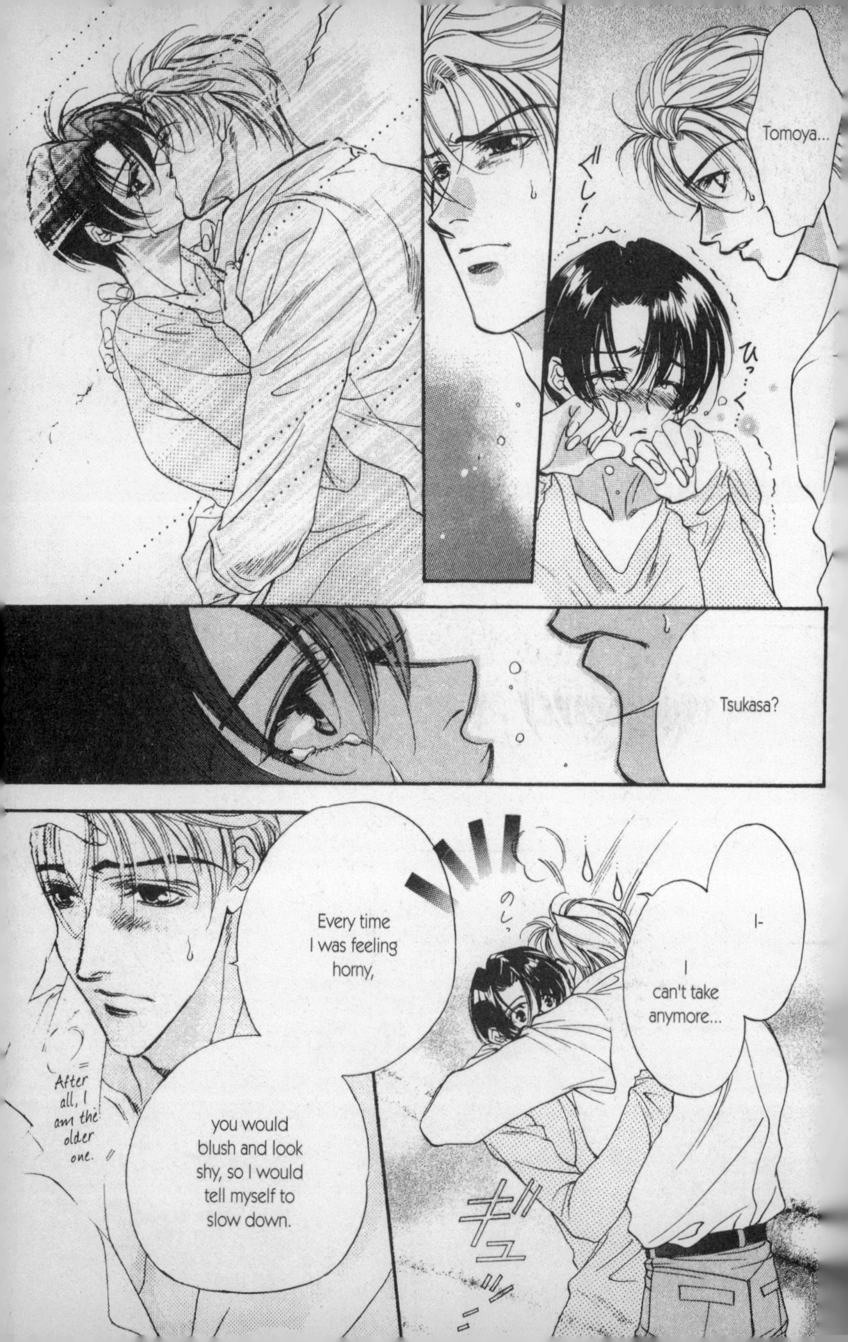

Tomoya...
ひっく
Tsukasa?
I-
I can't take anymore...
のし
Every time I was feeling horny,
you would blush and look shy, so I would tell myself to slow down.
After all, I am the older one.

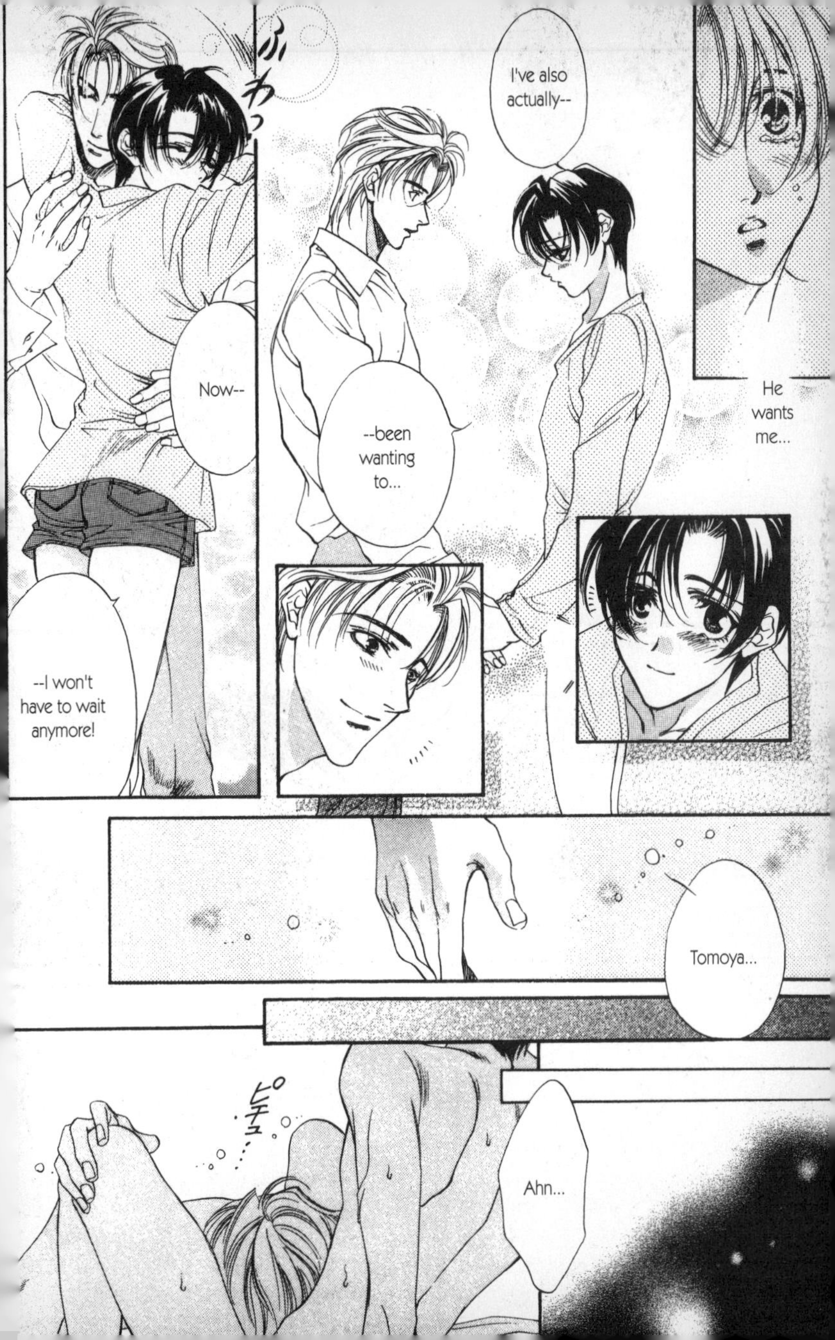
He wants me...
I've also actually--
--been wanting to...
ふわっ
Now--
--I won't have to wait anymore!
Tomoya...
Ahn...
ピチュ...

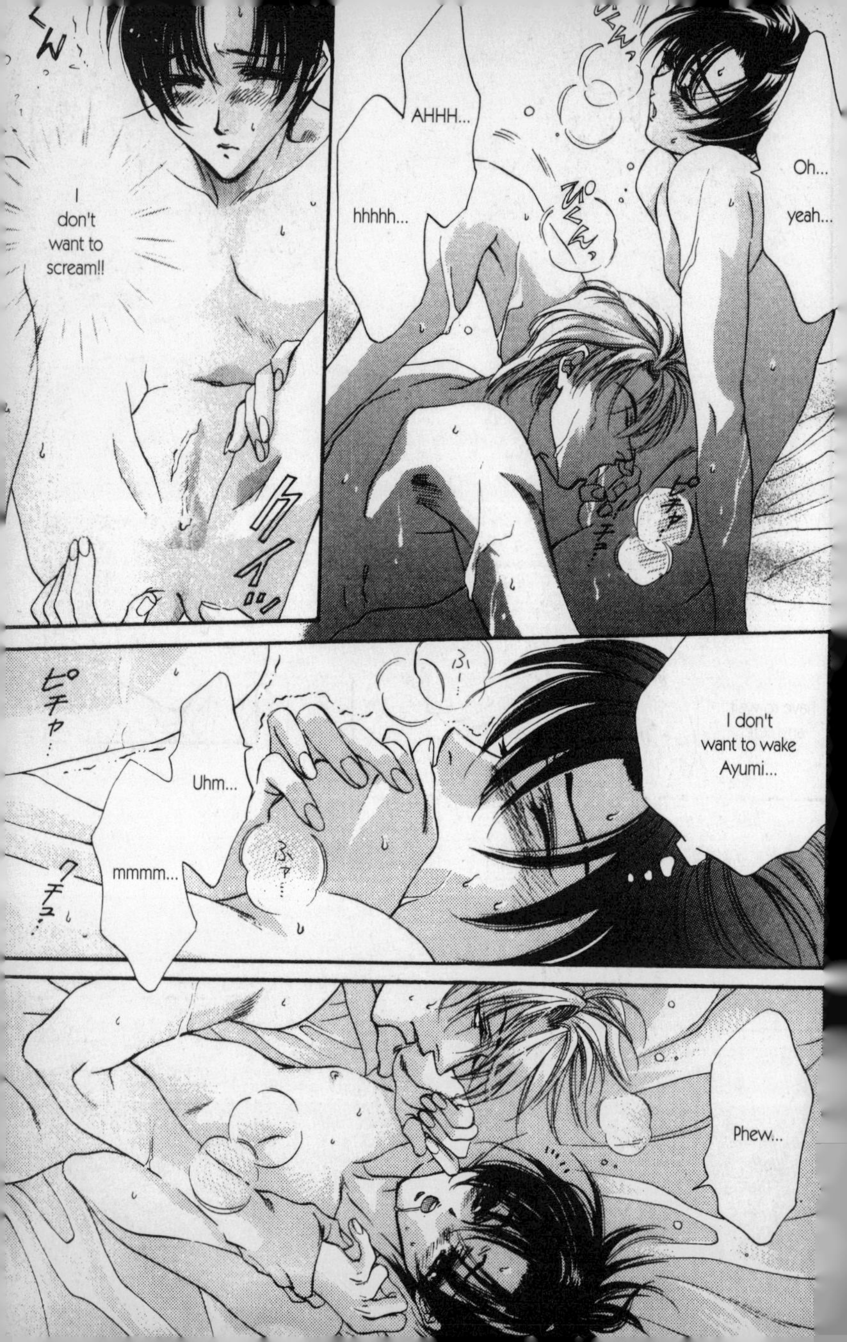

Oh... yeah...
AHHH... hhhhh...
I don't want to scream!!
I don't want to wake Ayumi...
Uhm... mmmm...
ピチャ…
クチュ…
Phew...

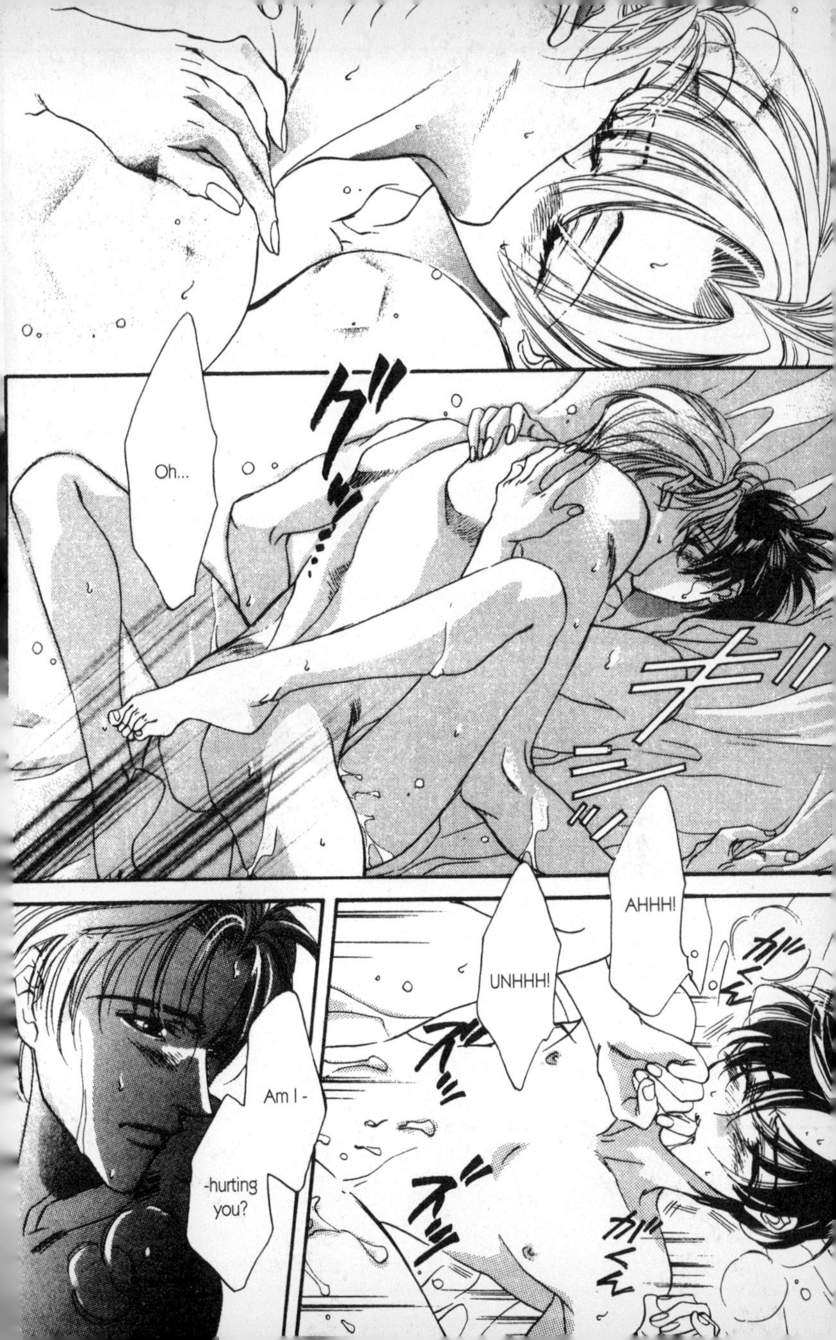
Oh...
AHHH!
UNHHH!
Am I -
-hurting you?

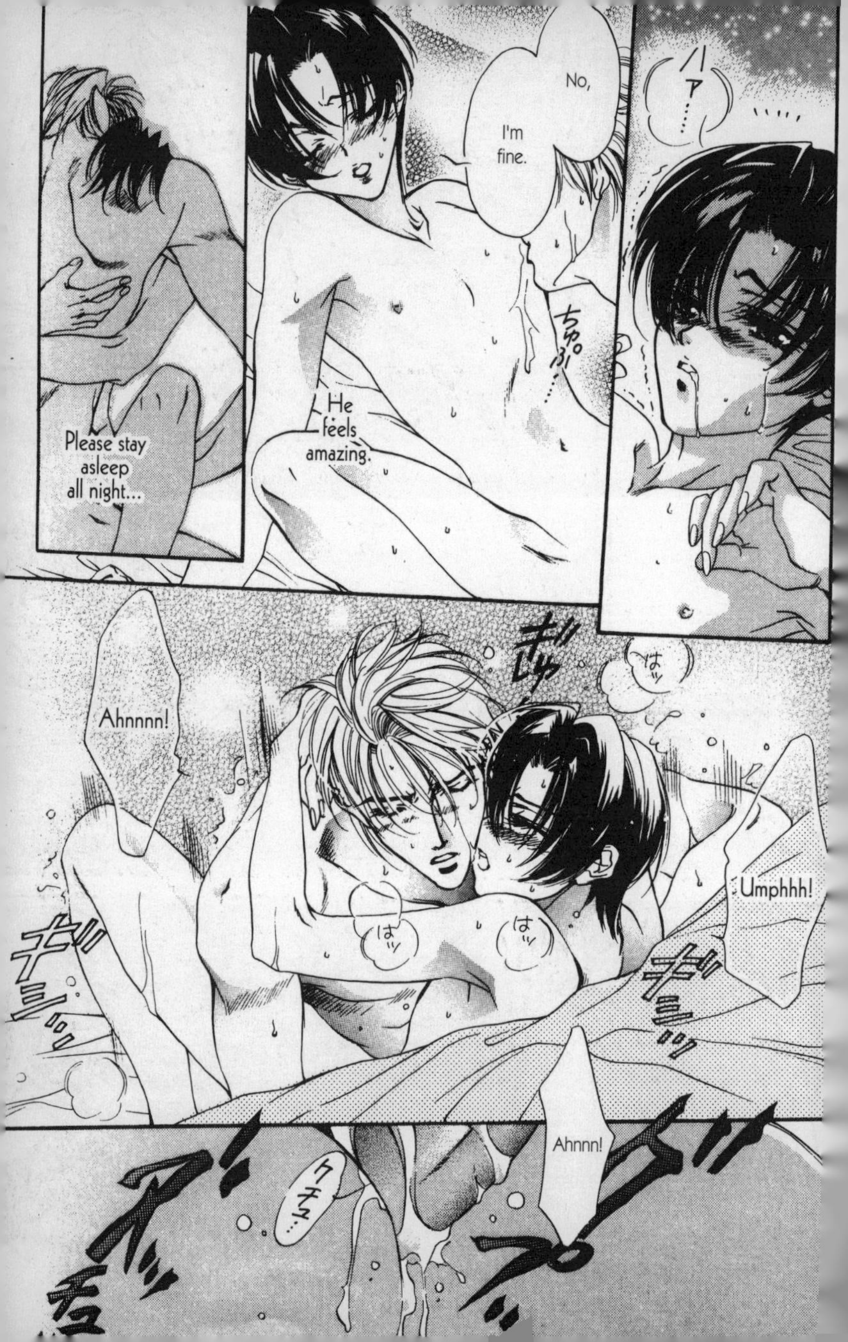
ハア……
No,
I'm fine.
ちゅぷ…
He feels amazing.
Please stay asleep all night…
はッ
Umphhh!
はッ
はッ
Ahnnnn!
Ahnnn!
クチュ…

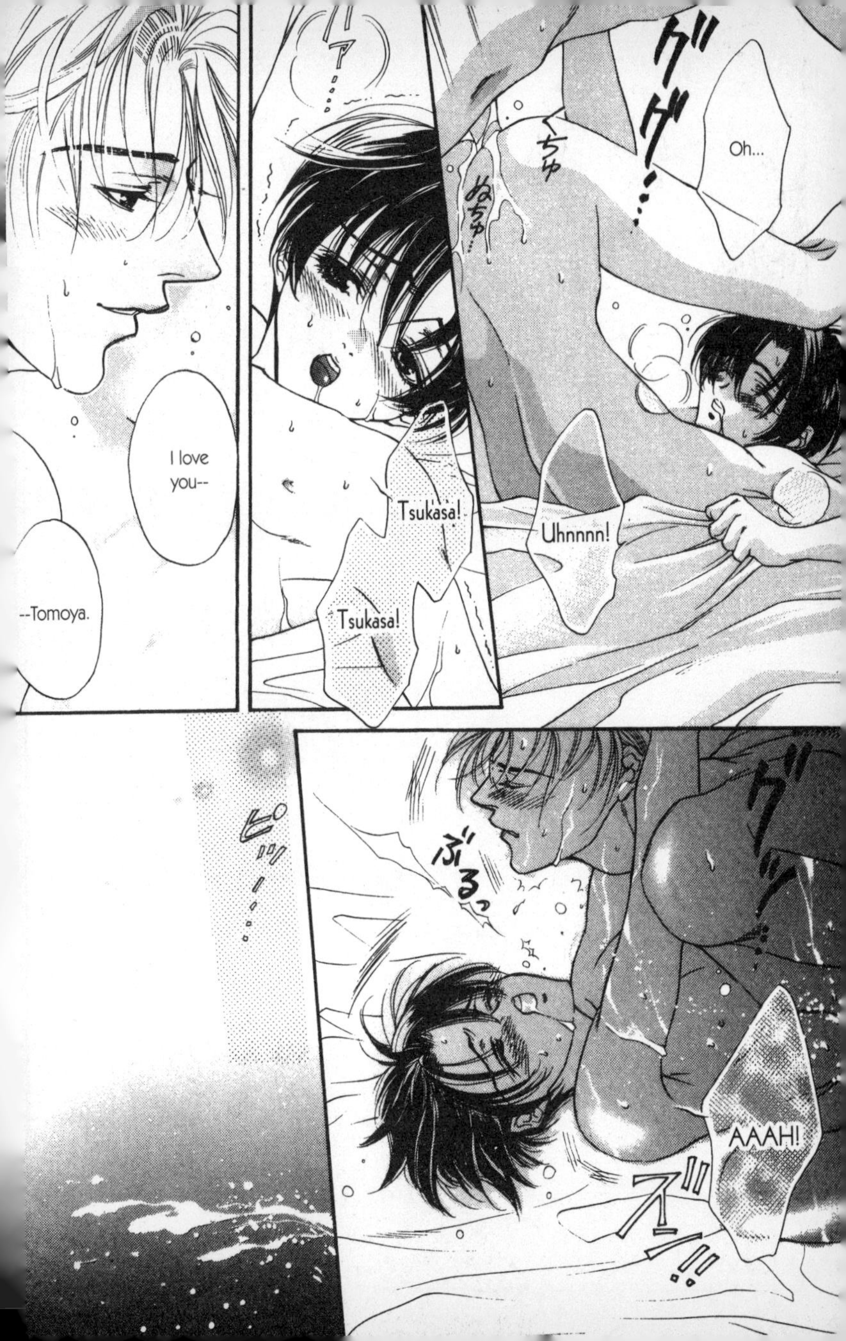

Oh...
くちゅ
ぬちゅ...
Uhnnnn!
Tsukasa!
Tsukasa!
I love you--
--Tomoya.
ぶるっ
AAAH!

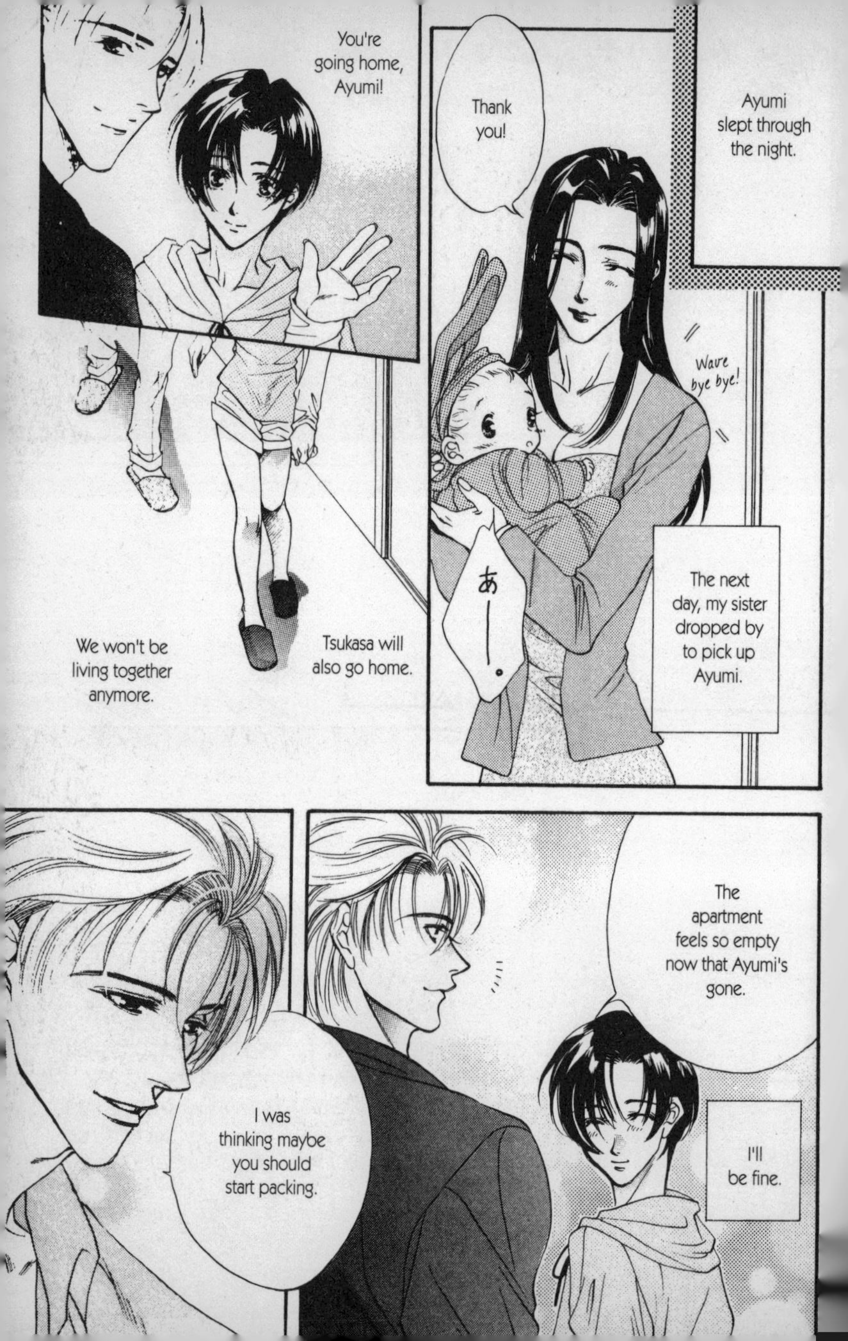
Ayumi slept through the night.
The next day, my sister dropped by to pick up Ayumi.
Thank you!
Wave bye bye!
あー。
You're going home, Ayumi!
Tsukasa will also go home.
We won't be living together anymore.
The apartment feels so empty now that Ayumi's gone.
I'll be fine.
I was thinking maybe you should start packing.

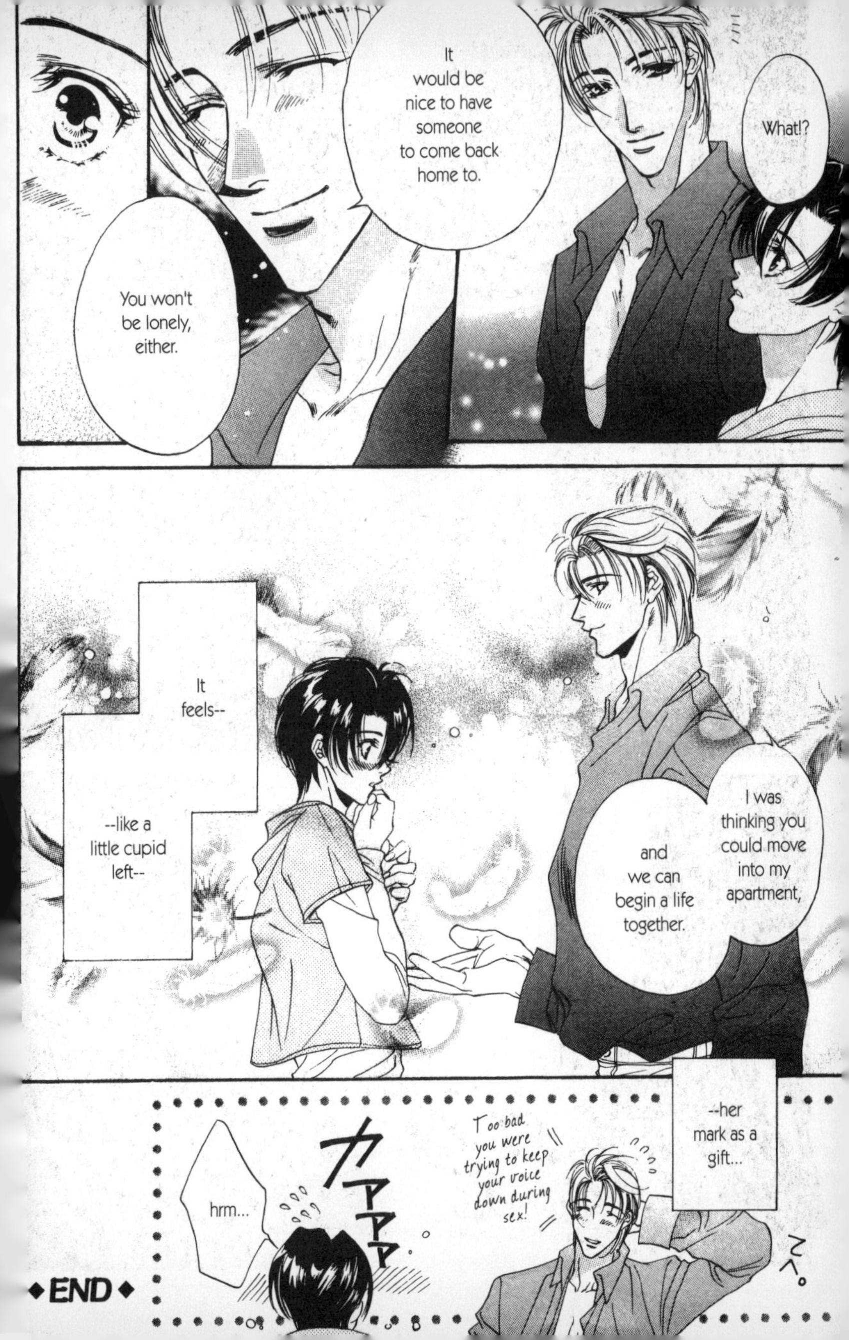
What!?
It would be nice to have someone to come back home to.
You won't be lonely, either.
I was thinking you could move into my apartment,
and we can begin a life together.
It feels--
--like a little cupid left--
--her mark as a gift...
Too bad you were trying to keep your voice down during sex!
カァァァ
hrm...
◆END◆

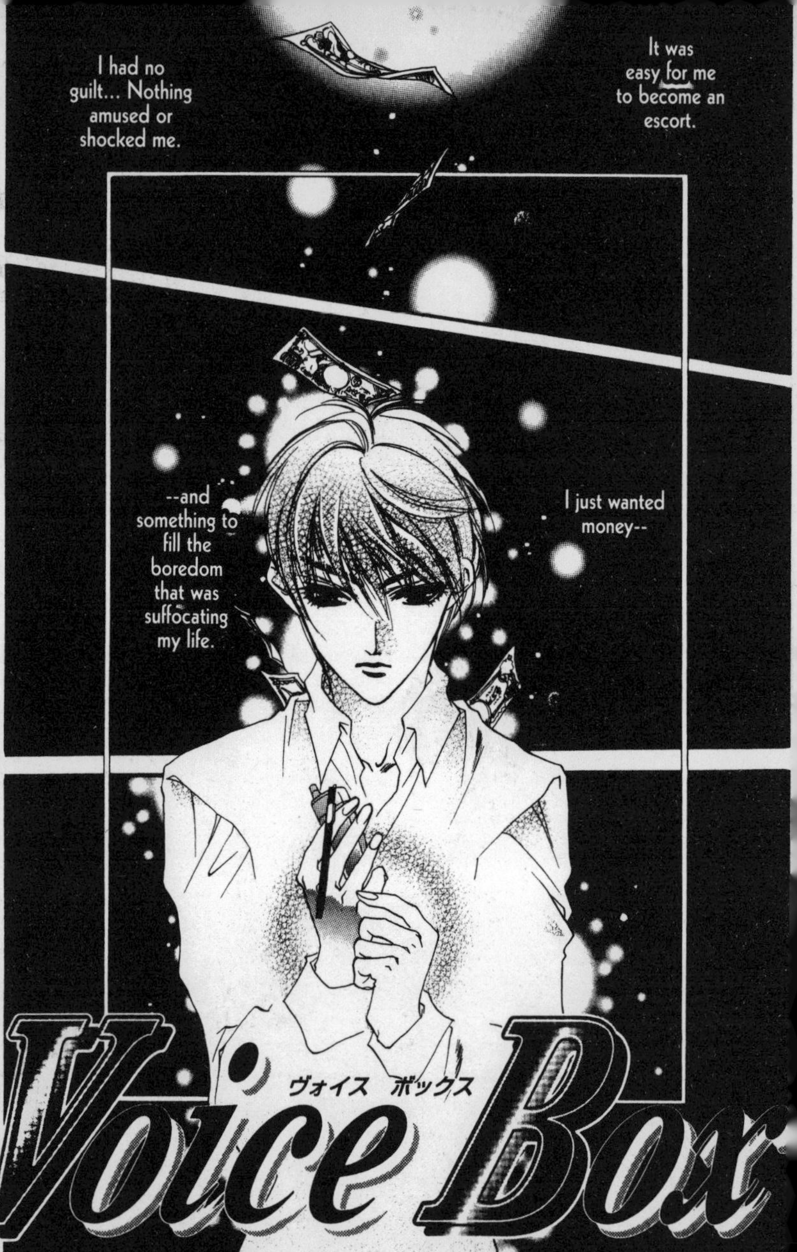
It was easy for me to become an escort.
I had no guilt... Nothing amused or shocked me.
I just wanted money--
--and something to fill the boredom that was suffocating my life.
Voice Box
ヴォイス ボックス

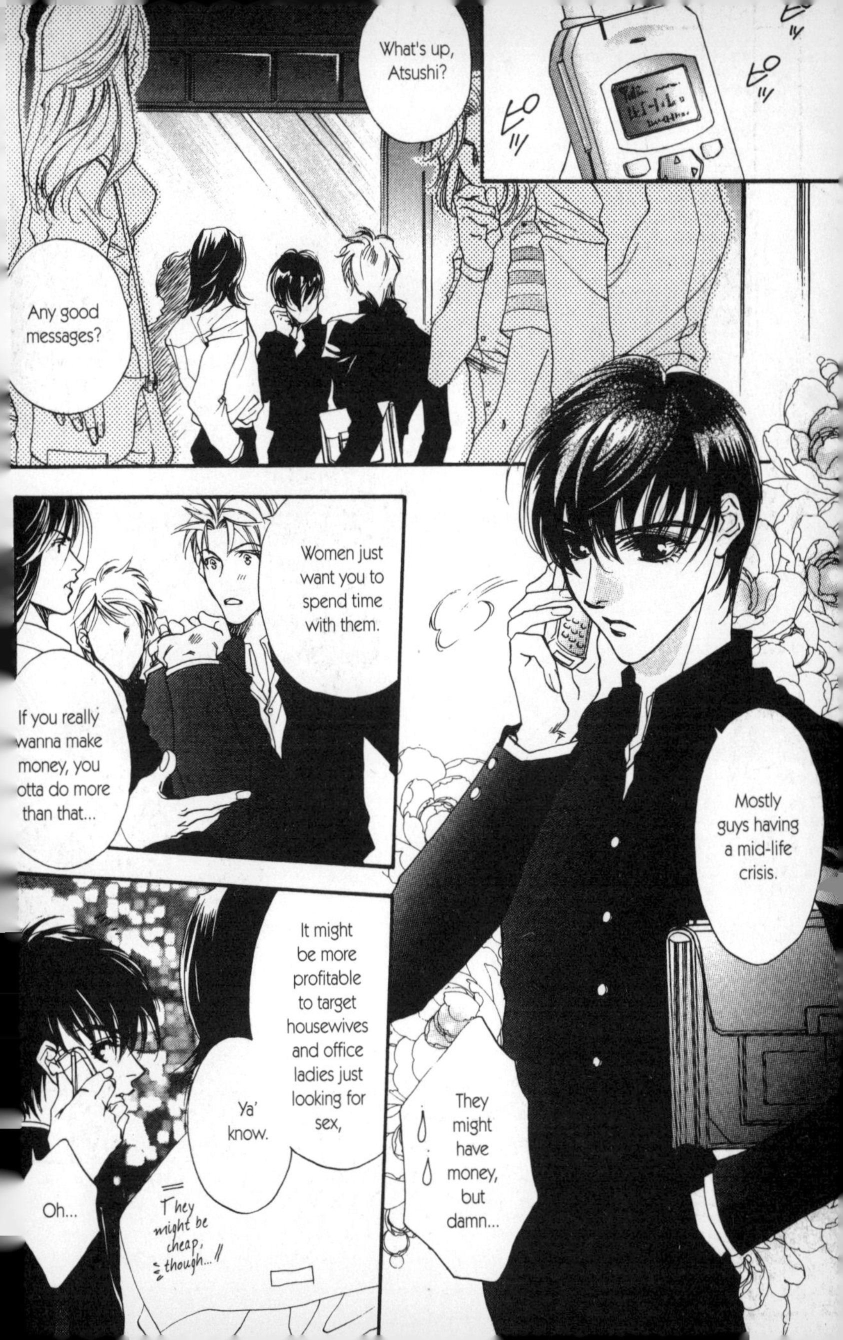

ピッ
ピッ
ピッ
What's up, Atsushi?
Any good messages?
Mostly guys having a mid-life crisis.
Women just want you to spend time with them.
If you really wanna make money, you otta do more than that...
It might be more profitable to target housewives and office ladies just looking for sex,
Ya' know.
They might have money, but damn...
Oh...
They might be cheap, though...!!

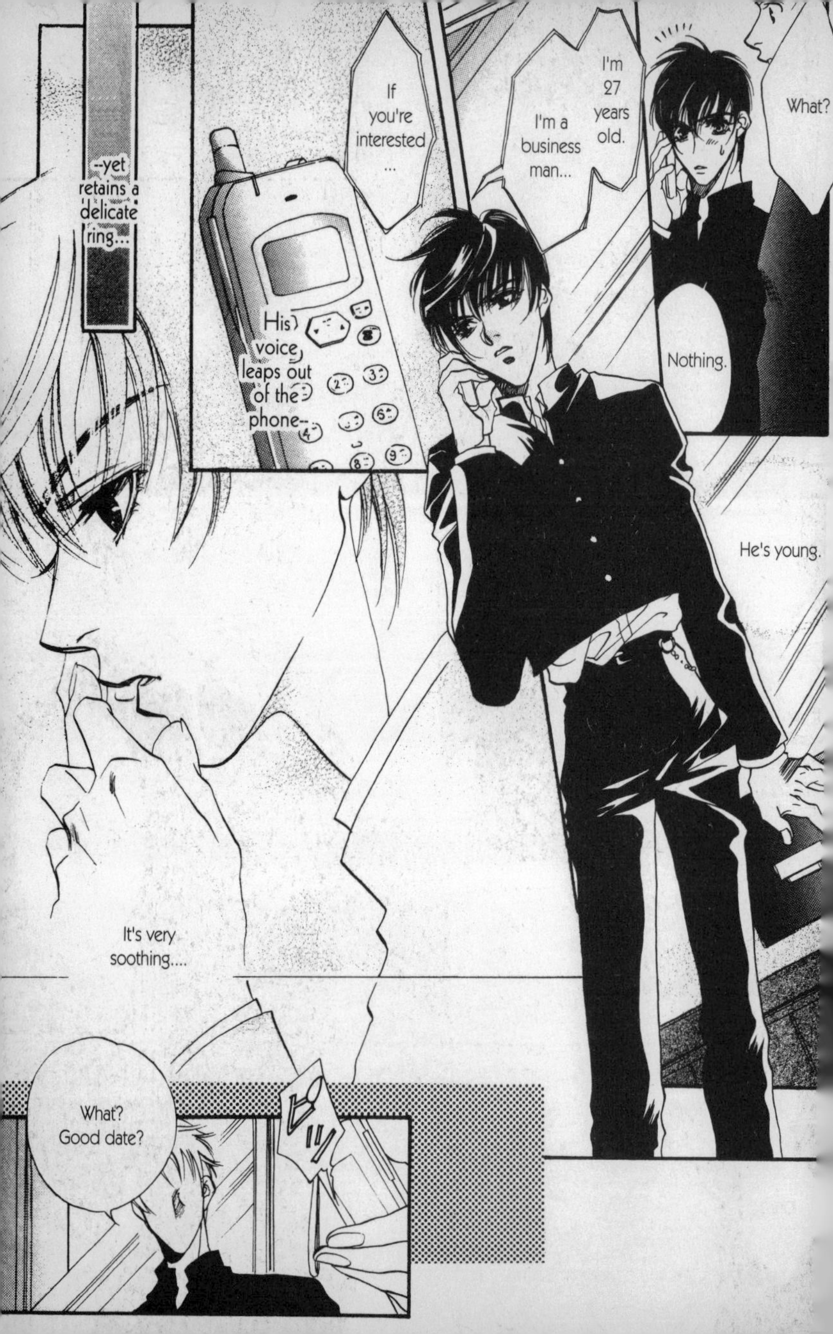

What?
Nothing.
I'm a business man...
I'm 27 years old.
If you're interested ...
His voice leaps out of the phone--
--yet retains a delicate ring...
He's young.
It's very soothing....
What? Good date?

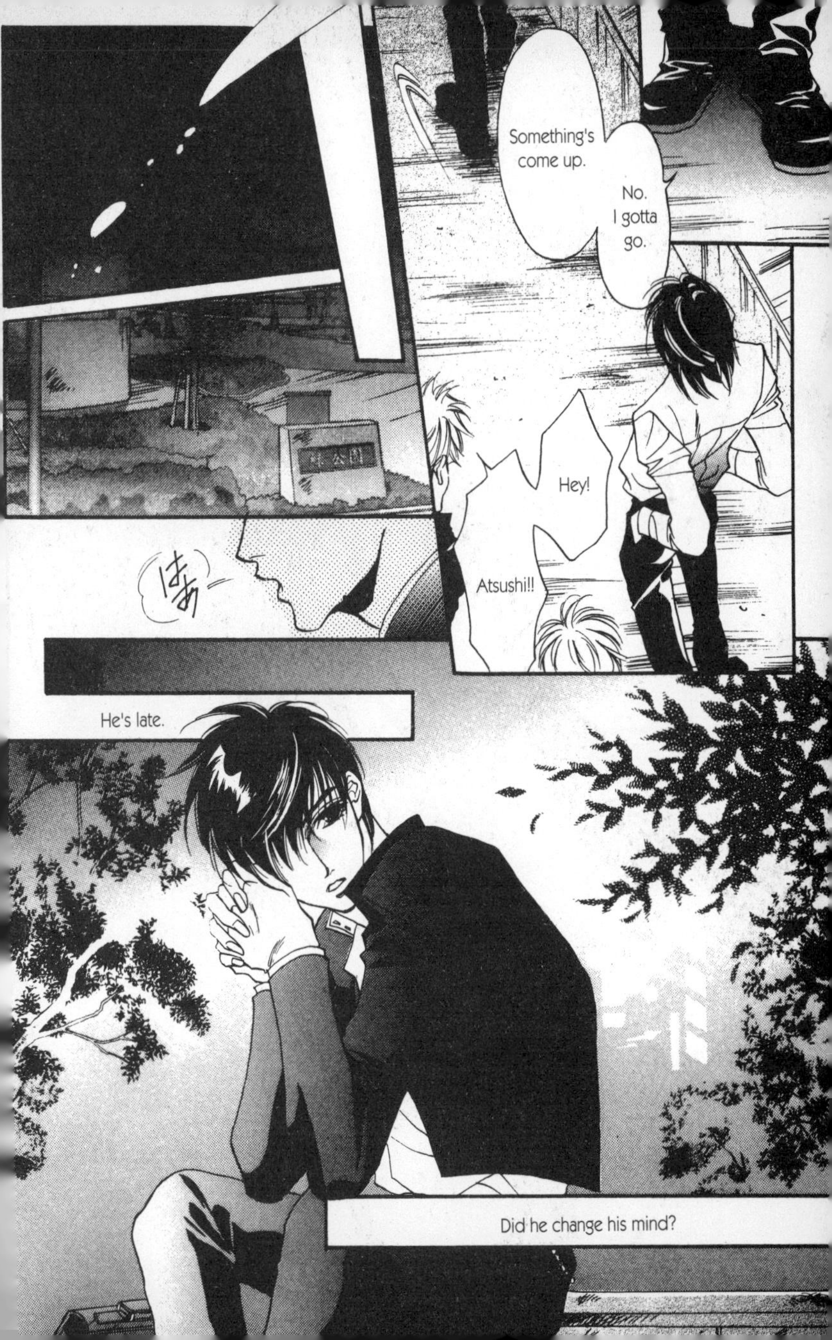
Something's come up.
No. I gotta go.
Hey!
Atsushi!!
はぁ
He's late.
Did he change his mind?

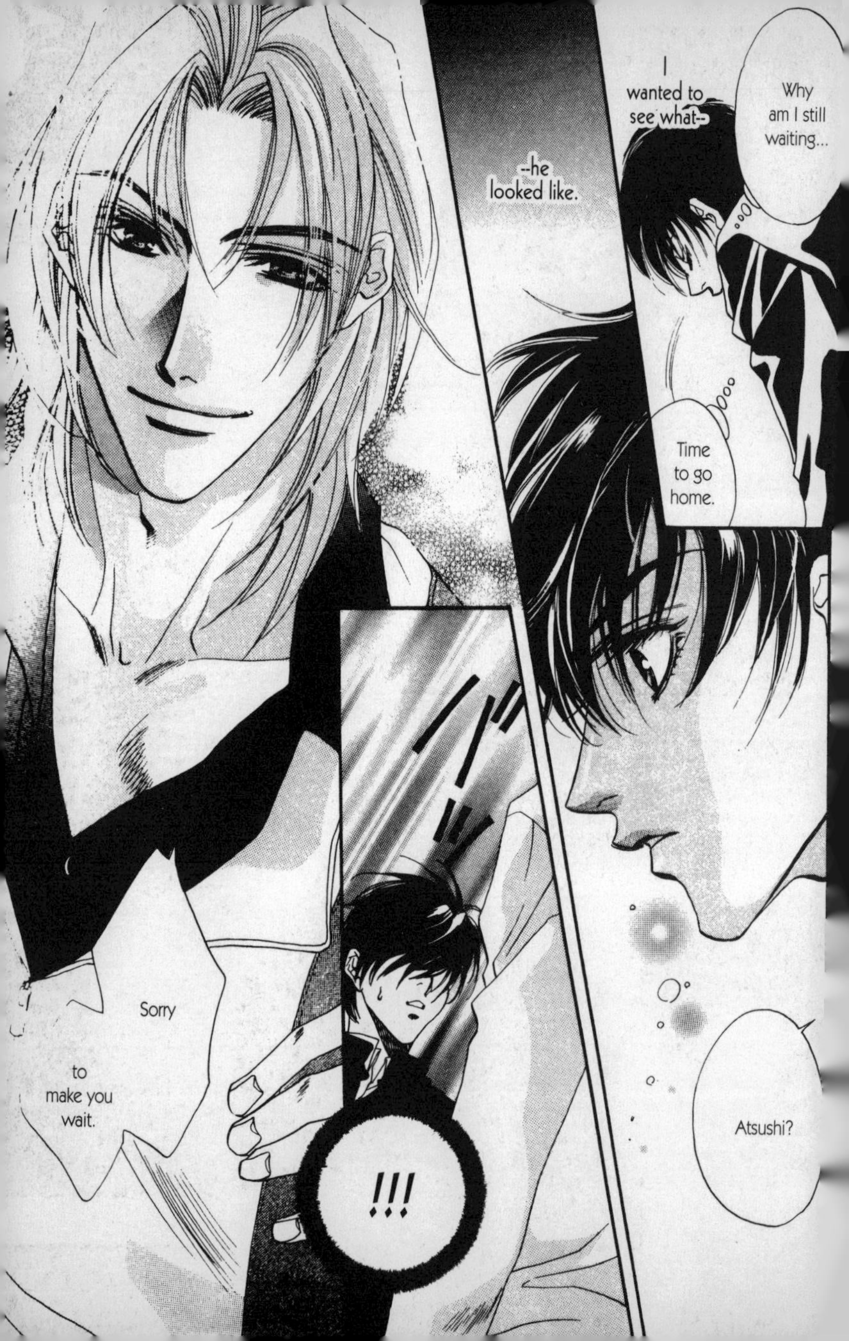
Why am I still waiting...
I wanted to see what--
Time to go home.
--he looked like.
Atsushi?
!!!
Sorry
to make you wait.

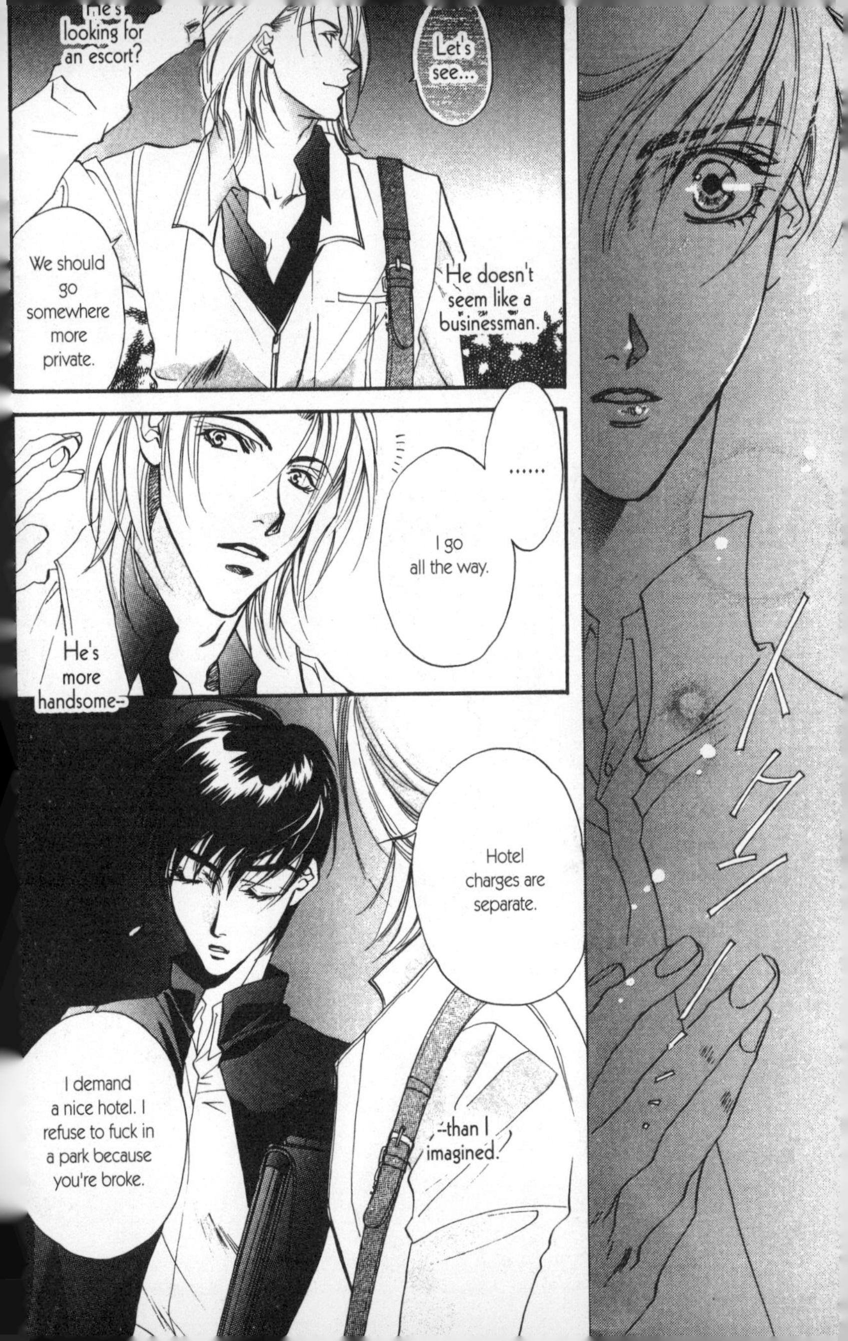
Let's see...
He doesn't seem like a businessman.
He's looking for an escort?
We should go somewhere more private.
......
I go all the way.
He's more handsome--
Hotel charges are separate.
--than I imagined.
I demand a nice hotel. I refuse to fuck in a park because you're broke.

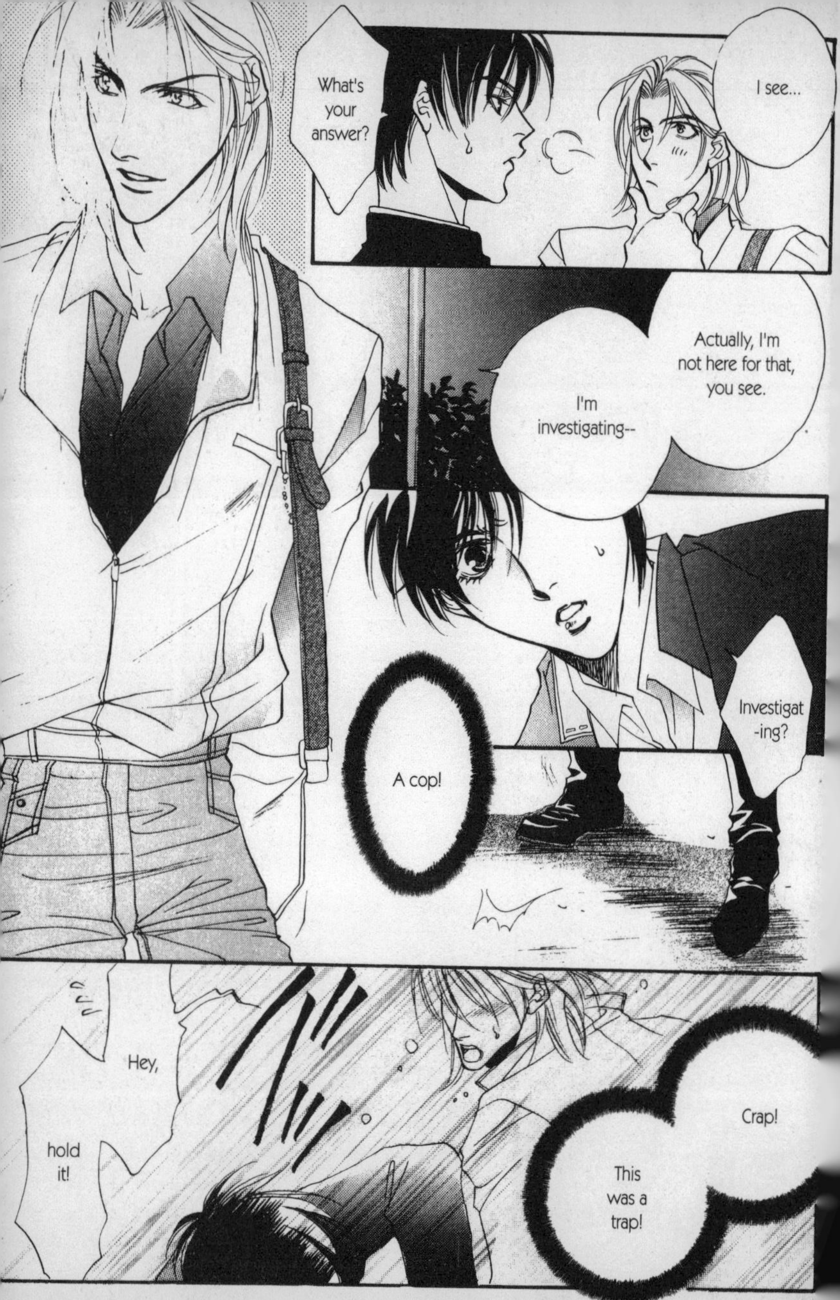
I see...
What's your answer?
Actually, I'm not here for that, you see.
I'm investigating--
Investigat -ing?
A cop!
Crap!
This was a trap!
Hey,
hold it!

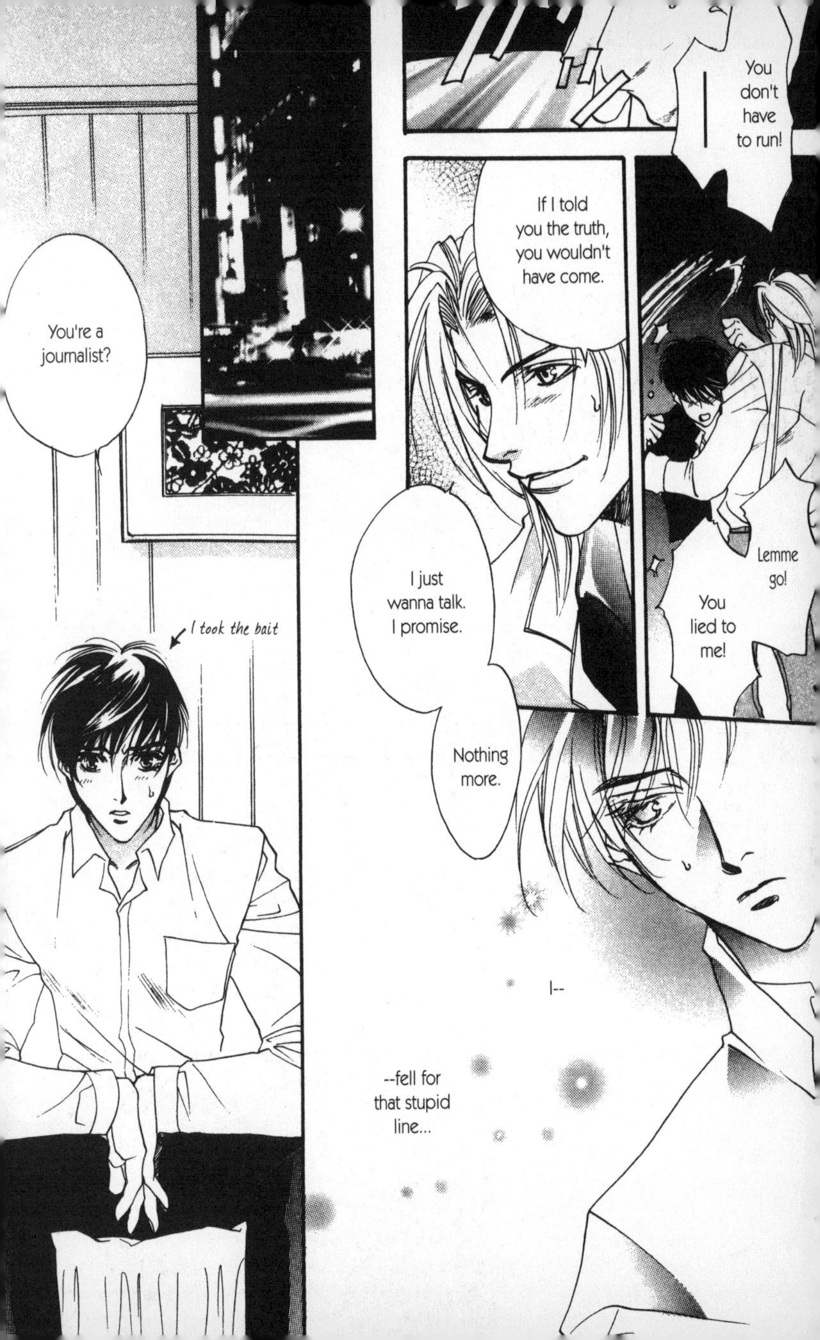
You're a journalist?
I took the bait
You don't have to run!
Lemme go!
You lied to me!
If I told you the truth, you wouldn't have come.
I just wanna talk. I promise.
Nothing more.
I--
--fell for that stupid line...

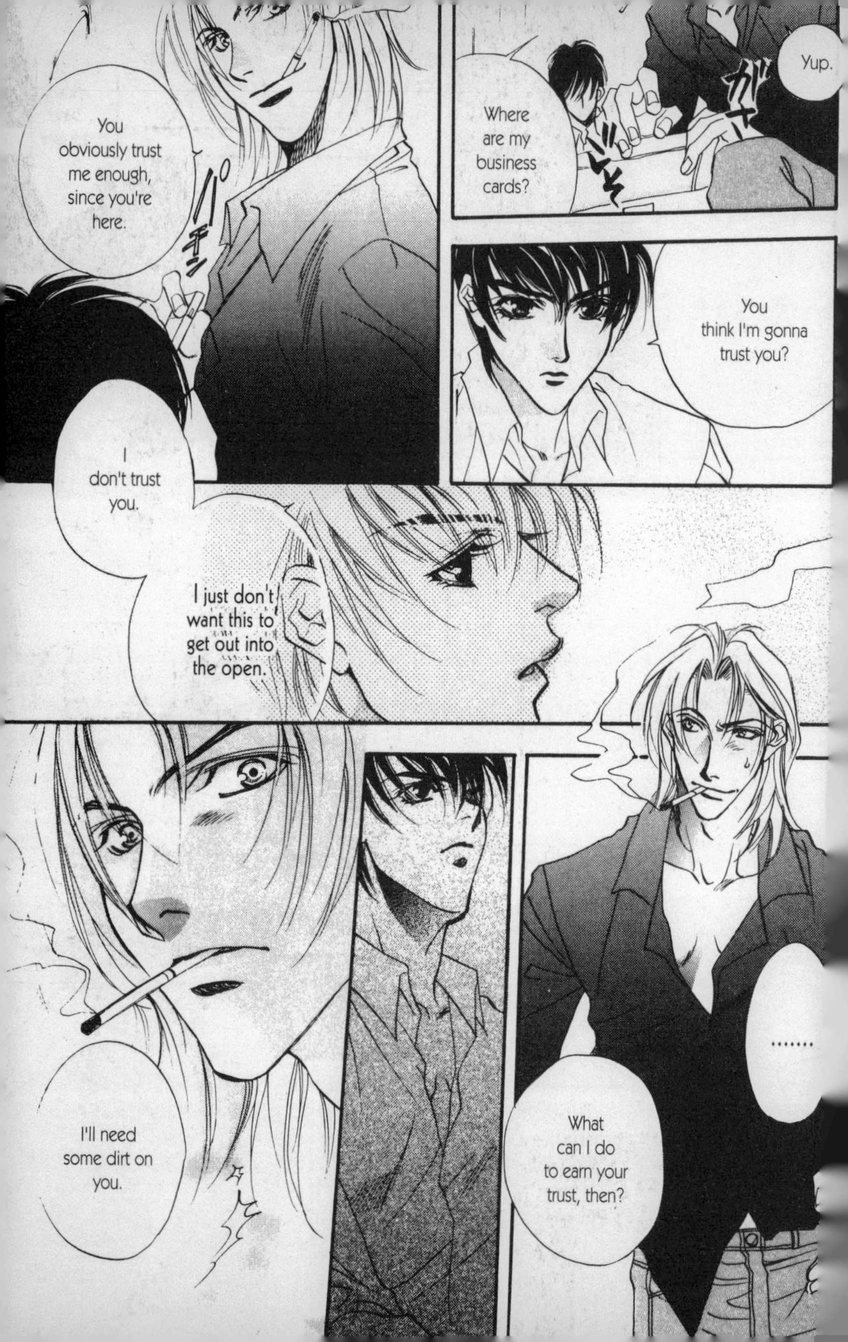

Where are my business cards?
Yup.
You think I'm gonna trust you?
You obviously trust me enough, since you're here.
I don't trust you.
I just don't want this to get out into the open.
......
What can I do to earn your trust, then?
I'll need some dirt on you.

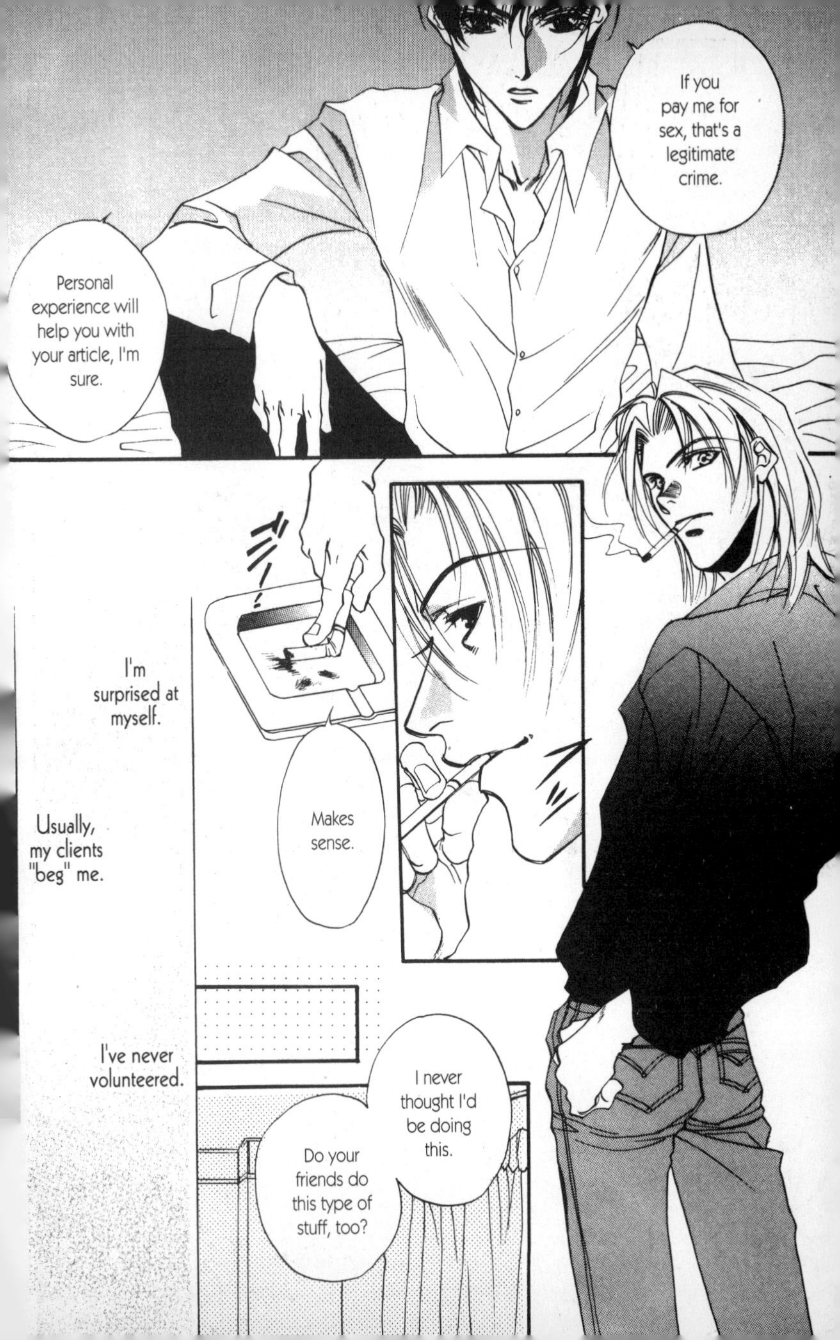
If you pay me for sex, that's a legitimate crime.
Personal experience will help you with your article, I'm sure.
Makes sense.
I'm surprised at myself.
Usually, my clients "beg" me.
I never thought I'd be doing this.
Do your friends do this type of stuff, too?
I've never volunteered.

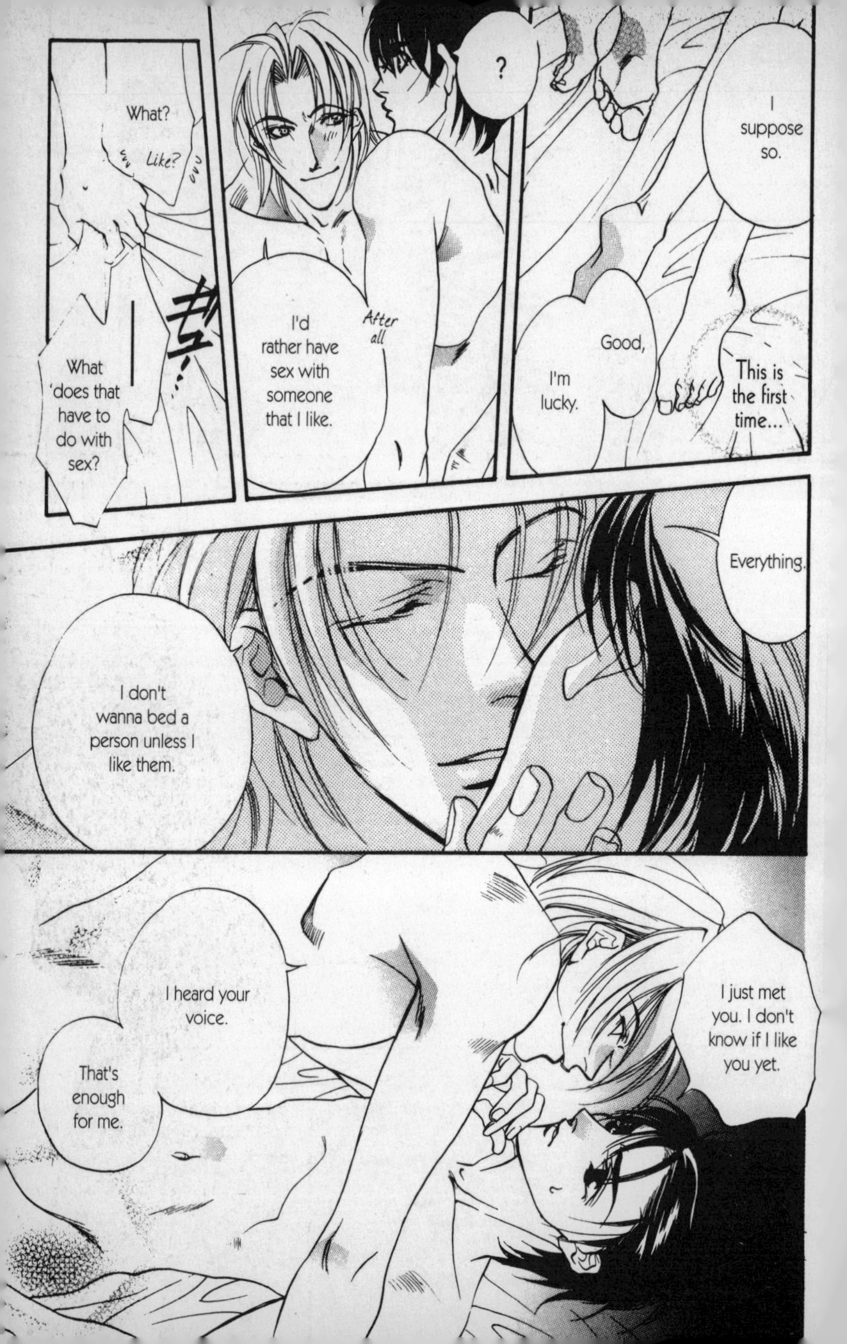
What?
Like?
What 'does that have to do with sex?
I'd rather have sex with someone that I like.
After all
?
I suppose so.
Good,
I'm lucky.
This is the first time...
Everything.
I don't wanna bed a person unless I like them.
I just met you. I don't know if I like you yet.
I heard your voice.
That's enough for me.

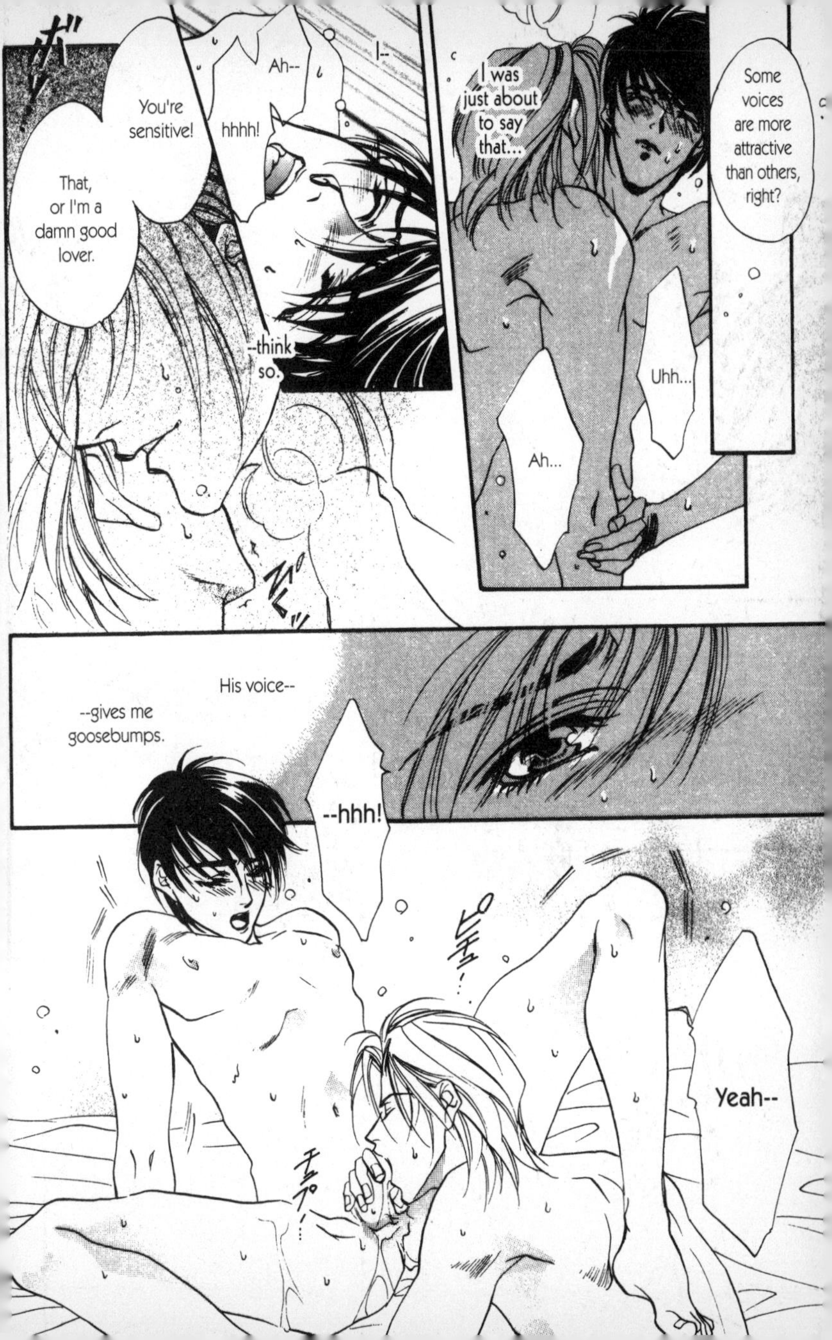
Some voices are more attractive than others, right?
I was just about to say that...
Uhh...
Ah...
I--
Ah--
hhhh!
You're sensitive!
That, or I'm a damn good lover.
--think so.
His voice--
--gives me goosebumps.
--hhh!
Yeah--

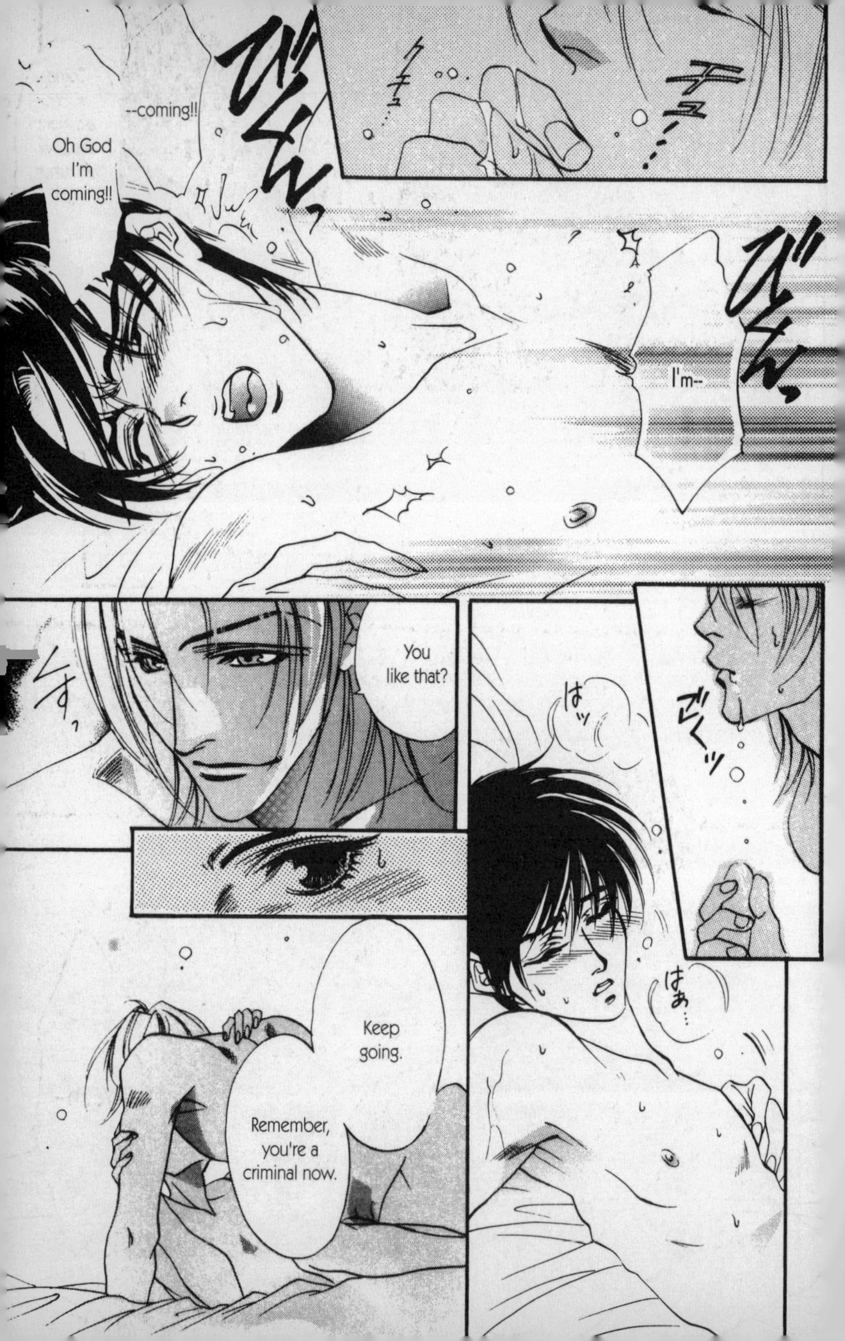

びくん
I'm--
びくん
--coming!!
Oh God I'm coming!!
ごくッ
はッ
You like that?
くすっ
はぁ…
Keep going.
Remember, you're a criminal now.

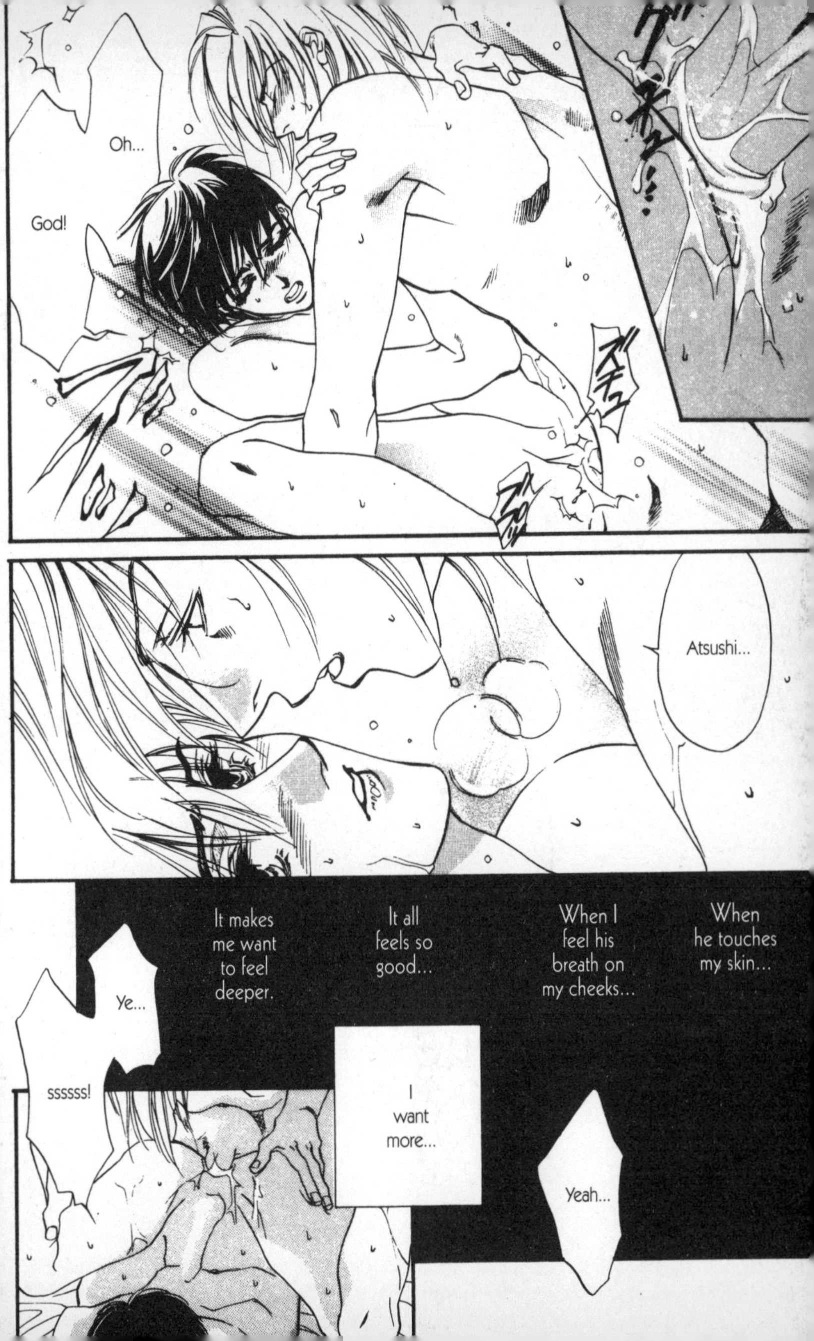
Oh...
God!
Atsushi...
When he touches my skin...
When I feel his breath on my cheeks...
It all feels so good...
It makes me want to feel deeper.
Yeah...
I want more...
Ye...
ssssss!

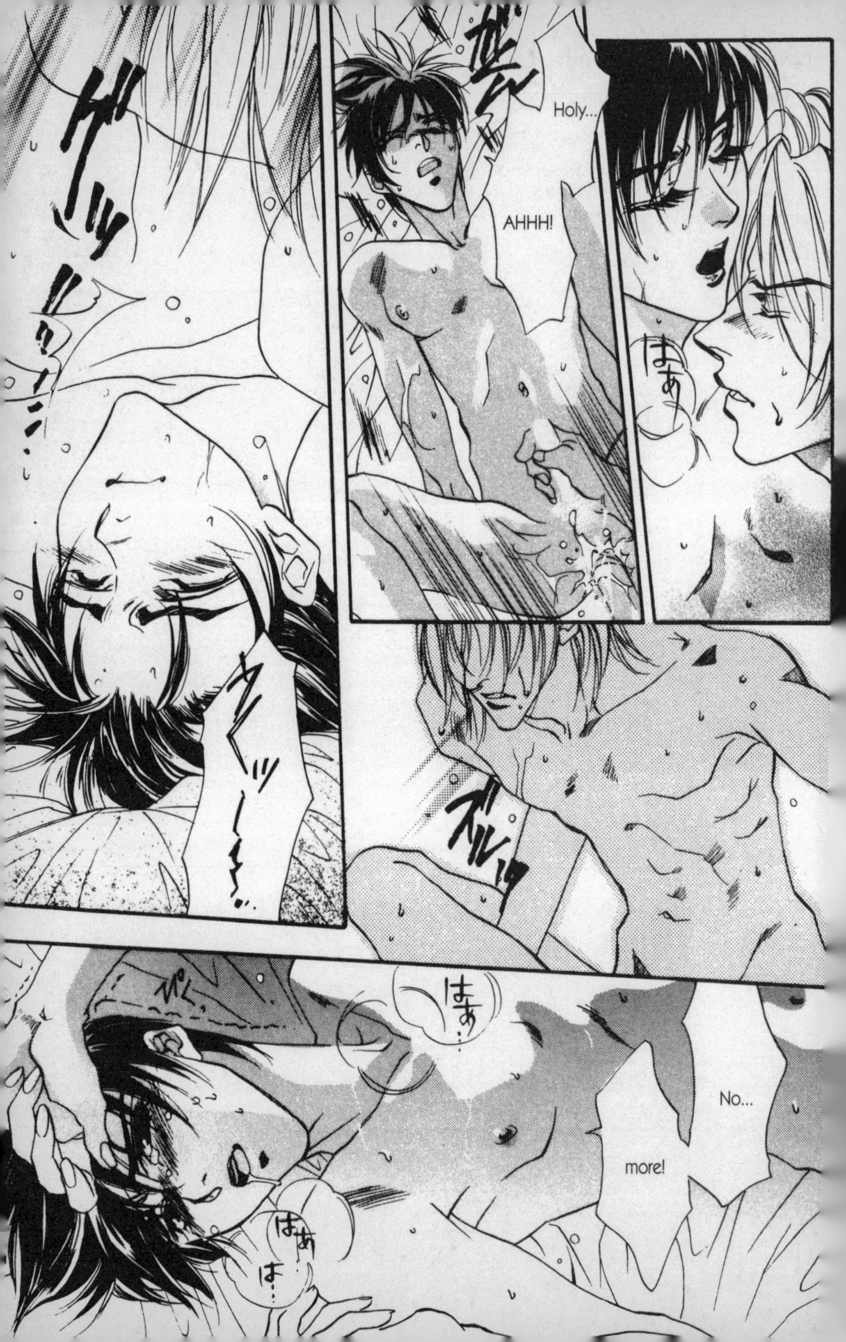
はぁ
Holy...
AHHH!
ザーッ!!
ズルッ
ぴく
はぁ…
No...
more!
はぁ は…

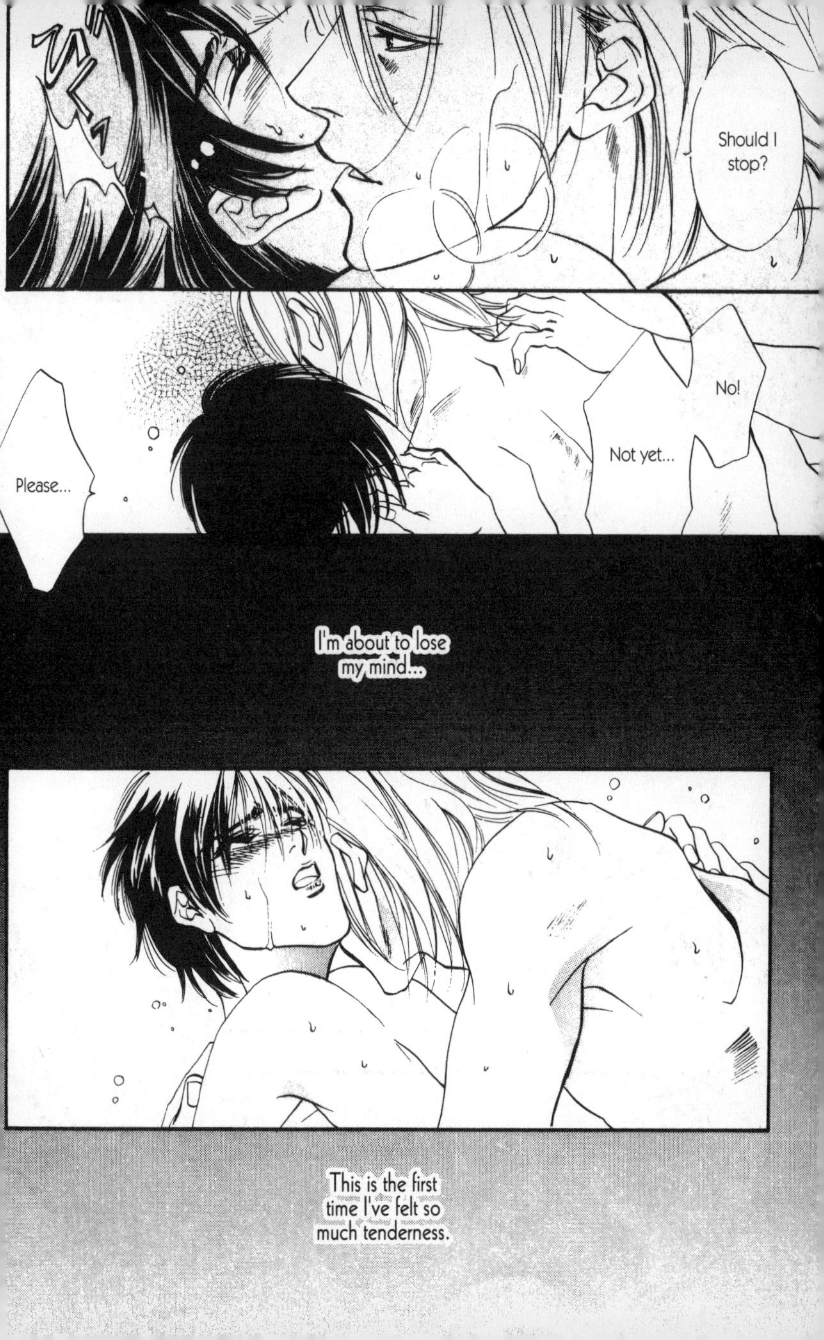
Should I stop?
No!
Not yet...
Please...
I'm about to lose my mind...
This is the first time I've felt so much tenderness.

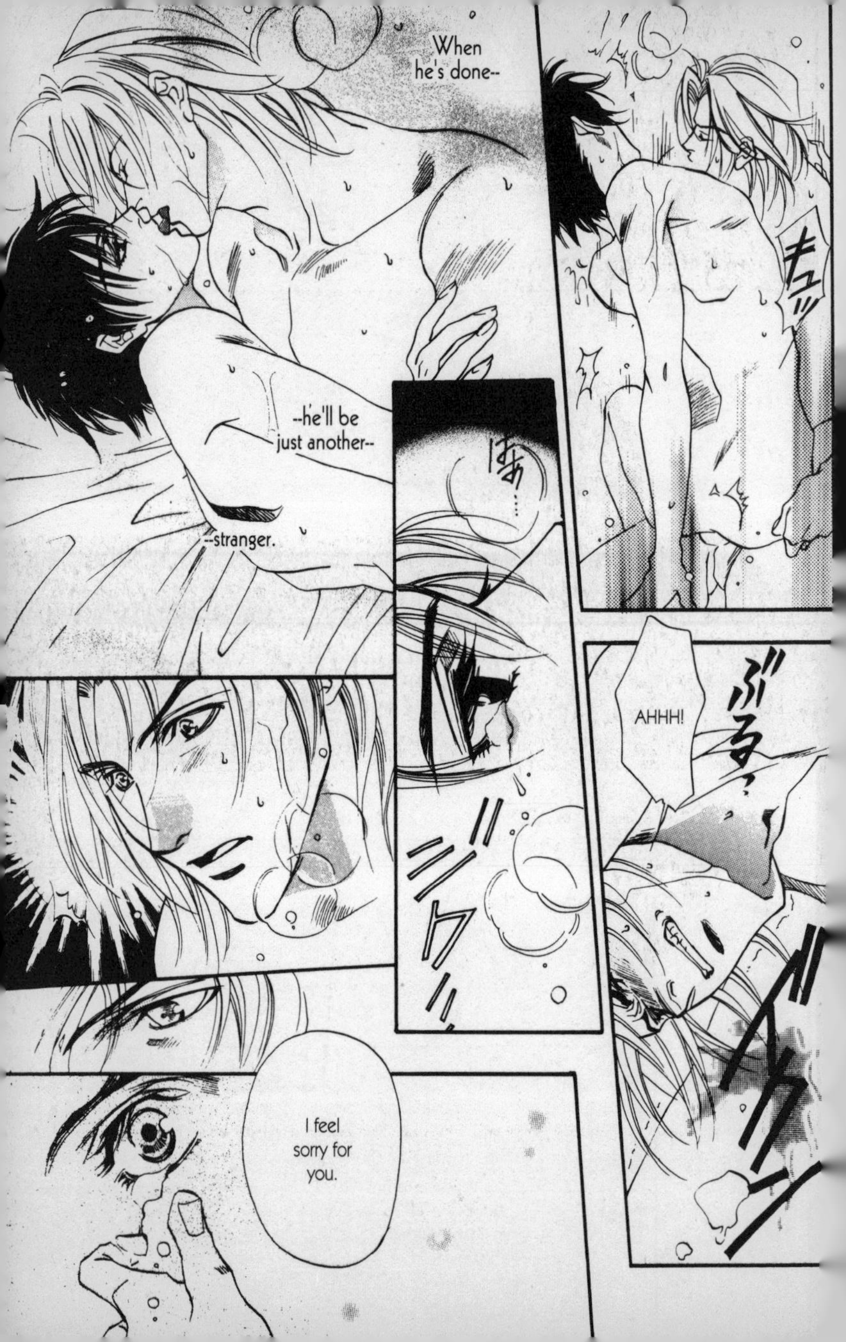
When he's done--
--he'll be just another--
--stranger.
AHHH!
I feel sorry for you.

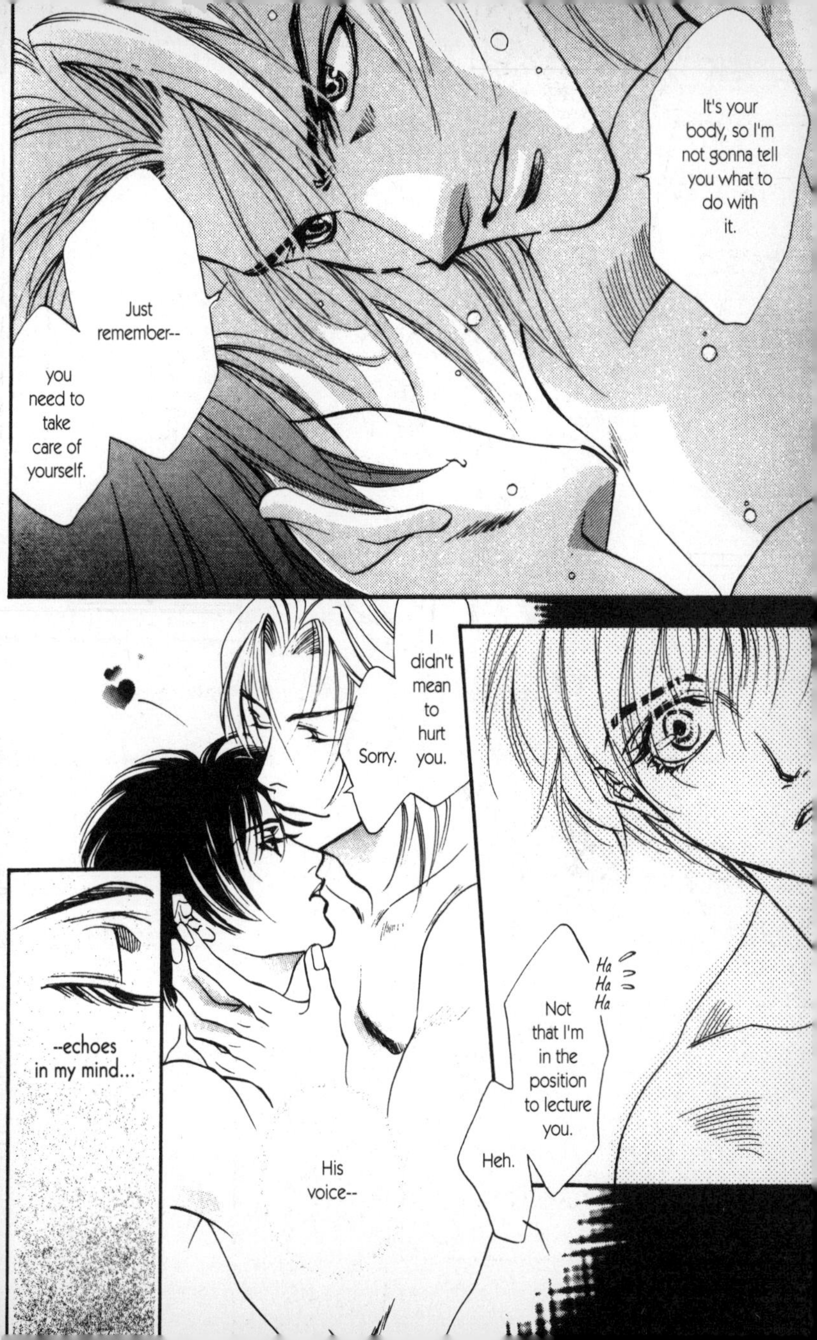
It's your body, so I'm not gonna tell you what to do with it.
Just remember--
you need to take care of yourself.
Ha Ha Ha
Not that I'm in the position to lecture you.
Heh.
I didn't mean to hurt you.
Sorry.
His voice--
--echoes in my mind...

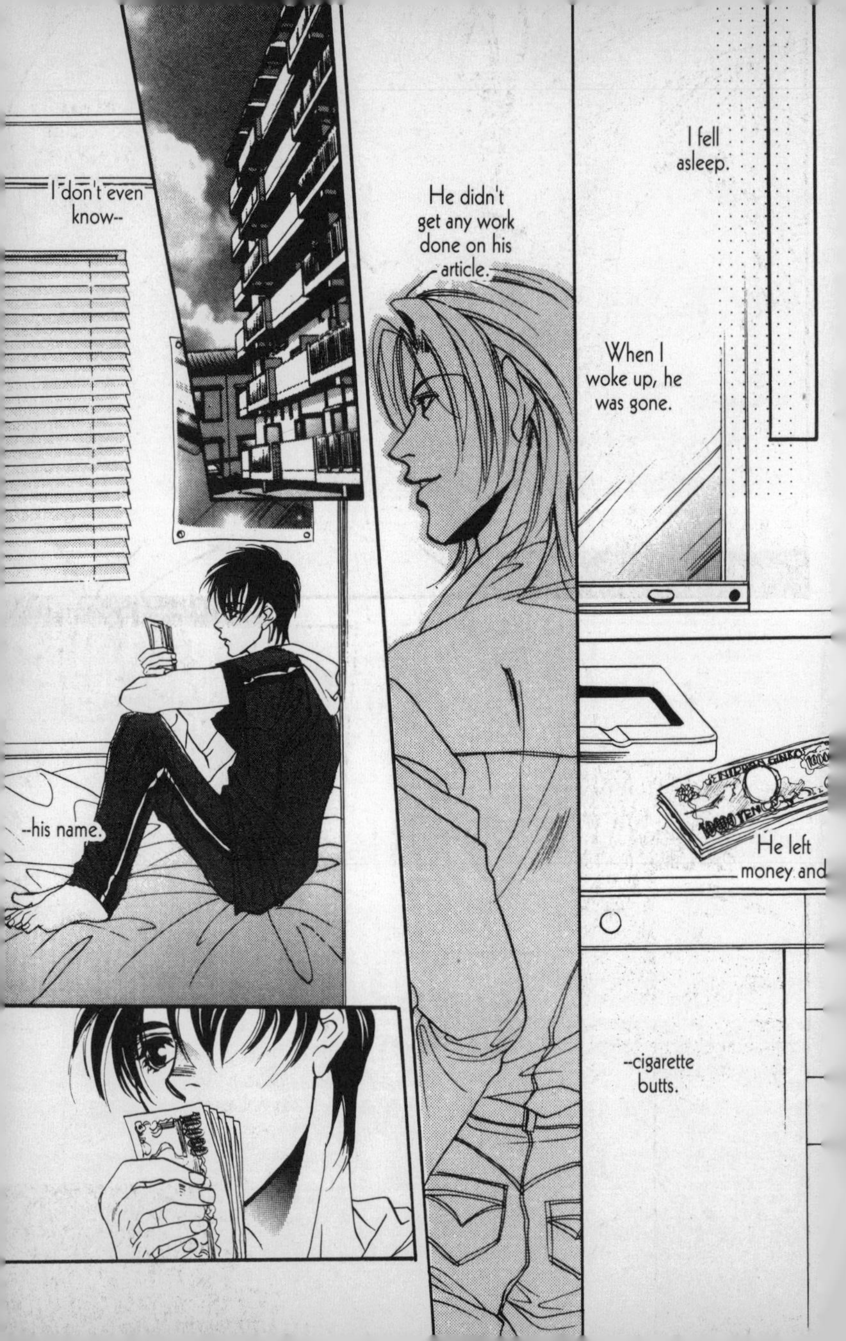
I fell asleep.
When I woke up, he was gone.
He left money and
--cigarette butts.
He didn't get any work done on his article.
I don't even know--
--his name.

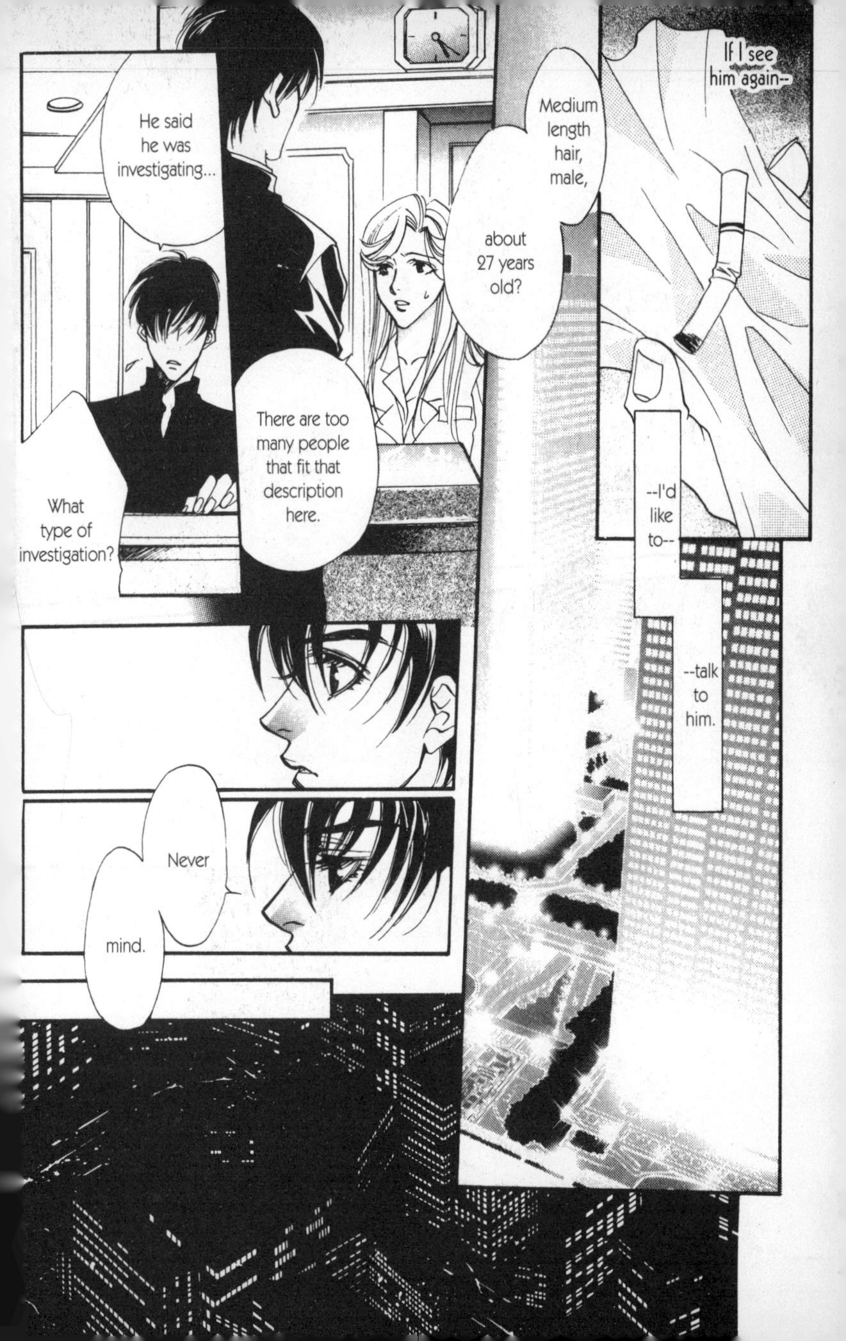
If I see him again--
--I'd like to--
--talk to him.
He said he was investigating...
Medium length hair, male,
about 27 years old?
There are too many people that fit that description here.
What type of investigation?
Never mind.

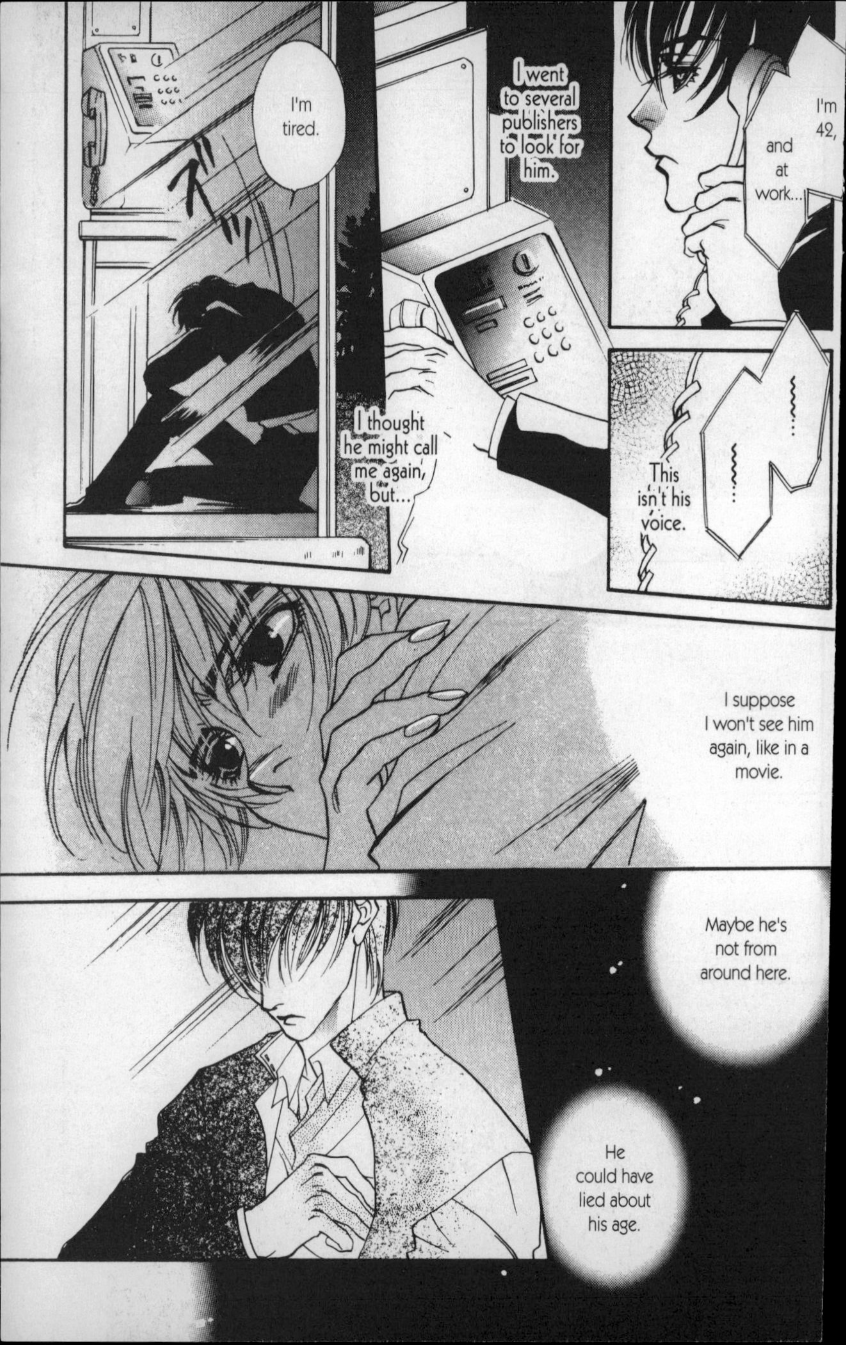
I'm 42, and at work...
......
......
This isn't his voice.
I went to several publishers to look for him.
I thought he might call me again, but...
I'm tired.
I suppose I won't see him again, like in a movie.
Maybe he's not from around here.
He could have lied about his age.

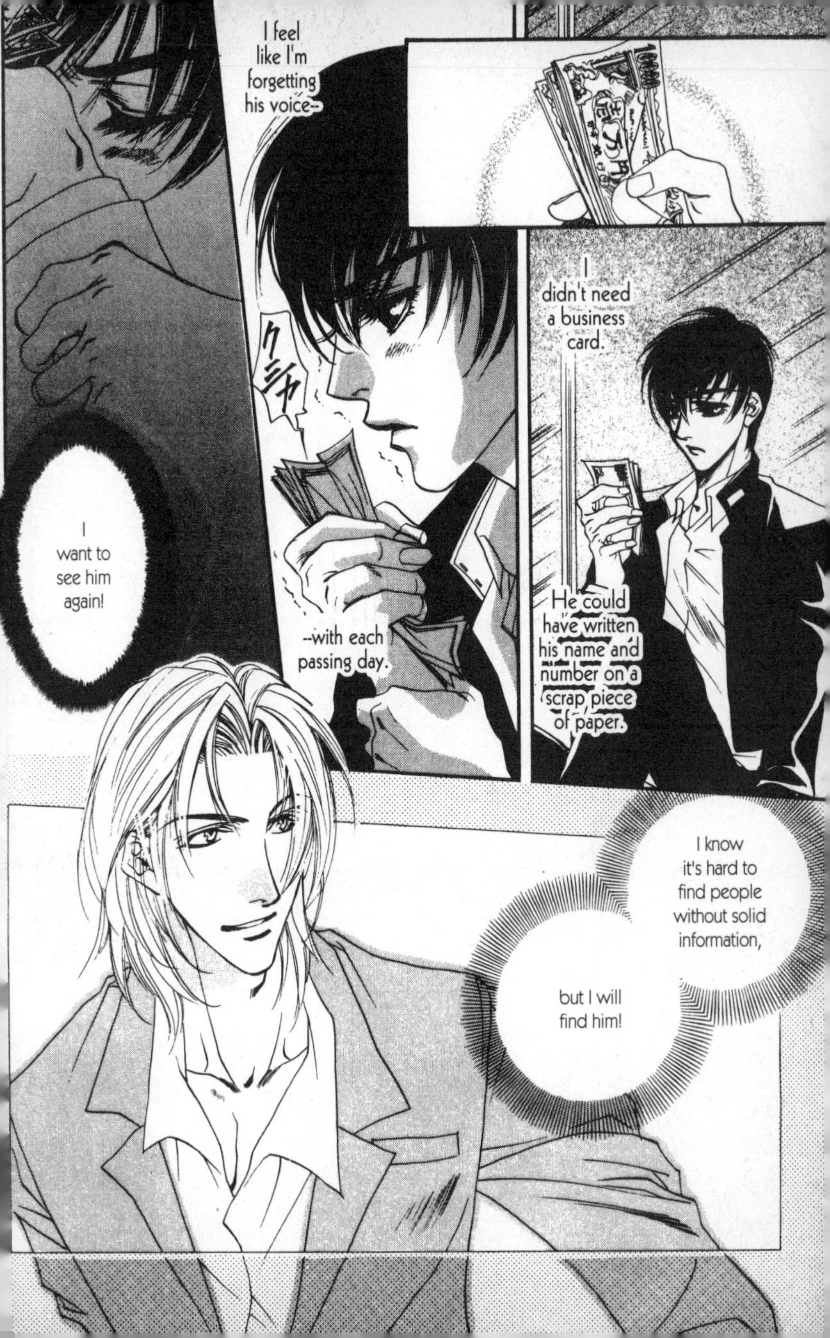
I didn't need a business card.
He could have written his name and number on a scrap piece of paper.
I feel like I'm forgetting his voice--
クシャ
--with each passing day.
I want to see him again!
I know it's hard to find people without solid information,
but I will find him!

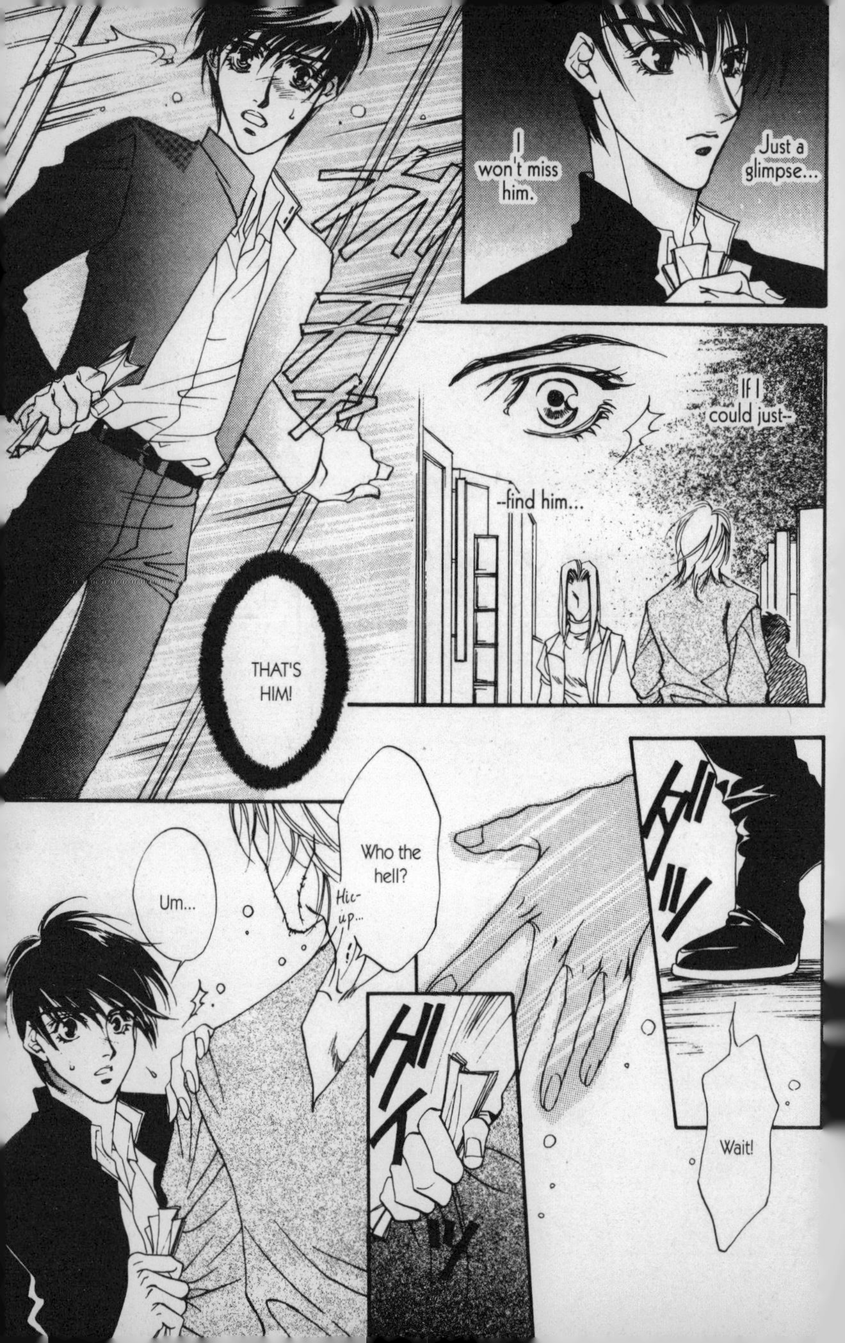
Just a glimpse...
I won't miss him.
If I could just--
--find him...
THAT'S HIM!
Wait!
Who the hell?
Hic-up...
Um...

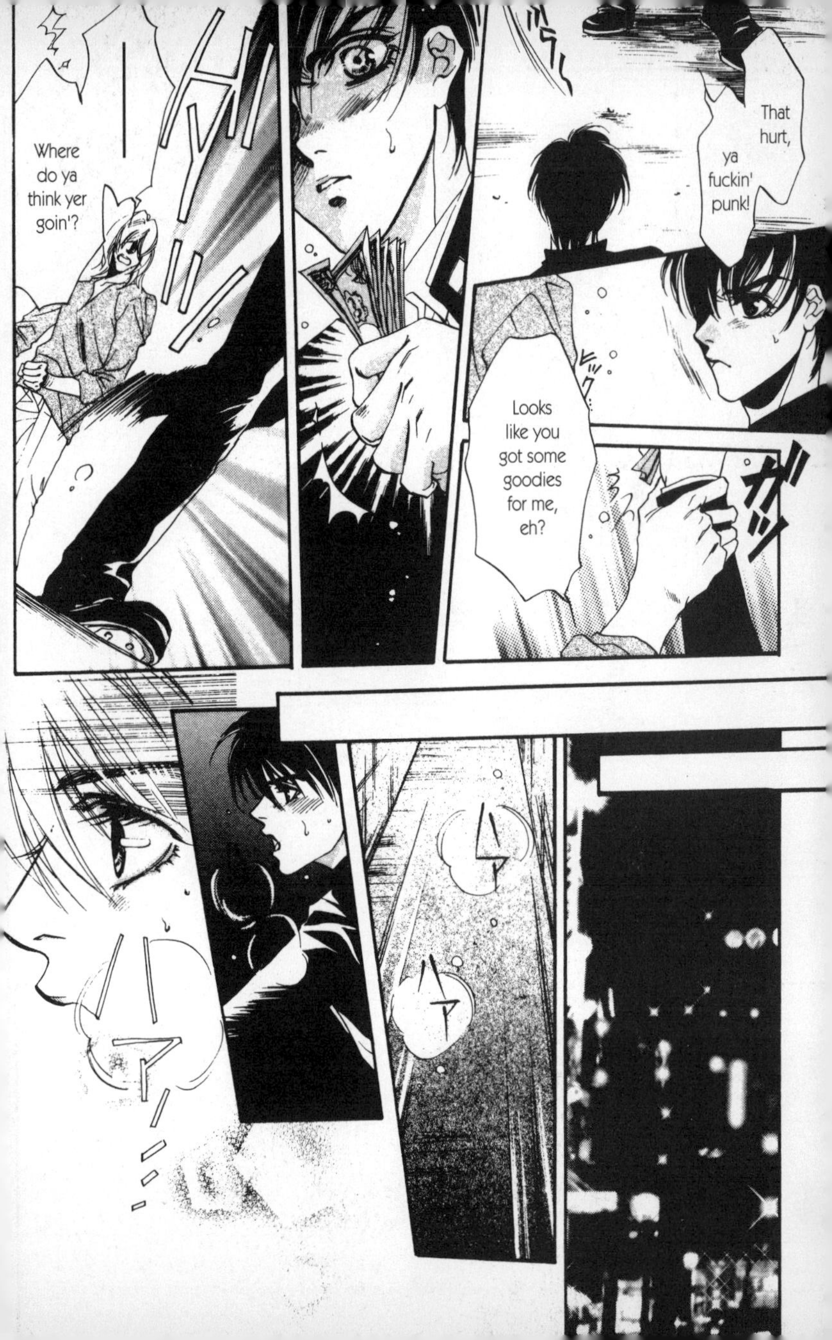
That hurt, ya fuckin' punk!
Looks like you got some goodies for me, eh?
Where do ya think yer goin'?

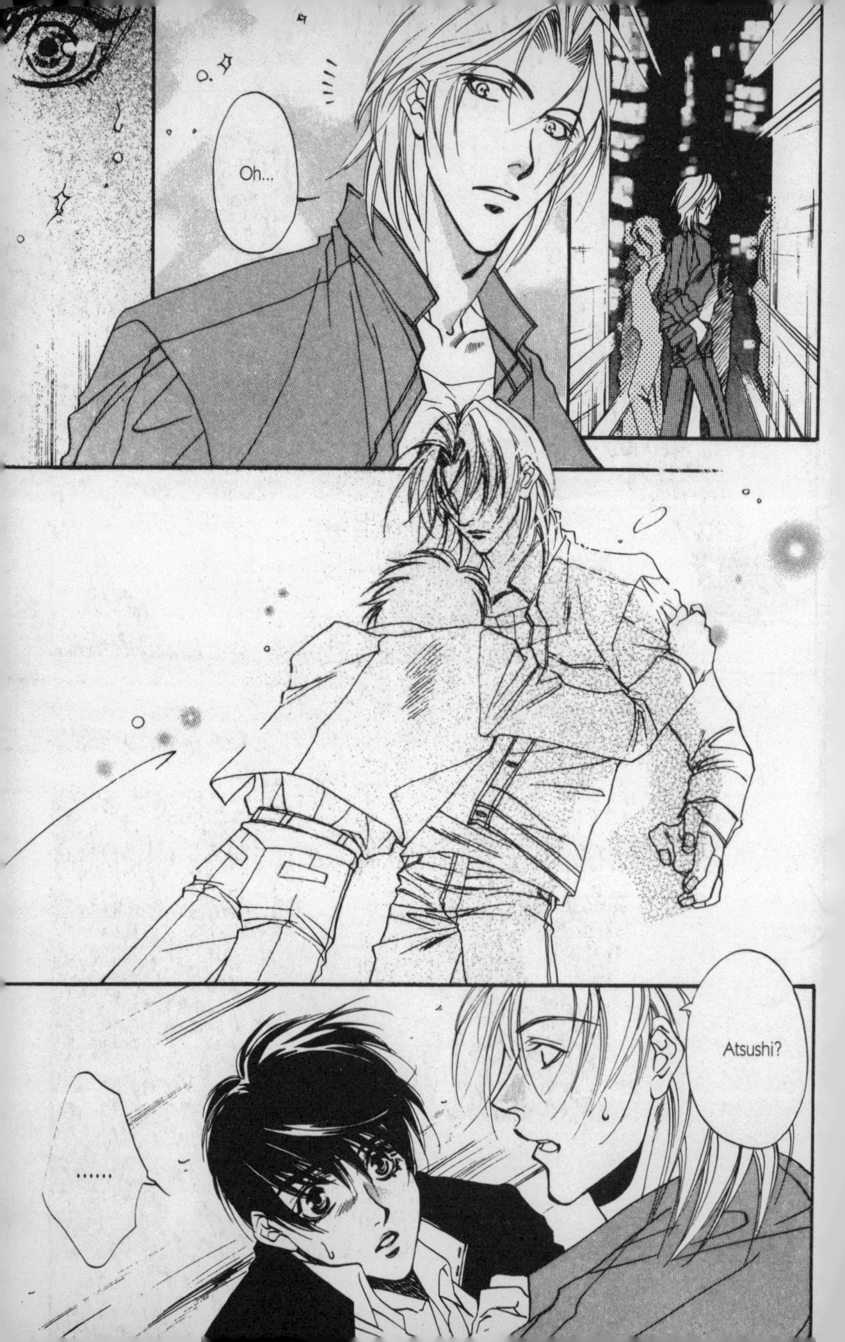

Oh...
Atsushi?
......

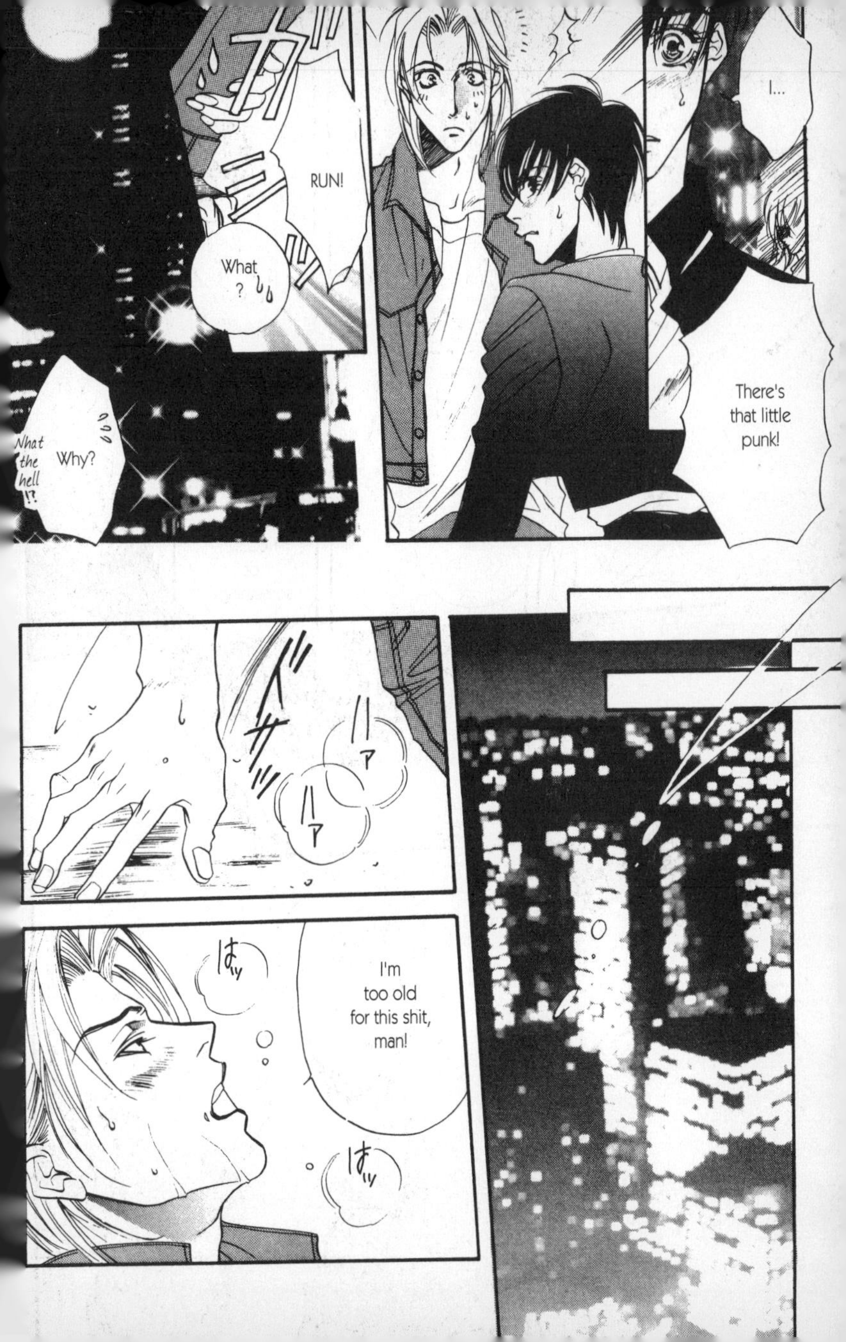
I...
There's that little punk!
RUN!
What ?
Why?
What the hell !?
I'm too old for this shit, man!

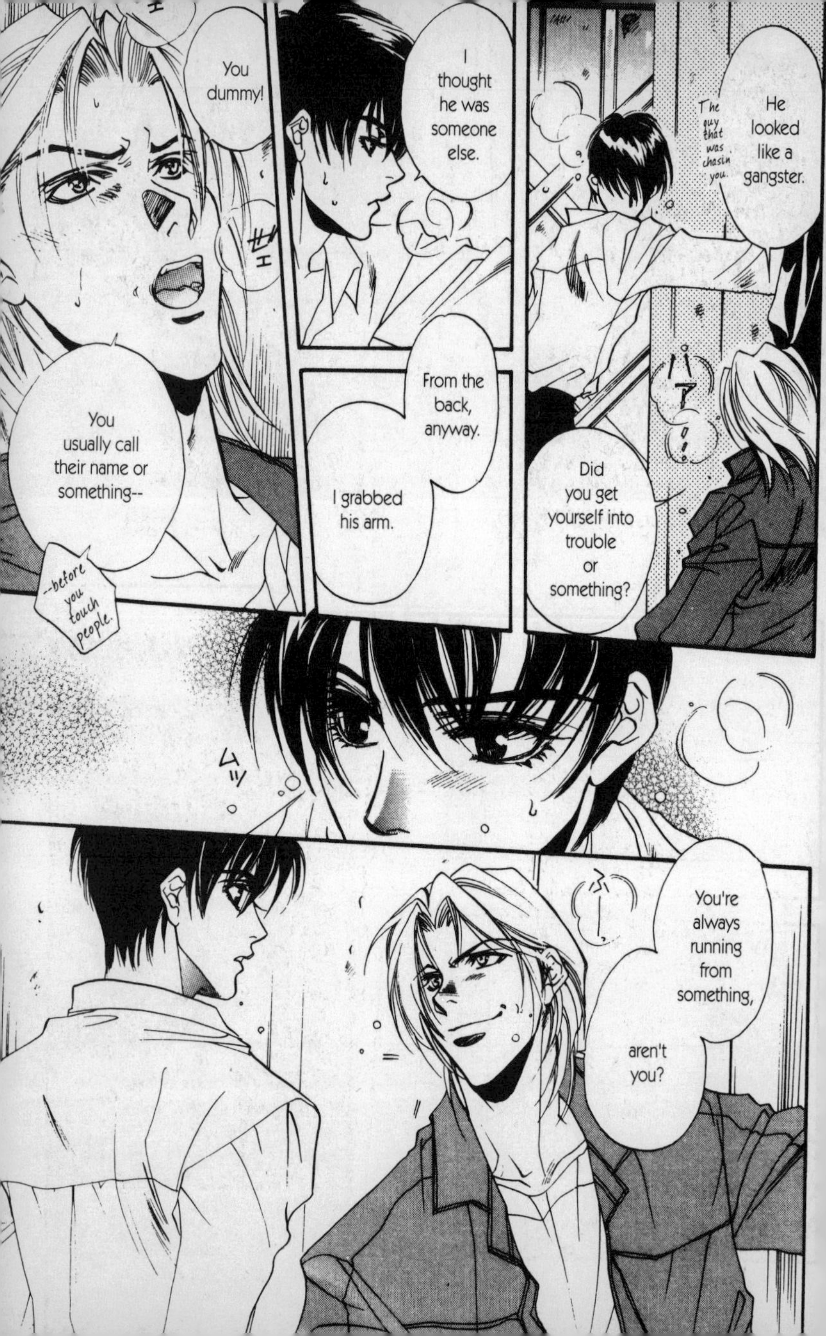
He looked like a gangster.
The guy that was chasin you.
Did you get yourself into trouble or something?
I thought he was someone else.
From the back, anyway.
I grabbed his arm.
You dummy!
You usually call their name or something--
--before you touch people.
You're always running from something,
aren't you?

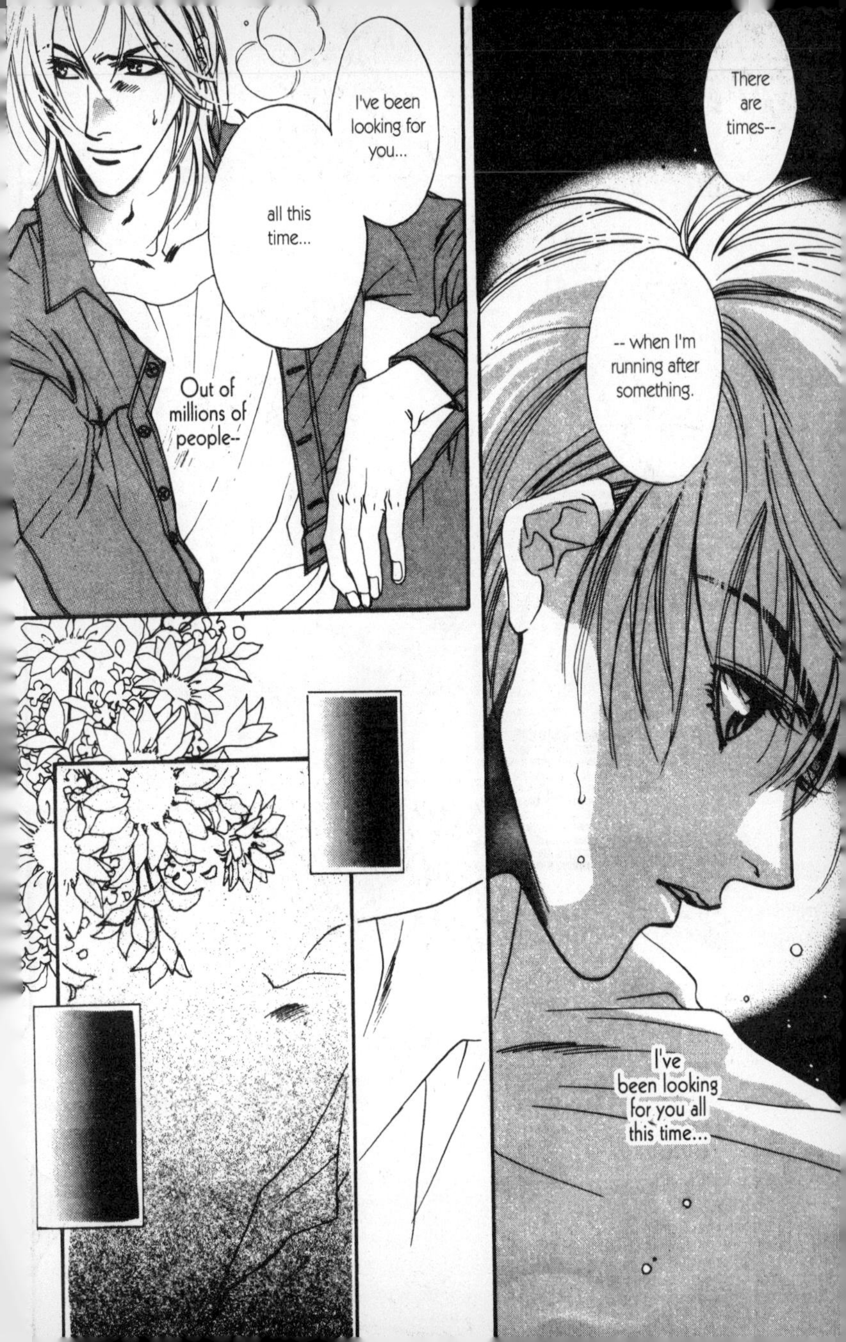
There are times--
-- when I'm running after something.
I've been looking for you all this time...
I've been looking for you...
all this time...
Out of millions of people--

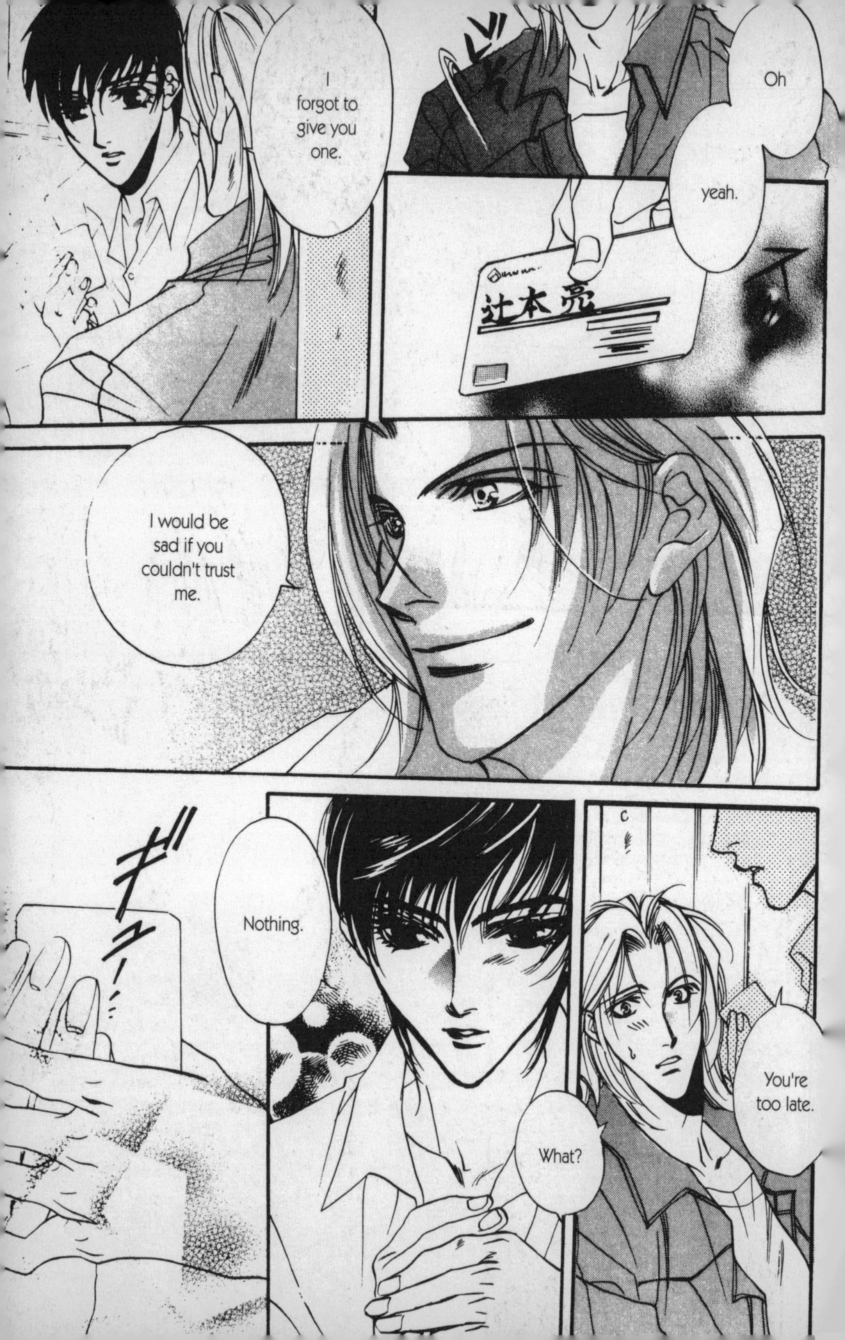

Oh
yeah.
I forgot to give you one.
辻本亮
I would be sad if you couldn't trust me.
You're too late.
What?
Nothing.

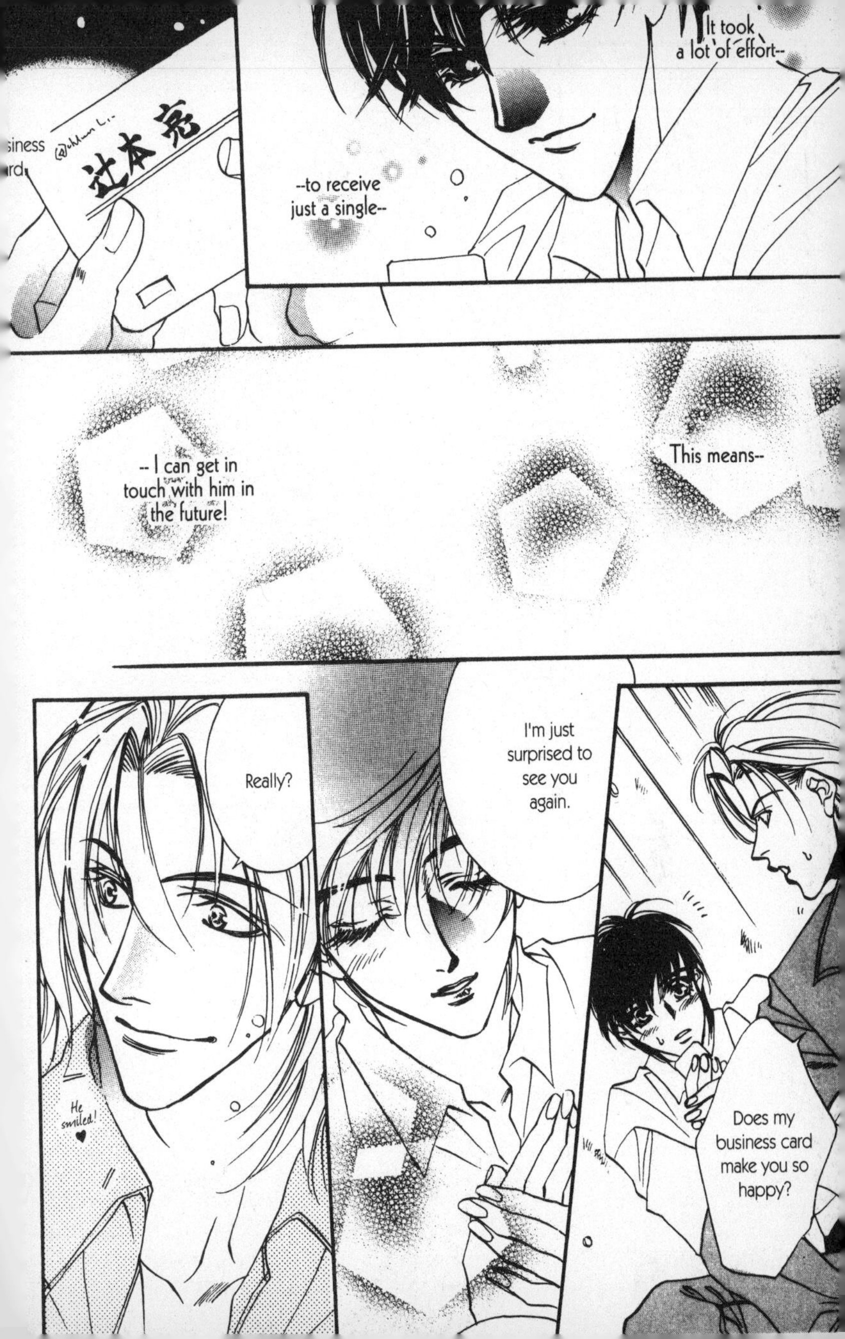
It took a lot of effort--
--to receive just a single--
辻本亮
This means--
-- I can get in touch with him in the future!
Does my business card make you so happy?
I'm just surprised to see you again.
Really?
He smiled! ♥

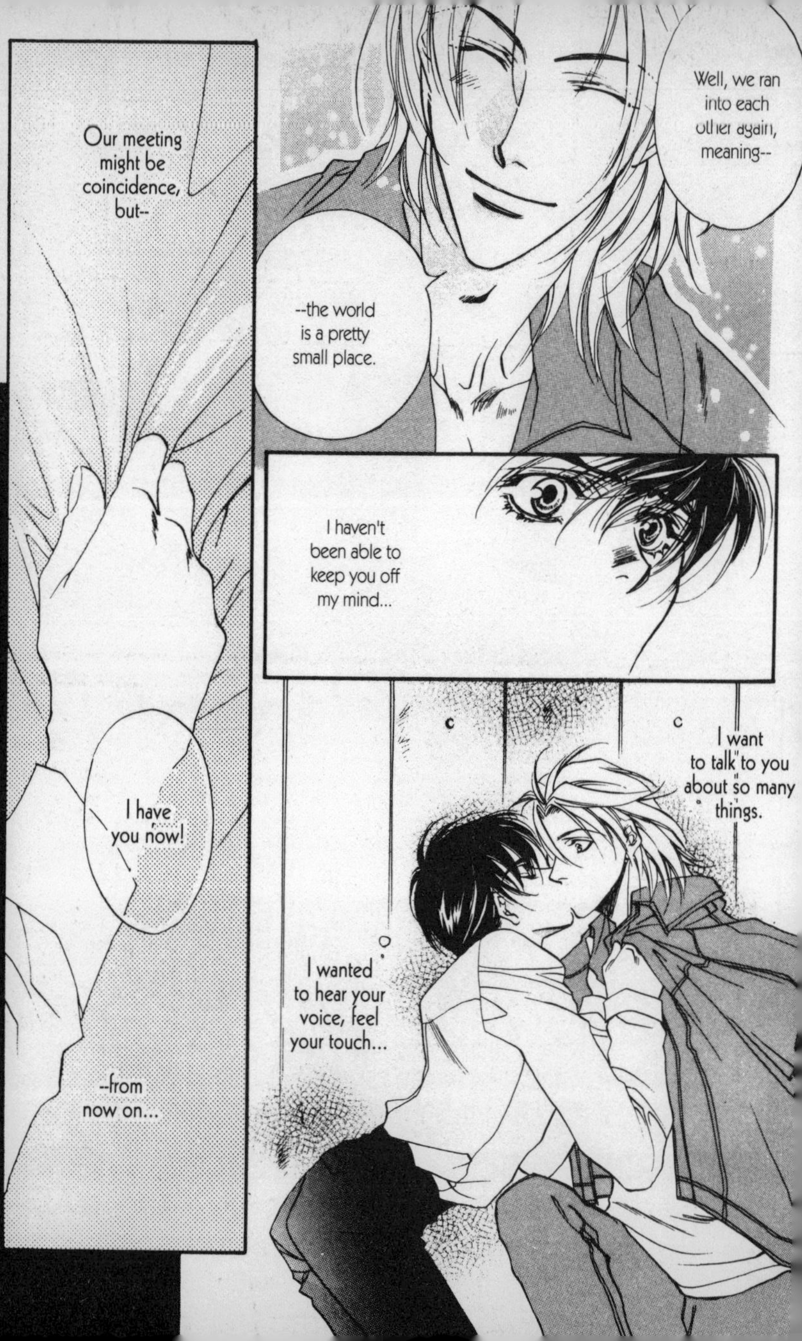
Well, we ran into each other again, meaning--
--the world is a pretty small place.
I haven't been able to keep you off my mind...
I want to talk to you about so many things.
I wanted to hear your voice, feel your touch...
Our meeting might be coincidence, but--
I have you now!
--from now on...

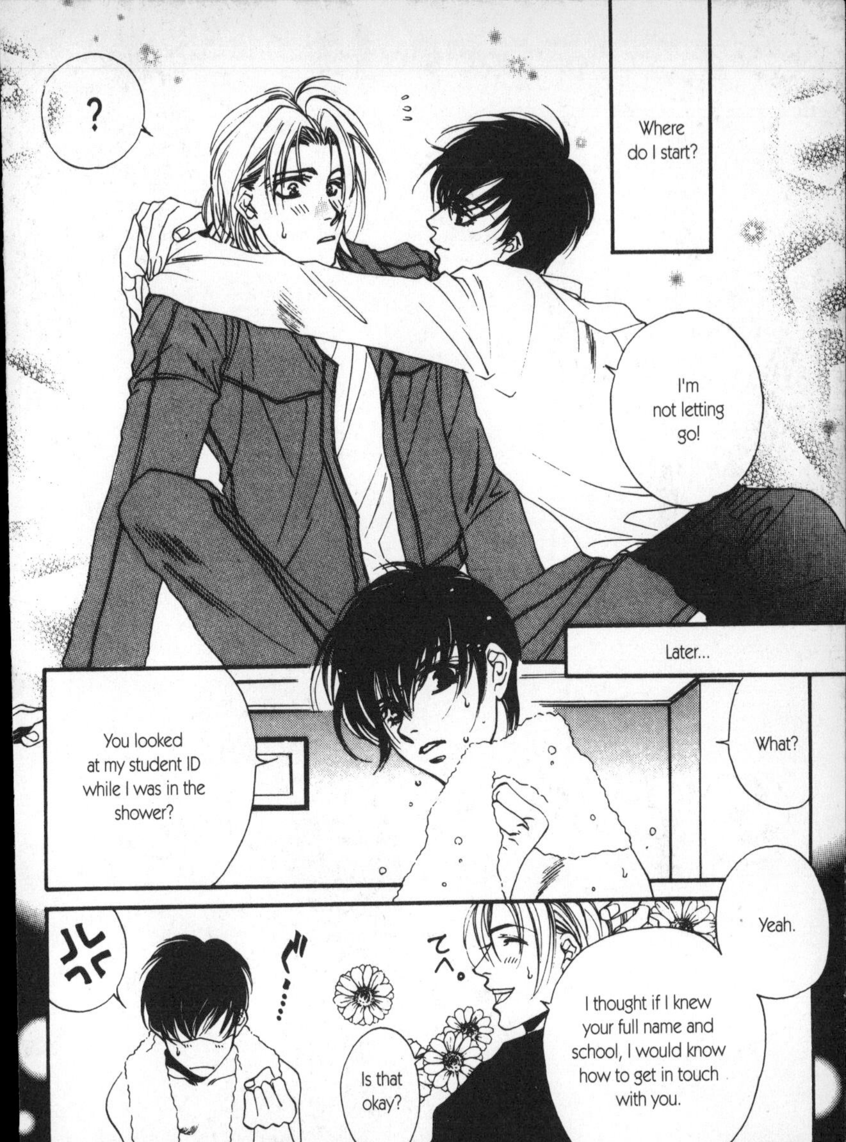
Where do I start?
?
I'm not letting go!
Later...
What?
You looked at my student ID while I was in the shower?
Yeah.
I thought if I knew your full name and school, I would know how to get in touch with you.
Is that okay?

Instead of catching him, maybe I got caught in his trap... ———

◆END◆

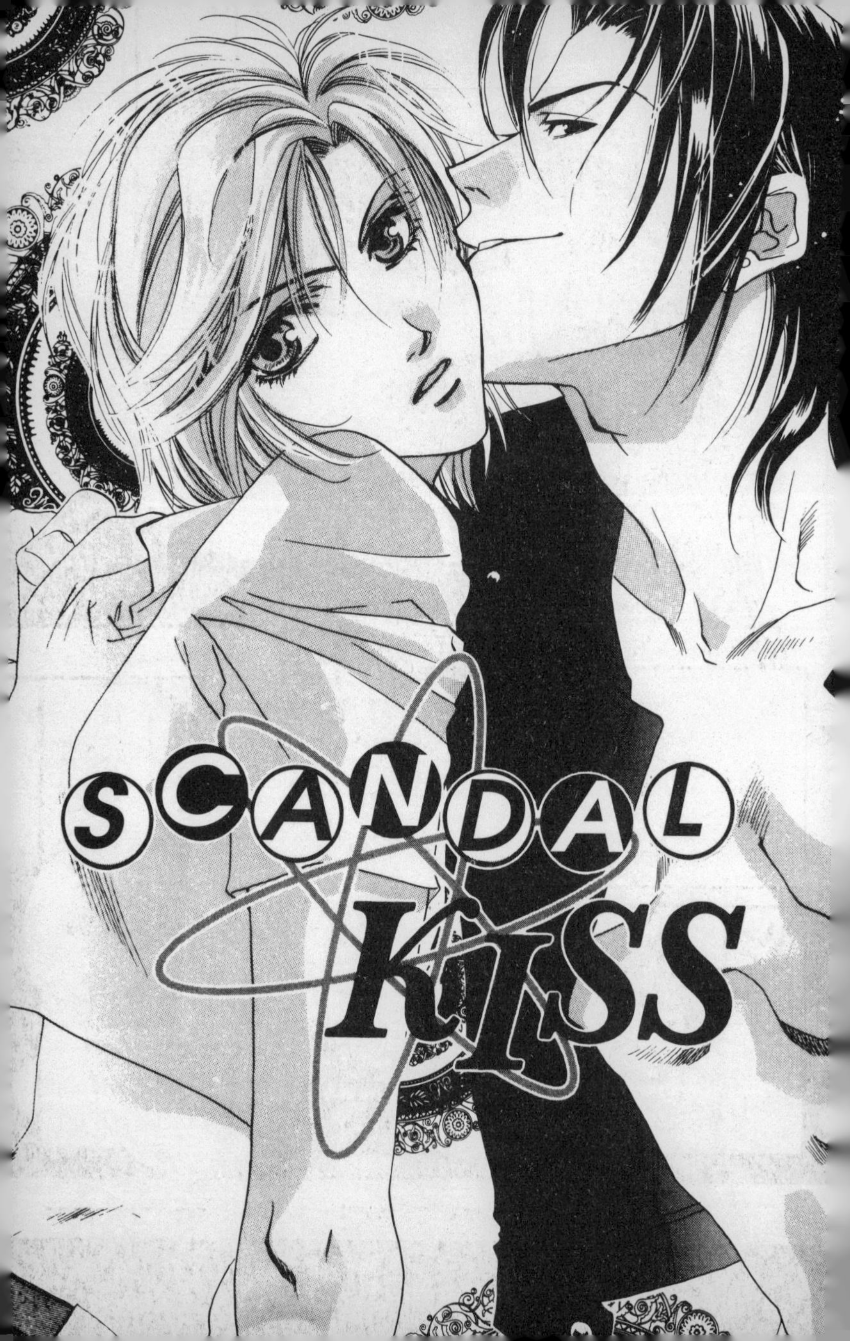
SCANDAL
KISS

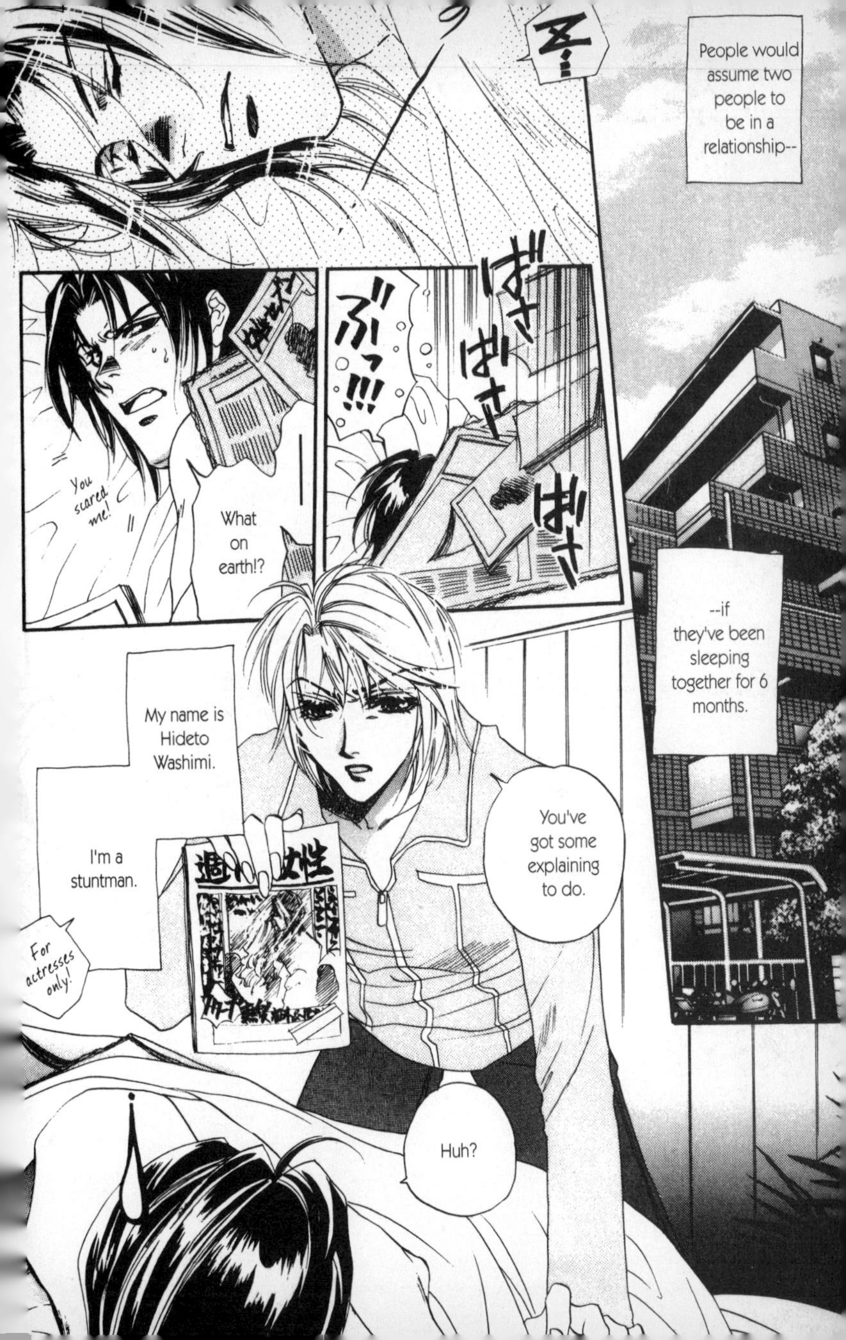

People would assume two people to be in a relationship--
--if they've been sleeping together for 6 months.
ぶっ!!!
What on earth!?
You scared me!
You've got some explaining to do.
Huh?
My name is Hideto Washimi.
I'm a stuntman.
For actresses only!

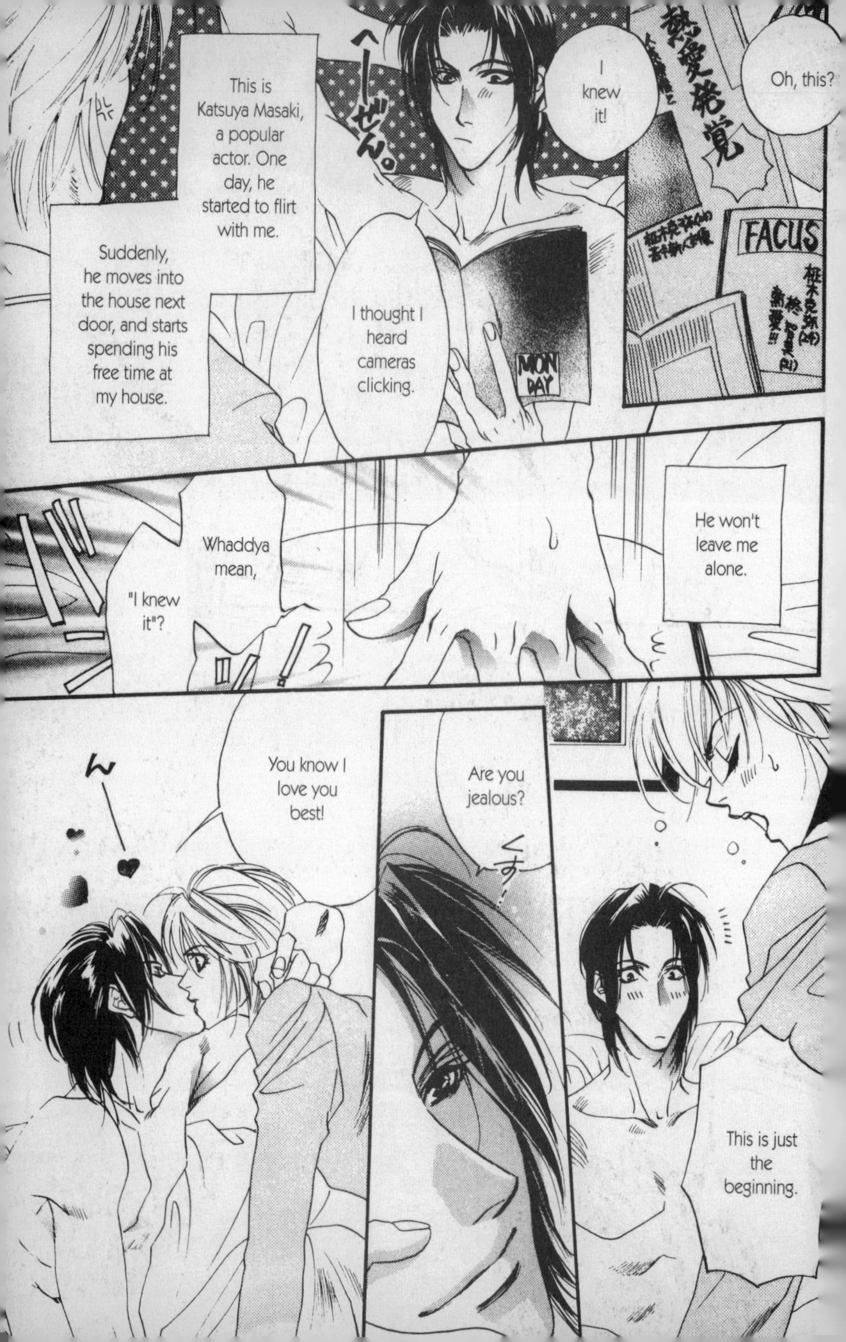
Oh, this?
熱愛発覚
FACUS
I knew it!
へーぜん。
This is Katsuya Masaki, a popular actor. One day, he started to flirt with me.
Suddenly, he moves into the house next door, and starts spending his free time at my house.
I thought I heard cameras clicking.
MON DAY
He won't leave me alone.
Whaddya mean, "I knew it"?
This is just the beginning.
Are you jealous?
くす…
You know I love you best!
ん—

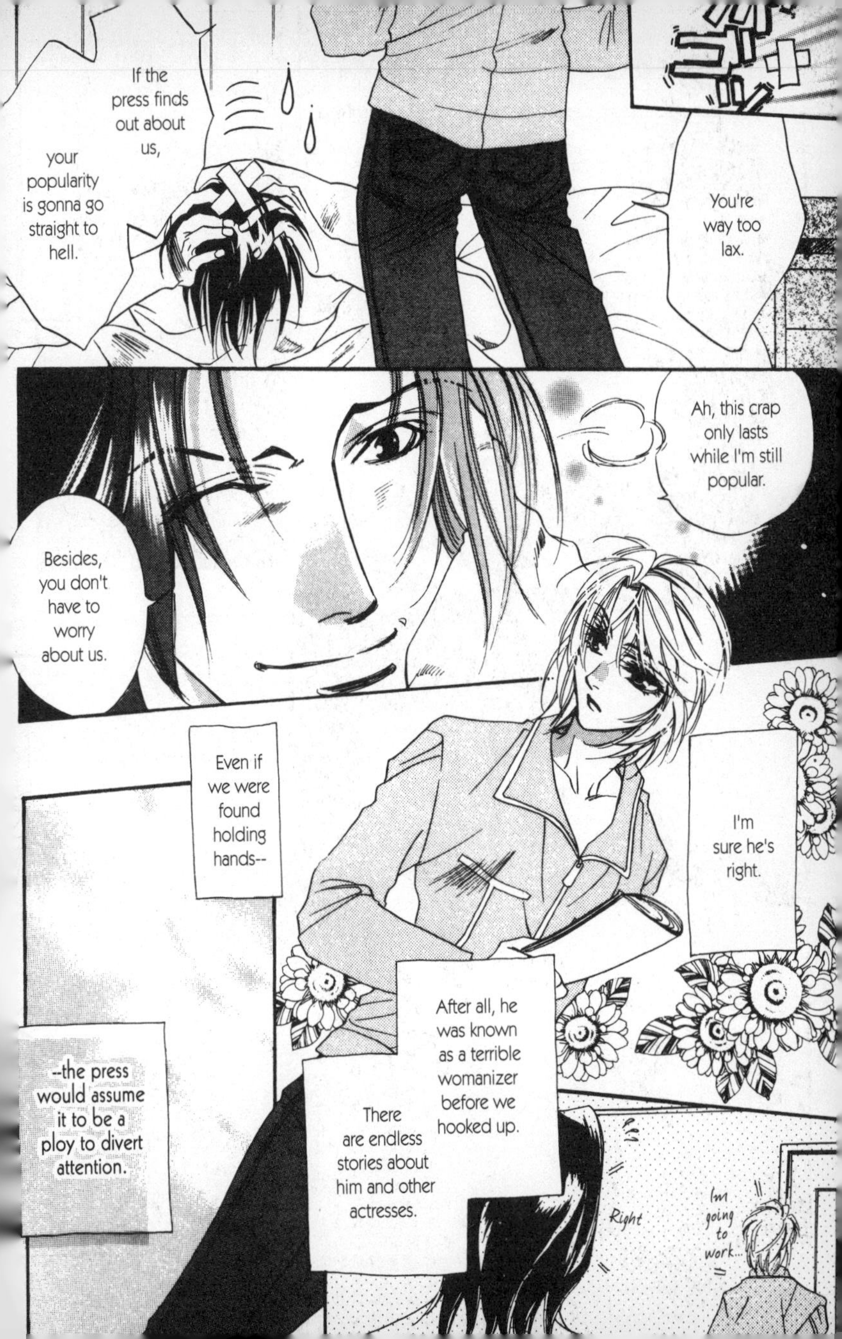
You're way too lax.
If the press finds out about us,
your popularity is gonna go straight to hell.
Ah, this crap only lasts while I'm still popular.
Besides, you don't have to worry about us.
I'm sure he's right.
Even if we were found holding hands--
--the press would assume it to be a ploy to divert attention.
After all, he was known as a terrible womanizer before we hooked up.
There are endless stories about him and other actresses.
I'm going to work...
Right

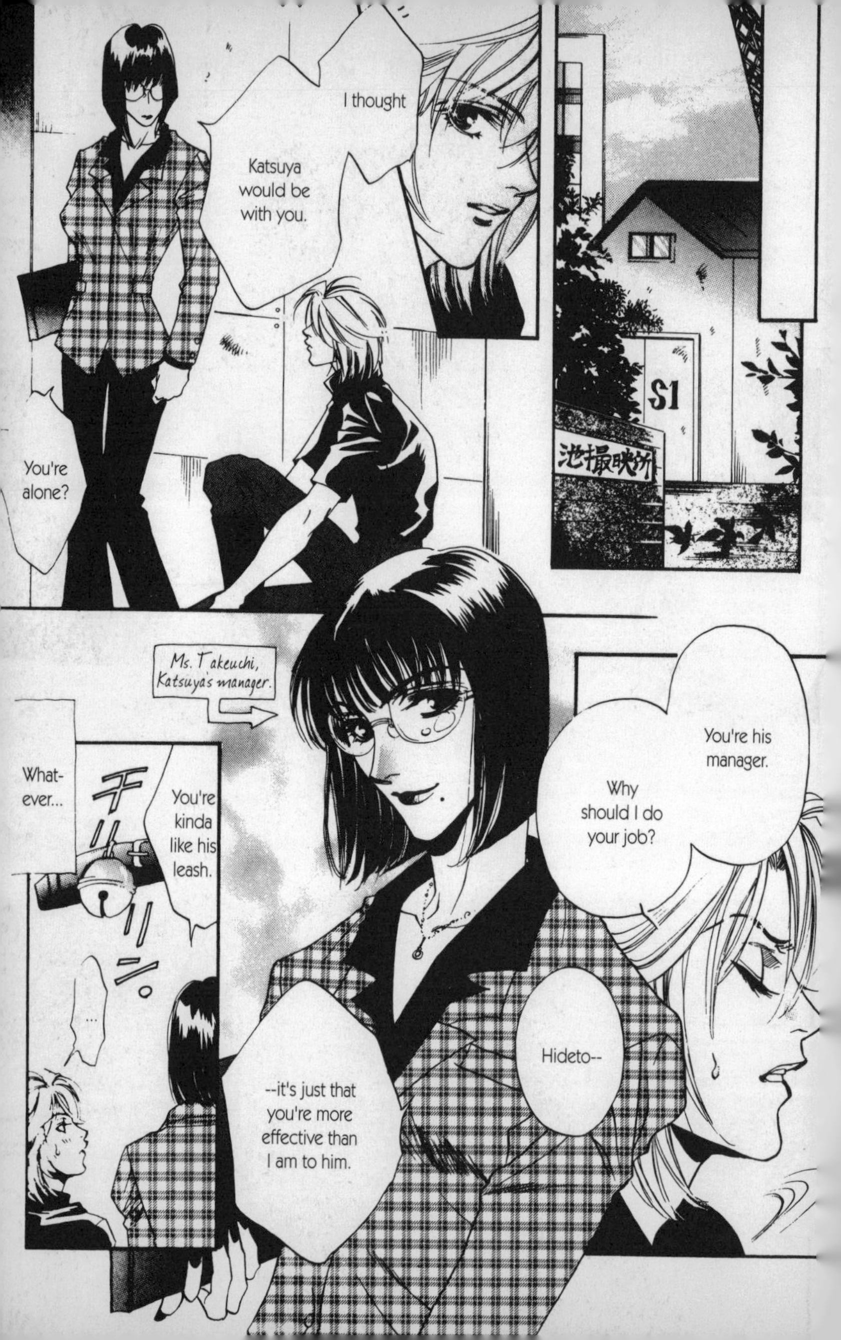
S1
池撮映所
You're alone?
I thought
Katsuya would be with you.
You're his manager.
Why should I do your job?
Hideto--
--it's just that you're more effective than I am to him.
Ms. Takeuchi, Katsuya's manager.
You're kinda like his leash.
What-ever...
チリリン。
...

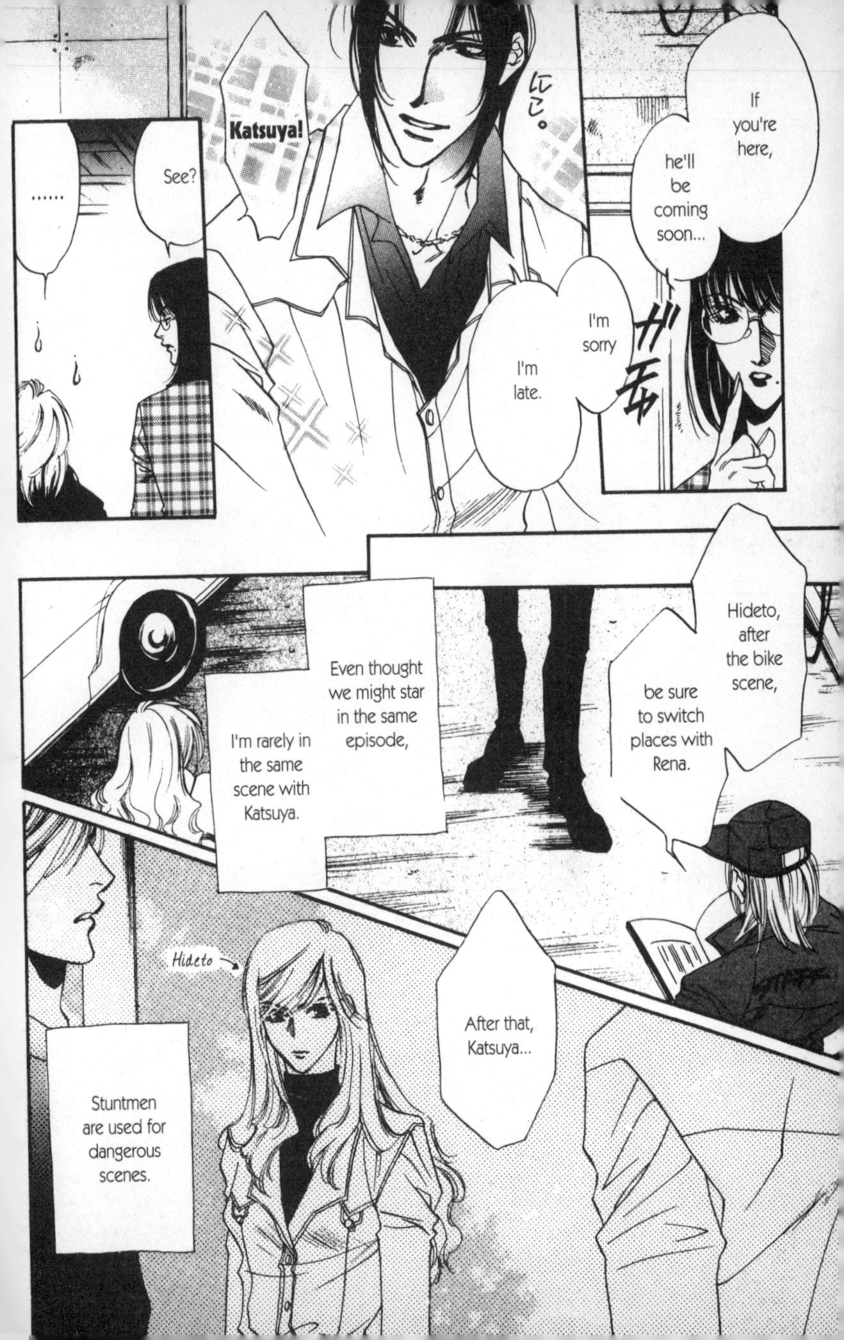

If you're here, he'll be coming soon...
ガチャ
Katsuya!
にこ。
I'm sorry I'm late.
See?
......
Hideto, after the bike scene, be sure to switch places with Rena.
Even thought we might star in the same episode, I'm rarely in the same scene with Katsuya.
After that, Katsuya...
Hideto
Stuntmen are used for dangerous scenes.

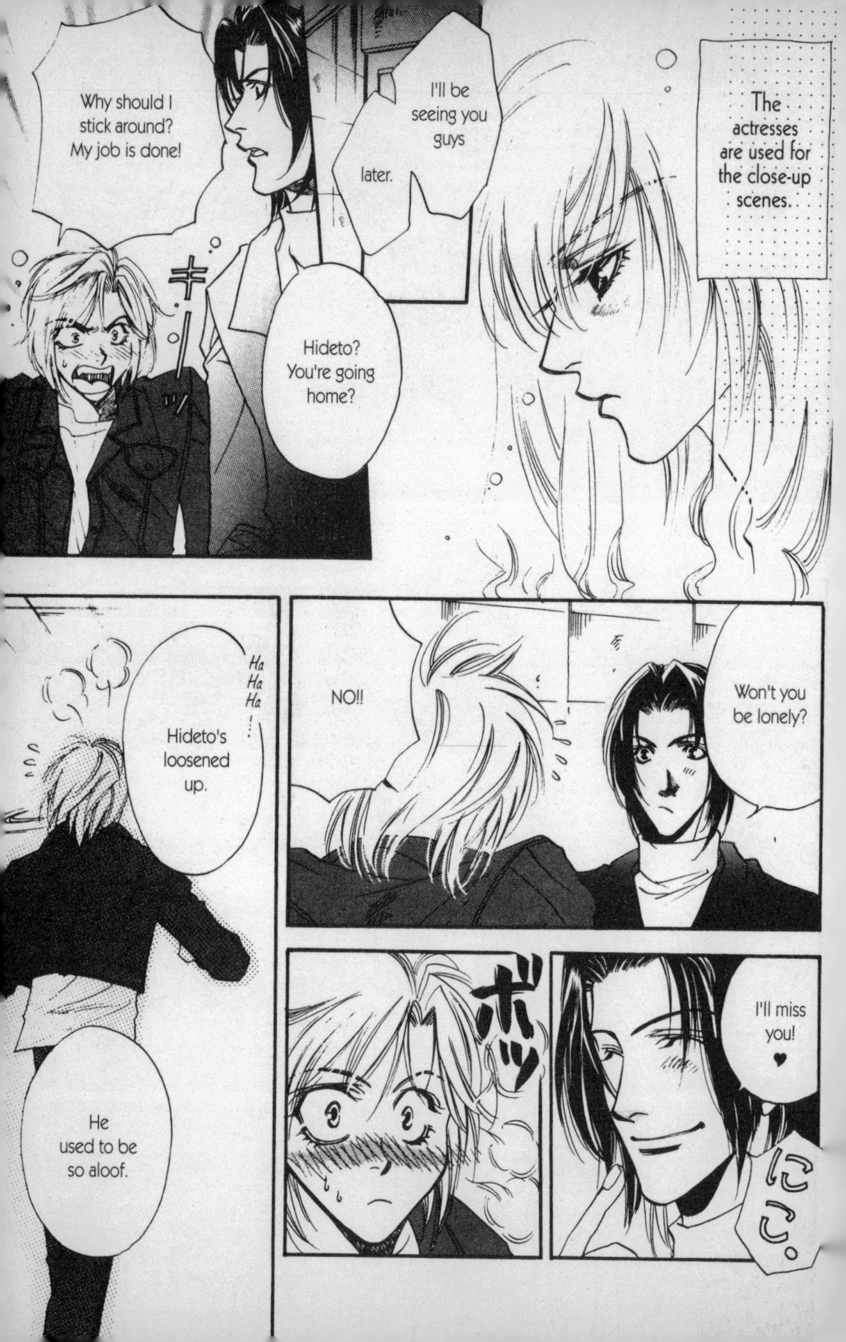
The actresses are used for the close-up scenes.
I'll be seeing you guys
later.
Why should I stick around? My job is done!
Hideto? You're going home?
Won't you be lonely?
NO!!
Ha Ha Ha!
Hideto's loosened up.
He used to be so aloof.
I'll miss you! ♥
ボッ
にこっ

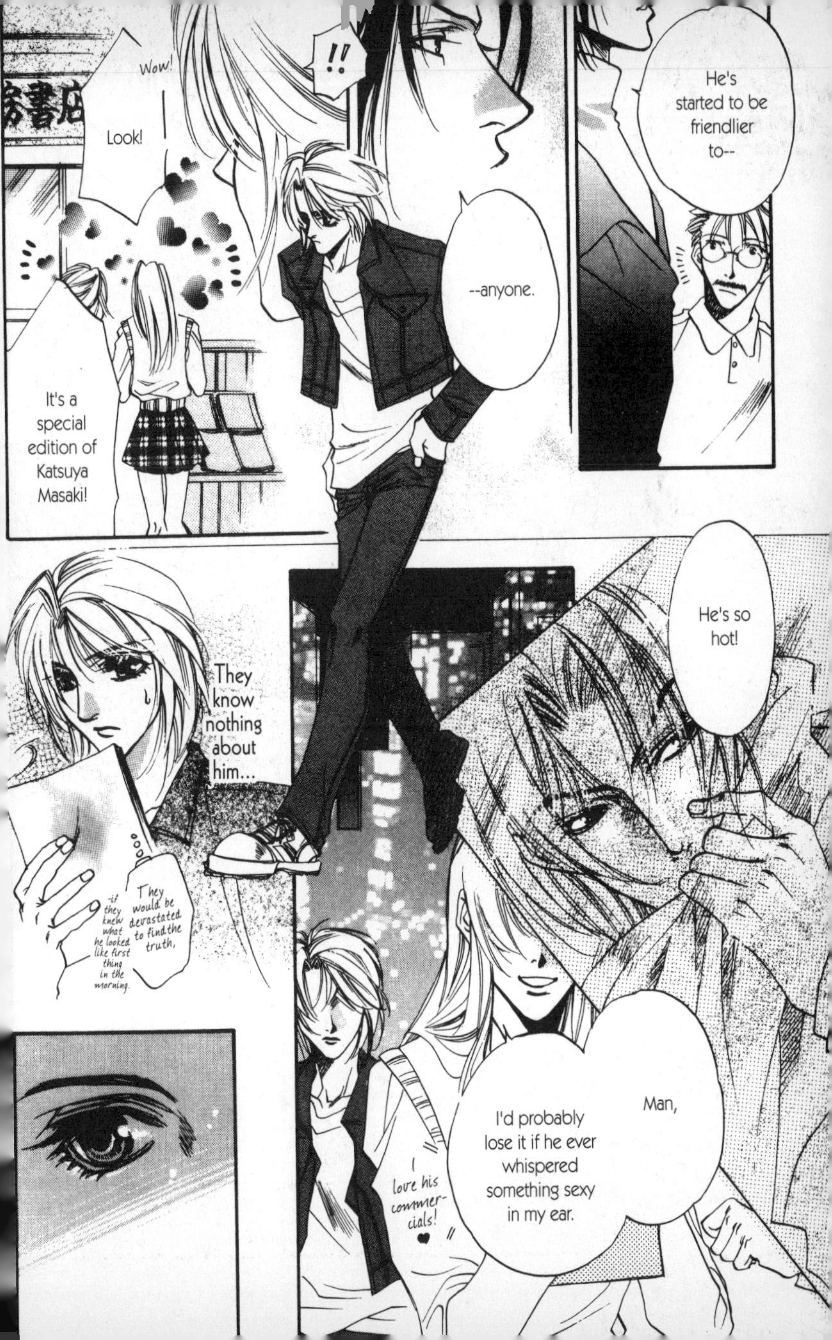

He's started to be friendlier to--
--anyone.
!!
Wow!
Look!
It's a special edition of Katsuya Masaki!
He's so hot!
Man,
I'd probably lose it if he ever whispered something sexy in my ear.
I love his commercials!
They know nothing about him...
They would be devastated to find the truth,
-if they knew what he looked like first thing in the morning.

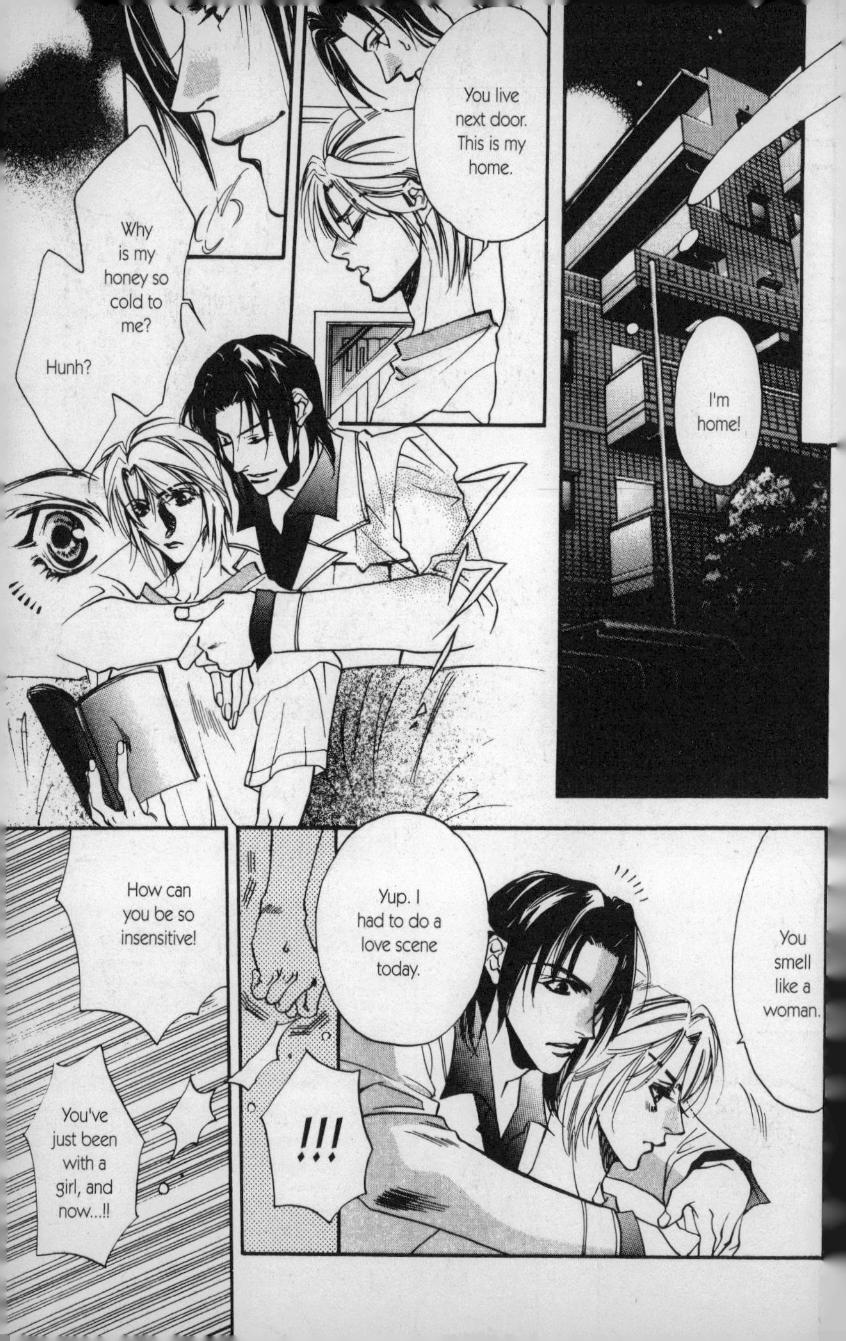
I'm home!
You live next door. This is my home.
Why is my honey so cold to me?
Hunh?
You smell like a woman.
Yup. I had to do a love scene today.
!!!
How can you be so insensitive!
You've just been with a girl, and now...!!

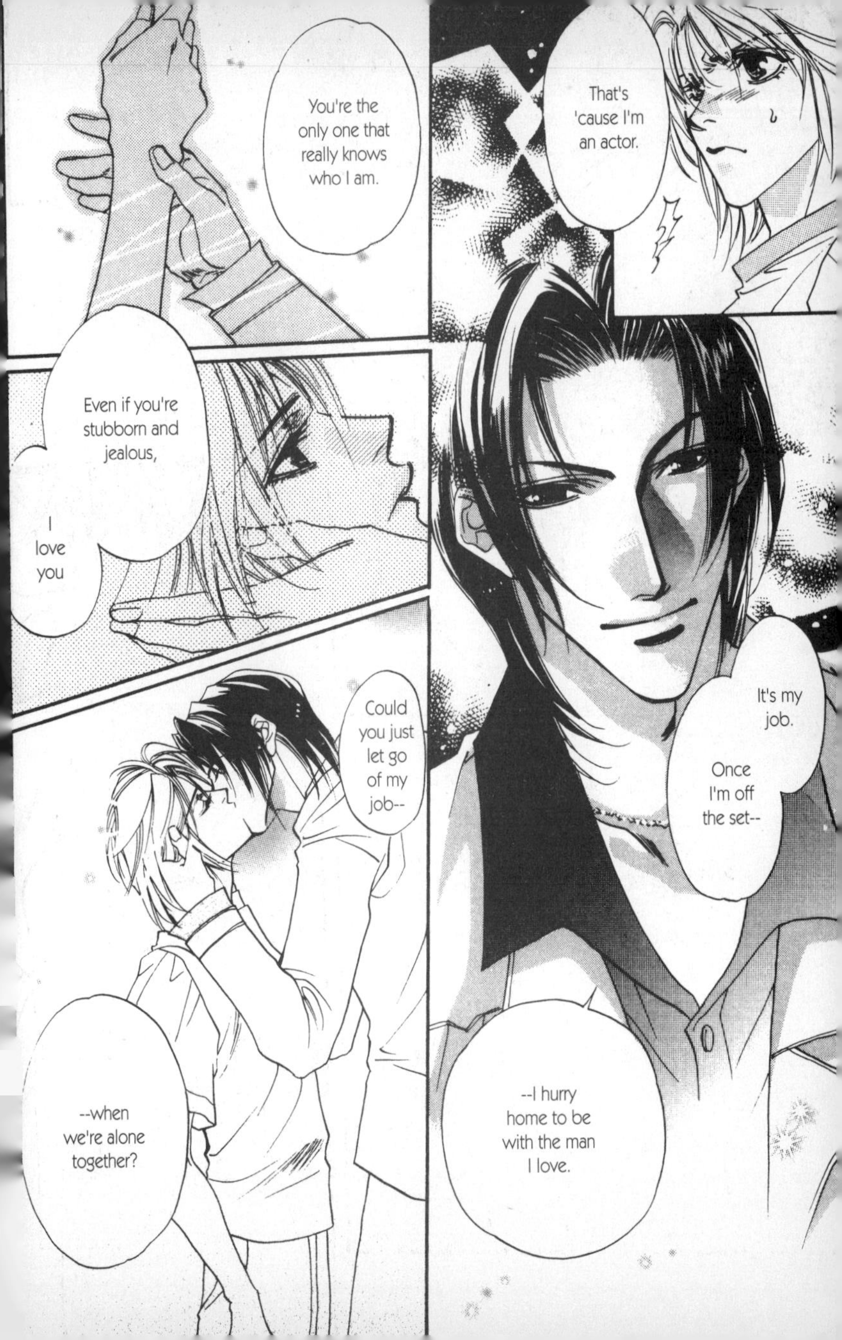
You're the only one that really knows who I am.
Even if you're stubborn and jealous,
I love you
Could you just let go of my job--
--when we're alone together?
That's 'cause I'm an actor.
It's my job.
Once I'm off the set--
--I hurry home to be with the man I love.

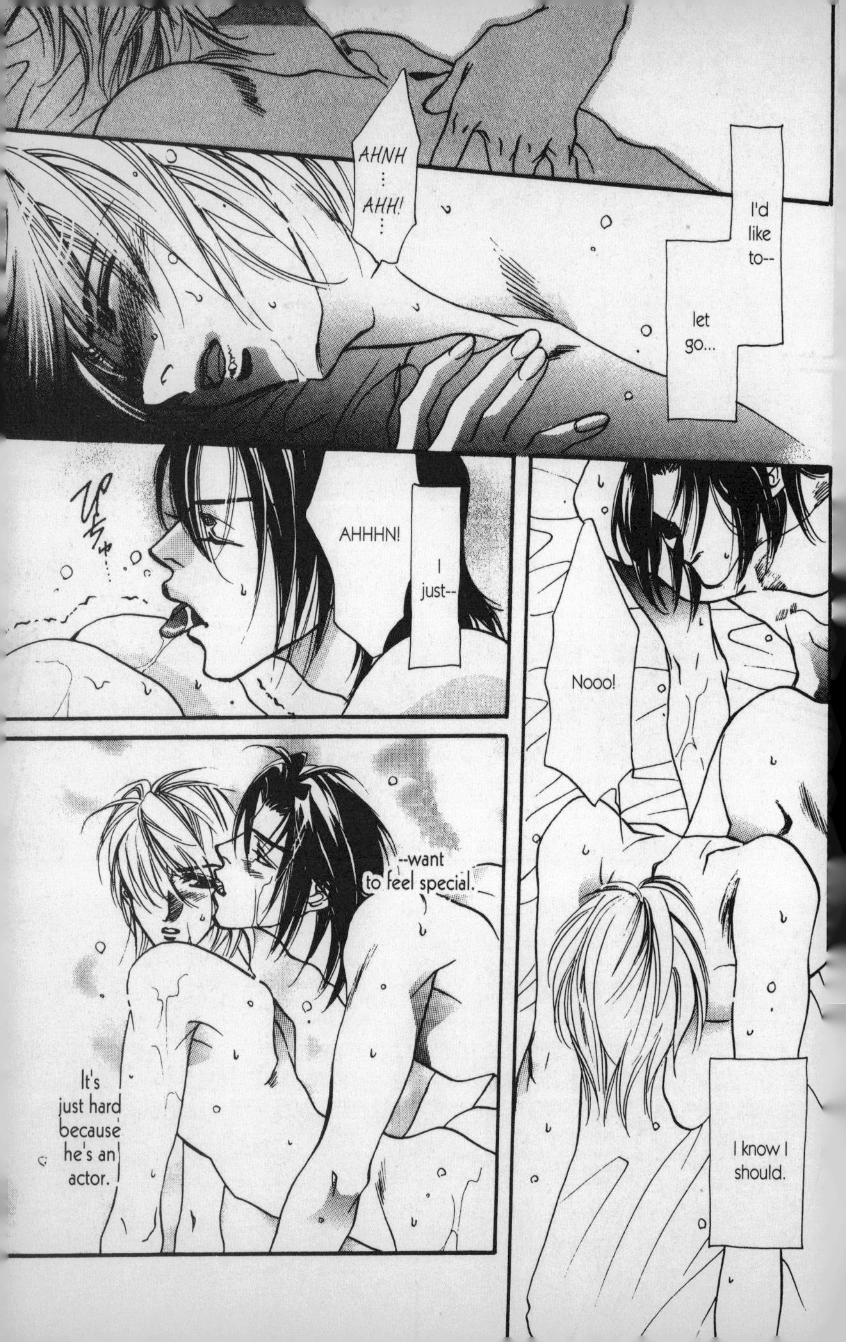
I'd like to--
let go...
AHNH ... AHH! ...
Nooo!
I know I should.
AHHHN!
ぴちゃ…
I just--
--want to feel special.
It's just hard because he's an actor.

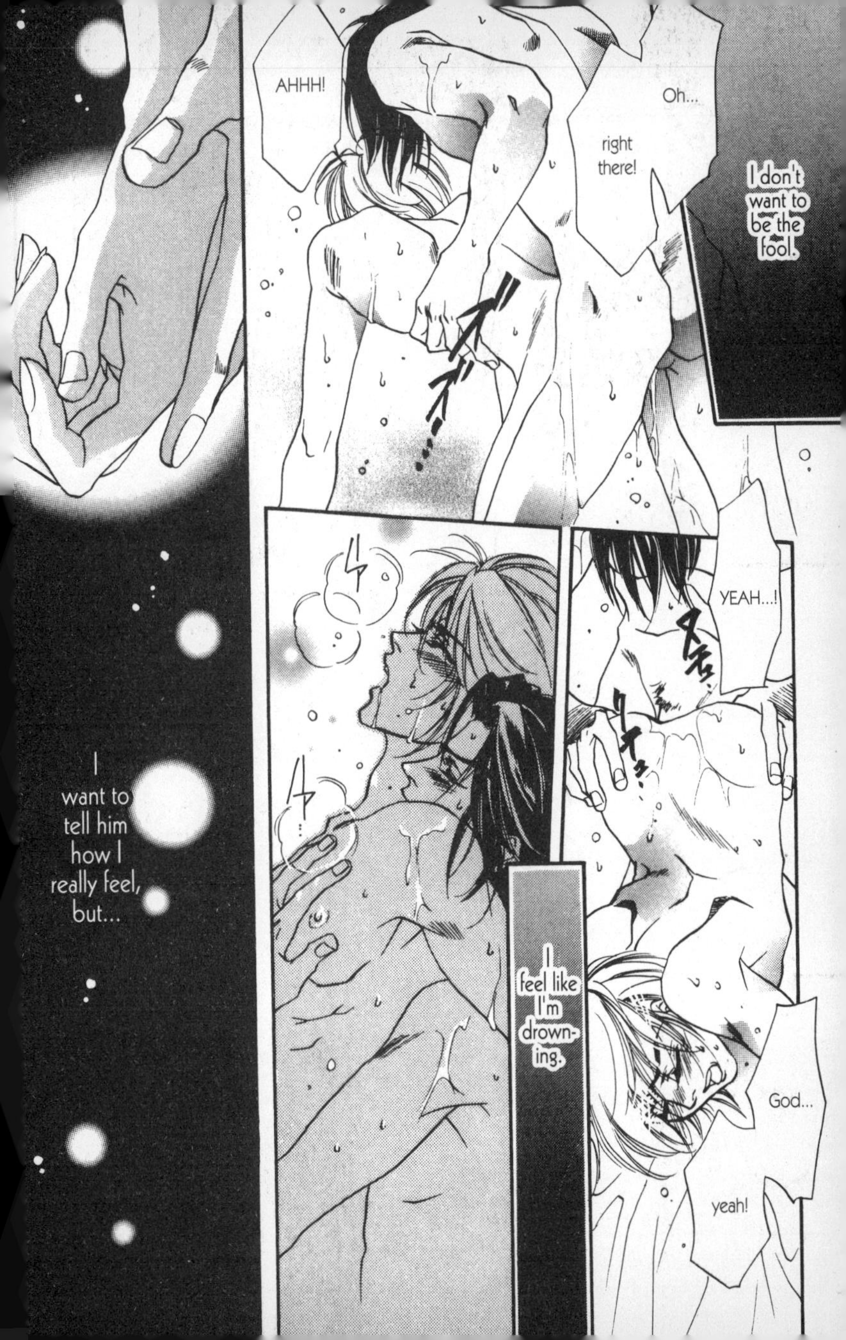

I don't want to be the fool.
Oh...
right there!
AHHH!
YEAH...!
God...
yeah!
I feel like I'm drown-ing.
I want to tell him how I really feel, but...

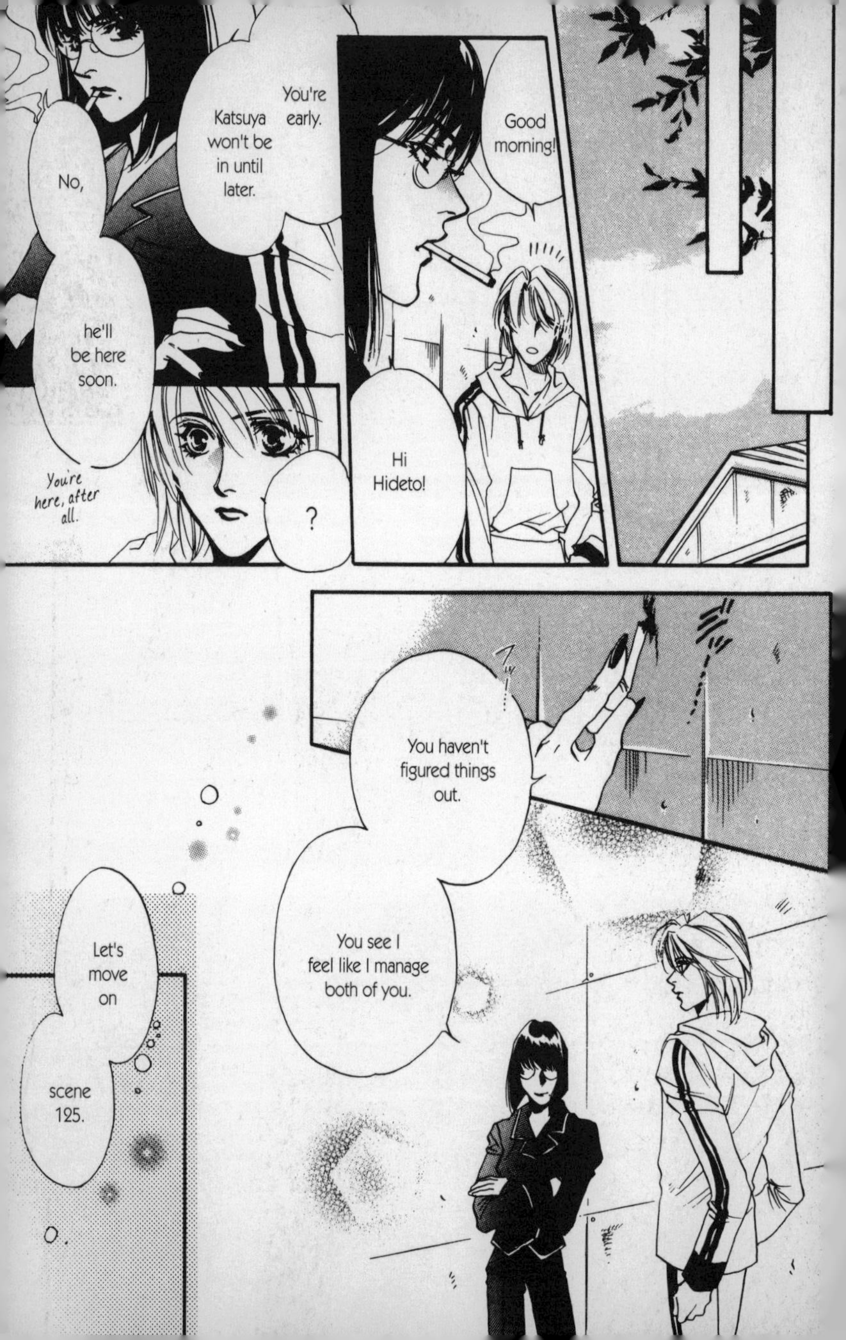
Good morning!
Hi Hideto!
You're early.
Katsuya won't be in until later.
?
No,
he'll be here soon.
You're here, after all.
フッ…
You haven't figured things out.
You see I feel like I manage both of you.
Let's move on
scene 125.

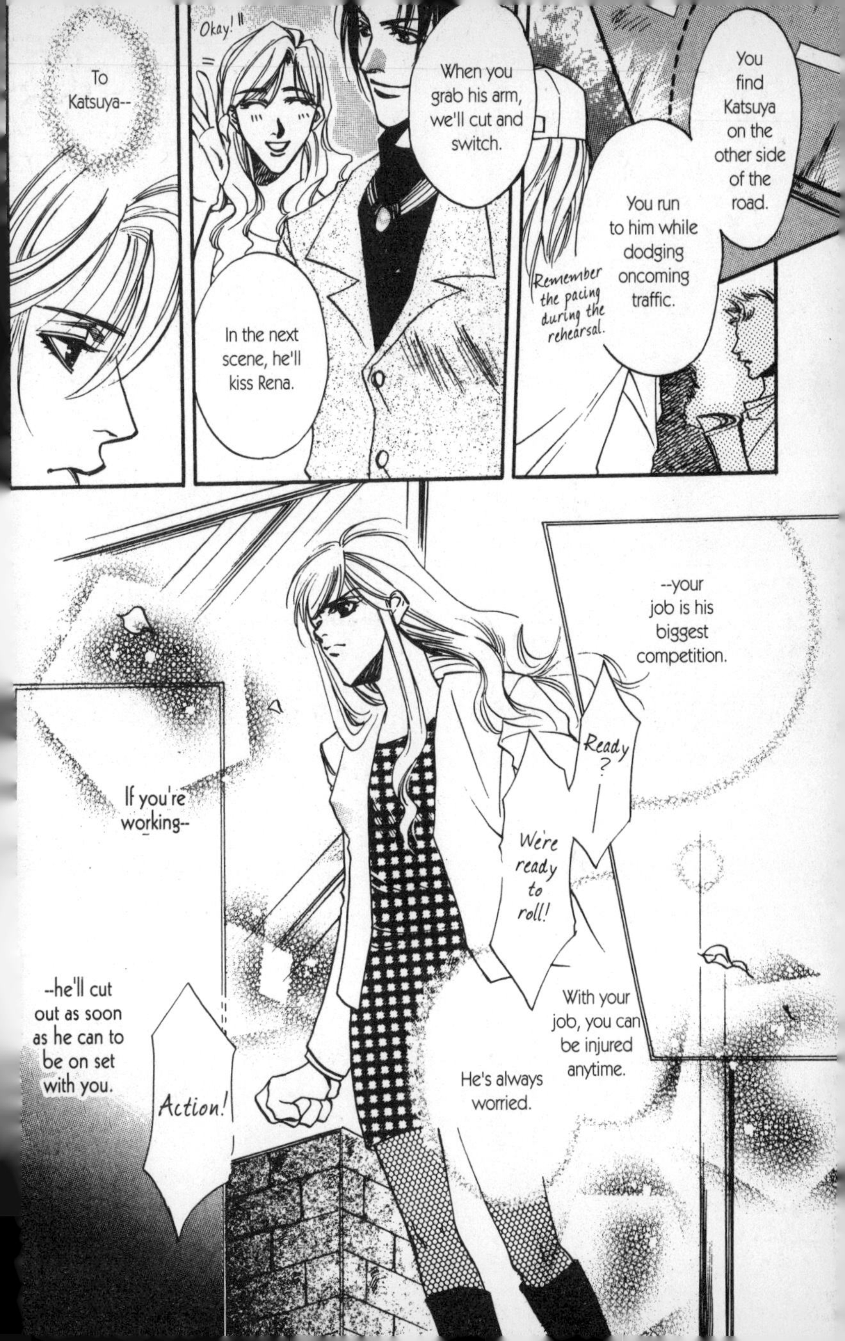
You find Katsuya on the other side of the road.
You run to him while dodging oncoming traffic.
Remember the pacing during the rehearsal.
When you grab his arm, we'll cut and switch.
In the next scene, he'll kiss Rena.
Okay!!
To Katsuya--
--your job is his biggest competition.
Ready?
We're ready to roll!
With your job, you can be injured anytime.
He's always worried.
If you're working--
--he'll cut out as soon as he can to be on set with you.
Action!

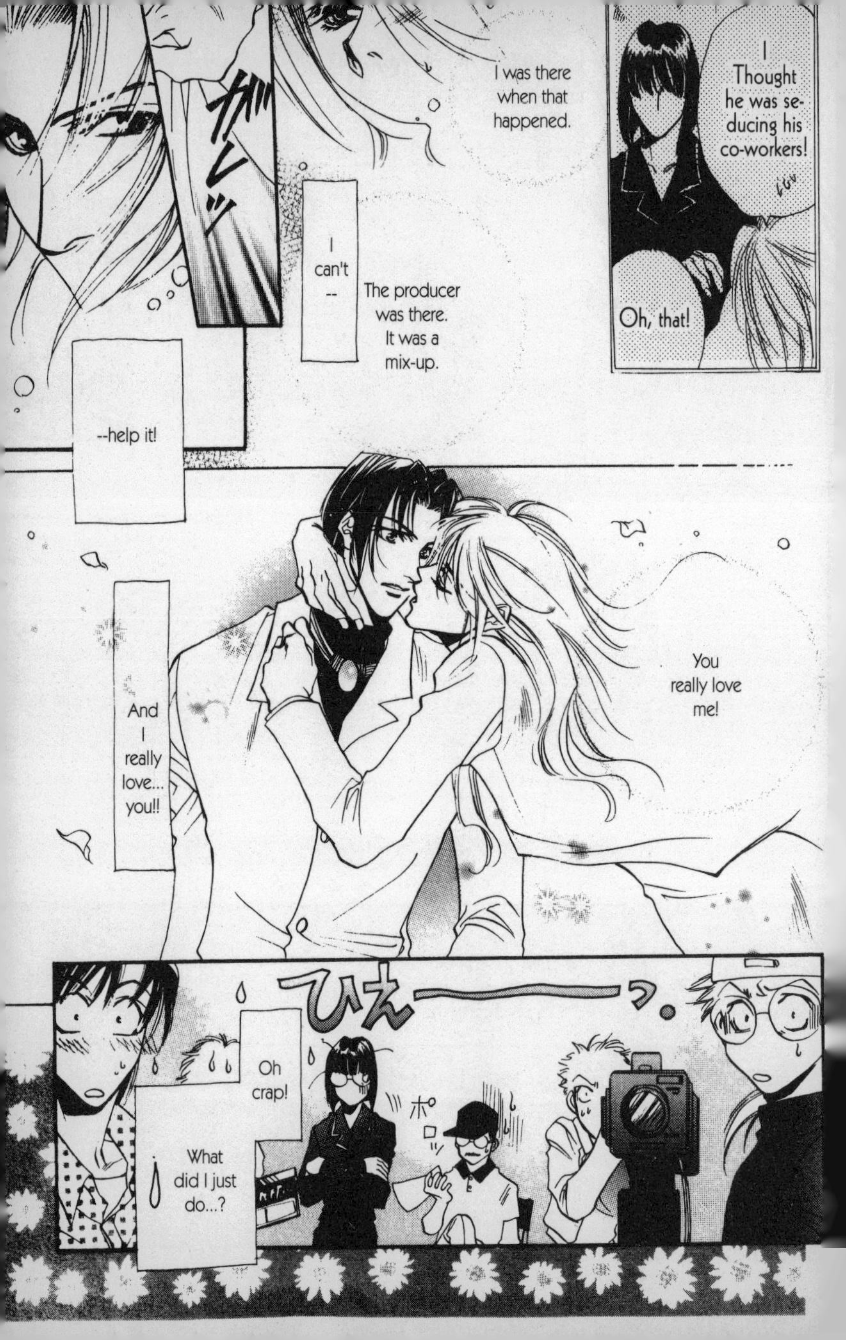
I Thought he was seducing his co-workers!
Oh, that!
I was there when that happened.
The producer was there. It was a mix-up.
I can't --
--help it!
You really love me!
And I really love... you!!
ひえ——っ。
Oh crap!
What did I just do...?

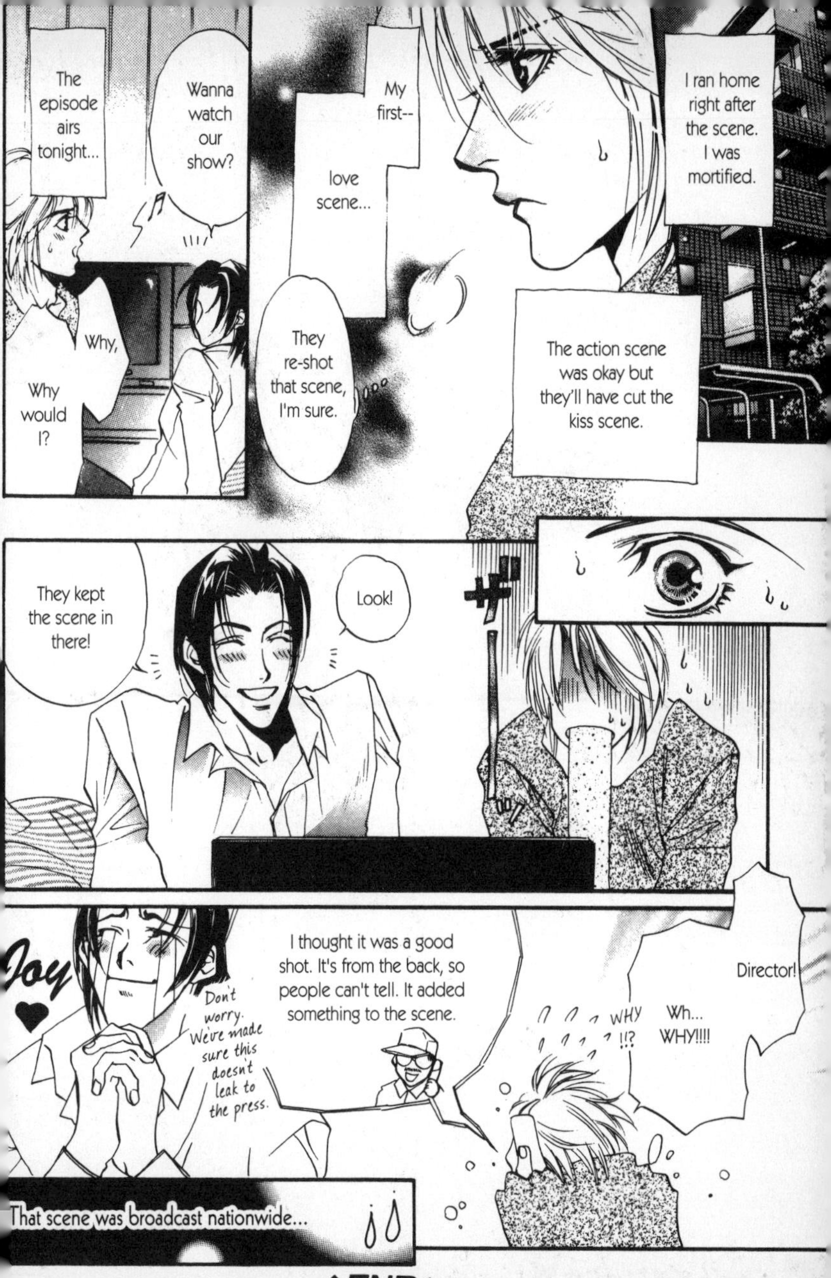

I ran home right after the scene. I was mortified.
The action scene was okay but they'll have cut the kiss scene.
My first--
love scene...
They re-shot that scene, I'm sure.
Wanna watch our show?
The episode airs tonight...
Why,
Why would I?
Look!
They kept the scene in there!
Director!
Wh... WHY!!!!
WHY !!?
I thought it was a good shot. It's from the back, so people can't tell. It added something to the scene.
Don't worry. We're made sure this doesn't leak to the press.
Joy
That scene was broadcast nationwide...

◆END◆

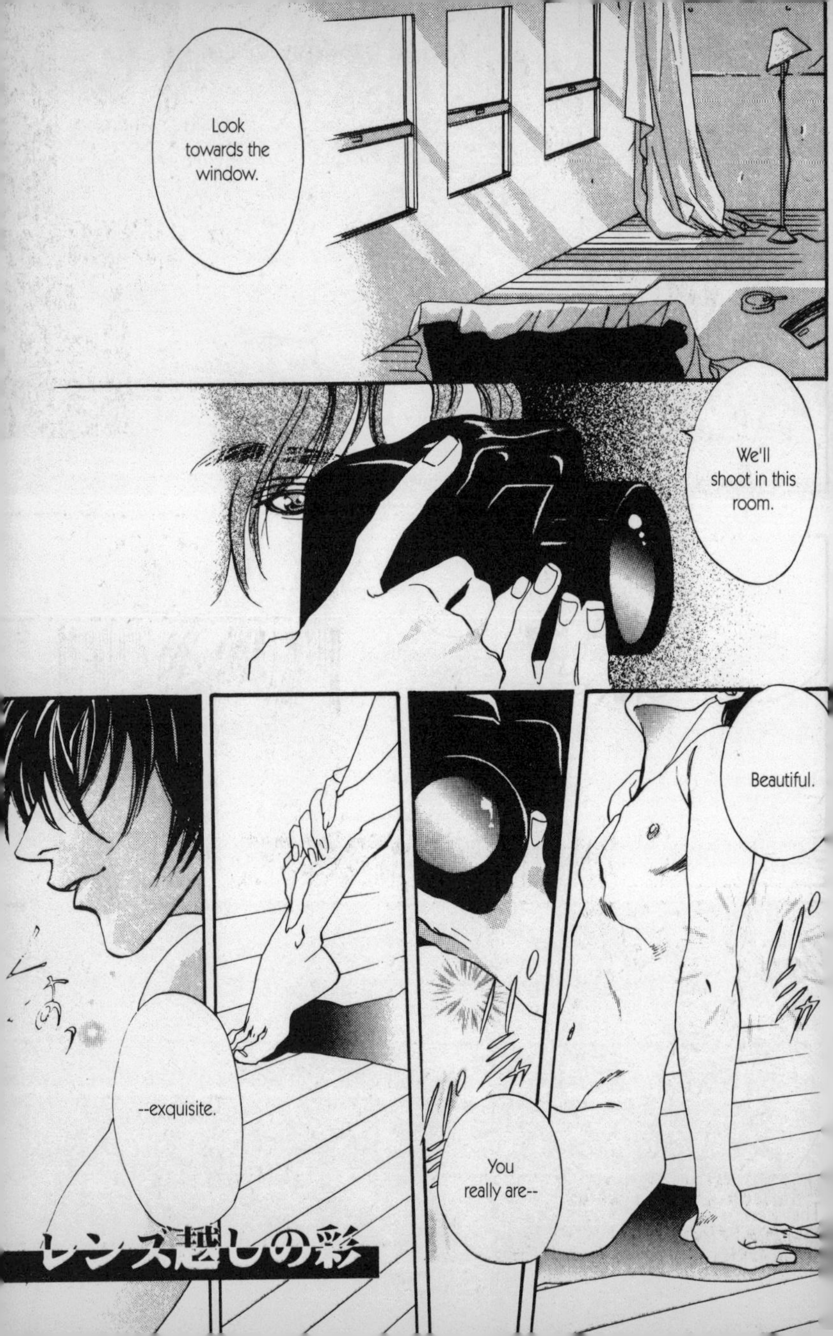
Look towards the window.
We'll shoot in this room.
Beautiful.
You really are--
--exquisite.
レンズ越しの彩

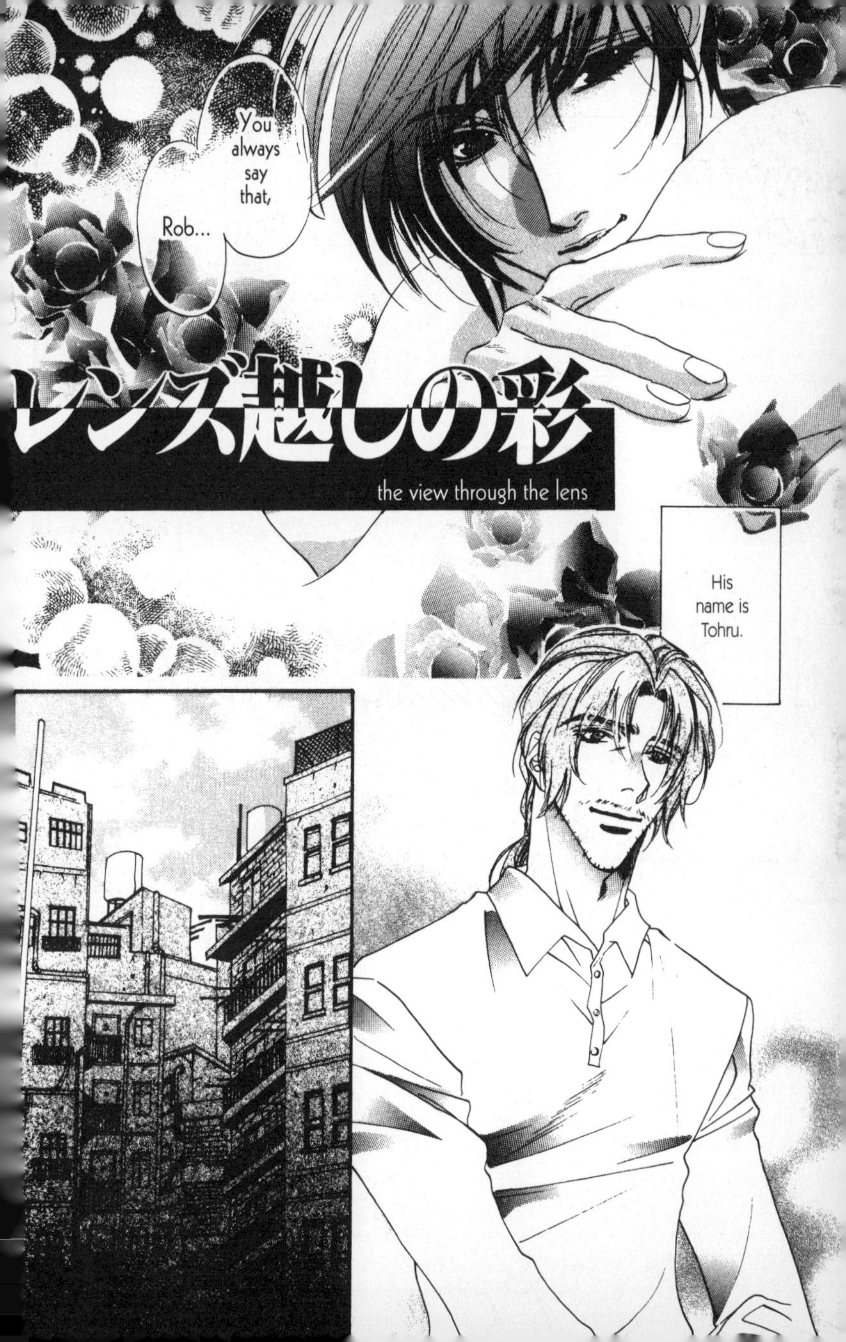

You always say that, Rob...
レンズ越しの彩
the view through the lens
His name is Tohru.

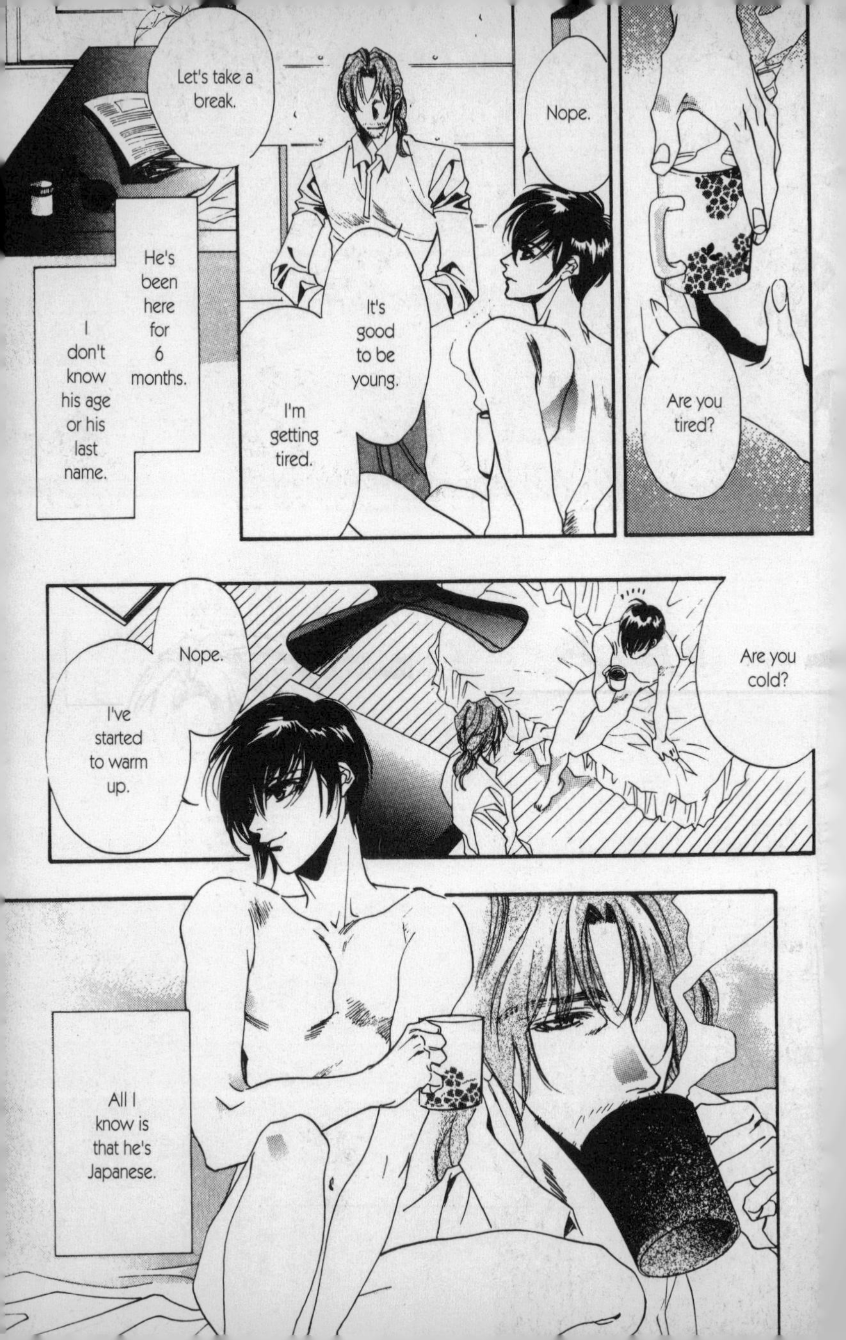
Are you tired?
Nope.
It's good to be young.
I'm getting tired.
Let's take a break.
He's been here for 6 months.
I don't know his age or his last name.
Are you cold?
Nope.
I've started to warm up.
All I know is that he's Japanese.

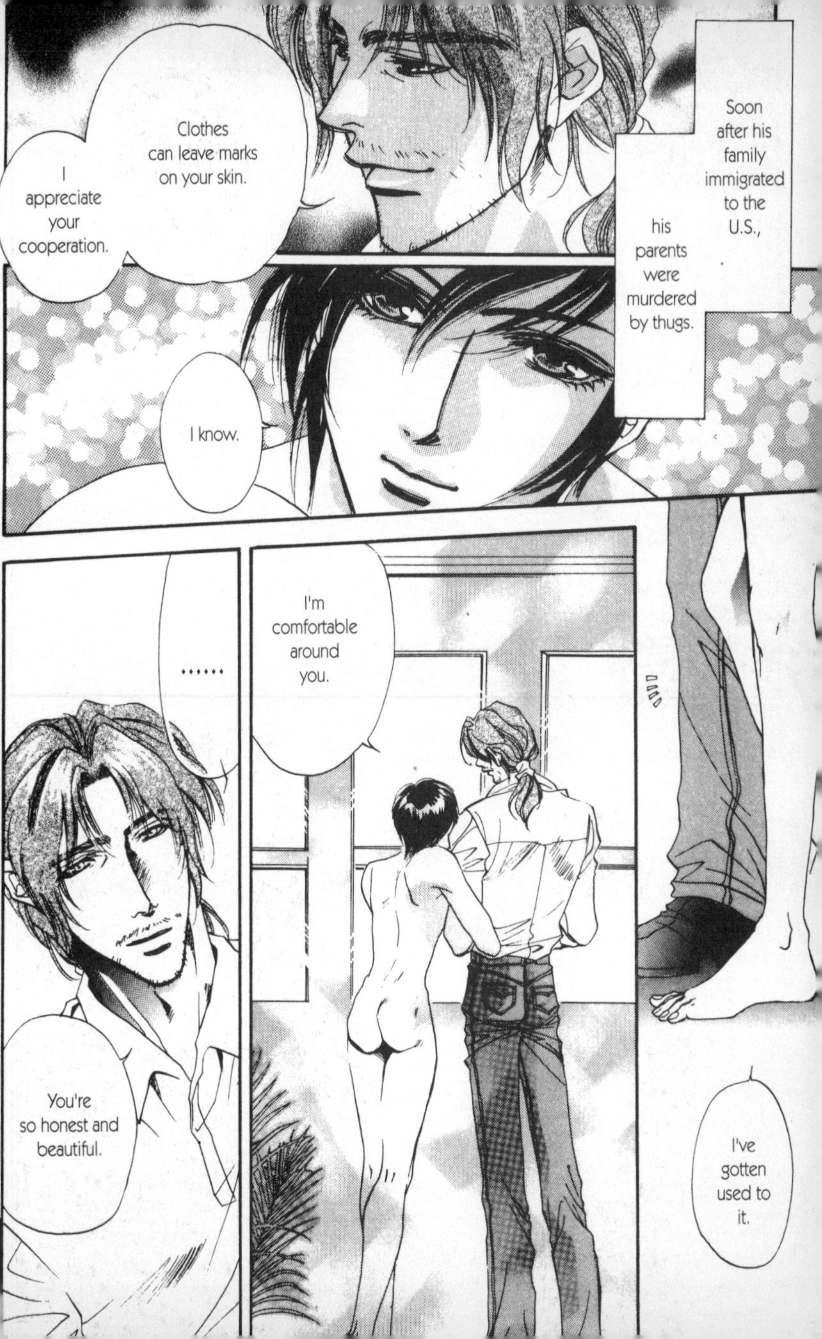
Soon after his family immigrated to the U.S.,
his parents were murdered by thugs.
Clothes can leave marks on your skin.
I appreciate your cooperation.
I know.
I'm comfortable around you.
......
You're so honest and beautiful.
I've gotten used to it.

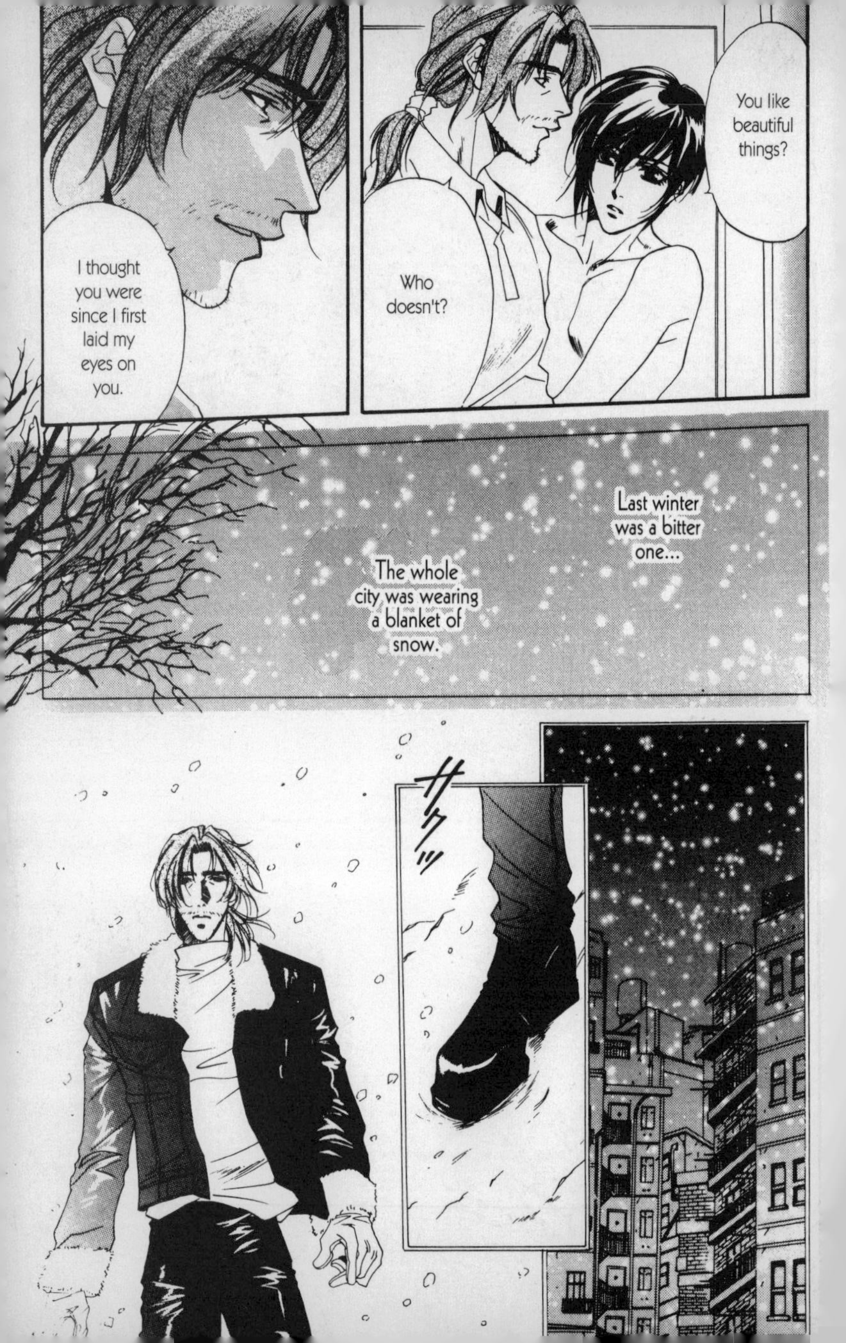
You like beautiful things?
Who doesn't?
I thought you were since I first laid my eyes on you.
Last winter was a bitter one...
The whole city was wearing a blanket of snow.
サクッ

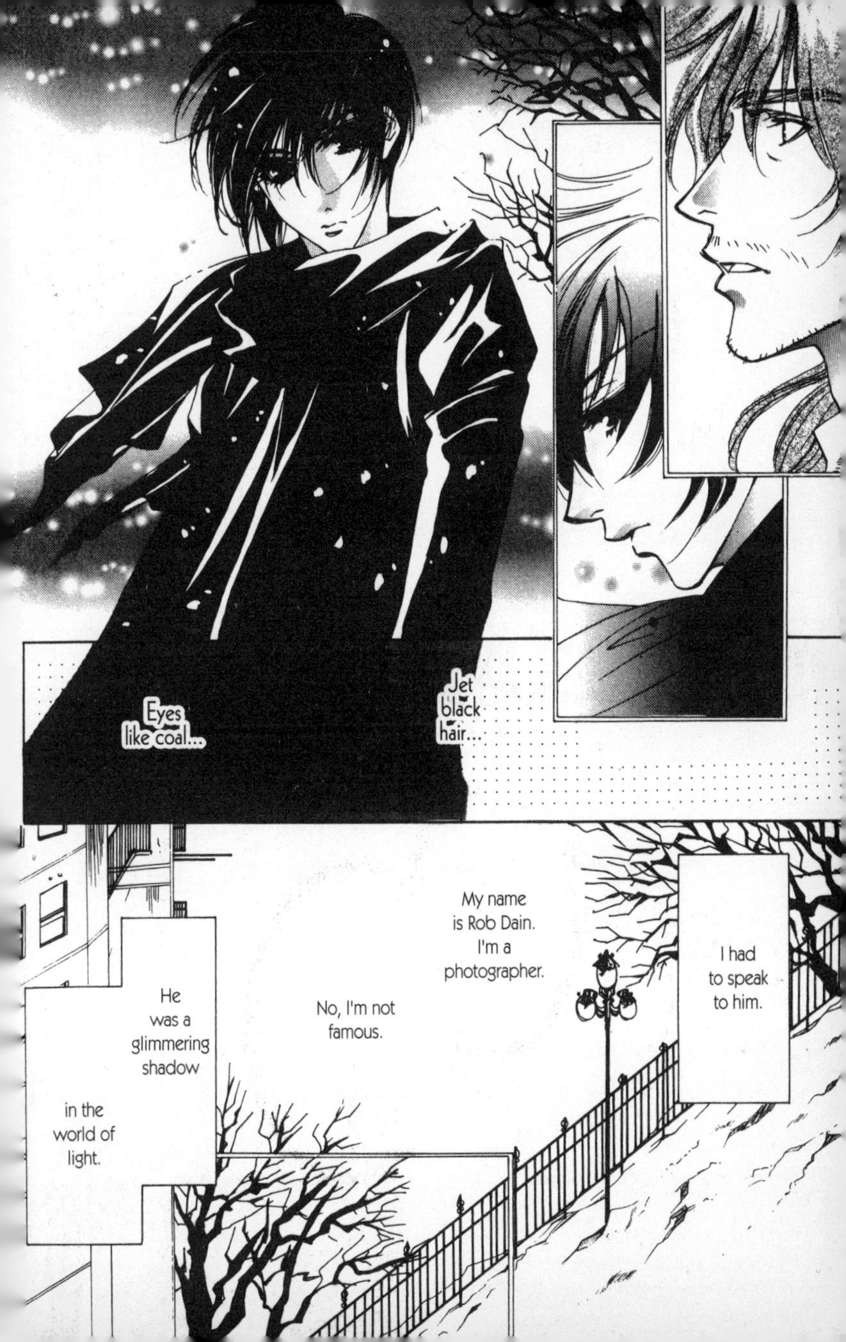

Jet black hair...
Eyes like coal...
I had to speak to him.
My name is Rob Dain. I'm a photographer.
No, I'm not famous.
He was a glimmering shadow
in the world of light.

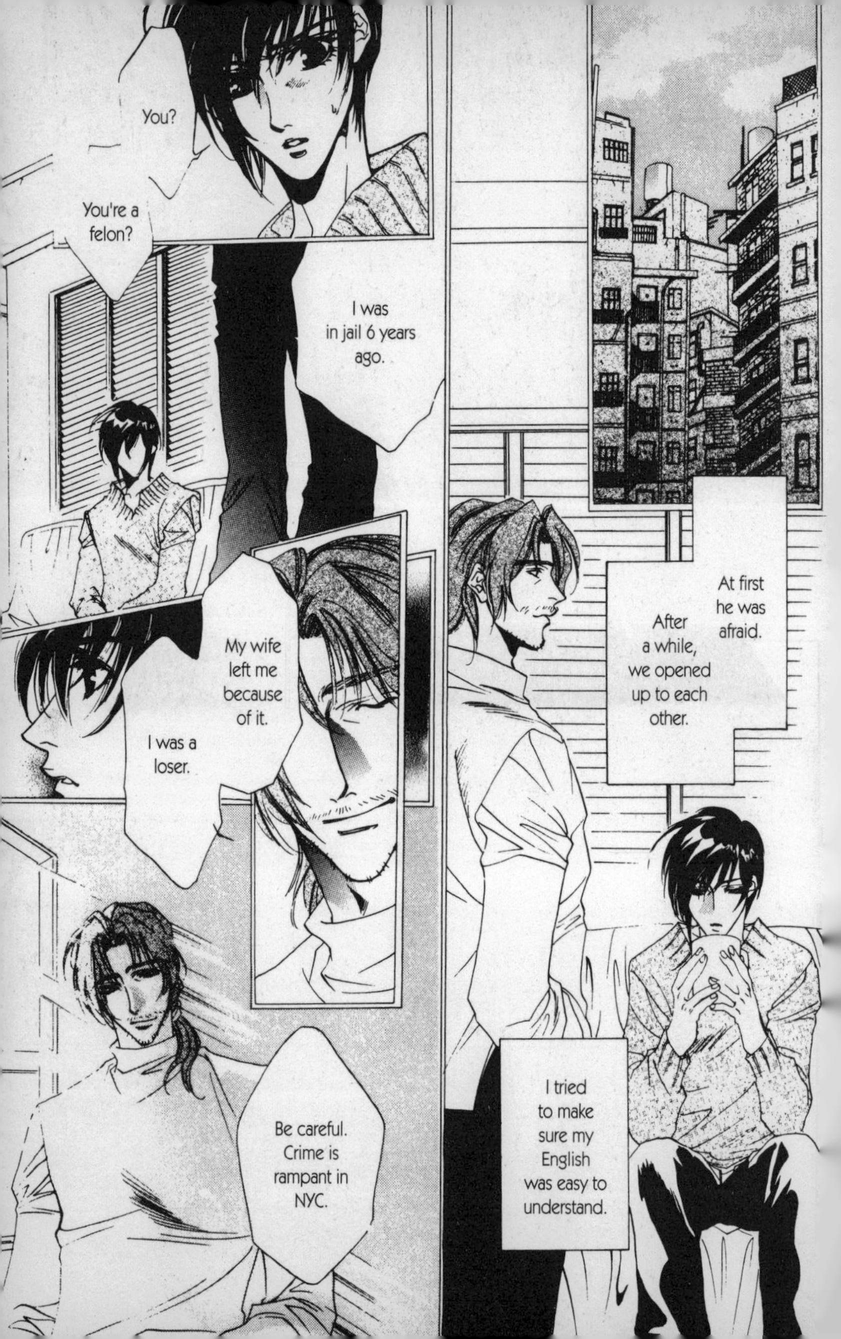
You?
You're a felon?
I was in jail 6 years ago.
My wife left me because of it.
I was a loser.
Be careful. Crime is rampant in NYC.
At first he was afraid.
After a while, we opened up to each other.
I tried to make sure my English was easy to understand.

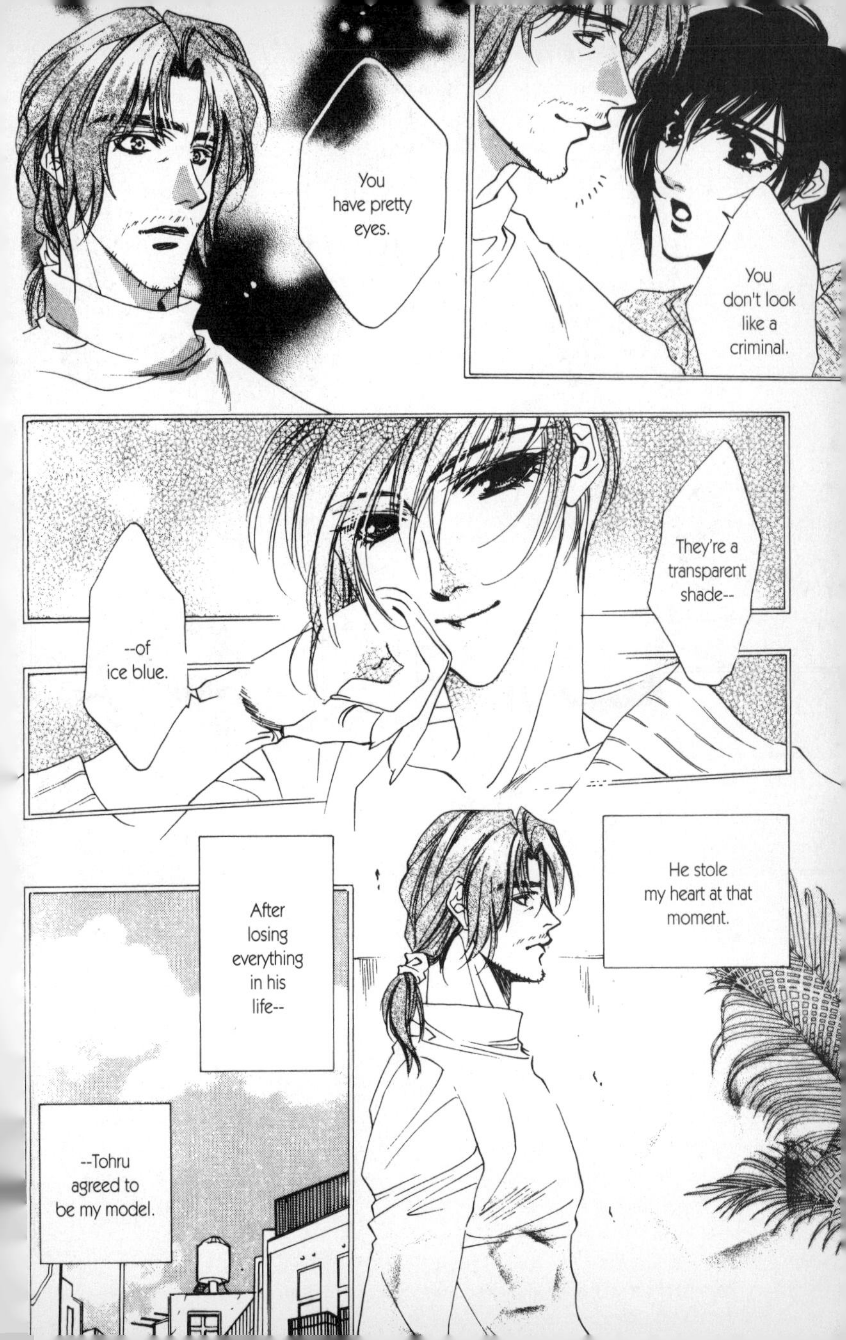
You have pretty eyes.
You don't look like a criminal.
They're a transparent shade--
--of ice blue.
He stole my heart at that moment.
After losing everything in his life--
--Tohru agreed to be my model.

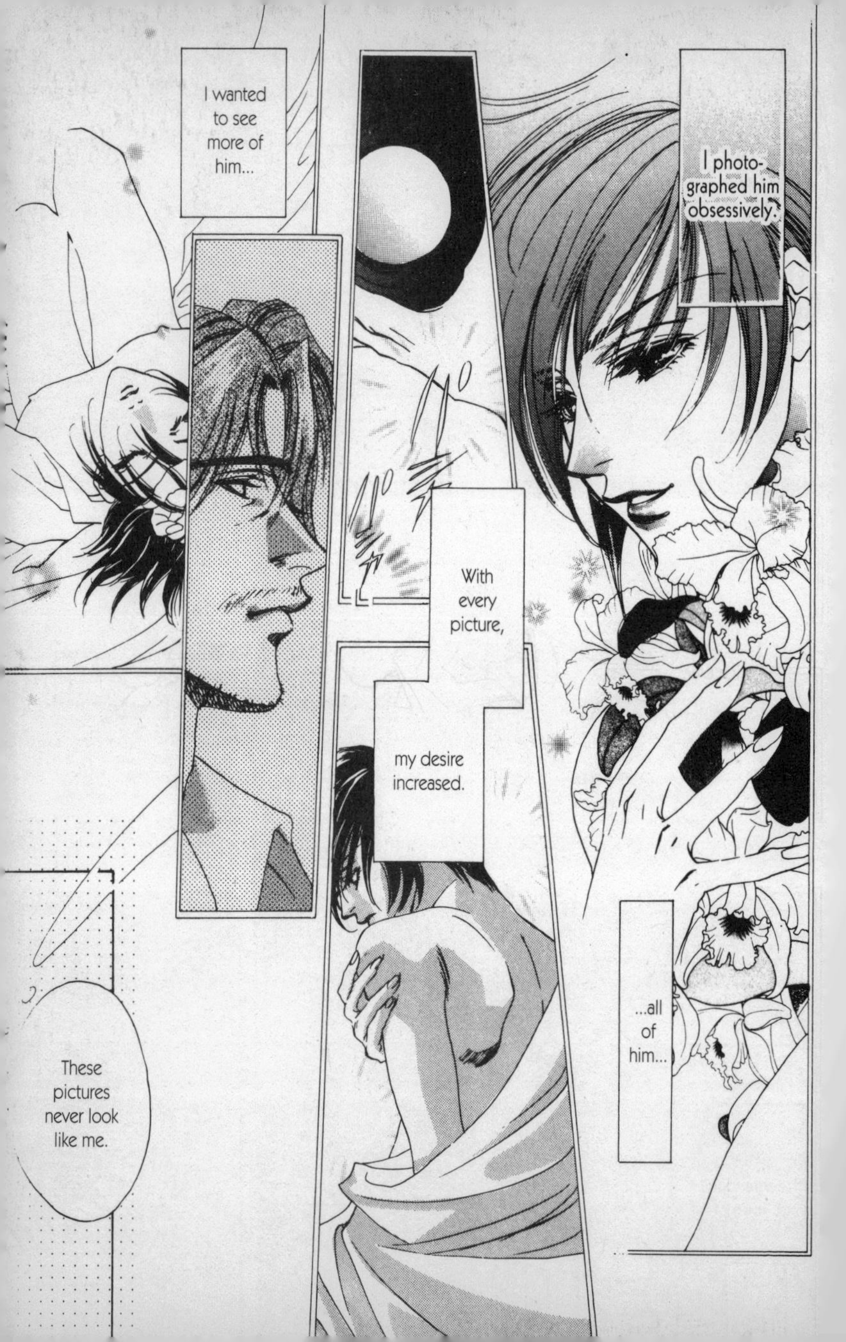

I photographed him obsessively.
With every picture,
my desire increased.
I wanted to see more of him...
...all of him...
These pictures never look like me.

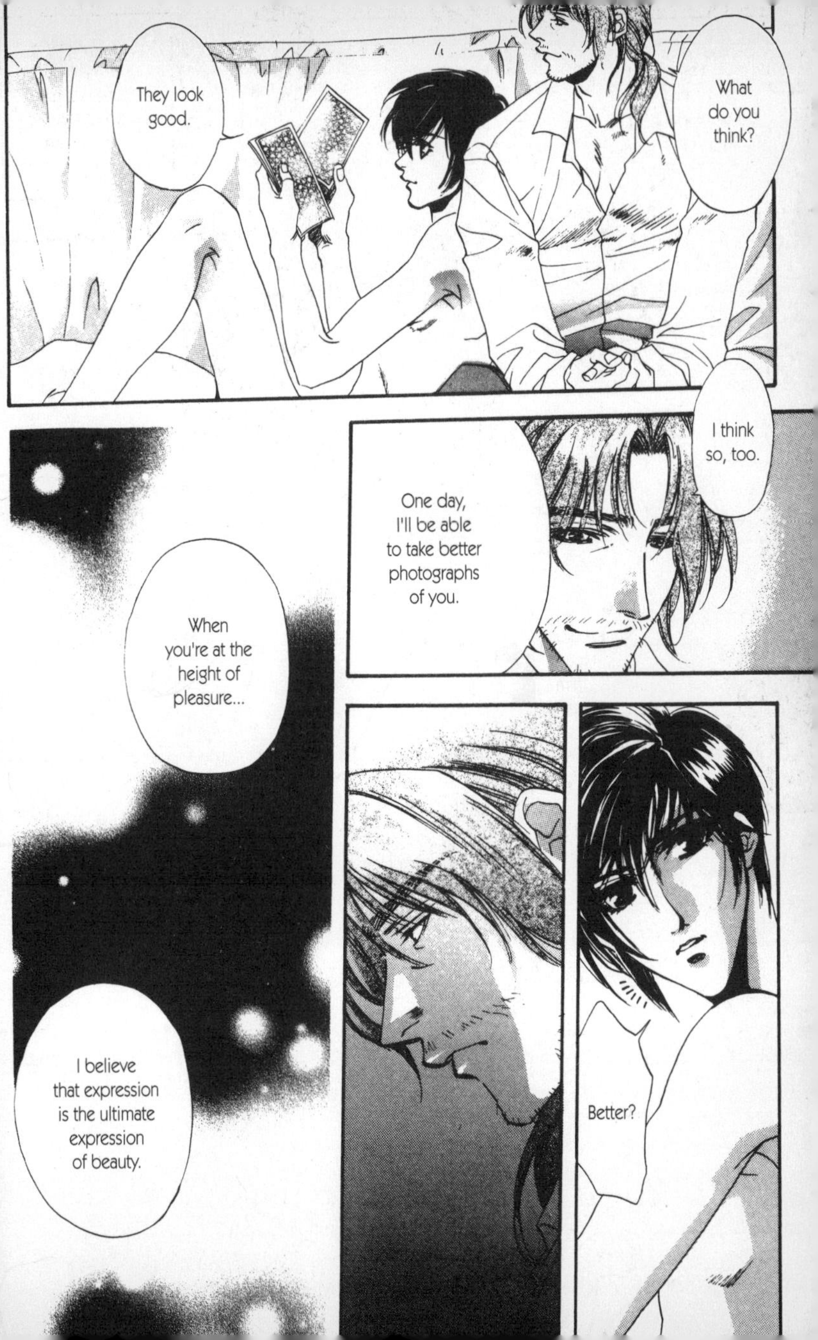
What do you think?
They look good.
I think so, too.
One day, I'll be able to take better photographs of you.
When you're at the height of pleasure...
Better?
I believe that expression is the ultimate expression of beauty.

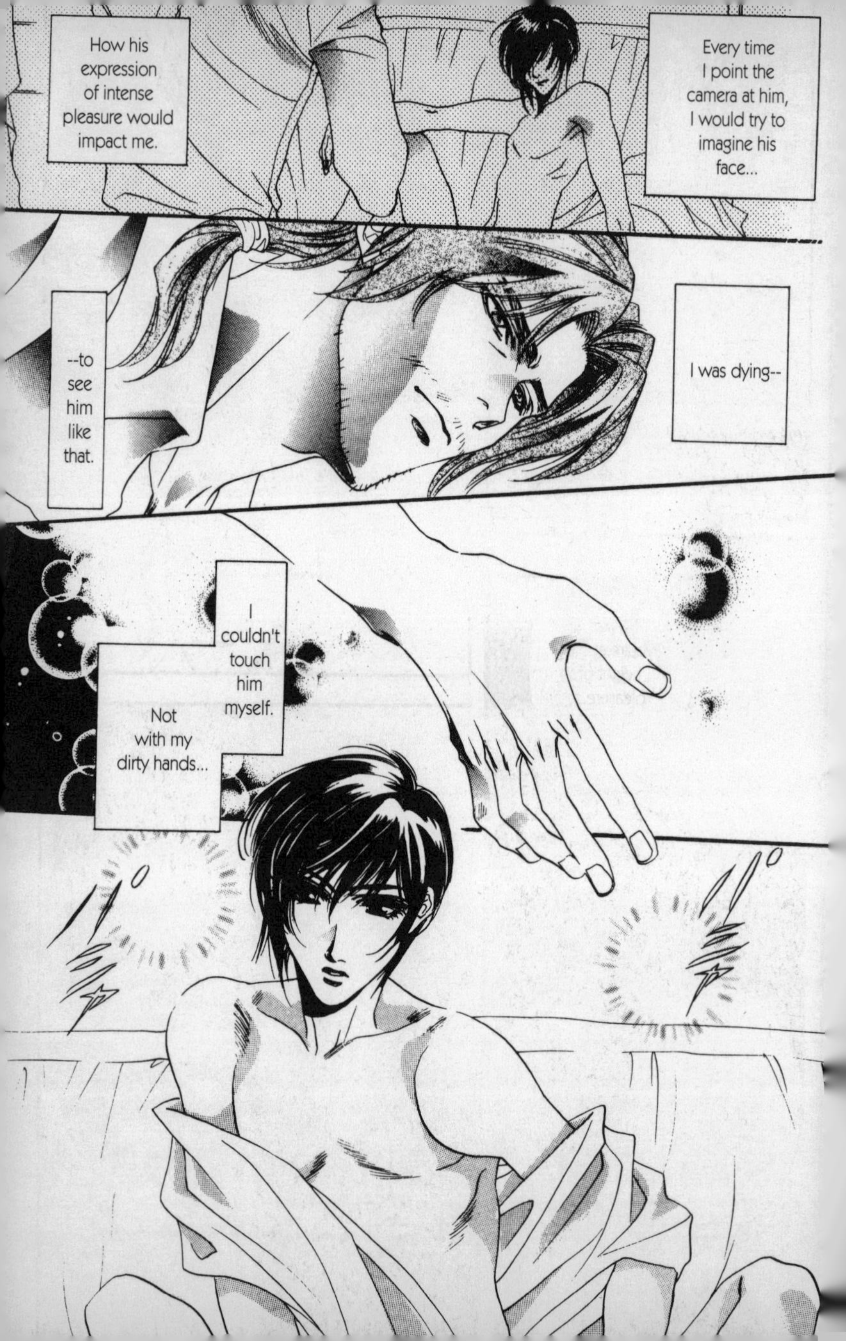
Every time I point the camera at him, I would try to imagine his face...
How his expression of intense pleasure would impact me.
I was dying--
--to see him like that.
I couldn't touch him myself.
Not with my dirty hands...

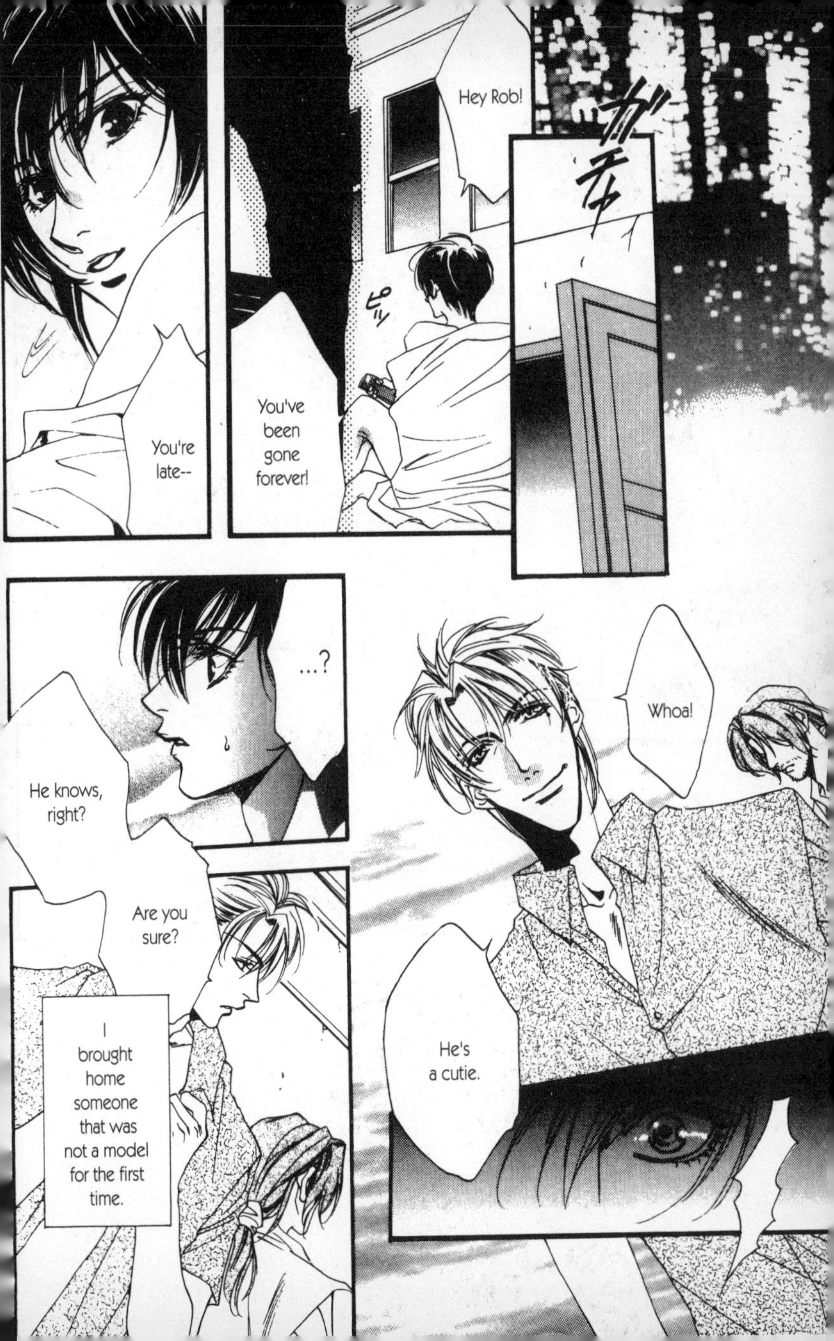
ガチャ
Hey Rob!
ピッ
You've been gone forever!
You're late--
Whoa!
He's a cutie.
...?
He knows, right?
Are you sure?
I brought home someone that was not a model for the first time.

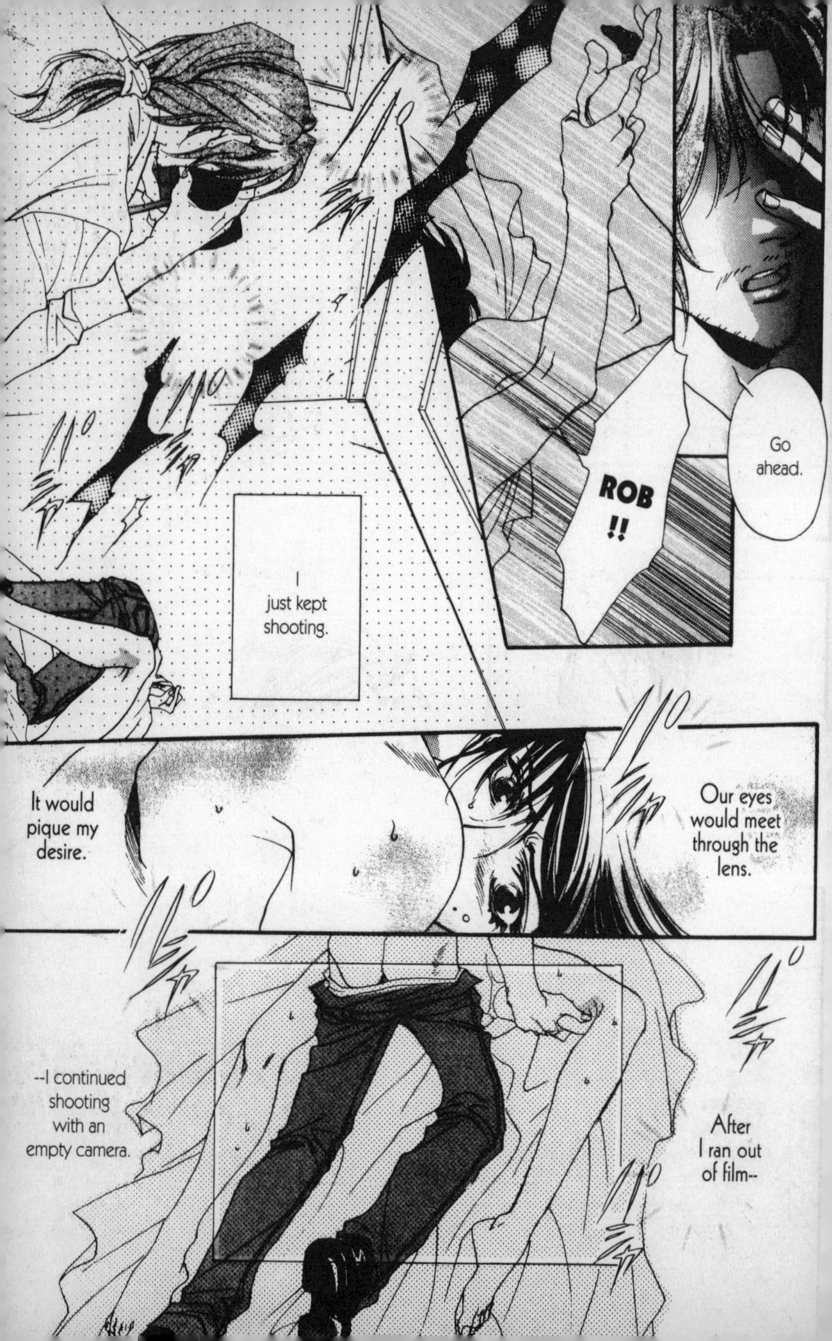

Go ahead.
ROB !!
I just kept shooting.
Our eyes would meet through the lens.
It would pique my desire.
After I ran out of film--
--I continued shooting with an empty camera.

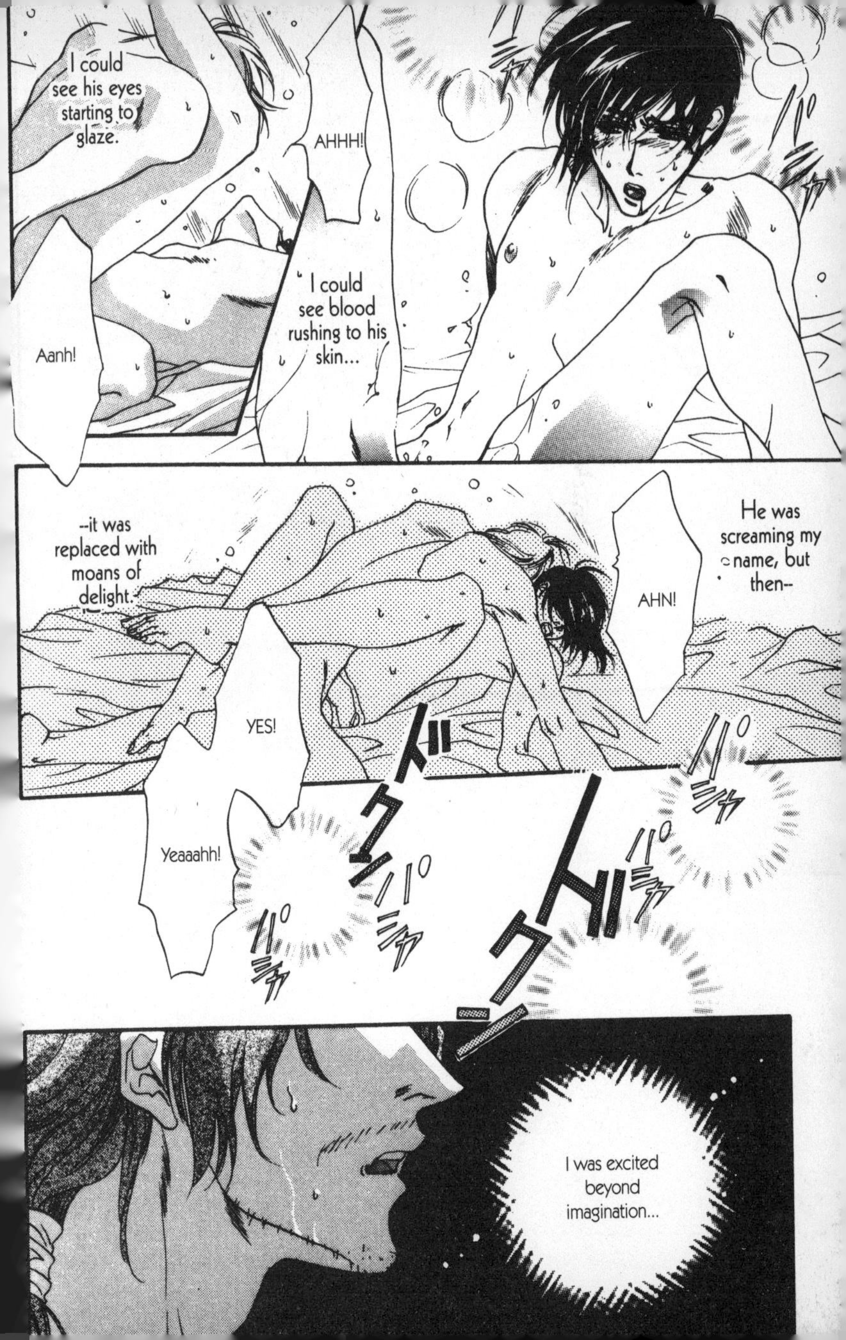
AHHH!
I could see blood rushing to his skin...
I could see his eyes starting to glaze.
Aanh!
He was screaming my name, but then--
AHN!
--it was replaced with moans of delight.
YES!
Yeaaahh!
I was excited beyond imagination...

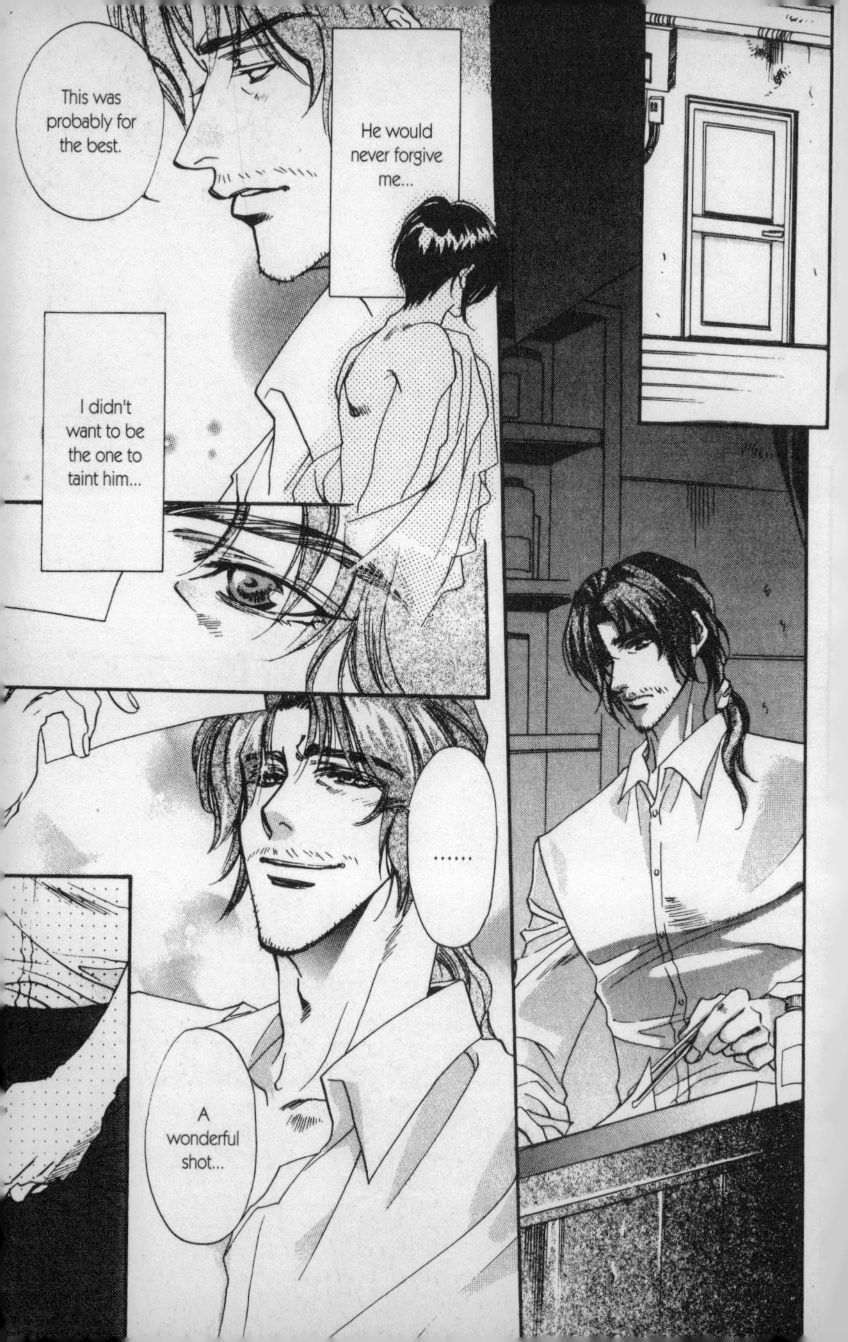
He would never forgive me...
This was probably for the best.
I didn't want to be the one to taint him...
......
A wonderful shot...

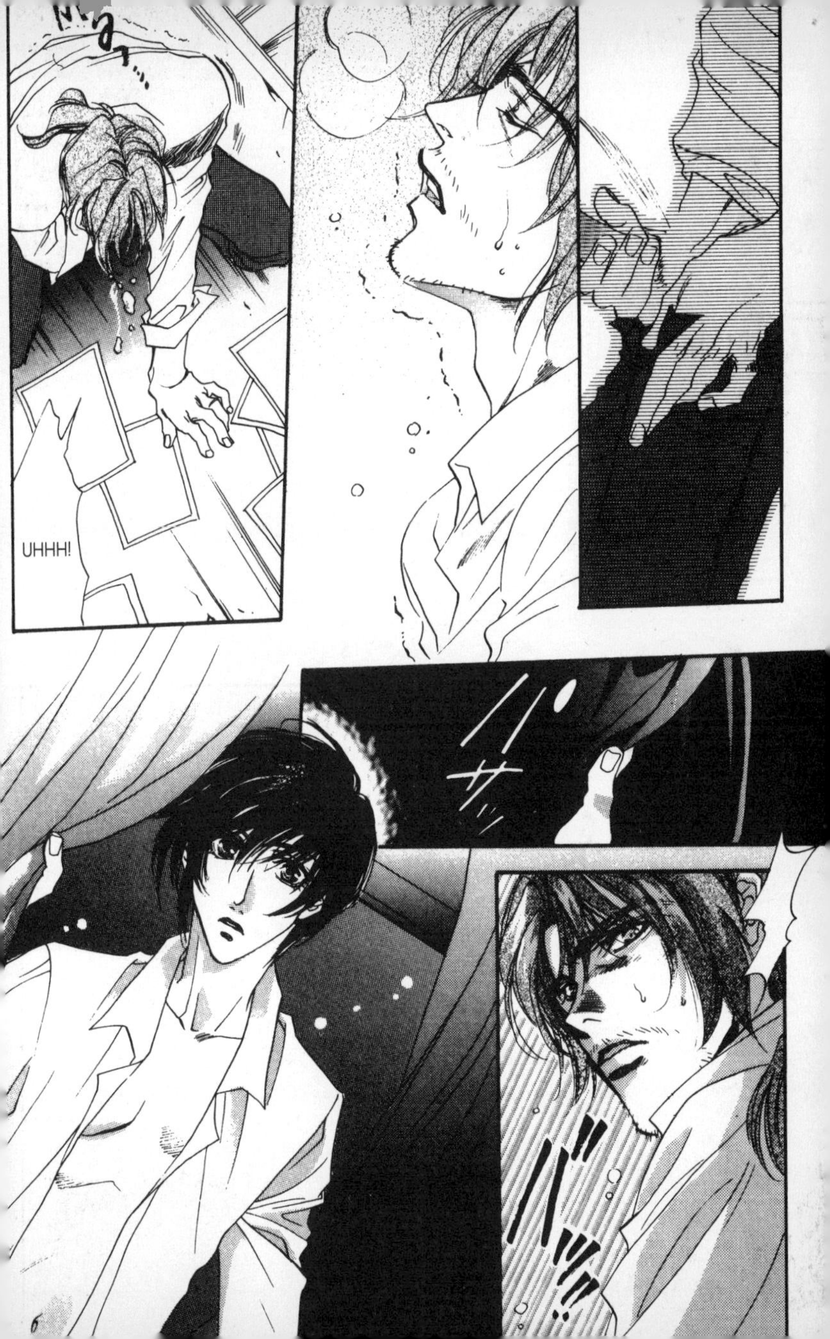
UHHH!

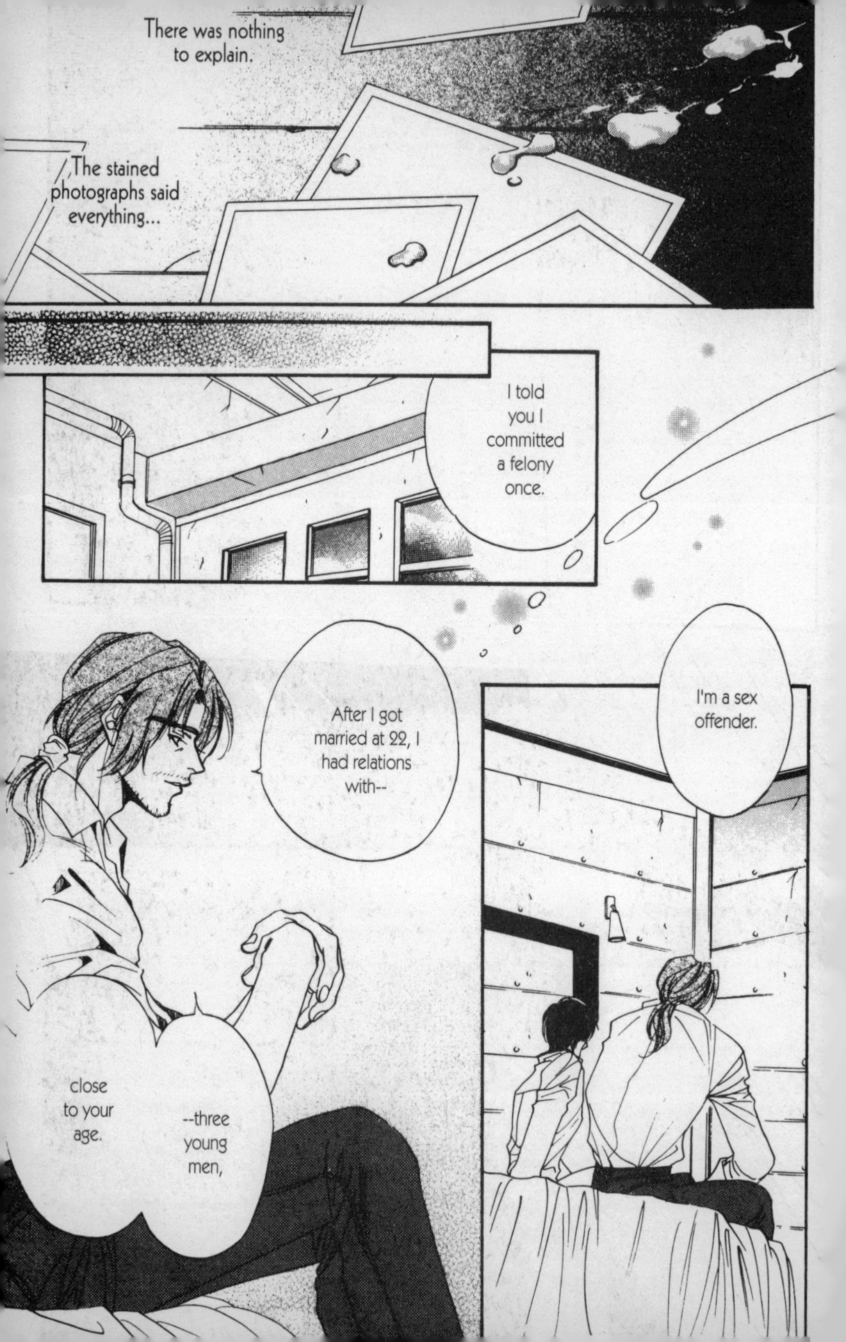
There was nothing to explain.
The stained photographs said everything...
I told you I committed a felony once.
I'm a sex offender.
After I got married at 22, I had relations with--
--three young men,
close to your age.

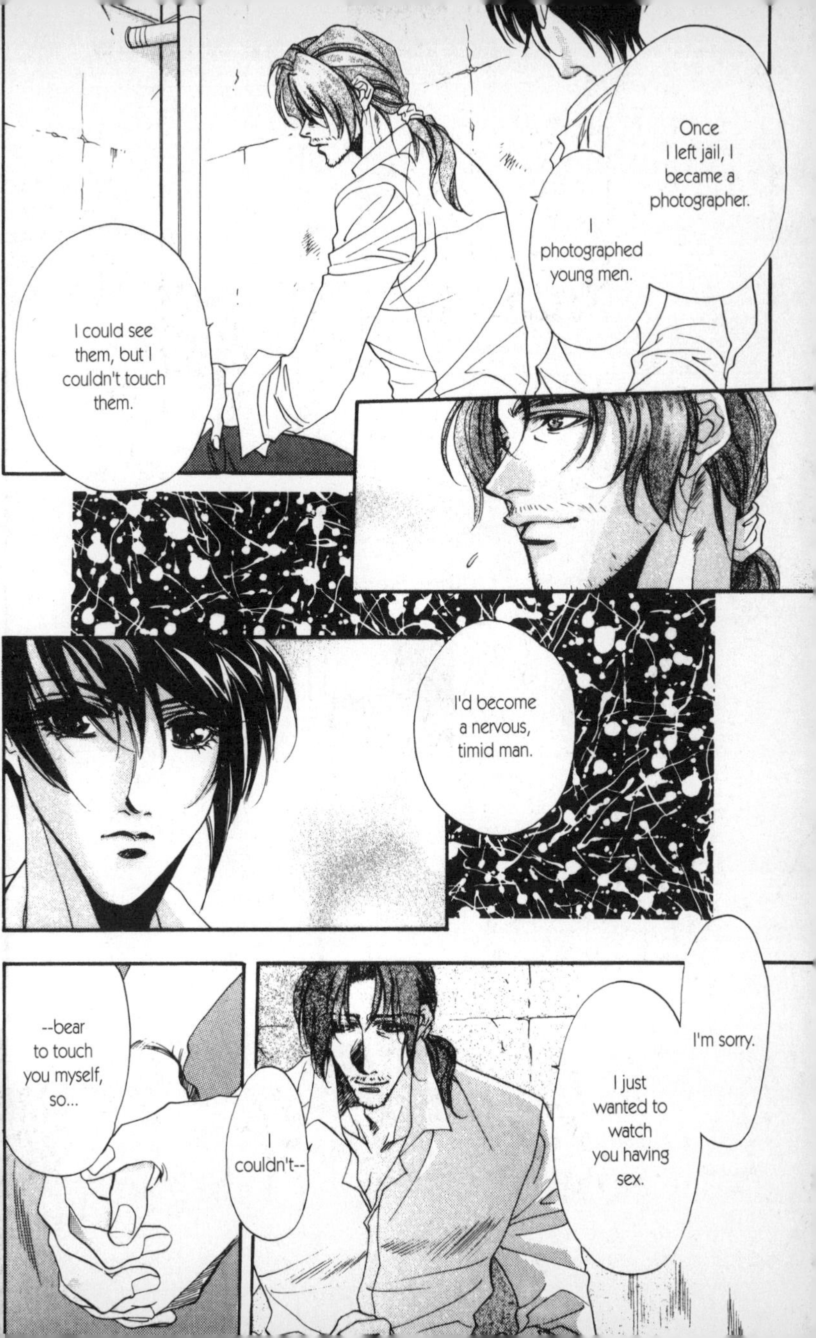
Once I left jail, I became a photographer.
I photographed young men.
I could see them, but I couldn't touch them.
I'd become a nervous, timid man.
I'm sorry.
I just wanted to watch you having sex.
I couldn't--
--bear to touch you myself, so...

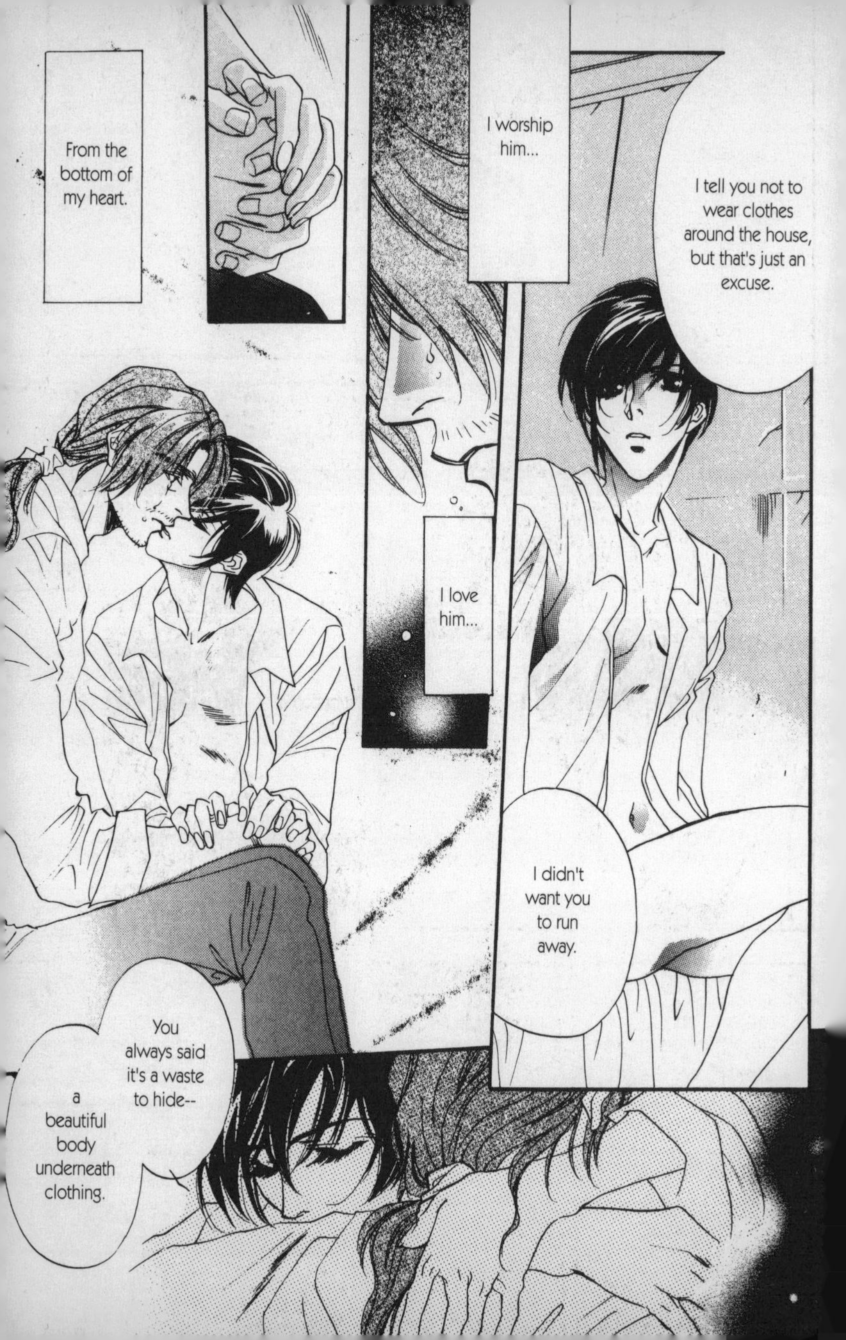
I tell you not to wear clothes around the house, but that's just an excuse.
I didn't want you to run away.
I worship him...
I love him...
From the bottom of my heart.
You always said it's a waste to hide--
a beautiful body underneath clothing.

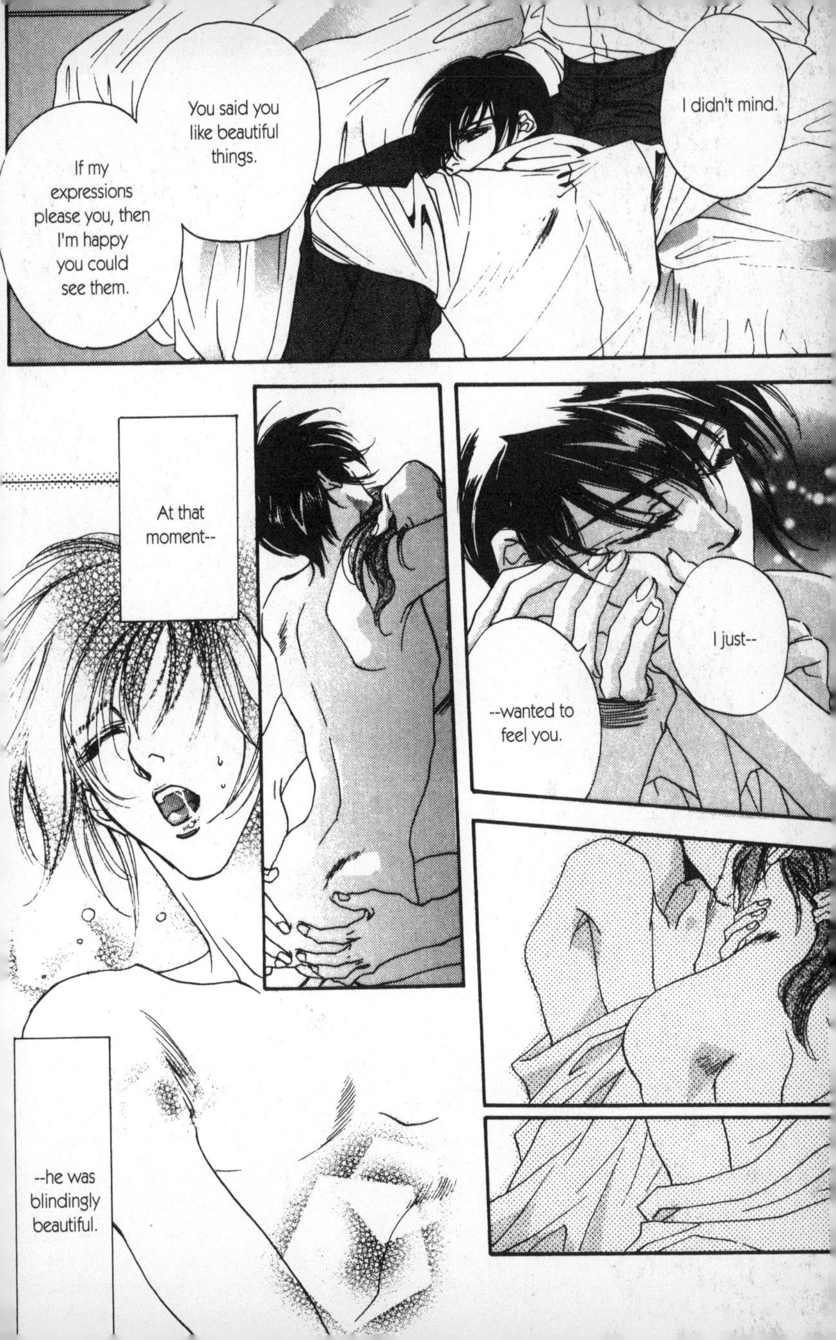
I didn't mind.
You said you like beautiful things.
If my expressions please you, then I'm happy you could see them.
I just--
--wanted to feel you.
At that moment--
--he was blindingly beautiful.

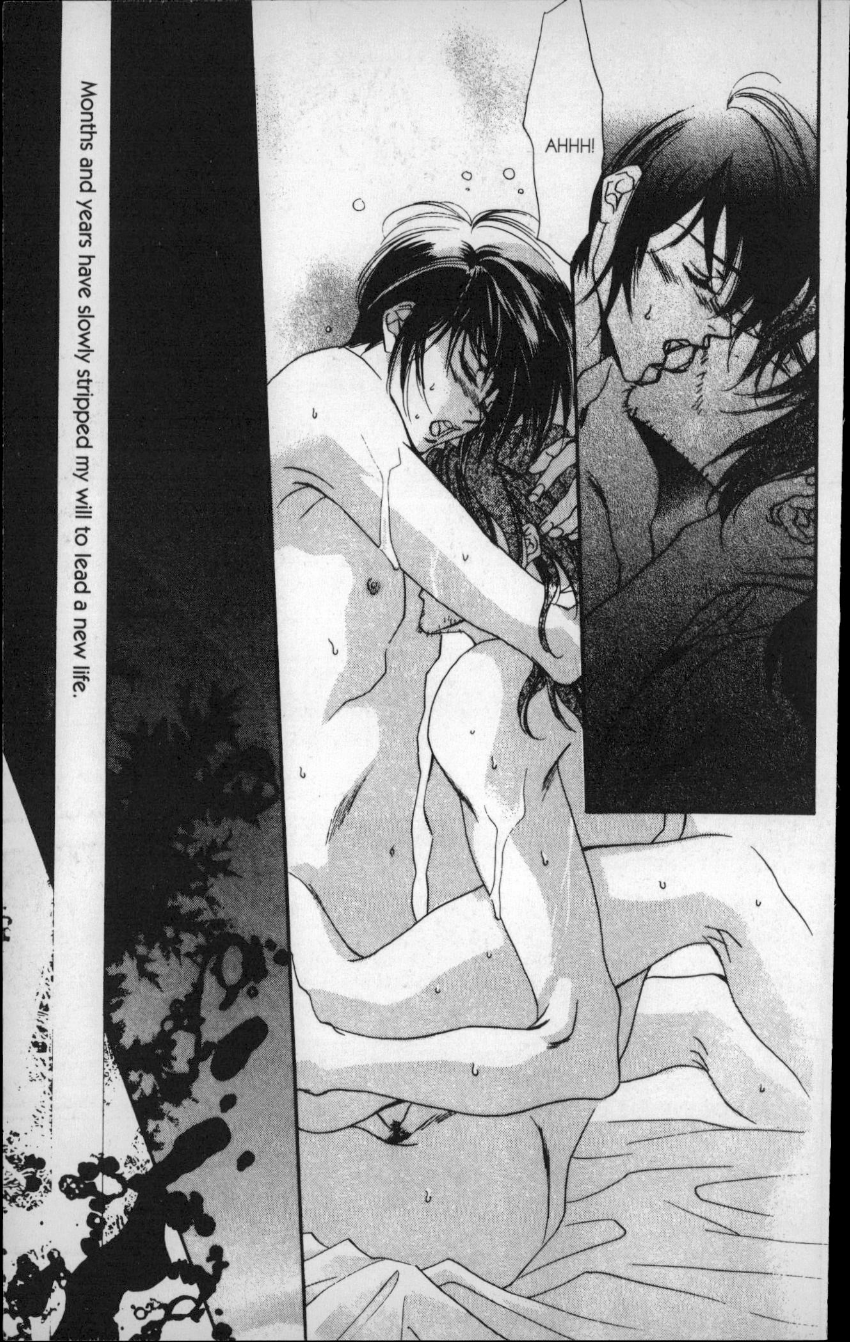
AHHH!
Months and years have slowly stripped my will to lead a new life.

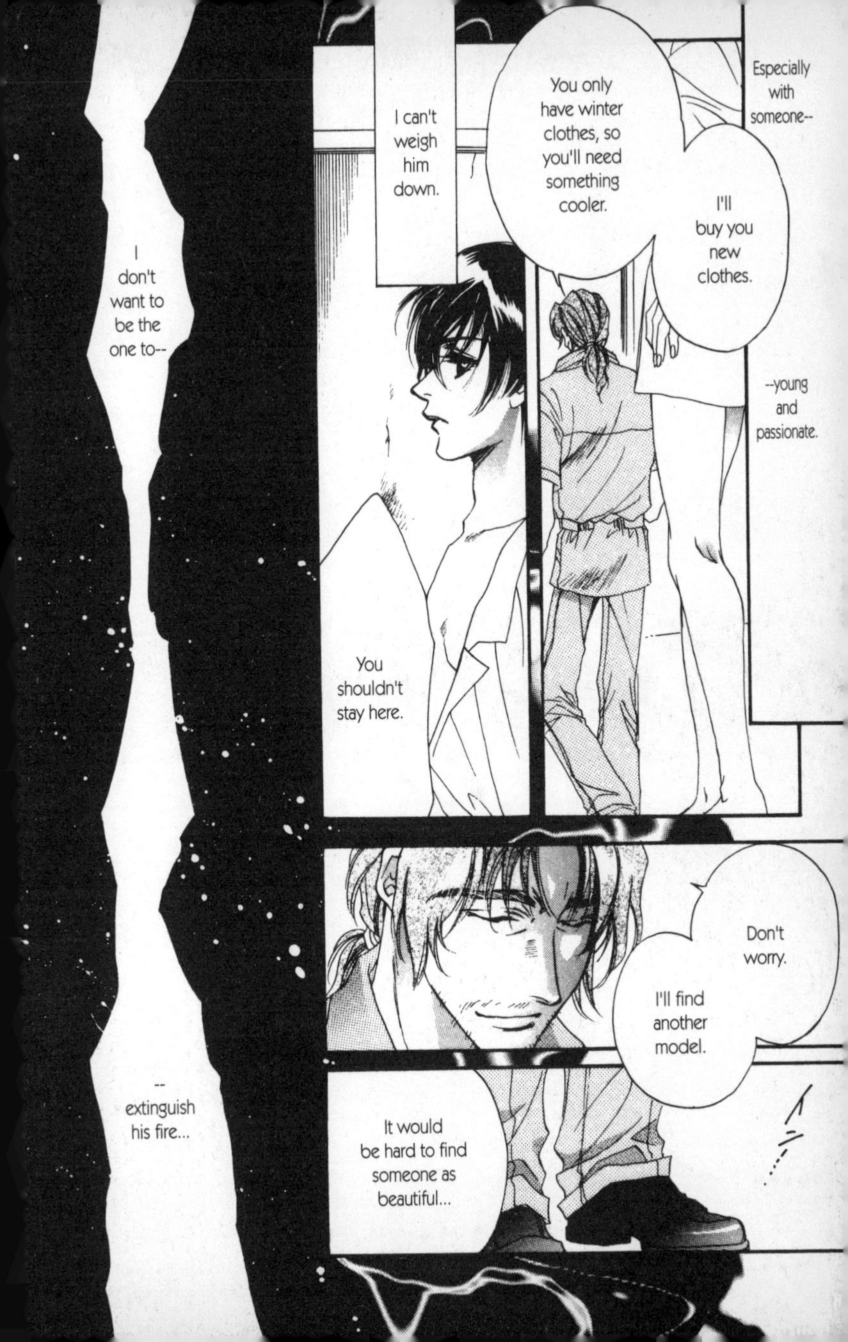
Especially with someone--
--young and passionate.
I'll buy you new clothes.
You only have winter clothes, so you'll need something cooler.
I can't weigh him down.
You shouldn't stay here.
I don't want to be the one to--
Don't worry.
I'll find another model.
It would be hard to find someone as beautiful...
--extinguish his fire...

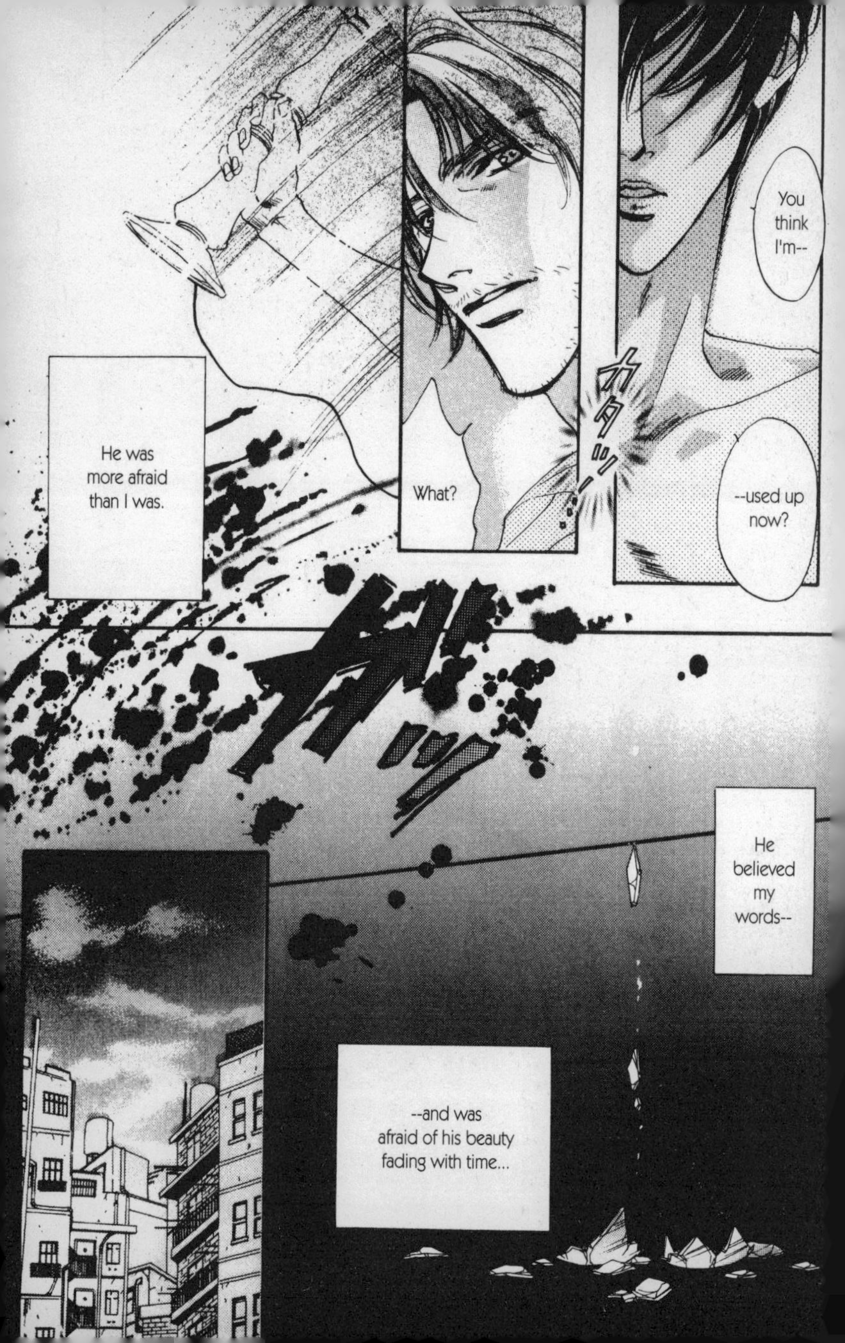
You think I'm--
--used up now?
What?
He was more afraid than I was.
He believed my words--
--and was afraid of his beauty fading with time...

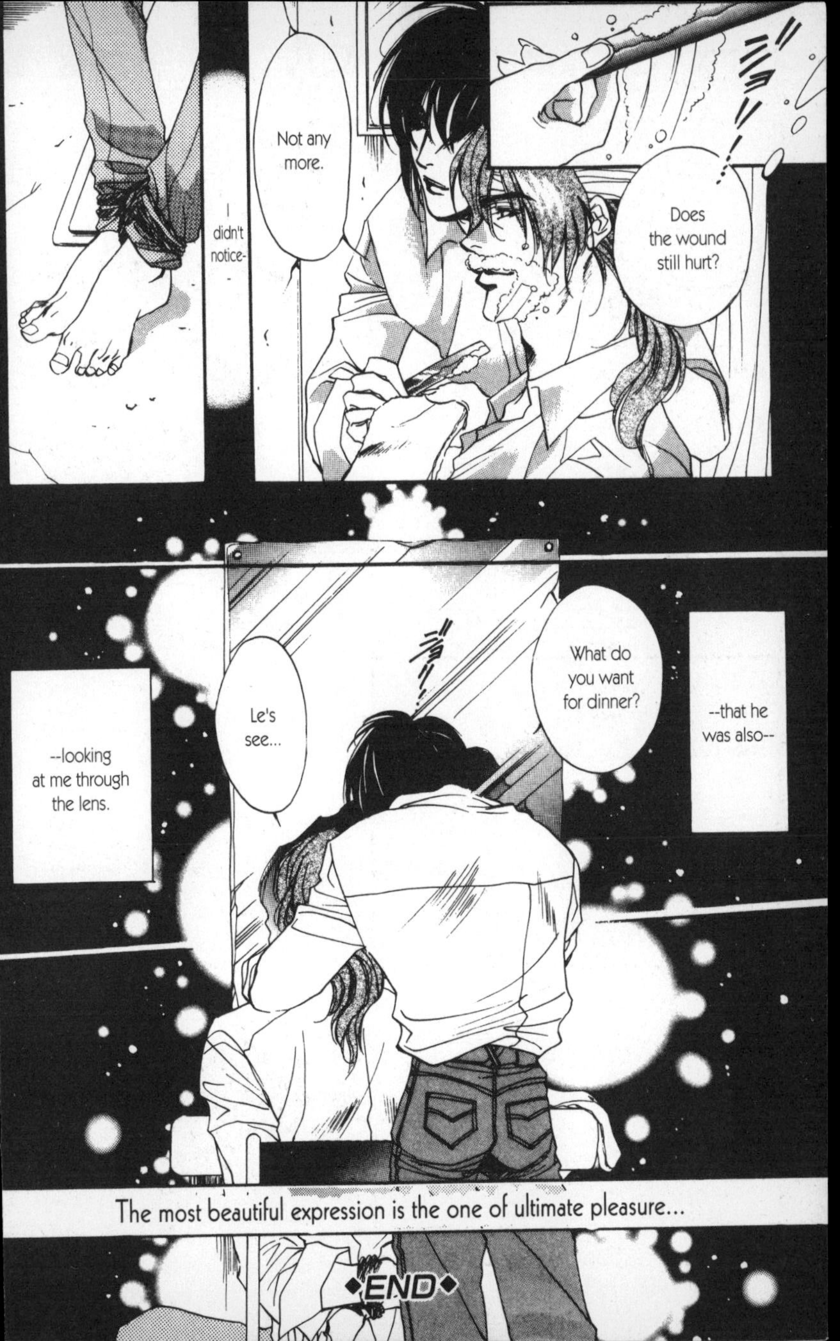
Does the wound still hurt?
Not any more.
I didn't notice-
--that he was also--
What do you want for dinner?
Le's see...
--looking at me through the lens.
The most beautiful expression is the one of ultimate pleasure...
END

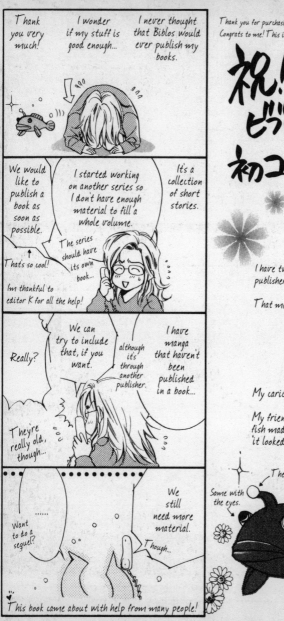

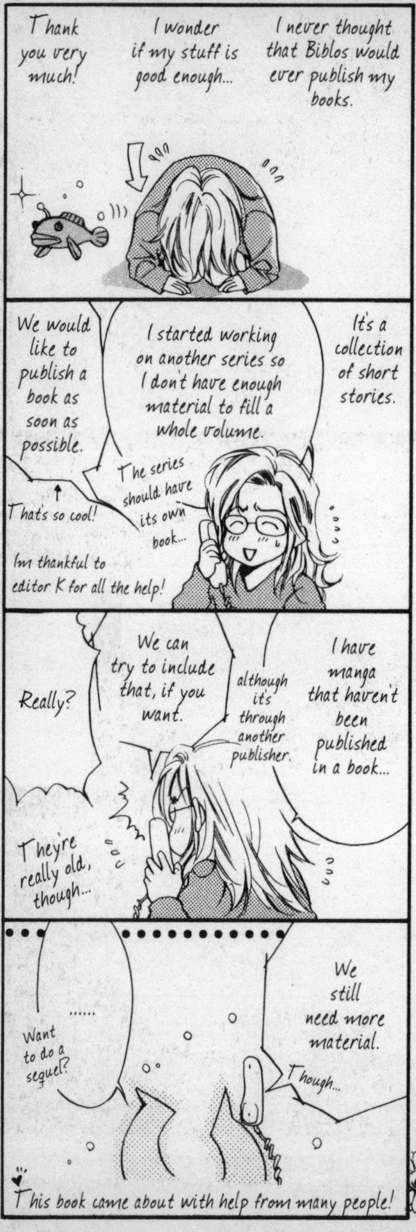
I never thought that Biblos would ever publish my books.
I wonder if my stuff is good enough...
Thank you very much!
It's a collection of short stories.
I started working on another series so I don't have enough material to fill a whole volume.
We would like to publish a book as soon as possible.
The series should have its own book...
That's so cool!
I'm thankful to editor K for all the help!
I have manga that haven't been published in a book...
although it's through another publisher.
We can try to include that, if you want.
Really?
They're really old, though...
We still need more material.
Though...
......
Want to do a sequel?
This book came about with help from many people!

Thank you for purchasing my very first comic!
Congrats to me! This is my first book from Biblos!

祝!! ビブロス刊から 初コミックス 出たよ。

いや、マジで。

I have two other books from other publishers.

That means I have a total of 3!

My caricature is a lantern fish.

My friend brought back a lantern fish made from red glass because 'it looked liked me.'

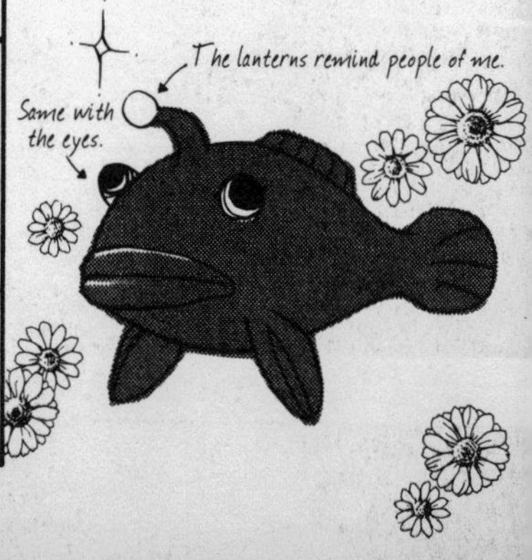
The lanterns remind people of me.
Same with the eyes.

The main story is about a young teacher and his student. It's a standard formula in yaoi manga, but it was my first time creating something along this vein. I wanted to make it sweet and romantic since it would be published through B-Boy. At first, I was thinking of a serious plot. The story was about a person losing his family through a medical mishap. The material was too difficult and it wasn't approved. As a result, I found myself devoid of ideas. What's different in the story is the fact that the younger guy is the more dependable, stronger partner. He'd become an ideal man and I'm proud of him! The bottom role, the teacher, was originally named Makoto. However, it wasn't used in the first episode, and by the time I was working on the sequel, I couldn't remember his name.

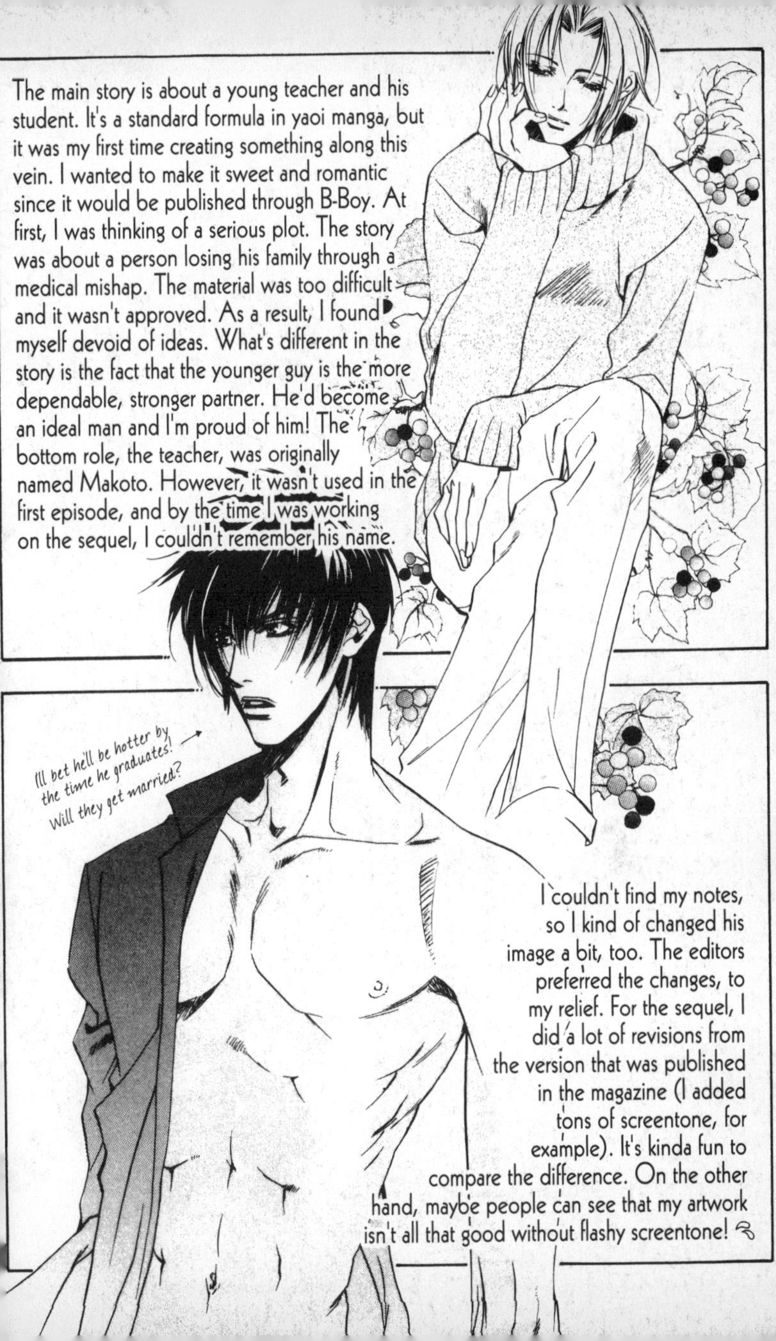
I'll bet he'll be hotter by the time he graduates!
Will they get married?

I couldn't find my notes, so I kind of changed his image a bit, too. The editors preferred the changes, to my relief. For the sequel, I did a lot of revisions from the version that was published in the magazine (I added tons of screentone, for example). It's kinda fun to compare the difference. On the other hand, maybe people can see that my artwork isn't all that good without flashy screentone!

Bloom!

I received this project from B-Boy Zip. The theme was going to be about a gay couple that were BOTH girly. I've done a lot of couples that were both masculine, but it was cool that they asked me to do something different! Go Biblos! I really enjoyed this project. I was thinking about two different plots. One was about a young man getting seduced by his stepfather. I was going to make the characters versatile, but the plot was nixed. They already had plenty of dramatic stories, so I decided to make this a comedy. It's definitely one of my more atypical stories.

Honey Happy Baby

I was doing a story about a baby. My former editor must have liked it since I was given this story to work on. It seems like I decided to fulfill the editor's request. However, that's not very unusual for me. My stories are often strange, so their requests are probably safer (laughs).

Voice Box

I wanted to redraw this. However, I didn't know where to start. Everyone around me was telling me that it was just fine. Someone even said it was quite nostalgic. Maybe it's strange to not want to change your work after 2 years. Back then, phone chat lines and voice mail was the rage. Now, with more e-mail and Internet access, voice mail is so outdated. I never thought cell phones would catch on like they have. The teen escort idea was not mine, but the characters are pretty typical of my books. I love these types of guys!

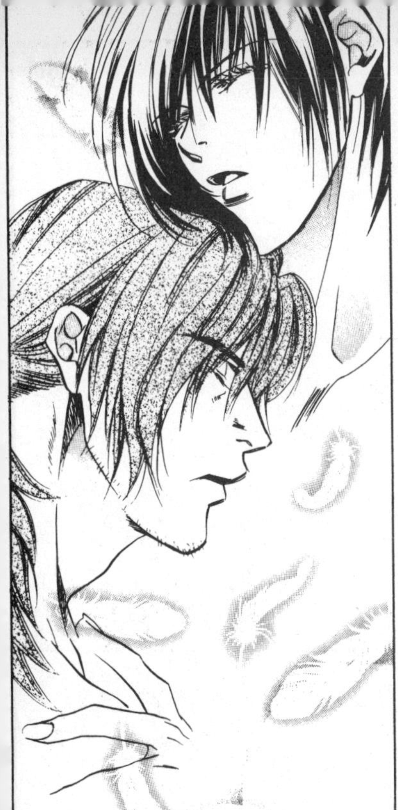

I wanted **"The View through the Lens"** to be about this man doting on another. Love between young people is often blind and passionate. I enjoy young love. However, doting brings up a pathetic image, or something more familial, like a grandfather doting on his grandkids. I actually like stubble on a guy, but I wondered if the younger readers would like it too.

Scandal Kiss was originally published by a different publisher. There's actually an episode that precedes the one here. If you're interested, please check out Secret Area- Kinryugu." (Sorry for the plug.) The story is a series, but each episode can also stand on its own. The theme was supposed to be about a dangerous man, but I wanted to add a twist. As a result, the more feminine character has the dangerous job.

I'm serious!

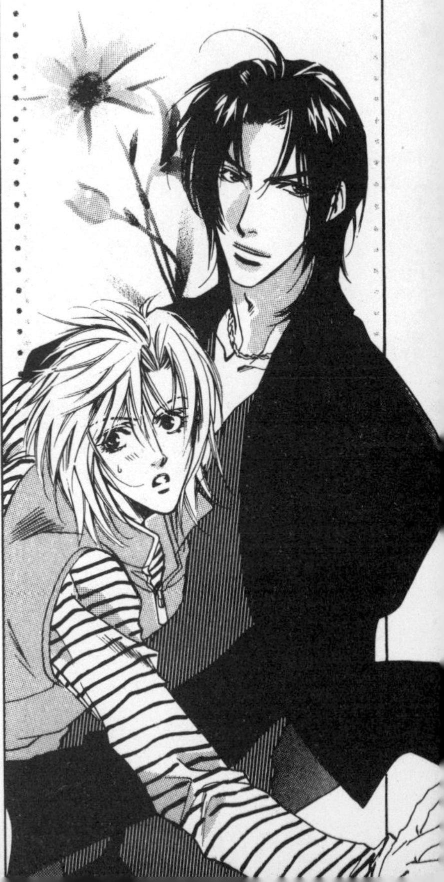

It's hard work,
but I love my job!

I'm sorry I haven't written back to my fans.

I DO read and keep all the fan letters!

I will continue to work hard for your support!

Let's hope I have more opportunities to work!

Special Thanx

Ayumi . M

Reiko . H

Thanks for your help!
Mom, Dad and Older sis
Former Editor K
Current Editor K-mura

..... and you ♡

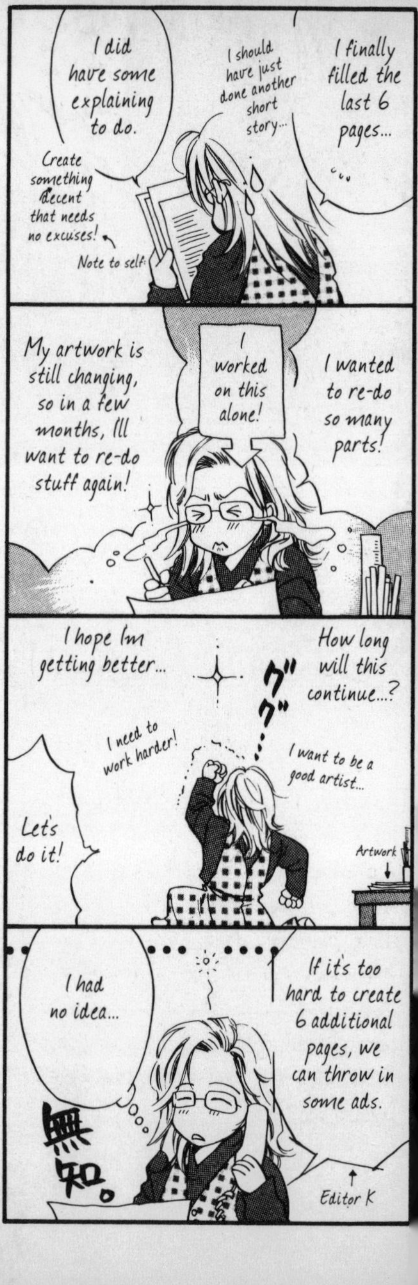

I finally filled the last 6 pages...
I should have just done another short story...
I did have some explaining to do.
...
Create something decent that needs no excuses!
Note to self:
I wanted to re-do so many parts!
I worked on this alone!
My artwork is still changing, so in a few months, I'll want to re-do stuff again!
How long will this continue...?
グ グ
I hope I'm getting better...
I want to be a good artist...
I need to work harder!
Let's do it!
Artwork
If it's too hard to create 6 additional pages, we can throw in some ads.
Editor K
I had no idea...
無知。

ROW.TAKAKURA
presents

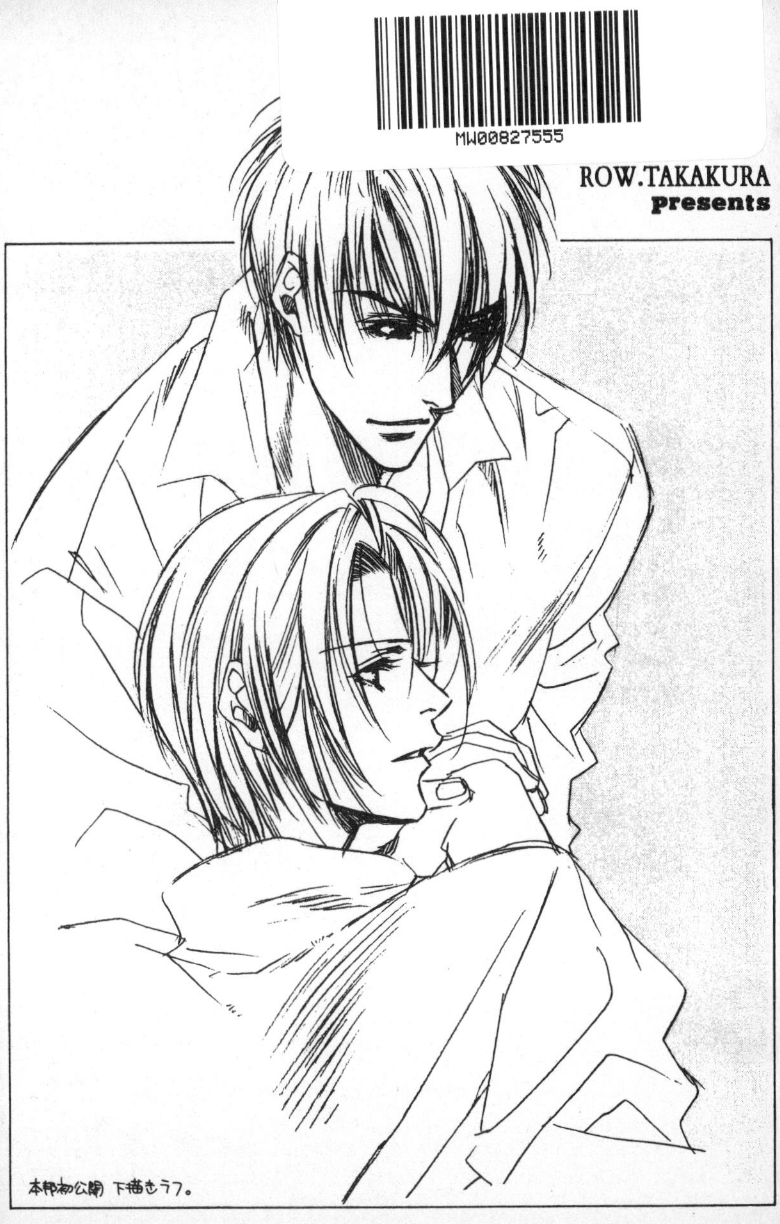

本邦初公開 下描きラフ。